Teaching Religion and Violence

AAR
AMERICAN ACADEMY OF RELIGION

TEACHING RELIGIOUS STUDIES SERIES

SERIES EDITOR
Susan Henking, Hobart and William Smith Colleges
A Publication Series of
The American Academy of Religion
and
Oxford University Press

Teaching Religion and Violence

Edited by Brian K. Pennington

OXFORD

UNIVERSITY PRESS

OXFORD
UNIVERSITY PRESS

Oxford University Press, Inc., publishes works that further
Oxford University's objective of excellence
in research, scholarship, and education.

Oxford   New York
Auckland   Cape Town   Dar es Salaam   Hong Kong   Karachi
Kuala Lumpur   Madrid   Melbourne   Mexico City   Nairobi
New Delhi   Shanghai   Taipei   Toronto

With offices in
Argentina   Austria   Brazil   Chile   Czech Republic   France   Greece
Guatemala   Hungary   Italy   Japan   Poland   Portugal   Singapore
South Korea   Switzerland   Thailand   Turkey   Ukraine   Vietnam

Copyright © 2012 by Oxford University Press, Inc.

Published by Oxford University Press, Inc.
198 Madison Avenue, New York, New York 10016

www.oup.com

Oxford is a registered trademark of Oxford University Press

Library of Congress Cataloging-in-Publication Data
Teaching religion and violence / edited by Brian K. Pennington.
p.   cm.
ISBN 978-0-19-537242-7
1. Violence—Religious aspects—Study and teaching.
I. Pennington, Brian K. (Brian Kemble)
BL65.V55T43   2012
201'.76332071—dc23   2011037958

1 3 5 7 9 8 6 4 2

Printed in the United States of America
on acid-free paper

CONTENTS

ACKNOWLEDGMENTS

This project has taken several years to bring to a conclusion, and I am grateful to many people who helped ensure that it was eventually published. Two contributors to the volume played other important roles: Aaron Hughes, who initially conceived this book, solicited some of the authors whose work is included and opened discussions with Oxford University Press before asking me to assume responsibility for it; and Amir Hussain, who served as my coeditor during the early phases of the project. Amir helped write the book proposal that finalized its scope and content, and his voice and his ideas about how to teach religion in an age of conflict are discernible throughout this volume. I am grateful for the many conversations we have had that gave the book its shape. Several of these essays were first drafted as papers for a panel in the Academic Teaching and the Study of Religion section at the American Academy of Religion's 2005 annual meeting. Michel Desjardins delivered a very thoughtful response at that meeting in which he proposed important correctives and offered welcome encouragement for our work. The editor of the AAR/OUP Teaching Religious Studies Series, Susan Henking, has been a champion of this project from the beginning and was particularly helpful to me in overcoming some of the strategic challenges involved in getting this volume to press, as was Jack Fitzmier of the AAR and OUP's religion editor, Cynthia Read. I have been fortunate to work at an institution, Maryville College, that is suffused by a culture that demands and supports good teaching and that truly understands what the scholarship of teaching means. I have learned a great deal about the craft of teaching and about pedagogy from colleagues across the disciplines. I am particularly grateful to students in various incarnations of my Religion 348, Religion and Violence course for challenging me on a daily basis to be a better teacher and for responding to my classroom efforts with seriousness, enthusiasm, and good humor. My division chairs during the time this book was compiled, Susan Schneibel and Peggy Cowan, have always worked with me to schedule my time in ways that allowed me to write and conduct research. Finally, academic marriages can present unusual challenges, but I could do very little of what I do, and certainly never as well, without the constant support and input of my wife, Amy Allocco. My daily sounding board and personal editor in chief, she is my most valued colleague and the too-often unacknowledged collaborator behind all of my work.

CONTRIBUTORS

Jason C. Bivins is an associate professor and is associate head of the Department of Philosophy and Religion at North Carolina State University. He is the author of *Religion of Fear: The Politics of Horror in Conservative Evangelicalism* (Oxford University Press, 2008) and *The Fracture of Good Order: Christian Antiliberalism and the Challenge to American Politics* (University of North Carolina Press, 2003). He is currently working on two monographs. The first is *"Spirits Rejoice!": Jazz and American Religion*, and the second is *Embattled Majority*, a genealogy of the rhetoric of "religious bigotry" in conservative Christian politics since the 1960s.

Randal Cummings teaches in the Religious Studies Department at California State University, Northridge. He has taught World Religions; Myth, Religion, and Culture; Religion and Literature; The Buddha and the Christ; Death and Afterlife; Hinduism; The Bible, Women and Religion, and the newly developed History of Religion/s: Social-Scientific Approaches to the Study of Religion. He has served as the director of online instruction at CSUN and on the executive board of directors of academic technology for the California State University System. He currently chairs the Art/s of Interpretation Group that meets annually at the American Academy of Religion.

Ken Derry is assistant professor in the Department of Historical Studies at the University of Toronto Mississauga. He has been teaching courses that variously involve connections between religion and violence since 1996 at the University of Toronto, where Ken received his PhD from the Centre for the Study of Religion. His dissertation concerned religion, colonialism, and mimetic violence in contemporary Canadian Native literature, and his published work includes the chapter "Indigenous Traditions" in OUP's *World Religions* (third edition), as well as examinations of the Epistle of Barnabas, John Woo's *The Killer*, and several stories by Thomas King. A continued, diverse focus on religion and violence in both literature and popular American film is central to Ken's current and planned research projects.

Michael Dobkowski received his MA and PhD degrees in history from New York University and is presently professor of religious studies at Hobart and William Smith Colleges and chair of the department. He is the author of *The Tarnished Dream: The Basis of American Anti-Semitism* (1979); *The Politics of Indifference: Documentary History of Holocaust Victims in America* (1982); and *Jewish American Voluntary*

Organizations (1986); and in 2007 he coauthored *Nuclear Weapons, Nuclear States and Terrorism*. He has cowritten and edited other volumes on the Holocaust, genocide, nuclear weapons, and anti-Semitism including *The Nuclear Predicament: Nuclear Weapons in the 21st Century* (2000) and *On The Edge of Scarcity* (2003). His main areas of interest include the American Jewish experience, Holocaust studies, religion and violence, terrorism, and anti-Semitism.

William French is an associate professor of theology at Loyola University Chicago. He graduated from Dickinson College, received his MDiv degree from Harvard University, and completed his PhD at the University of Chicago. At Loyola he serves with the Environmental Studies/Sciences Program and also the Peace Studies Program. His main research interests are religious ethics, ecological ethics and policies, and war and peace issues. He has written articles and book chapters on such topics as global climate change, land use issues, ecological security, just war theory, domestic gun control policy, the Catholic natural tradition, biblical views of creation, and comparative religious ethics. He is on the board of the National Catholic Center for Holocaust Studies.

Aaron W. Hughes is the Gordon and Gretchen Gross Professor and associate director in the Institute of Jewish Thought and Heritage at the State University of New York at Buffalo. He is the author of over fifty articles and nine books, including *Situating Islam* and *The Invention of Jewish Identity*. In 2004–5 he received a Student Union Teaching Excellence Award.

Amir Hussain is professor of theological studies at Loyola Marymount University in Los Angeles, where he teaches courses on Islam, world religions, and comparative theology. He is the editor of the third edition of the textbook *World Religions: Western Traditions* for Oxford University Press. For 2011 to 2015, he is the editor of the *Journal of the American Academy of Religion*.

Jeffrey J. Kripal holds the J. Newton Rayzor Chair in Philosophy and Religious Thought at Rice University, where he is also the chair of the Department of Religious Studies. He is the author of *Authors of the Impossible: The Paranormal and the Sacred* (Chicago, 2010); *Esalen: America and the Religion of No Religion* (Chicago, 2007); *The Serpent's Gift: Gnostic Reflections on the Study of Religion* (Chicago, 2007); *Roads of Excess, Palaces of Wisdom: Eroticism and Reflexivity in the Study of Mysticism* (Chicago, 2001); and *Kali's Child: The Mystical and the Erotic in the Life and Teachings of Ramakrishna* (Chicago, 1995). He has also coedited volumes with Wouter Hanegraaff on eroticism and esotericism, *Hidden Intercourse: Eros and Sexuality in the History of Western Esotericism* (University of Amsterdam Press, 2008); Glenn W. Shuck on the history of Esalen and the American counterculture, *On the Edge of the Future: Esalen and the Evolution of American Culture* (Indiana, 2005); Rachel Fell McDermott on a popular Hindu goddess, *Encountering Kali: In the Margins, at the Center, in the West* (California, 2003); G. William Barnard on the ethical critique of mystical traditions, *Crossing Boundaries: Essays on the Ethical Status of Mysticism* (Seven Bridges,

2002); and T. G. Vaidyanathan of Bangalore, India, on the dialogue between psychoanalysis and Hinduism, *Vishnu on Freud's Desk: A Reader in Psychoanalysis and Hinduism* (Oxford, 1999). His present areas of interest include the comparative erotics of mystical literature, American countercultural translations of Asian religious traditions, and the history of Western esotericism from ancient Gnosticism to the New Age. He is currently working on a book on the paranormal and American popular culture.

William Morrow (PhD, University of Toronto, 1988) is associate professor of Hebrew and Hebrew scriptures at Queen's School of Religion, Kingston, Ontario. As a graduate of Knox College (MDiv, 1978), he served the Presbyterian Church in Canada for two years in Elphinstone, Manitoba, and two First Nations communities. His publications deal with biblical law in its ancient Near Eastern contexts, the lament tradition, and the effects of violence on the development of biblical religion. His most recent book is *Protest Against God: The Eclipse of a Biblical Tradtion* (Sheffield Phoenix Press, 2006).

Anne Murphy is assistant professor and chair of Punjabi language, literature, and Sikh studies at the University of British Columbia. She received her PhD from Columbia University's Department of Religion in 2005 and her master's degree in Asian languages and literature from the University of Washington. She previously taught in the Religious Studies and Historical Studies Concentrations at the New School in New York City. Her research interests focus on the historical formation of religious communities in Punjab and northern South Asia, with particular but not exclusive attention to the Sikh tradition. She recently completed a book manuscript based upon her dissertation, titled *Materializing History: Representation and the Territorialization of the Sikh Past, 1711–1925*, which focuses on the construction of Sikh memory and historical consciousness around material representations and religious sites. She has edited a volume titled *Time, History and the Religious Imaginary in South Asia* (Routledge, 2011). Other research interests concern the formations of modern Punjabi literature, and particularly the articulation of the secular within it, and the historical formations of social service or *seva* within Sikh tradition. She conducted research on the latter topic as a senior fellow with the American Institute of Indian Studies in 2009–10 and recently received a grant for the project from the Social Sciences and Humanities Research Council of Canada.

Laurie L. Patton is dean of the Faculty of Arts and Sciences of Duke University and former Charles Howard Candler Professor of Religions at Emory University. She earned her BA from Harvard University and her PhD from the University of Chicago. She has authored over forty-five articles on the interpretation of early Indian ritual and narrative, comparative mythology, literary theory in the study of religion, and women and Hinduism in contemporary India. She is the author or editor of seven books: *Authority, Anxiety, and Canon: Essays in Vedic Interpretation* (1994); *Myth as Argument: The Brhaddevata as Canonical Commentary* (1996); *Myth and Method* (1996); *Jewels of Authority: Women and Text in the Hindu Tradition* (2002);

Bringing the Gods to Mind: Mantra and Ritual in Early Indian Sacrifice (2004); *The Indo-Aryan Controversy: Evidence and Inference in Indian History* (ed., with Edwin Bryant, 2005); *Notes from a Mandala: Essays in the Indian History of Religions in Honor of Wendy Doniger* (ed., with David Haberman, 2010). She has also published a book of poetry, *Fire's Goal: Poems from a Hindu Year* (2003) and a translation of the *Bhagavad Gītā* (2008).

Brian K. Pennington is professor of religion at Maryville College in Maryville, Tennessee. He is a member of the board of directors of the American Academy of Religion and of its executive committee, and he serves on the board of directors of the Society for Hindu-Christian studies. Pennington holds a BA degree from Georgetown University and a PhD from Emory University. Currently he is developing a book manuscript, *God's Fifth Abode: Emergent Religion in the Indian Himalayas*, a study of religious change in the north Indian city of Uttarkashi, an ancient hub of a major Himalayan pilgrimage circuit. His earlier book, *Was Hinduism Invented? Britons, Indians, and the Colonial Construction of Religion*, was also published by Oxford University Press (2005), and he is coeditor, along with Amy Allocco, of *Ritual Innovation in South Asia*.

Brian Daizen Victoria is a native of Omaha, Nebraska, and a 1961 graduate of Nebraska Wesleyan University in Lincoln, Nebraska. He holds an MA in Buddhist studies from Sōtō Zen–affiliated Komazawa University in Tokyo, and a PhD from the Department of Religious Studies at Temple University. In addition to a second, enlarged edition of *Zen at War* (Rowman and Littlefield, 2006), Brian's major writings include *Zen War Stories* (RoutledgeCurzon, 2003); an autobiographical work in Japanese titled *Gaijin de ari, Zen bozu de ari* (As a Foreigner, as a Zen Priest), published by San-ichi Shobo in 1971; *Zen Master Dōgen,* coauthored with Professor Yokoi Yūhō of Aichi-gakuin University (Weatherhill, 1976); and a translation of *The Zen Life* by Sato Koji (Weatherhill, 1972). Brian is a professor of Japanese studies and director of the AEA Buddhist Studies in Japan program at Antioch University.

Paul Younger studied at Banaras Hindu University and Princeton University, and worked briefly with Jaya Prakash Narayan and the Boodan movement. Since 1964, he has taught at McMaster University in Hamilton, Ontario, and he and his family have raised sheep on their farm nearby. His most recent books are *The Home of Dancing Śivan: The Traditions of the Hindu Temple in Citamparam* (1995); *Playing Host to Deity: Festival Religion in the South Indian Tradition* (2002); and *New Homelands: Hindu Communities in Mauritius, Guyana, Trinidad, South Africa, Fiji and East Africa* (2010).

Teaching Religion and Violence

Introduction

BRIAN K. PENNINGTON

Probably few topics in religious studies capture, on the one hand, the ambiguities and challenges of the discipline and, on the other, its contemporary indispensability as successfully as the intersection of religion and violence does. For its ability to highlight the problem of defining religion, for underscoring religion's inseparability from power and politics, for pointing out the contested and internally plural nature of all religious traditions and identities, for suggesting the religious functions of popular culture, and for revealing the historical mutability of religious expression and identity, religious violence flags many of the distinctive and defining questions addressed by the discipline. For those very reasons it is also an excellent topic for initiating students into the practices of religious studies and cultivating a heightened appreciation for the nuances and complexities that characterize religion in all of its historical manifestations. Advancing beyond a superficial understanding of religious violence demands that students develop a level of competence in the use of such diverse interpretive tools as textual exegesis, historical reasoning, and psychological analysis; it demands that they recognize the multiple perspectives that mature observation of religious phenomena must adopt, including the sociological, political, ethnographic, literary, and historical, to name only a few. In short, the subject of religion and violence can provide a model for teaching students how to conduct interdisciplinary, humanistic inquiry. The essays collected in this volume sketch the landscape of that topic and propose a variety of tools, resources, and approaches that instructors can utilize to make studying religious violence an intellectually and morally transformative experience for students of religious studies.

In the post-9/11 cable news era, the challenges of communicating the subtlety of violent themes and the complexity of causes and motivations in any instance of violence are significantly heightened. Whether one is teaching an entire course on religion and violence or some other topical course in which violence receives substantial or attention, it can be difficult to overcome the cumulative effect of pulsating images and sound-bite news coverage to stimulate real critical analysis among students reared in that media climate. An effective undergraduate pedagogy invites students to move beyond simplistic and binary accounts of conflict to modes of discourse that are more richly descriptive, analytical, and explanatory. Teaching a course on violence demands a rigorous and probative pedagogical stance that confronts common misconceptions and insists that students attempt to understand the nature and causes of religious violence without recourse to essentialisms and trite plotlines. Any "explanation" our courses provisionally produce we will ultimately judge to be fragmentary, partial, and unsatisfactory, but that, of course, is in the very nature of teaching and learning in the humanities, where we often come up against the intricacies of human culture and the resistance of human experience and motivation to reductive analysis.

If critical thinking and historical judgment have been tools of the study of religion since its founding, the environment in which we pursue those goals has dramatically shifted. In the second half of the twentieth century, academics and pundits announced the death of God, declared the decline of religion, and advanced some form of the secularization thesis. The first decade of the twenty-first century taught us quite different lessons: that religion remains an active force in the world; that few developing or developed societies jettison religious belief and ritual as an expression of the modern; and that religious fundamentalisms and neotraditionalisms have proven effective and compelling means for resisting globalization and the infiltration of Western social and political values. The fusion of guerrilla tactics and otherworldly discourses has delivered a potent reminder of the tenacity of religious cosmologies and unleashed the terrifying demons that colonialism spawned.

In fact, many people now see religious violence as one of the defining traits of our postmodern and postcolonial world. What average, North American people on the street "know" about religious communities outside the continent is very often tied to conflict. They may not be able to accurately explain the different practices or histories of Sunni and Shia Muslims, but they can often report that those groups are locked in cycles of recrimination in Pakistan and Iraq. They may have no awareness at all of the texture of shared religious life in places like Sri Lanka but recall a decades-long civil war between Hindus and Buddhists. Although religion reporting has improved dramatically since 9/11, on countless occasions over the last decade I found myself complaining again and again about a radio or television story, often from the United States' best news sources, that reported a conflict between groups it identified by their religious or sectarian affiliation without ever explaining the historical relationship between these groups, their fundamental differences, or factors other than their religious identities that might have been in play. Even as politically and historically complex a crisis as the horror that gripped the Darfur region of Sudan was typically reported according to the well-established narrative of religious communities at odds. There is a common Aristotelian structure to these stories and a mythic aura to the violence they portray.

It is in an interpretive environment shaped by these media realities that instructors today must teach courses that deal with religious identities and communities. We routinely face students' prejudices and poorly informed assumptions about individual religious traditions and the roles that religion plays in human societies. These prior conceptions might assume that a particular religion promotes violence more than others, that "hijacked" religion makes people violent but uncorrupted religion seeks peace, or that there are simple and obvious solutions to the production of religious violence, such as counterforce or a return to a founder's original teachings. Frustrating though this environment may be, the best instructors I know welcome the opportunity that resurgent public and student interest in religion offers for engaging them in more probing and disciplined reflection on religious discourses, authorities, and cosmologies, including the questioning of the very categories used to narrativize conflict between them: religion, violence, Hindu, Muslim, and so on.

Such interest is also an entry point for examining how religious figures and texts themselves have understood the nature of violence. The question of the moral status of force, harm, and killing is central to religious thought. The problems of suffering and the cessation of life have been painstakingly investigated in texts from every religious tradition. These concerns, however, are not only moral but also metaphysical because they confront the ubiquity of harm and death and strive to conceptualize their place in the cosmic order. The authoritative sources of every religious tradition and community avail themselves of multiple and competing interpretations, and they have often inspired a perplexing range of opinions about such issues as war, sacrifice, self-defense, the maintenance of social order, and the coercive propagation of belief and practice. To get a full picture of the scope of the questions and responses to such concerns that sacred texts and commentaries have articulated, a broadly historical consideration of religion itself, individual religious traditions, and the concept of violence is necessary. Many of the essays in this volume are dedicated to providing instructors just these kinds of historical and conceptual maps of particular traditions' diverse ways of reasoning about these questions.

Teaching, however, entails far more than the delivery of content, and this volume also presents strategies and models for encouraging critical thinking among students. Dissecting the etiologies of religious violence requires the kind of careful distinctions that instructors must work hard to communicate in the best of classroom circumstances. When serious and sustained analysis is forestalled by a well-founded horror or a simplistic understanding of the causes of conflict, the task of critical analysis becomes still harder. Discussion of religious violence, especially contemporary religious violence, can also incite vigorous student debate that pits the partisans of one tradition against those of another or secular humanism's despisers of religion against the champions of faith and morals. Essays in this volume are written with these kinds of pedagogical challenges in mind to help instructors teaching in today's variably and variously religious classrooms to equip their students to think critically about religious violence.

TEACHING, RELIGION, AND VIOLENCE

None of the three terms that anchor this book unambiguously signifies any discrete or static reality; each is, in itself, the subject of serious debate; and each circulates, moreover, in a distinct semantic field. Most important to note at this point, however, is that each of these terms—religion, violence, and teaching—means something different in the vernacular realm of everyday speech than it does in the academy's domain of specialized terminology, ritualized practice, and linguistic self-consciousness. Teaching, for most of us, means not transmitting data but cultivating intellectual habits. Our incoming students often find that success in college involves acculturating to new and often alien pedagogies. Much of our undergraduates' academic development consists in developing not only an expanded vocabulary but an expanded lexical field for the vocabulary that they have already acquired in the realm of vernacular speech. As instructors of these students, we model the unfamiliar ways of teaching that challenge them, insist that they adopt new habits of learning, and urge them to reconsider their understanding of such everyday concepts as culture, text, history, religion, and violence. The existence of competing and only partially overlapping languages inside and outside the academy demands that the college and university teacher is fluent in both and has an actual plan for training students conversant in only one to read, write, and speak the other.

To drive the point home: outside the academy, "religion" implies far more and "violence" far less than they do among those with advanced graduate degrees, command of historical sources, and facility in multiple languages. For the undergraduates entering our classrooms, religion has a self-evident character that is observable across history and human cultures, while violence involves only acts that inflict pain or draw blood.

The very category of religion, however, has long been under fire by many scholars whose academic appointments and professional livelihoods would appear to depend on it. The essays here show great appreciation especially for two sets of these critical voices: those that decry, to quote one, the "widespread scholarly use of the term 'religion' and the common presumption that it designates a private site of inner experience," and those that work to undermine the foundations of the world religions paradigm that structures most of our departments and the catalogs of the publishers who supply their textbook needs.[1] From the standpoint of teaching, however, there are important questions that this critical literature raises but almost never addresses. There is too little consideration, much less actual scholarship, dedicated to what those who have to face a lecture hall of undergraduates uninitiated into the language and practice of higher criticism might do about the wide gulf between vernacular and academic ways of describing human culture.[2] Moreover, a large body of work has expanded our understanding of what might or should be considered violence to include a range of interventions in human freedom, transgressions against human dignity, and symbolic as well as actual injury and death. The imposition of gender norms, structural poverty, and hate speech involve no direct physical harm to individuals but lend themselves to an analysis that foregrounds force and coercion. In this volume we employ more expansive notions of both of these concepts. In our assessment, the public violence of American football is religious while the existential terror intended by Christian evangelical Halloween Hell Houses is an act of violence.[3]

This volume aims to connect a sizeable academic literature on religious violence to the needs of college and university instructors who have to translate the language and concepts of highly specialized scholarship for the early twenty-first-century North American undergraduate.[4] We all know that the skill sets necessary for being a good scholar and a good teacher do not precisely overlap (a fact that is sometimes painfully on display when we or our departments invite big-name speakers to address our students, who then accomplish little beyond confusing and boring a room full of twenty-year-olds). The contributors to this volume, therefore, discuss not only what scholarship tells us we must teach, but how to teach it. They address the gap between what good scholarship (including their own) demonstrates, and what good teaching accomplishes in order that undergraduates can come to understand theoretical scholarship's application and implications. The findings of a recent important study of award-winning college teachers are especially relevant here. Its authors concluded that effective college teaching consistently displays a set of common characteristics: it is based on a careful assessment of student needs; it fosters students' ability to learn on their own; it ensures their mastery of fundamental concepts before introducing advanced content; it establishes the real-world relevance of course material; and it challenges common beliefs and misconceptions.[5] Pursuing these objectives would require those of us who teach religion and violence to meet students where they are when we find them, to engage them in material that will move them, to monitor their comprehension carefully, and to do these things as a first act on behalf of their transformation as thinkers and social actors.

THE ORGANIZATION OF THE VOLUME

The book is organized into two sections. The first, Traditions, addresses topics and methods appropriate for teaching violence in particular religious traditions. These essays provide the historical overview, typologies, and pedagogical strategies that their authors have developed for teaching Hindu, Jewish, Buddhist, Christian, Muslim, and Sikh traditions. They will be useful to instructors in a variety of teaching contexts: those developing or revising courses on violence in specific religious traditions, those wishing to introduce the place, interpretation, or practice of violence into a topical course in a specific tradition or an overview course on a specific tradition, and those who are offering a course covering a particular historical period of a tradition. In addition, the separate chapters addressing some of the world's "major" religious traditions will make pedagogical material on violence readily accessible to those teaching comparative courses. While many of the authors in this volume resist the world religions paradigm—some of us, indeed, have written or write here in opposition to it—because this book is aimed at the teacher, this section corresponds to the way the discipline and most religion departments conceptualize the field.

In fact, this volume recognizes that many questionable ideas about the relationship of religion to violence stem from the very categories established by religious studies discourses. Collectively, the various chapters of the first sec-tion are motivated by an interest in the classroom dismantling of uncritical and ahistorical ideas that regularly attach themselves to the concepts Hinduism, Islam, and so forth. Students often bring to our courses commonplace assump-tions derived from the world religions paradigm that regard religions as largely conservative social forces whose primary function is to pronounce the beliefs and obligations that orient individuals within traditions inherited in toto from the past. These creedal and moral traditions, according to this conception of religion, establish continuity across time and place for those who claim adher-ence to a "faith." Coherence and stability are regarded as the hallmarks of the world's major religions while sectarianism, innovation, and reinterpretation are aberrations. The chapters in the Traditions section confront these ideas by identifying fissures and debates within communities that courses might cover with the aim of training students to think more contextually and historically about violence as well as religion. These essays demonstrate that consideration of force, harm, and armed conflict has given rise to a range of positions and perspectives within every religious tradition,[6] and, moreover, that violence and related concepts intersect with a great variety of topics treated by religious studies, from sacrifice to social injustice to holy war.

This book also confronts a second implication of the idea that religions are cohe-sive entities separable from other elements of psychological or social life. A common and unexamined presumption regards religion as an ideally pure and distinct ele-ment of human culture that is defiled or degraded when it is touched by political or social concerns. This notion imagines that religion is, in its essential form, a wholly benign entity or positive good. On this view, religious practitioners may manipu-late religious ideas to further their political or violent intentions, but, in doing so, they undermine and contaminate some of the crowning insights of human civiliza-tion. This volume, on the other hand, promotes pedagogy that can effectively make the case with students that religion is not a sui generis thing in itself whose fol-lowers, unfortunately, exploit it for political or other motives,[7] but rather is always already fully implicated in social and economic systems that may either oppose or promote violence.

Arranged in historically chronological order, the Traditions section begins with my own essay on the complicated relationship between the contemporary concepts of Hinduism and violence. From the earliest Sanskrit texts to the present, the ques-tion of the moral status of harm and killing has informed a central thread of Hindu discourse. The rejection of animal sacrifice in the late Vedic period and Gandhian nationalism in the twentieth century represent only two of the many historical in-stances in which we hear voices advocating the avoidance of harm in opposition to Hindu voices that argue for the cosmological or political necessity of violence. The millennia-long debate on *ahiṃsā* (nonviolence) that can be reconstructed from Indic materials provides especially rich material for developing and assessing students' critical reasoning. The diverse voices that have contributed to this debate also make Hindu history an important resource for training students to attend closely to the social and political context of all religious ideas.

Michael Dobkowsky's essay, "'A Time for War and a Time for Peace': Teaching Religion and Violence in the Jewish Tradition," adopts a similar historical and topical approach to suggest to instructors the range of Jewish sources on the role and moral status of violence. Jewish traditions have often committed themselves to the sanctity of life, but powerful currents also recognize the reality and sometimes moral necessity of violent death, as well as the transformative power of suffering. Dobkowsky argues that life is of supreme, but not infinite, value in Jewish thought, as both Jewish history and literature perceive that justice and lasting peace may require force and bloodshed. He recommends collaborative learning strategies with students, especially engagement with the Talmud and Tanach, to draw them into rabbinic reasoning on war and the elusive state of wholeness and peace that Jewish traditions have called "shalom."

In chapter 3 Brian Victoria discusses the task of convincing a media-consumptive generation that the popular representations of Buddhism actually erase its history of fomenting and rationalizing violence. Associated in the popular imagination with the Dalai Lama, compassion, and meditation, Buddhism actually has a long history of entanglement with state power and military conflict that challenges students to unlearn the normative and sanitized versions of Buddhist teachings that suppress this side of the story. Victoria details a series of what he calls Buddhism's "enabling mechanisms," the subtle manipulations of doctrine or practice that provide justifications of violence with the ideological grounding necessary to legitimate them. Present in all religious discourses of violence, these enabling mechanisms effectively claim divine sanction and give rise to what we can properly call, in this case, Buddhist violence.

In chapter 4 William Morrow recommends a pedagogy based on real-world problem solving as an effective means of motivating students to organize bodies of polyvalent data and to come to terms with Christianity's historical connections to violence. Morrow's problem-based learning emphasizes developing both taxonomies and associated theories of religiously sanctioned violence through case studies of specific texts, rituals, or incidents. The object of these exercises is to guide students in the discovery of the complexity of religious violence and the diverse array of explanations available for any particular instance of it. Christianity's investment in the discourses of redemptive sacrifice as well as its supersessionist self-understanding have contributed to its implication in various forms of violence, a relationship that Morrow illustrates with respect to martyrdom, war, heroic asceticism, collective persecution, colonialism, and sacrificial ritual.

In the years since 9/11, Amir Hussain has observed a shift in North American public discourse from a pervasive Islamophobia to a more pronounced hatred of Islam he names "misoislamia." His essay in chapter 5 provides historical and textual background for understanding and addressing this shift and for teaching a range of topics that typically emerge in countless classroom situations today when the purportedly necessary connection between Islam and violence arises. The life of Muhammad, the Qur'an, and the spread of Islam are often cited as evidence of the tradition's violent character. Hussain explains how he approaches these topics and what sources he uses to equip students with much more informed ideas about Islam than they would commonly imbibe from media sources. He also treats many of the political, military, and cultural events of the last several decades that are most relevant to the teaching of contemporary Islam.

For reasons that have to do with both its narratives of origin and its more recent history, the Sikh tradition is one also haunted by associations with religiously sanctioned violence. In chapter 6 Anne Murphy challenges the ready acceptance by scholars and the media of a connection between religious motives and violent actions on the part of Sikhs. The overrepresentation of Sikh violence in these sources (the ones most commonly used by students) stands in sharp contrast to the relative absence of state violence against Sikhs in the same sources. Murphy questions the religious-secular binary that enables the linkage between Sikhs and violence and that continues to inform the cultural memory and self-understanding of second- and third-generation Sikhs in North America.

In this book's second section, Approaches, eight experienced undergraduate teachers discuss non-tradition-based courses they offer in which the intersection between religion and violence is central. Some take us inside the classroom to show what they and their students actually do; others take us through the rationale and objectives that drive course content and structure. Each offers some alternative to the Tradition X and Violence paradigm and presents ideas for promoting student learning about the diffusion of religious themes into the social, cultural, and political spheres. These essays convey the intellectual creativity and intuition of teachers who have developed exciting methods for demonstrating the wide applicability of the questions and concepts explored in this volume. It introduces teaching strategies that could be employed across the field of religious studies broadly conceived and liberates religion and violence from the topic's moorings in discrete traditions provided in the first section. Each essay is, at the same time, grounded in specific sources, materials, contexts, or teaching experiences.

Opening the Approaches section in chapter 7, Aaron Hughes describes the rationale behind his course called Religious Space and Violence and details his delivery of the subject matter. His pedagogical aims revolve around prompting students to think of religion in terms of human cultural production and the sociorhetorical legitimation that religious discourse performs rather than in terms of the interior spirituality that students commonly identify with religious life. Hughes takes the contested city of Jerusalem as his course's central case study. His emphasis on method and theory and his use of sources that offer students competing ways of conceiving both religion and space help dismantle the essentialisms that inflame global conflict and shape students' worldviews.

In chapter 8 Ken Derry describes his use of film to highlight the "semantic tension and ambiguity" that is endemic in religious traditions and in artistic depiction of them. Because students feel empowered and qualified to interpret film in ways that they may not with texts, film's religion-like capacity to construct social identity and generate myth lends itself especially well to collaborative, classroom analysis as well as to interpretive writing. In Derry's examination of six cinematic explorations of physical, structural, and mythic violence—from superhero fantasies to films depicting the postcolonial state of indigenous peoples—we see how his teaching methods uncover and critique both the ways that religiously themed violence is represented in film and the ways that film is implicated in normalizing religious violence. Derry dwells in the concrete, opening his pedagogical strategies and sources to suggest how film might activate students' learning of theory in semester-length courses or those that would choose to employ it selectively.

Randal Cummings's essay "Teaching Religion, Violence, and Pop Culture" explains how his course Myth, Religion, and Culture uncovers violent themes in contemporary music, advertising, television, and film with which students may be widely familiar. While little of this material displays overt religious content, Cummings mines it to illustrate the dominant theories of religious violence in the field of religious studies. Using a range of data borrowed from the everyday experience of his students, from bumper stickers on the road to the low-wage lifestyles of the American working class, Cummings trains his students to see religion and violence all around them.

The pedagogical payoff of teaching U.S. religious history in terms of violence is the subject of Jason C. Bivins's contribution in chapter 10. The dominant account of religion in America, found in both popular and academic histories, is one that foregrounds pluralism. Bivins argues that this story represses episodes and movements that reveal a darker underside to American religious life. Rather than treating the "bad stuff" as exceptions to a prevailing tale of a social order constructed around diversity, he teaches the intersections of religion, violence, and politics in the United States to situate another narrative alongside the normative one in students' minds. Imagining alternative histories, he finds, helps to sharpen their critical thinking capacities while also functioning as an intervention in the patterns of violence that this narrative reveals.

The relationship between religious traditions and violence may often be marked by negation, a point students seldom fail to note, and this volume on teaching could not responsibly conclude without exploring the pedagogy of the religious rejection of violence. A massive literature on peace making has continued to develop as a backdrop to the twentieth and twenty-first centuries' large-scale wars, arms races, and terrorist attacks. As the preeminent modern voice condemning all violence on the basis of religious conviction, Mohandas Gandhi has come to signify the position that the essence of religious faith is a commitment to peaceful coexistence. Paul Younger's essay in chapter 11 explains how he complicates that picture by moving students from a similar notion—that religion is largely about "self-cultivation and the quest for truth"—to show them what Gandhi himself realized as the Indian independence movement unfolded: that the postcolonial era would entail a strong and dangerous linkage between religion and state. Younger details how his course, taught to largely diasporic South Asians in Canada, presents Gandhi not simply as a pacifist motivated by a deep spirituality but as a postcolonial strategist wrestling with how to effectively dislodge colonial power. His students come to see that political and social conflict during independence inaugurated a decisive shift that fashioned religion as the primordial trait of a specific people and the natural basis for its polity. Century-old debates about Indian society, religion, and politics take on new relevance as his students examine the issues and movements that shaped their parents' and grandparents' lives and the subsequent experience of their generation.

If Gandhi represents the religious rejection of violence as the polar contrast to religious justifications of violence, other religious voices have historically taken a middle stance, finding that certain circumstances and injustices might demand the use of force as a proper moral response. In chapter 12 William French describes his experience teaching a course on the most prominent of the Western religious traditions to stipulate the conditions necessary for the moral use of armed force, the just war tradition, whose roots are in medieval Catholic theology. His course trains students in critical thinking about violence by emphasizing the careful analysis of wartime logic and the restraint of violence that this theological tradition has demanded. French involves them in creative moral reasoning by exploring with them the possible expansion of the theory's criteria, on the basis of the planet's accumulated experience of one hundred years of modern warfare, to include a consideration of postwar concerns as part of the assessment of an action's moral status.

The post-9/11 years have seen an upsurge in the overt targeting of scholars and artists by groups who would silence the criticism and interpretation of religious traditions by those who do not speak from within them. The two authors of chapter 13, one the former department chair of a faculty member attacked by religious activists opposed to his work, and the other the author of a book assailed by a similarly offended audience, Laurie L. Patton and Jeffrey J. Kripal respectively, have firsthand experience of the threat of religious violence.[8] Their dialogue on what those experiences have taught them about the scandal that religious studies teaching and scholarship represent to some segment of religious practitioners concludes this volume. Patton and Kripal discuss three topics essential for students conducting critical and historical analyses of religious violence: the nature of authorship in the humanities and the liberal arts; the Christian and Jewish character of critical theorizing about religion; and the necessary offense that the study of religion poses to religious communities. They conclude each section with a set of generative discussion questions for instructors to pose to students thinking broadly about the critical work of the religious studies scholar in an age of conflict and terror.

NOTES

1. Russell T. McCutcheon, "The Tricks and Treats of Classification: Searching for the Heart of Authentic Islam," in *Religion, Terror, and Violence: Religious Studies Perspectives*, ed. Bryan Rennie and Philip L. Tite (New York: Routledge, 2008), 87, 90; Tomoko Masuzawa, *The Invention of World Religions: Or, How European Universalism Was Preserved in the Language of Pluralism* (Chicago: University of Chicago Press, 2005).
2. See my response to Masuzawa's book, "*World* Religions or World *Religions*? A Response to Tomoko Masuzawa," *Council of Societies for the Study of Religion Bulletin* 35/1 (Fall 2006): 9–11, and her response to me and three other critics that

follows, "Author's Response—Review Symposium on *The Invention of World Religions*." In fairness to McCutcheon, he has discussed at length how one might dismantle the received categories of religious studies with students, but, in my judgment, his attempts fall short of actually addressing the gulf I am talking about and do not take seriously the pervasiveness and tenacity of these very categories in the world outside of the critical study of religion. Except for one very good short section on a classroom exercise he has students conduct on category formation, his description of his courses discusses the content of the readings and the structure of the course alone, i.e., not how to help undergraduates connect with abstruse theory; see the four chapters that constitute part IV of McCutcheon, *Critics Not Caretakers: Redescribing the Public Study of Religion* (Albany: State University of NewYork Press, 2001), 153–236; the category formation exercise is discussed on 230–31.

3. Following the examples examined in Eric Bain-Selbo, *Game Day and God: Football, Faith, and Politics in the American South* (Macon, GA: Mercer University Press, 2009), 53–68; and Jason Bivins, *Religion of Fear: The Politics of Horror in Conservative Evangelicalism* (New York: Oxford University Press, 2008), 129–68.

4. There is a small body of literature on the pedagogy of religious violence. See the series of short articles edited by Tazim R. Kassam in the American Academy of Religion's *Religious Studies News*, "Spotlight on Teaching: Teaching about Religion and Violence," *RSN* 18/4 (October 2003); also see Andrew O. Fort, "Teaching Liberal Arts Undergraduates about Hinduism amid Theoretical and Political Contestation Today," *Teaching Theology and Religion* 9/3 (2006): 156–64. The journal *Method and Theory in the Study of Religion* has long shown commitment to teaching and has published a few pieces that gesture toward the pedagogical contextualization of religious conflict within a nexus of historical and political factors; see, e.g., J. P. Burris, "Text and Context in the Study of Religion," *Method and Theory in the Study of Religion* 15/1 (2003): 28–47; Michael L. Satlow, "Disappearing Categories: Using Categories in the Study of Religion," *Method and Theory in the Study of Religion* 17/4 (2005): 287–98; Ivan Strenski, "Why Is It Better to Know Some of the Questions Than All of the Answers?" *Method and Theory in the Study of Religion* 15/2 (2003): 169–86. More explicitly about teaching is Amir Hussain, "Teaching Inside-Out: Teaching Islam," *Method and Theory in the Study of Religion* 17/3 (2005): 248–63. Finally, Omid Safi has written a reflective piece about teaching Islam on and in the aftermath of 9/11: "Teaching Islam through and after September 11: Towards a Progressive Muslim Agenda," in *Religion, Terror, and Violence: Religious Studies Perspectives*, ed. Bryan Rennie and Philip L. Tite (New York: Routledge, 2008), 201–20.

5. David Kember, with Carmel McNaught, *Enhancing University Teaching: Lessons from Research into Award-Winning Teachers* (New York: Routledge, 2007).

6. R. Scott Appleby, *The Ambivalence of the Sacred: Religion, Violence, and Reconciliation* (Lanham, MD: Rowman and Littlefield, 2000), 33–41.

7. *Sui generis* is a phrase now associated especially with the work of Russell T. McCutcheon. See especially *Manufacturing Religion: The Discourse on Sui Generis Religion and the Politics of Nostalgia* (New York: Oxford University Press, 1997).

8. Paul B. Courtright's *Gaṇeśa: Lord of Obstacles, Lord of Beginnings* (New York: Oxford University Press, 1985) was initially attacked by Hindu activists during the time that Patton was chair of his department. Kripal's *Kali's Child: The Mystical and the Erotic in the Life and Teachings of Ramakrishna* (Chicago: University of Chicago Press, 1998) came under fire around the same time. Both remain the objects of frequent petitions and protests.

BIBLIOGRAPHY

Appleby, R. Scott. *The Ambivalence of the Sacred: Religion, Violence, and Reconciliation*. Lanham, MD: Rowman and Littlefield, 2000.

Assman, Jan. *The Price of Monotheism*, trans. Robert Savage. Stanford, CA: Stanford University Press, 2010.

Bain-Selbo, Eric. *Game Day and God: Football, Faith, and Politics in the American South*. Macon, GA: Mercer University Press, 2009.

Bivins, Jason C. *Religion of Fear: The Politics of Horror in Conservative Evangelicalism*. New York: Oxford University Press, 2008.

Burris, J. P. "Text and Context in the Study of Religion." *Method and Theory in the Study of Religion* 15/1 (2003): 28–47.

Cobban, Helena. "Religion and Violence." *Journal of the American Academy of Religion* 73/4 (2005): 1121–39.

Courtright, Paul B. *Gaṇeśa: Lord of Obstacles, Lord of Beginnings*. New York: Oxford University Press, 1985.

Fort, Andrew O. "Teaching Liberal Arts Undergraduates about Hinduism amid Theoretical and Political Contestation Today." *Teaching Theology and Religion* 9/3 (2006): 156–64.

Hussain, Amir. "Teaching Inside-Out: Teaching Islam." *Method and Theory in the Study of Religion* 17/3 (2005): 248–63.

Juergensmeyer, Mark. *Terror in the Mind of God: The Global Rise of Religious Violence*, 3rd rev. and updated ed. Comparative Studies in Religion and Society 13. Berkeley: University of California Press, 2003.

Kassam, Tazim R. "Spotlight on Teaching: Teaching about Religion and Violence." *Religious Studies News* 18/4 (October 2003): i–xii.

Kember, David, with Carmel McNaught. *Enhancing University Teaching: Lessons from Research into Award-Winning Teachers*. New York: Routledge, 2007.

Kripal, Jeffrey J. *Kali's Child: The Mystical and the Erotic in the Life and Teachings of Ramakrishna*. Chicago: University of Chicago Press, 1998.

Masuzawa, Tomoko. *The Invention of World Religions: Or, How European Universalism Was Preserved in the Language of Pluralism*. Chicago: University of Chicago Press, 2005.

McCutcheon, Russell T. *Critics Not Caretakers: Redescribing the Public Study of Religion*. Albany: State University of New York Press, 2001.

———. *Manufacturing Religion: The Discourse on Sui Generis Religion and the Politics of Nostalgia*. New York: Oxford University Press, 1997.

———. "The Tricks and Treats of Classification: Searching for the Heart of Authentic Islam." In *Religion, Terror, and Violence: Religious Studies Perspectives*, ed. Bryan Rennie and Philip L. Tite, 81–95. New York: Routledge, 2008.

Pennington, Brian K. *Was Hinduism Invented? Britons, Indians, and the Colonial Construction of Religion*. New York: Oxford University Press, 2005.

———. "*World* Religions or World *Religions*? A Response to Tomoko Masuzawa." *Council of Societies for the Study of Religion Bulletin* 35/1 (Fall 2006): 9–11.

Safi, Omid. "Teaching Islam through and after September 11: Towards a Progressive Muslim Agenda." In *Religion, Terror, and Violence: Religious Studies Perspectives*, ed. Bryan Rennie and Philip L. Tite, 201–20. New York: Routledge, 2008.

Samman, Khaldoun. "Towards a Non-essentialist Pedagogy of Islam." *Teaching Theology and Religion* 8/3 (2005): 164–71.

Satlow, Michael L. "Disappearing Categories: Using Categories in the Study of Religion." *Method and Theory in the Study of Religion* 17/4 (2005): 287–98.

Seeman, Don. "Violence, Ethics, and Divine Honor in Modern Jewish Thought." *Journal of the American Academy of Religion* 73/4 (2005): 1015–48.

Smith, Wilfred Cantwell. *On Understanding Islam: Selected Studies.* The Hague: Mouton, 1981.

Stern, Jessica. *Terror in the Name of God: Why Religious Militants Kill.* New York: Harper-Collins, 2003.

Strenski, Ivan. "Why Is It Better to Know Some of the Questions Than All of the Answers?" *Method and Theory in the Study of Religion* 15/2 (2003): 169–86.

PART ONE

Traditions

CHAPTER 1

Striking the Delicate Balance

Teaching Violence and Hinduism

BRIAN K. PENNINGTON

In the middle of a recent semester in which I was teaching my biannual advanced undergraduate seminar called Religion and Violence, one of my finest students, a young woman who had excelled in the course until then, stopped in my office a few minutes before class was due to begin. We had been reading Sudhir Kakar's *The Colors of Violence*, a psychoanalytic portrait of Hindu-Muslim riots in the Indian city of Hyderabad in 1990, and watching portions of filmmaker Rakesh Sharma's documentary of the 2002 religious riots in the state of Gujarat, *Final Solution*. At first in a steady voice, but then haltingly, through tears, she told me, "I cannot come to class today, and I don't know when I can come back. Last year I was raped, and I can't handle this course anymore." As she briefly narrated (for only the second time, she said) that awful episode, a wave of shame came over me as I recognized my share of responsibility for her current anguish. Although previously unaware of her assault, I had compelled her to directly confront the narratives of both perpetrators and victims of physical and sexual violence and to imagine rape as a tool of terror. My sense of culpability deepened as she explained that she found the classroom atmosphere itself threatening due to the ignorance and insensitivity openly displayed by other (mostly male) students. A year later, another mature and dedicated student whose senior thesis on the religious elements of late twentieth-century genocide and ethnic cleansing I was supervising broke down my office, overcome by the personal accounts of terror and slaughter she was reading. She struggled for the rest of the year to complete a seventy-five-page thesis whose sources profoundly saddened her.

The distress these students experienced under my instruction and the ways their stories unfolded over subsequent months have come to signify for me some of the

pedagogical quandaries I face in teaching religion and violence. How does one negotiate the demand for a cool analysis of social forces when the material under scrutiny
is often graphic and horrifying? How can an instructor lead effective discussion in a
classroom populated by students with disparate life experience, some who know violence as a terrifying reality and others who are naive about its contours and lingering
effects? How can I myself manage delicate political and personal classroom dynamics
when my own interest in the material is motivated by a generally unconcealed anger
at the communal politics of India and a dismay that many people whom I love and
work with there participate in those politics? What is my responsibility to the victims
of violence, past and present? How can I introduce students to the many causes and
motives of religious violence without thereby normalizing or rationalizing it?

RELIGION, VIOLENCE, AND PEDAGOGY

This essay presents a topical approach to teaching Hinduism and violence. It is one I
have found helpful for orienting course content and student learning with respect to
those very pedagogical questions. My strategy is to represent religious violence in its
many diverse forms, to give voice to perpetrators and victims, and to assess a range
of motives for violence, from the reluctantly desperate to the vile. I rely on students'
capacity to expand their critical thinking skills, to complexify and nuance their
understanding of received concepts such as religion and violence, and to develop the
empathy and understanding that characterizes the scholarly traditions of the humanities. I aim, in short, to strike a delicate balance between two sets of countervailing
pedagogical demands that Hindu thought makes of me. I work toward the violence of
the contemporary period by conducting a historical survey to engage students in discussion and analysis that balance the tradition's powerful rationalizations of violence
against its equally compelling demands for the renunciation of violence. Additionally,
I take students through a series of readings, films, discussions, and exercises that
engage their empathic capacity as well as their analytic skills. Victim testimony,
graphic documentary footage, and hate speech can be disturbing to students (indeed,
one hopes they are) but are, to my mind, critical counterparts to the primary and
secondary literature that treats violence at some remove from actual trauma.

My course on religion and violence foregrounds Hinduism, the religious tradition
with which I am most familiar, but that is not its sole and exclusive emphasis. I also
spend considerable time teaching method by examining the many ways in which
violence might be conceived and studied. In this essay I underscore a number of
approaches and concepts I employ to help students develop a vocabulary for characterizing the religious violence of Hinduism, most of which would be easily adaptable
to teaching about other traditions. While its suggestions might be useful in developing graduate-level seminars, it emphasizes the undergraduate classroom setting,
where the tasks of fostering an invigorating and sensitive learning environment fall
largely to the instructor. Teaching Hinduism and violence effectively and in a manner
that appropriately reflects the depth of Hindu concern for violence—a concern
developed and refined over many centuries—requires a sensibility for the complexity

of Hindu thought on the matter and for the students' level of awareness of these complexities. A reasonably accurate and nuanced sketch of the subject can be achieved by a judicious choice of perspectives and materials, depending on the amount of time given to Hinduism in any particular course on violence.

"Harm" (Sanskrit: *hiṃsā*) is a subject on which Hindu traditions have ruminated for millennia. Perhaps no religious tradition has as complex and well developed a discursive approach to violence. Because both violence and its renunciation have been central concerns of Hindu discourse and practice from the Vedic period (c. 1500–900 B.C.E.), provoking as many sharp divergences in Hindu thought as widely accepted doctrines, virtually nothing can be said universally or generally about Hinduism and violence. For the purposes of trying to convey some of this complexity while also addressing the milieu of the twenty-first-century North American college classroom, I have identified three areas of pedagogical concern that I aim to keep distinct as students and I progress through a semester. The first section of this essay on topical considerations identifies some specific means by which Hindu texts have historically approached violence. In this section, I describe some of the rubrics under which I present Hindu violence to my undergraduates. In the next section on conceptual considerations I try to represent the substance of the second-order reflections that emerge in the later moments of a course, when the very act of pairing "religion" and "violence" starts to provoke more sophisticated student responses. It is these questions that establish the major instructional goals I pursue in my course. In the last section, on pedagogy, I describe just a few of the activities and assignments that I use to address those goals and that play a significant role in structuring the learning environment my students encounter.

TOPICS IN THE HISTORY OF HINDUISM AND VIOLENCE

The Hindu tradition has perceived and evaluated violence in a great many ways, and various Hindu voices have argued for and against the use of violence at different times and under different circumstances. A historical approach to Hindu thought on these questions ought to lead students to an awareness of the multiple contexts and agendas that have shaped the millennia-long Hindu conversation about the nature and role of violence. I organize my course on the principle that a deep contextualization of these Hindu discourses, that is, one that situates any particular understanding of the nature and moral status of violence in a concrete political and social milieu, is a powerful antidote to the simplistic ideas about religion, war, terrorism, and ethnic conflict cultivated in the mass media that constitutes such a formative influence on our students' lives. Violence is not any one thing, and the concept may include quite different acts and episodes. Students sometimes resist the idea that violence could include anything other than guns, bombs, fists, or box cutters. To encourage interdisciplinary and critical thinking, however, I make sure students encounter violence in very different kinds of sources and take stock of its more subtle, less overt expressions. In Hindu traditions, we find coercive and destructive acts as well as reflection on their nature and moral status in philosophical texts, ritual, myth, art, and in the politics of identity, past and present. I begin the course with my own typology of Hindu violence. This partial typology roughly corresponds to a periodization of Hindu history and provides a schematic backdrop to the course. Much of the semester consists of reading and discussion about the topics I introduce in the first couple of sessions. While the categorization is selective and reflects my own interests and training, I have students consider Hindu violence in the following forms.

Sacrificial Violence and Its Denial

The oldest texts of the Hindu tradition, the Vedas, already indicate a certain uneasiness about the violent sacrificial rites they appear to have inherited. There is some evidence for earlier human sacrifice,[1] but the violence of the earliest preserved Vedic sacrifices consists in the immolation of some animal victim. Even in the act, however, the texts themselves exhibit an unmistakable but muted ambivalence about the taking of animal life, at first because of the negative consequences associated with killing, later because of the spread of the teachings about karma, the law of moral cause and effect, and ahiṃsā, the avoidance of harm to another creature, often somewhat misleadingly glossed as "nonviolence."[2] This bifurcated consciousness begins to appear at the same time as the rise of asceticism and the appearance of Buddhism and Jainism, related movements that each elevated the ideal of ahiṃsā to a primary moral principle. In the Vedic corpus, early qualms about violence are most apparent in the Brāhmaṇas, commentaries and ritual instructions appended to the Saṃhitās, the oldest Vedic hymns, which express fewer such scruples. In these later layers, priests are enjoined to lead the sacrificial victim outside the altar precincts when it is killed. Further, the animal must be killed by suffocation to minimize the spill of blood and to muffle its cries of anguish (Śatapatha Brāhmaṇa 3.8.1–2). Eventually, vegetable offerings were substituted for the animal victim. All of these developments clearly indicate an ongoing struggle over the necessity and fruitfulness of animal sacrifice.

Scruples aside, the conduct of Vedic sacrifice (*yajña*) was a fundamental cosmic and social obligation borne by Brahmin priests qualified to offer it, for it played an essential role in the integration and maintenance of the universe.[3] It could also be marked by an agonistic drive, as, for example, when sacrificers or their sponsors tried to harness the powers obtained through these sometimes very costly and complex rituals for their material or political advantage.[4] The Ṛg Veda (c. 1500–1200 B.C.E.) depicts a worldview steeped in sacrificial themes and practices. Although it is found in a later layer of the text, the famed hymn the Puruṣasūkta (RV 10.90) explains that the cosmos itself proceeded out of the sacrifice of the primal person, Puruṣa. The violence of the sacrifice is here constitutive and creative: from Puruṣa's quartered body come both the matter and structure of the cosmos, as well as the four main caste groups, and from the sacrifice come the Vedas themselves, including the formulas and chants of sacrificial ritual. It is not, however, that sacrifice simply provides the materials from which the universe will be formed.

Sacrifice is the very logic and essence of cosmic (and, therefore, social) order, as is evident in the recursive and self-referential nature of the originary act itself: Puruṣa sacrifices himself to produce the goods of sacrifice, the hymns that describe, justify, and extol the sacrifice, and the system of social organization based on sacrifice. As the text puts it, "With the sacrifice, the gods sacrificed to the sacrifice" (RV 10.90.16).[5] The selection, immolation, and distribution of the offering are sanctified acts that replicate and participate in the generation of the universe, elevating sacrifice to the ultimate human act.

The Vedas, therefore, recognize that the order they undergird is founded in violence and preserved in violence. Simultaneously and paradoxically, however, the Ṛg Veda performs a denial of the violence of the sacrifice. The discussion of this paradox comes at an early moment in my course, and it marks the students' first encounter with a theme they will come to know well: violence is seldom, if ever, celebrated as a religious end in itself but is, on the other hand, repeatedly rationalized, denied, or normalized so it no longer appears as pure violence. The animal victim of the aśvamedha (the horse sacrifice that declares and commemorates a king's supremacy), for example, is told, "You do not really die through this, nor are you harmed. You go to the gods on paths pleasant to go on" (RV 1.162.21). Officiants also show their discomfort with the violence. The animal victim is led outside the sacred enclosure, and at the moment of slaughter the other priests turn their backs. The Vedic rationale for blood sacrifice is too richly embedded in an intricately sketched cosmos to suggest, as Houben and van Kooij have, that such denials and evasions put us "dangerously close to a great ruse to get a thirst for violence satisfied under cover of praiseworthy morals."[6] Nevertheless, in the Ṛg Veda one detects an incipient rationalism or unacknowledged embarrassment creeping in; perhaps the less-than-full embrace of slaughter reflects a "magico-ritualistic" fear on the part of the priests of ill effects that may rebound upon them.[7] Whatever its source, the early Vedas display a deep ambivalence about the violence of the sacrifice; they employ a battery of euphemisms and deflections to deny the reality of the violent death that sacrifice requires.[8] It would be too simplistic to argue that sacrifice is merely killing, but those who claim that it should be understood primarily as "not taking but giving life" also fail to appreciate the moral complexity the Vedic authors seem to sense.[9] The text's apparent need to deny or at least normalize violence signals its obvious concern for the ethical aspects of sacrificial slaughter.[10] Sacrifice is real violence, I tell my students, not only because it culminates in the deliberate death of an animal, but because its perpetrators and apologists betray their simultaneous fascination and revulsion. Vedic hymns of sacrifice are strongly affected by both the power and horror of sacrifice, and they are caught between reveling in and rejecting its transgressive character. Comprehending sacrifice requires taking stock of both drives. As others have observed, "making the violence in sacrifice sacred and making it euphemistic have, . . . in ways that are not unmarked by ethical qualms, been in constant tension with each other since ancient times."[11]

In addition to the embryonic ethical critique we can discern in the Vedas, it is also important to emphasize, lest we or our students romanticize or exoticize sacrificial violence as some mystical and mysterious ancestral practice, that a whole inequitable economy of power and wealth is also preserved by means of the sacrifice. First, an astonishing level of what a more cynical eye might regard as sheer avarice and exploitation is encouraged in the texts.[12] Two of the chief ends of the sacrifice are the rewards the sacrificer seeks, especially in terms of cattle, and the destruction of one's economic and political rivals. Second, the ideological basis of the caste system lies in Vedic sacrifice, whereby only the purest classes and the ritual's chief beneficiaries, Brahmin priests, are permitted to offer it, empowering them to demand the protection and services of the other three lower castes.

Violence Versus Nonviolence (Ahiṃsā)

Whereas the first section of the course emphasizes the paradox of a cosmology that views sacrificial slaughter as both essential and morally troubling, the next section examines the fuller development of a nonviolent ethic. I hope that students soon begin to understand how a shared metaphysical perspective and cultural worldview can produce quite divergent conclusions about actual practice. The concept of nonviolence is often considered a hallmark of South Asian religious thought. Ahiṃsā, which more literally means "noninjury," developed its moral connotation and the associated belief that harming other creatures entailed karmic consequences beginning around the eighth century B.C.E. Whether ahiṃsā emerged within Vedic thinking or as an ascetic rejection of the violence and ritualism of Vedic practice, the internalization of the sacrifice and the associated suppression of blood sacrifice mark an important moment in the dialectical relation between violent and nonviolent Hinduisms.[13] The repression of the violent elements of Vedic sacrifice was undertaken in the period of the later Upaniṣads to the Yogasūtras,[14] while animal sacrifice would continue to be practiced in some quarters and occasionally experienced revival.[15] (It is important to note that non-Vedic animal sacrifice is not uncommon in popular Hinduism in India today.) This period, 500 B.C.E.–200 C.E., effectively laid the groundwork for centuries of later commentary and debate in Hindu traditions over the use of violence. Roughly contemporaneous with the appearance of Buddhism and Jainism, the composition of the Upaniṣads and the development of ascetic practices in early Hindu communities represented a transformation and transmutation of Vedic ritual. The sacrifice continued to be a model on which communion with supernatural entities was imagined, but with several turns to its logic. First, the sacrifice was metaphorized and interiorized such that various mental actions were imaginatively correlated with those of Vedic sacrifice, and "the individual person's own inner being [became] the true sacrificial arena."[16] In effect, one could perform the sacrifice mentally, with the material elements of the ritual (e.g., the food offerings) now imagined as elements of the cosmos, human consciousness, or the body. The Bṛhadāraṇyaka Upaniṣad, one of the earliest of the Upaniṣads (seventh–sixth century B.C.E.), illustrates the new line of reasoning: "the dawn, verily, is the head of the sacrificial horse, the sun the eye, the wind the breath, the open mouth the . . . fire; . . . The rising (sun) is the forepart, the setting (sun) the hind part, when he yawns then it lightens, when he shakes himself, it thunders, when he urinates, then it rains" (1.1.1). Second, directly or implicitly, the violence of the sacrifice was rejected. While the Bṛhadāraṇyaka Upaniṣad subtly associates injury and violence with karmic penalty and consequent rebirth (1.5.14), the roughly contemporaneous Chāndogya Upaniṣad does so directly (8.15).[17] In all likelihood, the widespread ascetic antiritualism of the late Vedic period (i.e., from the fifth century) formed the root of later ideologies of nonviolence, when the fairly muted anxiety of the earlier Vedic period burgeoned into an argument for substitutionary vegetable sacrifice and an ethic of nonviolence.[18] Ahiṃsā slowly took hold in Vedism, as we have seen, but never fully, and whether it arose within Vedic circles or was appropriated from Buddhist, Jain, and ascetic communities in general is unclear. Houben sees a mixed picture over the 2,000 years that begin with the Ṛg Veda. A gradual move away from sacrificial violence and even the most veiled reference to human sacrifice as a theoretical possibility is clearly evident during the period of antiritualistic, ascetic forest communities associated with the Upaniṣads and the early forms of Buddhism and Jainism. A period of revival of sacrificial violence and its justification followed the fall of the Mauryan Empire (second century C.E.), but this revival itself then gave way to a more enduring rejection of sacrificial violence and the eventual adoption of ahiṃsā and vegetarianism as Brahminical norms.[19] Michaels argues that ahiṃsā emerged when the Aryan migration was complete and opposition to Brahminism and the prominence of Brahminical sacrifice could arise.[20]

A related shift in early Hinduism was the widespread substitution of vegetal offerings for blood sacrifice. While Vedism turned on the principle that sacrifice and its associated violence fed the cosmic furnaces that generated life, settled agricultural societies that followed the long, slow Aryan migration opened up new conceptual possibilities at the same time as asceticism and anti-Brahminical and ascetic ideologies were taking hold.[21] Philosophical reflection on Vedic sacrifice concluded that elements of *yajña* were homologous with cosmic principles and forces, and substitution was therefore logically possible and ideologically unproblematic. In later Hinduism, the earlier ethical qualms noted above became the very reason for vegetal substitution.[22] Through most of post-Vedic Hindu history, therefore, rice cakes have been offered as stand-ins for living offerings, and today the shattering of a coconut symbolizes the breaking of one's own skull and the individual ego it houses.[23]

Rājadharma and Legitimate Violence

As Houben and van Kooij observe, religions rarely promote violence as an end in itself but generally find justification for it as an undesirable but necessary evil.[24] Accordingly, many Hindu texts and commentaries fully accommodate violence that preserves or advances social stability. In classical Hindu thought, the right and obligation to employ violence to secure the socioreligious order falls to the members of the second, or Kshatriya, caste. When used judiciously, dispassionately, and for the preservation of order and the defense of piety, violence and force are the king's dharma—his duty—and this "legitimate" violence is solely his prerogative, dele-gated to those he commissions. An important source for Hindu thinking on the problem of royal might is the Indian epic tradition. In their discrete episodes and larger themes, the Sanskrit epics the Mahābhārata and Rāmāyaṇa are deeply con-cerned about the apparent necessity of force for the protection of the virtuous and innocent. On the one hand, violence is unambiguously karmic; that is, the perpe-trator of harm can expect to pay for the act according to the relentless laws of karma, regardless of motive. On the other hand, the king's failure to secure his subjects' protection and ability to perform their dharma signals his neglect of his own dharmic duties. The king and his warriors are caught in a double bind: to shrink from the violence required to maintain a virtuous kingdom is a great shame and a dereliction of caste duty, and yet the fruits of kingship are poisoned by their associ-ation with violence and bloodshed.[25] Contemplating the cost of the righteous war he is about to wage, the Mahābhārata's Arjuna became paralyzed thinking about the ethical paradox and initially refused to fight in the epic's most famous episode, the Bhagavad Gītā. Similarly, King Rama, the hero of the Rāmāyaṇa, did penance for killing the demon Ravana who kidnapped his wife. The ambivalence of Hindu thinking on the issue of violence is apparent here: royal muscle is the umbrella under which ascetics and Brahmins may pursue the ostensibly higher path of ahiṃsā. Only by means of Kshatriya violence is the renouncer's nonviolence even possible. Framed another way, under such a conceptual regime, nonviolence is, si-multaneously, impossible and the highest moral ideal.[26]

Passages from the Dharmaśāstras, classical legal discourses contemporary with the epics, link these disparate castes and discourses in an effort to resolve the par-adox. Chapter 7 of the Mānava Dharmaśāstra (The Laws of Manu) argues that the king's rod (or *daṇḍa*) symbolizes the legitimate violence necessary for nonviolence: the two require one another for the mutual rationalization they provide.[27] Arjuna had explicitly extolled the king's legitimate and necessary use of force himself, declaring, "*Daṇḍa* is dharma itself," and signaling the claim that its judicious and dispassionate use was the very essence of royal duty.[28] In the Hindu tradition, the great Mahābhārata war is therefore considered an elaborate sacrificial undertaking that provides for the order and stability of the cosmos.[29] The Brahmin and Kshatriya ideologies of violence, ultimately irreconcilable, establish their pact in the logic of the sacrifice. The insoluble questions of legitimate violence are, if not put to rest, at least set aside by associating its performance with the sanctity and mystery of the *yajña*. Killing in the spirit of pure sacrifice for a righteous cause allows one to over-look the violent nature of the act and the suffering it directly causes.[30]

Because it meets the paradox of legitimate violence head on and lends itself to a variety of interpretations on that issue, the Bhagavad Gītā remains an unmatched teaching resource on the subject of the religious sanction of violence. Its treatment of the contradictory Hindu impulses evident from the Vedic texts forward—the preservation of a just order and the avoidance of all harm—has been the subject of centuries of commentary. The most important modern debates erupted in the Independence movement in which rival interpretations of the Bhagavad Gītā by Mahatma Gandhi and Bal Gangadhar Tilak were composed and widely circulated.[31]

The former advocated ahiṃsā and the latter armed confrontation with the British. Tilak read the Gītā's call to perform one's duty without attachment to the fruits of that action in a fairly literal manner. His *Gītā Rahasya* was a manifesto calling for armed resistance to the British inspired by the Gītā's endorsement of Arjuna's righteous war.[32] Mahatma Gandhi, Tilak's antagonist, read the text allegorically, seeing its apparent endorsement of legitimate force as a metaphor for selfless action that did not gratify itself by succumbing to violence.[33] As an introduction to Hindu conceptions of violence and duty, the Bhagavad Gītā and its interpreters provide an excellent resource for pursuing the question of whether religious war can serve a general, higher good.[34]

The Self-Inflicted Violence of Asceticism

Hindu conceptions of violence cannot be adequately explored without taking full account of the prominence of nonviolence in the historical development of Hindu traditions. Similarly, the range of students' understanding of Hindu violence would be limited if violence were considered only when it is directed at others. The internalization of violence in the form of harm inflicted on oneself as an expression of surrender to God or in a fierce pursuit of divine merit represents a common theme in the theory and practice not only of popular, devotional Hinduism, as indicated above, but also of ascetic practices. Depriving oneself of food, causing deliberate pain or discomfort, holding a limb in one position until it withers, living in rugged or exposed conditions, and bathing in icy waters are all practices of self-inflicted harm that ascetics have undertaken to elevate their consciousness above the plane of physical existence and its limitations. We have already seen that in the case of bloody Vedic sacrifice, violence was perpetrated on some animal victim, and the resulting benefits accrued to both the sacrificer and the victim, whose suffering and death were denied or explained away and whose enjoyment of the fruits of its immolation was said to take place in some transcendent realm. The period of the Upaniṣads saw a rejection of this sacrificial violence in favor of transforming one's body or mind into the site of the oblation. In ascetic transmutations of this sacrificial logic, the problematic violence was not denied, but fully embraced, such that pain and reward were rendered identical and both accrued to the sacrificer-victim, the one who, through self-abnegation or mortification, did harm to the self.

The substitutions that allowed a shift from blood to vegetal sacrifice showed the innovation possible when the elements of the rituals, long sanctified already, were understood metaphorically or allegorically. A pumpkin could represent a head, for example, and the rituals of sacrificial exchange could be steadfastly observed in a milieu of rising discomfort with blood sacrifice. Similarly, self-denial and rigorous self-mortification in pursuit of merit and power indicate the obvious extension of a substitutionary logic that allowed an animal victim to stand in for the sacrificer in the first place, or a vegetal substitute for the animal.[35] One might see these transmutations as means by which the chain of karmic causes and effects is terminated: in ascetic harm to the self no sin is incurred; the individual willingly absorbs the violence, and its consequences are therefore inverted so the acts are rewarded in the accumulation of spiritual energy believed to constitute the fruits of asceticism.[36] These energies confer, among other things, the ability to bless or curse, and so one could also understand ascetic discipline as a sleight of hand that acquires for the adept a coercive power he previously could not have possessed.[37] The life of the renunciant might appear to be one of self-denial, but, under such a view, its potential tangible benefits come into focus. To problematize the concept of violence/nonviolence further, one might consider with students the various ways that Hindu ascetics, among whom the vow of ahiṃsa is primary and binding, have also fomented or participated in violence themselves.[38]

Fierce Gods and Their Divine Violence

In its climactic scene of divine self-revelation, The Bhagavad Gītā's eleventh chapter also gives insight into Hindu thinking on the violent nature of being itself. When Krishna's ultimate form displays itself voraciously destroying and consuming members of both rival armies, it silences Arjuna's moral quibbling by pointing out the ubiquitous, universal violence that is a part of every people's experience. Theistic traditions must ultimately attribute the plain facts of death and suffering to the deity in some respect, but the theodicies of some monotheistic traditions try to shield their gods from full culpability for evil. In the nondualistic schools of Hindu thought, however, the alternative that God must, at some level, be responsible for apparent violence, injustice, and cruelty can be explored.

In its literature, art, and ritual Hinduism confronts the reality of undeserved and inexplicable violence squarely. Observing Krishna's cosmic form wreaking its havoc, Arjuna exclaims, "As moths that fly to their full will rush to death in the blazing fire, so, too, worlds rush to death in your mouths" (11.29). Fierce or angry deities feature in other religious mythologies, but Hinduism is noteworthy in that many of its divine personalities, particularly certain goddesses, are identified primarily in terms of their violence, often extravagant and excessive. Goddess worship and theologies of divine feminine violence are common throughout Hindu India, but especially in the eastern region of Bengal and in south India. An especially fierce form is Kali, who emanates from the brow of the powerful goddess Durga as "pure violence" to vanquish the demons who threaten cosmic and social stability.[39] In some regions, popular devotion to the goddess addresses her as a prevalent actor in social and individual life, but one who is often believed to demand painful devotions from her followers and whose potential malevolence requires regular ritual control.[40] Appropriately contextualizing the capricious violence of the Hindu divine for students, especially the feminine divine, can be difficult. Many non–South Asian students can readily dismiss artistic motifs that depict belts of severed human heads and seemingly cartoonish displays of gore as infantile or primitive.

David Shulman has examined many of these violent themes, and his analyses offer alternative interpretations of violent myth and ritual that engage tales of divine cruelty without entertaining an apologetics for a terrifying cosmology. His understanding of the relationship between cosmic violence and devotional religion is applicable to Hindu concepts of the divine as well as to rituals that inflict violence on the self. In the tale of Ciruttontar, a fervent devotee of Shiva who sacrifices his son and cooks him for the god, Shulman does not find that the south Indian devotionalism reflected in the story either explains or justifies the divine appetite for cruelty. It depicts, rather, "the terror that is the truth of divinity," a terror that, nevertheless, resides in conjunction with divine compassion.[41] Each is characteristics of the Hindu divine, and the paradox remains unresolved and irresolvable. The "all-devouring absolute," depicted also in the hierophany scene of the Bhagavad Gītā, is at the heart of Hindu conceptions of deity, as is God's gracious intimacy.[42] On the one hand, these figures are expressions of the knowledge that the natural order is founded in and based upon sex, violence, and decay,[43] but their worship is also correlated with violent rituals of self-mortification,[44] warfare,[45] and, particularly in earlier centuries, robbery and murder.[46] Devotion to violent gods, it seems, has been both impetus and response to actual physical violence.

Devotional Violence

Contemporary devotional Hinduism, especially that practiced by non-Brahmin castes and in rural areas, offers numerous examples of the means by which nonascetic devotees may inflict violence on themselves or others.[47] Menacing spirits of the dead and threatening goddesses can be placated with bloody offerings,[48] piercings and fire walking can avert pox associated with the goddess,[49] and the merit obtained through pilgrimage can be enhanced when the devotee proceeds in painful ways—barefoot, by prostration, or without sleep. While the notion that supernatural personalities and the cosmos as a whole can be capricious and cruel is pervasive in Hindu India, the sometimes malevolent and always dangerous energies that pulse through and animate the universe are commonly engaged, addressed, managed, manipulated, or dispersed through such dramatic ritual expression. Possession by the deity, moreover, can be experienced as favor as well as trauma, for when the goddess takes residence in one's body, it can be profoundly disruptive to personal and domestic life. The north and south Indian concepts of śakti, dangerous feminine energy that nourishes and drives the universe, are associated with female sexuality as well as blood.[50] The well-attested convergence of these themes in Hindu ritual and text can open up classroom space for pursuing the overlapping semantic fields with respect to sex and violence as well as the relation between concrete social experiences of Hindu women and those forms of violent religious devotionalism exhibited predominantly (but not exclusively) by women.[51] When dealing with the socially marginal roles played by many Hindu women, I believe it is especially important to direct classroom analysis and discussion toward the concrete contexts in which women experience violence or participate in violent ritual expression, particularly through ethnographic literature, as a means of circumventing the universalizing tendencies of North American college students, which often render the developing world and its religions as uniformly oppressive to women.

Students can also rapidly and deftly deploy a "religion as the refuge of the dispossessed" analysis when confronted with such beliefs, particularly when the practitioners are poor and illiterate. The anxious striving to placate a menacing force can appear irrational, indulgent, and escapist. Nevertheless, however limited its purchase on the texts, images, and rites in question, a student's hypothesis that poverty and ignorance provide sufficient explanation of dangerous, emotional, and even self-mortifying religious practices can prove an entry point into a more nuanced discussion of the genesis and meaning of devotional religious practice that does harm to oneself. There is evidence, for example, that experiences of war and personal violence lead to rises in vows and rites that involve self-inflicted harm such as fire walking, swinging from metal hooks run through the flesh, and so forth. This kind of data suggest a more subtly rendered interpretation in response to students' somewhat crude formulations, namely, that violent themes in religion allow an exploration of the existential issues surrounding random, unmerited violence and injustice.[52] Another option for lending more nuance to students' analyses is to examine the conjunction of violence and eroticism. This relationship is clearly evident in the iconography and mythology of the ten Mahāvidyās—of whom Kali is one—the most powerful embodiments and exemplars of *śakti*, cosmic feminine energy.[53]

Violence, Nonviolence, and the Production of the Modern Nation-State

In my experience, the great majority of students studying religious violence for the first time initially conceive it largely in terms of the politicized violence of the postcolonial era and the media's most common rubrics for packaging religiously themed conflict: terrorism directed at Western targets and sectarian or interreligious conflict mobilized by identity politics. One could easily spend an entire course analyzing this contemporary violence, even if it were focused solely on India, South Asia, or Hinduism. If a course, however, examines Hinduism and violence more broadly and in a variety of historical instantiations, as this essay advocates, students encountering modern, politicized religious violence will display a heightened capacity to think critically about a variety of possible causes, motives, and meanings of the religious violence that the North American news media only seems to deliver according to familiar plot lines. To promote these objectives, I wait until late in the semester to take up historically recent episodes of conflict between Hindus and India's religious minorities.

Contemporary religious violence in India can be approached from a number of angles, and grappling with its multiple sources and outcomes is the primary means by which students can come to awareness of the complexity of the modern production of violence. First to consider may be the politics of communalism in India and the demographic factors that drive it. In India, religion and nationalism operate under a symbiotic pact whereby they share leadership and also supply one another ideological legitimacy and visions of a utopian society.[54] Ainslee Embree has pointed out that the link between religion and the Indian nation has been forged and exploited by the two most successful nationalist movements in independent India and that each, although ostensibly the other's rival, has been implicated in communal violence. Tolerant "neo-Hinduism," embodied especially by Gandhi, staked its future on the essentialist claim that all religions have truth at their core. Gandhian nationalism promoted tolerance of all religions as a fundamental Indian value, but, by relying heavily on a Hindu vocabulary, this discourse alienated many Muslims and seemed implicitly to deny them full status as citizens.[55] Gandhi's neo-Hinduism was also largely responsible for the post-Independence construction of India as a pluralist state with a secular constitution, a fierce thorn in the side of those religious communities who do not share its liberal and universalist commitments. "The grimmest commentary on the irrelevance of the neo-Hindu solution," Embree writes, "is given in the bitter religious riots" that have plagued India since Independence.[56] The other strand of Hindu nationalism has come from the radical Hindu right. Its direct provocation of Muslims and other religious minorities, whom it sees largely as second-class occupants of a Hindu land, appeals quite consciously to urban Indians, those most beset by modernity's challenges to tradition.[57] Espousing an agenda signaled by the term "Hindutva" (or "Hinduness"), religious nationalists have transformed the ascetic renouncer, whose position and power in classical texts had been predicated upon his repudiation of desire, into a political agent. By tradition, sadhus and babas are politically and socially disinterested renouncers of all worldly aims. Sponsored by Hindu nationalist organizations and using the power of the media in the 1990s, some renouncers attained celebrity status and aggressively pursued power on behalf of those political parties and forces that nursed the notion of Hindus as a besieged majority in a secular state that "panders" to minorities.[58]

The emergence of the nation-state has introduced both new forms and new scales of religious violence to the world. The process of state formation itself is largely the project of monopolizing violence and curtailing its use among free individuals. The more recent rise of the postcolonial nation-state has often involved internal struggles for power within multiethnic and multireligious societies. Configured as the organic expression of a communal identity constituted on linguistic and religious bases, the modern nation-state may incite or inspire violence directed at the outsider within. Conversely, pluralism, secularism, and the state itself are often the targets of religious practitioners who feel themselves alienated from the production of power and the distribution of its resources. All of these twentieth- and twenty-first-century global dynamics have been powerfully evident in South Asia. Religious radicals in India have attempted to seize power through democratic means but, given the plurality of any Indian identity and of Hinduism itself, always by forcefully delineating certain images, divine personalities, or texts as "fundamental" to a national Hindu identity. In 1991, well before the outbreaks of communal violence later that decade, Daniel Gold analyzed the production of nationalist ideology by prominent religious organizations.[59] For the Arya Samaj and the Rashtriya Swayamsevak Sangh, the Vedic corpus and the Hindu god Rama respectively were pressed into service as totems that became "foci for allegiance" and helped nurture sharp distinctions in communal identities that could be exploited by those who held or sought political power.[60] In the Indian context, until the modern period a ruler's exercise of power was governed by the rules of *rājadharma*, the right and obligation of the king and the king alone to employ the *daṇḍa* (staff, i.e., coercive force) to safeguard the social order he imposed.[61] The contemporary Indian state, whether administered by the Hindu nationalist Bharatiya Janata Party or the ostensibly secular Congress Party, has regularly availed itself of a new capacity both to incite violence against its own citizens and to construct that violence in ways that further the agendas of its perpetrators, largely Hindu, whose interests it represents.[62]

Right-wing Hindu politics often legitimate episodes of Hindu violence by calling them a "natural" reaction to various Muslim offenses, past or present. This was the explanation offered by Narendra Modi, chief minister of the west Indian state of Gujarat, for the rioting in 2002 that left roughly 2,000 people dead, most of them Muslims, after the burning of a train car that killed fifty-eight Hindu activists. Mob violence of this sort, however, has followed established patterns since Independence. Dozens of studies and reports have documented the production of right-wing Hindu violence against religious minorities. Paul R. Brass has analyzed the ways in which "institutionalized riot systems" have emerged in some regions prone to violence. These systems involve politicians, police, and local leaders who conspire to prepare for rioting by distributing flyers and spreading rumors that raise Hindu-Muslim tension and create an atmosphere of impending conflict. The same leaders plan the subsequent mob action in advance, see it through to a conclusion that further isolates and ghettoizes Muslims, and then produce a postriot narrative that erases their roles and attributes the origins of the mob action to other sources, often a spontaneous and "natural" Hindu outrage over some Muslim provocation. Brass and Christophe Jaffrelot have examined the role of specific institutions and actors who foment and benefit from communal violence. These studies undercut the narrative of religious identities in interminable conflict and demonstrate that communal violence in India is more often organized than spontaneous and is typically directed toward specific ends. Many other factors contribute to the local and national atmospheres that make communal riots possible, including the construction of communalized versions of Indian history that aim to give historical legitimation to the grievances that lead to riots, the cultivation of Hindu nationalist sentiments and an exclusivist national identity by political leaders, and the diversion of state power, including the police, to provide material support to the Hindu side in any outbreak.[63] All are the work of specific organizations and not, as they are made to appear, the manifestation of prevailing political sentiment or the product of ancient communal identities.[64] In independent India, most political violence is rational and preplanned but made to appear as the eruption of mob rage.

Hinduism also provides the mythological resources that embolden those who strategically employ religious violence and allow them to cast their acts as episodes in a cosmic war of good versus evil played out on the stage of history.[65] We have already had occasion to see how the Bhagavad Gītā and Mahābhārata can be cited by individuals or groups who might endorse the use of violence. Lord Rama, the protagonist of the other Hindu epic, the Rāmāyana, has become one major icon of the Hindu right. In defense of Rama's mythological birthplace, a crowd of protesters destroyed the Babri Masjid, a sixteenth-century mosque in the city of Ayodhya, in 1992 and have engaged in other acts of mob violence, especially in support of the reclamation of Rama's purported birth site on which that mosque was said to have been built by Muslim conquerors five centuries ago.[66] Well into the first decade of the twenty-first century, this event and the Babri Masjid site continue to be flashpoints for actual conflict and fodder for political leaders of all stripes.

The psychology of the mob and of individual rioters provides another window onto contemporary religious violence. Sudhir Kakar's 1996 psychoanalytic portrayal of riots and rioters in Hyderabad still stands as a definitive psychological treatment of the Indian communal riot, and its narrative style and individual profiles work particularly well with undergraduate students.[67] Kakar's study of the play of rumor, the heightened sense of communal identity that occurs during rioting, and the moral imaginations of both perpetrators and victims paints a captivating and rather haunting landscape of the personal and social worlds that inspire mob action. The psychoanalytic method, with its particular understanding of the etiology of human action, its concern for the relationship between personal and social realities, and its capacity to speak the language of moral discourse provides a helpful classroom complement to political (and often politicized) approaches to religious nationalism and its violence.[68]

Most of the religious violence witnessed in independent India has occurred between Hindus and Muslims. Students are often interested in the less frequent but just as horrifying episodes of violence between Hindus and other, non-Muslim religious communities in India. In this volume, Anne Murphy discusses 1984 rioting that targeted Sikhs. There have also been significant but regionally isolated clashes between Hindus and Christians. In the late 1990s and again in 2007–8, the state of Orissa was the site of extended violence between Hindus and Christians, on which academic literature is just emerging.[69]

THREE PEDAGOGICAL ISSUES

The foregoing topics and others an instructor might introduce, such as violence against women, the rules of warfare, vegetarianism, and so forth, are naturally central to planning and delivering any course. Careful selection of subject matter cannot take place without also considering the pedagogical goals one judges to be most important. These goals will themselves be determined by other factors: one's training and methodological leanings, the nature of one's department and institution, and the relationship of the specific course under development to others in the curriculum, to name a few. All teaching, that is to say, is at once personal and institutional. I teach at a small liberal arts college with a large, required general education core that emphasizes critical thinking, problem solving, historical and cultural contextualization, and ethical decision making. Furthermore, I teach in the Bible Belt of the American South, where there is not only little visible diversity across religious communities, but dominance by a single form of regional Christianity (the conservative, evangelical variety associated with the churches of the

Southern Baptist Convention but now increasingly seen in a growing number of nondenominational churches). Even though only a minority of our students belongs to these communities, this cultural homogeneity, fairly striking to new-comers from other parts of the United States, has often fully socialized them into the presumption that all religions are rather homogeneous. The major pedagogical objectives I contemplate have developed in this institutional context. While I aim, therefore, to teach my students a good deal about Hinduism and violence, I am also just as concerned to cultivate the critical skills and interdisciplinary instincts necessary for analyzing the intersections of religion and violence broadly and for appreciating the value of interdisciplinary approaches to the study of religion. In the specific professional setting I find myself, therefore, my main, overarching priorities for this course are to lead students in developing critical awareness about three related issues: the internally contested nature of religious traditions, the particularity of religious violence, and the social, civic, and hermeneutical perils of essentialism.

The Internally Contested Nature of All Religious Traditions

In many important and fundamental respects, Hinduism is a fiction,[70] but so are its sister concepts in the family of world religions, like Christianity and Buddhism. Although they may be important heuristic devices, these ideas permeate Western consciousness and languages. Intrareligious conflict, therefore, is often seen as anomalous rather than being the very character and meaning of religion as a social reality. One of the religious studies instructor's basic tasks is to make students aware of the internally contested nature of virtually all religious communities, claims, and institutions. When discussing the question of violent religions and religious violence, R. Scott Appleby's advice is particularly apt: it is better to think of every ostensibly cohesive religious tradition as more like a sustained argument over the significance and meaning of that religion's sources.[71] No religious tradition speaks with one voice about the use or eschewal of violence, and no religious voice represents that religion's perspective on violence (as no such perspective exists). This is particularly the case in Hinduism. From ancient Vedic sacrifice to contemporary justifications of communal attacks on Muslims, a powerful tradition of the rationalization of violence presents a strong and recurrent counter-point to Hinduism's storied philosophies of nonviolence. Hindu traditions have produced a spectrum of positions on the nature and moral character of violence, each of them representing itself as authentic and portraying others as false or mis-guided. Disagreements and divergent perspectives on these issues could not be more starkly evident over the many centuries of Hindu history my course surveys, yet our culture, our students, and I myself cling to such categories of analysis as Hinduism. I hope that by the end of a term, I have loosened some of their attach-ment to the idea that religions exist as observable entities in the world out there and reshaped their concept of religion as something that is defined by, rather than corrupted by, conflict.

The Particularity of Religious Violence

In addition to knowing what Hinduism's many textual sources and general teachings say about the nature and moral status of harm, I want students to develop some awareness of how acts of religious violence are always the products of specific social, political, and historical configurations. While understanding the different ways in which a tradition might conceive of violence is critical, so is an appreciation of the contingent etiology of any act of violence. My first step in cultivating such an appreciation in students is a classroom exercise in which I assign groups to each read a different, brief account of some newsworthy event: a terrorist attack, an episode of ethnic cleansing, a sectarian riot, a hate crime, and so on. I ask them to identify or imagine a possible set of causes, contributing factors, and circumstances that provoked the event and then to divide these into two columns, the religious and the nonreligious factors. They quickly find, of course, that it is exceedingly difficult to separate out religious from nonreligious elements or motivations in any act of violence, for, in the end, such a distinction will rest on one's particular definition of religion.[72] Is a hate speech targeting a religious minority delivered during a close-fought election campaign an expression of religion or politics? Is a suicide bombing conducted by a poor and unmarried young man for which he is promised not only a martyr's paradise but also a large cash payment to his mother making a religious or financial decision? There is no single or correct answer to such questions, and as students explore the possibilities, they begin to deconstruct the received wisdom that religion, however understood, is in itself an especially pervasive cause of violence. Their attention shifts from, for example, Hinduism and the role of its texts or leaders to social, material, and political causes. In comparing their lists, they start to see how distinctive their episodes are and how they all depend on a host of individual circumstances all being present. This exercise in isolating the specific contributions of religion to the global problem of large-scale violence, therefore, always fails, but that is exactly the point. It starts to lead the student toward a comprehension of the complexity of a question he might earlier have thought quite simple, namely, "how does religion promote violence?" A free-ranging classroom discussion on the question can amplify the effect. What one student sees as an appeal to religious tradition, a defense of a sacred site or practice, or response to a divine command, another sees as transparent rationalization, a thirst for revenge, or a political calculation. As students become more aware of the almost instinctual reification of religion that our language and culture promote, they are better equipped to analyze and interpret specific acts of religious violence and see them as highly contextual episodes.

If, however, any religious act can also be described or explained by reference to context-specific, nonreligious factors, is religion itself responsible for religious violence? Doesn't this mean that religion is actually not the problem? In terms of developing students' critical thinking and their skills in social and historical analysis, this question about religion's culpability may be the most persistent and fruitful issue raised in a term. Students will have read authors who argue that religion causes conflict only when its social functions—such as its construction of utopian futures, its provision of certain social institutions, and its ability to legitimate any act or institution—intervene.[73] Mine will also have read Mark Juergensmeyer (whose work as a student resource Aaron Hughes and William Morrow both discuss in this volume), who maintains that religion itself is to blame, for it articulates a "transcendent moralism" that justifies violent acts, cultivates the "ritual intensity with which they are committed," and develops the "images of struggle and transformation" that promote the waging of cosmic war on the human plane.[74] Because a clear answer to the question of whether religion itself or any particular religion such as Hinduism necessarily possesses the potential for violence requires a carefully constructed case that takes these complexities into account, I always include some version of it as a final exam essay, less to test the students' responses than to assess their critical thinking on the problem (see Figure 1.1).

The Social, Civic, and Hermeneutical Perils of Essentialism

When the same question is posed in a slightly different way, another problem comes into focus: at their core, are religions benign quests for enlightenment and salvation that are occasionally hijacked by forces of evil, or is religion's inherent violence masked by its deceptively noble teachings? My students have routinely voiced both positions, assuming that there are originary and essential expressions of a tradition's particular genius. For those well disposed toward religion, Christianity is fundamentally about love and forgiveness; Hinduism about tolerance and spiritual insight; Islam about submission and obedience; Buddhism about compassion and renunciation, and so on. Paradoxically, perpetrators and victims of communal violence articulate parallel but inverse essentialist formulations that they share with a different group of students: Muslims are fanatical jihadists, Christians ardent evangelicals, Jews the oppressors of Palestine, and so forth. Many undergraduates, moreover, just as commonly believe that all religions really aspire to the very same things: harmony and salvation on the one account, hegemony and moral conformity on the other; for them, the distinguishing features of different religions are just window dressing for their underlying common aspirations. Our incoming students' street knowledge about religion and religions mitigates against the goals of historical and critical analysis, just as the partisans of religious conflict resist dialogue and meaningful civic engagement. The roots of both problems lay in the habits of homogenizing the other and collapsing difference into which too many of us are socialized. Interreligious violence itself and the persistent misdiagnosis of its origins each proceeds out of these faulty, essentializing assumptions.[75] Answering the question of religious violence by blaming historical accretions to or corruptions of a religion's transcendent, foundational insights betrays an acceptance of religions' customary rhetoric about themselves as an analysis of the origins and causes of violence. Likewise, a late-semester, knee-jerk condemnation of religion as essentially detrimental to human coexistence points to an absence of critical thinking about the complex cultural mechanisms that generate violence. The traditions of liberal education in the humanities have always confronted habits of thought, language, and perception like these directly. One of my chief standards for measuring my

---

Hinduism and Violence

Final Exam

Instructions: Answer each of the following two questions. I will not prescribe upper or lower word limits to your essays, but you should aim to answer each question both comprehensively and succinctly. Percentage values should indicate suggested relative length of responses. Essays will be evaluated according to their degree of precision, their overall development, the extent to which they are informed by course material, and their general merits as free-standing essays. There may be some overlap in your responses, but you should try to minimize it so you are not rehearsing the same material or arguments; if desirable, in one essay you may refer to your responses in another.

> Throughout the semester we have encountered groups, individuals, and ideas that try to justify the violence that they perform or promote. Write an essay in which you identify some general strategies that we have studied for justifying or rationalizing religious violence. Your choice of strategies should involve you in discussion of different periods of Hindu history. Examine each of these categories of justification by illustrating with specific material from our course readings (40%).

> We have also seen that "history," far from being a fixed set of events in the past that one could try to recover through various sources, is also a malleable political tool that can be invented or reinvented for the purposes or needs of any contemporary party. Write an essay in which you examine specific ways that some Hindu groups we have studied employ history as a tool for creating contemporary group identity, fostering conflict, or attaining political advantage (40%).

> Does religion necessarily contain the capacity for violence? Why or why not? (20%)

Figure 1.1 Final Exam.

course's success is the sophistication with which students can articulate what they have unlearned during the semester. To the degree that they can convince me that they are at least more aware of habitual patterns in their conception of religion and religions, I am satisfied that we have made important progress.

TWO COURSE ARTIFACTS

I have focused this essay on the reasoning that informs how I structure and deliver my course on Hinduism and violence, and I have aimed to give an overview of the major topics it covers and the objectives that drive the syllabus. Space limitations

Table 1.1 HISTORY OF HINDUISM AND VIOLENCE

Period	Representative texts	Selected issues
Early Vedic, 1500–800 B.C.E.	Ṛg Veda 1.162, 1.163, 10.90	The role of sacrificial violence in sustaining the cosmic order The fate of the sacrificial victim
Late Vedic, 800–400 B.C.E.	Chāndogya Upaniṣad 3.16–3.17, 8.5, 8.15	Emerging qualms about sacrificial violence
	Kauṣītaki Upaniṣad 2.5	Ascetic self-violence Early hints of ahiṃsā ethic
Epics and Dharmaśāstras, 400 B.C.E.–500 C.E.	Synopses of Mahābhārata 11 (Strī Parva, The Book of the Women) and 12 (Śāntī Parva, The Book of Peace)	Relationship between Brahmin nonviolence and Kshatriya violence
	Bhagavad Gītā, chs. 1–2 and 11	Arguments for and against dharmic violence
	Laws of Manu 7	King's dharma
Medieval, 500–1500	Bhāgavata Purāṇa 7.15	Vegetarianism Continuing ambivalence about animal sacrifice
Colonial and Imperial India, 1600–1915	Rammohan Roy, "Address to Lord William Bentinck" Bal Gangadhar Tilak, "The Shivaji Festival"	Accommodation of and resistance to imperial violence
Independence Movement, 1915–1947	V. D. Savarkar, *Hindutva: Who is a Hindu?*	Exclusivist identities and communal violence
	Mohandas Gandhi, *My Experiments with Truth*	Satyāgraha

prevent me from doing more, but in this last section, I provide two artifacts from the course as more immediately practical suggestions to those who are approaching a similar teaching assignment for the first time or rethinking an existing course. They come from documents my students encounter at two quite different moments, the very beginning and the very end of the semester.

Table 1.1 represents a rough periodization of Hindu history that I hand students in the first week, keyed to the major topics in Hinduism and violence as I present them. The middle column includes a handful of primary sources that are easily available in translation and that help students see that very different ideas about the use of violence are products of certain historical debates and that all of these often competing ideas still coexist in the tradition. Most of the passages are brief, intended only to give them a sense of one period's way of framing violence, but the table as a whole aims to sketch the course's bigger picture for them. They read much more through the semester, especially in secondary literature, and the bibliography at the end of this essay identifies many of my assigned texts as well as other resources on Hinduism and violence.

Second, I share the most recent version of my final exam (Figure 1.1). It requires three essays of different lengths, and I give it in take-home format to allow students the time and space to develop their responses carefully. As I hope the questions clearly communicate, I am much more interested at the end of the semester in their critical thinking on the questions of Hinduism/religion and violence than their recall of specific historical facts or developments. (My midterm exam is typically designed to assess their command of the "facts.")

CONCLUSION

I began this essay by recounting two emotional conversations with students who had attained some level of awareness about the stark and terrifying realities of religious violence that my course readings, lectures, and films had merely signified. As I have thought about those vulnerable office moments, including my own responses to them, I have wondered if, the pain and awkwardness aside, they suggest I was doing something right. Wendy Doniger once argued that sacrificial ritual both heightens and formalizes our consciousness of death, but that this formalization also introduces new anxieties that the attempt to tame violence by a structured and controlled encounter with it will fail.[76] Whether or not she is right, I wonder if good teaching about religion and violence might induce similar experiences in our most engaged students and reflect this same dialectic relationship between fear and formalism. As instructors, we can attempt to model an analysis removed from the experience of violence and hope, in that way, to produce a mature and incisive understanding of its motives and performances. The aim of college teaching in the humanities and social sciences often is, after all, to rationalize human experience, to isolate its formal and causative features, and thereby to demystify it. As in the cases of my troubled students, however, and perhaps in the case of long-dead Aryan sacrificers, our formalization may well fail to accomplish its objectives because awareness of the reality of pain, suffering, and killing is and should be terrifying. While the language of religious violence aims to normalize injury, harm, and death,[77] our languages of humanistic pedagogy can formalize and contextualize violence with the opposite aim, namely, to render it aberrant and unnecessary, precisely because its causes and motives can be brought to light.

NOTES

1. Roy E. Jordaan and Robert Wessing, "Construction Sacrifice in India, 'Seen from the East,'" in *Violence Denied: Violence, Non-violence and the Rationalization of Violence in South Asian Cultural History*, ed. Jan E. M. Houben and Karel R. van Kooij, Brill's Indological Library 16 (Leiden: Brill, 1999), 211–47.
2. Michael Witzel, "Vedas and Upaniṣads," in *The Blackwell Companion to Hinduism*, ed. Gavin Flood (Oxford: Blackwell, 2003), 80, 82.

3. William K. Mahony, *The Artful Universe: An Introduction to the Vedic Religious Imagination* (Albany: State University of New York Press, 1998), 104–36.

4. E.g., J. C. Heesterman, *The Inner Conflict of Tradition: Essays in Indian Ritual, Kinship, and Society* (Chicago: University of Chicago Press, 1985), 45–58; Laurie L. Patton, *Bringing the Gods to Mind: Mantra and Ritual in Early Indian Sacrifice* (Berkeley: University of California Press, 2005), 117–41.

5. All quotations from the Ṛg Veda refer to Wendy Doniger O'Flaherty's translation, *The Rig Veda* (London: Penguin, 1981).

6. Jan E. M. Houben and Karel R. van Kooij, "Introduction," in *Violence Denied*, ed. Houben and van Kooij, 8–9.

7. Jan E. M. Houben, "To Kill or Not to Kill the Sacrificial Animal (Yajña-Paśu)? Arguments and Ethical Perspectives in Brahminical Ethical Philosophy," in *Violence Denied*, ed. Houben and van Kooij, 119.

8. Boris Oguibénine, "On the Rhetoric of Violence," in *Violence/Non-violence: Some Hindu Perspectives*, ed. Denis Vidal, Gilles Tarabout, and Eric Meyer (New Delhi: Manohar, 2003), 73–76. A tendency persists among some Hindu apologists to deny the historical primacy or reality of blood sacrifice. See, e.g., Subhash Kak, *The Aśvamedha: The Rite and Its Logic* (Delhi: Motilal Banarsidass, 2002).

9. Axel Michaels, *Hinduism: Past and Present*, trans. Barbara Harshav (Princeton, NJ: Princeton University Press, 2004), 153.

10. Laurie L. Patton, "Telling Stories about Harm: An Overview of Early Indian Narratives," in *Religion and Violence in South Asia: Theory and Practice*, ed. John R. Hinnells and Richard King (London: Routledge, 2007), 19.

11. Denis Vidal, Gilles Tarabout, and Éric Meyer, "On the Concepts of Violence and Nonviolence in Hinduism and Indian Society," in *Violence/non-violence*, ed. Vidal, Tarabout, and Meyer, 15–16. Similarly, Kathryn McClymond argues that sacrifice may involve killing, but that sacrificial deaths are not violent because they aim to minimize suffering, in *Beyond Sacred Violence: A Comparative Study of Sacrifice* (Baltimore: Johns Hopkins University Press, 2008), 60–64.

12. Bruce Lincoln, *Death, War, and Sacrifice: Studies in Ideology and Practice* (Chicago: University of Chicago Press, 1991), 167–75.

13. Hugh B. Urban, "The Power of the Impure: Transgressing, Violence, and Secrecy in Bengali Śakta Tantra and Modern Western Magic," *Numen* 50/3 (2003): 280–82.

14. On the question of the origins of asceticism and a summary of debates on the question, see Henk W. Bodewitz, "Hindu Ahiṃsā and Its Roots," in *Violence Denied*, ed. Houben and van Kooij, 17–44.

15. Houben, "To Kill or Not to Kill."

16. Mahony, *The Artful Universe*, 45. An early articulation of this idea is found in the Kauṣītaki Upaniṣad, 2.5.

17. See also Joseph A. Magno, "Hinduism on the Morality of Violence," *International Philosophical Quarterly* 28/1 (March 1988): 81–82; Houben, "To Kill or Not to Kill," 116–17.

18. Bodewitz, "Hindu Ahiṃsā and Its Roots," 40–41.

19. Houben, "To Kill or Not to Kill."

20. Michaels, *Hinduism*, 153.

21. Ibid.

22. Brian K. Smith and Wendy Doniger, "Sacrifice and Substitution: Ritual Mystification and Mythical Demystification," *Numen* 36/2 (December 1989): 208.

23. On vegetal substitution, see McClymond, *Beyond Sacred Violence*, 65–91.

24. In their introduction to *Violence Denied*, 2.

25. Danielle Feller Jatavallabhula, "Raṇayajña: The Mahābhārata War as a Sacrifice," in *Violence Denied*, ed. Houben and van Kooij, 98.
26. Madeleine Biardeau, "Ancient Brahmanism, or Impossible Non-violence," in *Violence/Non-violence*, ed. Vidal, Tarabout, and Meyer, 95.
27. Ibid., 85–91.
28. Ibid., 93.
29. Jatavallabhula, "Raṇayajña," 69–103.
30. Tamar C. Reich, "Sacrificial Violence and Textual Battles: Inner Textual Interpretation in the Sanskrit *Mahābhārata*," *History of Religions* 41/2 (November 2001): 142–69.
31. Mohandas Gandhi, *The Bhagavad Gita According to Gandhi*, trans. John Stroheier (Albany, CA: Berkeley Hill Books, 2007); Bal Gangadhar Tilak, *Śrīmad Bhagavad Gītā Rahasya or, Karmayogaśāstra*, trans. Bhalchandra Sitaram Sukthankar (1935; reprint, New Delhi: Asian Educational Services, 2007).
32. Tilak, *Śrīmad Bhagavad Gītā Rahasya*.
33. A recent edition of Gandhi's discourses on the Gītā has been translated by John Stroheier, *The Bhagavad Gita According to Gandhi*.
34. See Biardieu, "Ancient Brahmanism," 102. An excellent summary and comparison of various pre-Independence thinkers' interpretations of the Gītā, including Tilak's and Gandhi's, is Satya P. Agarwal's *The Social Role of the Gītā: How and Why* (Delhi: Motilal Banarsidass, 1993).
35. Smith and Doniger, "Sacrifice and Substitution."
36. Oguibénine, "On the Rhetoric of Violence," 65–83.
37. Vidal et al., "On the Concepts of Violence and Non-violence," 16–17.
38. Véronique Boullier, "The Violence of the Non-violent, or, Ascetics in Combat," in *Violence/Non-violence*, ed. Vidal, Tarabout, and Meyer, 41–61. See also Paul Dundas, "The Non-violence of Violence: Jain Perspectives on Warfare, Asceticism, and Worship," in *Religion and Violence in South Asia*, ed. Hinnells and King, 41–61.
39. Sarah Caldwell, *Oh Terrifying Mother: Sexuality, Violence, and Worship of the Goddess Kali* (New Delhi: Oxford University Press, 1999), 122.
40. Ibid., 16.
41. David Shulman, *The Hungry God: Tales of Filicide and Devotion* (Chicago: University of Chicago Press, 1993), 33.
42. Ibid., 39.
43. David R. Kinsley, *Hindu Goddesses: Visions of the Divine Feminine in the Hindu Religious Tradition* (Berkeley: University of California Press, 1985), 173.
44. Paul D. Younger, *Playing Host to Deity: Festival Religion in the South Indian Tradition* (New York: Oxford University Press, 2002), 34–46, 147–50; Amy L. Allocco, "Snake Goddesses and Anthills: Modern Challenges and Women's Ritual Responses in Contemporary South India" (PhD diss., Emory University, 2009); Joanne Punzo Waghorne, *Diaspora of the Gods: Modern Hindu Temples in an Urban, Middle-Class World* (New York: Oxford University Press, 2004), 163–69.
45. Patricia Lawrence, "Kali in a Context of Terror: The Tasks of a Goddess in Sri Lanka's Civil War," in *Encountering Kali: In the Margins, at the Center, in the West*, ed. Rachel Fell McDermott and Jeffrey J. Kripal (Berkeley: University of California Press, 2003), 100–123.
46. Martine Van Woerkens, *The Strangled Traveler: Colonial Imaginings and the Thugs of India*, trans. Catherine Tihanyi (Chicago: University of Chicago Press, 2002), esp. 109–85.

47. William P. Harman, "Negotiating Relations with the Goddess," in *Dealing with Deities: The Ritual Vow in South Asia*, ed. Selva J. Raj and William P. Harman (Albany: State University of New York Press), 25–41.

48. Caldwell, *Oh Terrifying Mother*, 141.

49. Harman, "Negotiating Relations"; Allocco, "Snake Goddesses and Anthills."

50. Caldwell, *Oh Terrifying Mother*, 15–16.

51. Caldwell's fieldwork was among communities in which women are prohibited from participating in possession rites, but her work suggests compelling social and psychological hypotheses about what such rights mean to women; *Oh Terrifying Mother*, 188, 237–39.

52. Patricia Lawrence, "Kali in a Context of Terror: The Tasks of a Goddess in Sri Lanka's Civil War," in *Encountering Kali: In the Margins, at the Center, in the West*, ed. Rachel Fell McDermott and Jeffrey J. Kripal (Berkeley: University of California Press, 2003), 100–123.

53. David R. Kinsley, *Tantric Visions of the Divine Feminine: The Ten Mahavidyas* (Berkeley: University of California Press, 1997), 244–45.

54. Ainslee T. Embree, *Utopias in Conflict: Religion and Nationalism in Modern India* (Berkeley: University of California Press, 1990), 7.

55. Ibid., 43–46, 70.

56. Ibid., 46.

57. Ibid., 46–55.

58. Harbans Mukhia, "Communal Violence and the Transmutation of Identities," in *Religion, Religiosity and Communalism*, ed. Praful Bidwai, Harbans Mukhia, and Achin Vanaik (New Delhi: Manohar, 1996), 28. Contrast this contemporary rhetoric of violence among sadhus with Véronique Bouillier's reconstruction of the medieval development of sects of sadhus commissioned to use violence to protect the ascetics' community: "The Violence of the Non-violent, or, Ascetics in Combat," in *Violence/Non-violence*, ed. Vidal, Tarabout, and Meyer, 27–63.

59. Daniel Gold, "Organized Hinduisms: From Vedic Truth to Hindu Nation," in *Fundamentalisms Observed*, ed. Martin E. Marty and R. Scott Appleby (Chicago: University of Chicago Press, 1991), 531–93.

60. Ibid., 578.

61. See Jos Gommans, "The Embarrassment of Violence in Europe and South Asia, c. 1100–1800," in *Violence Denied*, ed. Houben and van Kooij, 287–315.

62. On the state's involvement in violence, see the many essays and reports in Siddharth Varadarajan, *Gujarat: The Making of a Tragedy* (New York: Penguin, 2002); on the construction of communal violence, see Paul Brass, *Theft of an Idol: Text and Context in the Representation of Collective Violence* (Princeton, NJ: Princeton University Press, 1997).

63. See ibid.; Asghar Ali Engineer, "Communal Violence and the Role of Law Enforcement Agencies," in *Religion, Religiosity and Communalism*, ed. Bidwai, Mukhia, and Vanaik, 127–42.

64. See Christophe Jaffrelot, "Opposing Gandhi: Hindu Nationalism and Political Violence," in *Violence/non-Violence*, ed. Vidal, Tarabout, and Meyer, 299–324.

65. Mark Juergensmeyer, *Terror in the Mind of God: The Global Rise of Religious Violence* (Berkeley: University of California Press, 2001), 146–66.

66. Pradip Kumar Datta, "VHP's Ram: The Hindutva Movement in Ayodhya," in *Hindus and Others: The Question of Identity in India Today*, ed. Gyanendra Pandey (New York: Penguin, 1993), 46–73.

67. Sudhir Kakar, *The Colors of Violence: Cultural Identities, Religion, and Conflict* (Chicago: University of Chicago Press, 1996).
68. On these matters, see also Thomas Blom Hansen, *The Saffron Wave: Democracy and Hindu Nationalism in Modern India* (Princeton, NJ: Princeton University Press, 1999), which uses Slavoj Žižek as a resource for portraying the social and psychological character of the riot, 202–13.
69. News reports on these events are widely available, but the scholarly literature is just emerging; e.g., Chad M. Bauman, "Reporting Violence: Media Accounts of Hindu-Christian Violence in Orissa and Beyond," paper delivered at the annual meeting of the American Academy of Religion, November 3, 2008.
70. Among many good works, see John Llewellyn, ed., *Defining Hinduism: A Reader.* (New York: Routledge, 2006); and my own *Was Hinduism Invented? Britons, Indians, and the Colonial Construction of Religion* (New York: Oxford University Press, 2005).
71. R. Scott Appleby, *The Ambivalence of the Sacred: Religion, Violence, and Reconciliation* (Lanham, MD: Rowman and Littlefield, 2000), 33–41.
72. It is perhaps more analytically useful, then, ultimately to proceed as Hansen does, by viewing radical religious ideologies as the products of neither religion nor politics exclusively or in some cooperative design, but of "public culture," that "public space in which a society and its constituent individuals and communities imagine, represent, and recognize themselves through political discourse, commercial and cultural expressions, and representations of state and civic organizations." Riots, to take one example, therefore, are not "pathological parentheses in a sea of normality" but "points of condensation" where everyday knowledge and experience of one's own tradition and of the communal other interact with received religious narratives, images, and ideologies; Hansen, *The Saffron Wave*, 203–5.
73. Jonathan Fox, *Ethnoreligious Conflict in the Late Twentieth Century: A General Theory* (Oxford: Lexington Books, 2002), 103.
74. Juergensmeyer, *Terror in the Mind of God*, 10.
75. Pennington, *Was Hinduism Invented?*, 183–87.
76. Wendy Doniger, *Tales of Sex and Violence: Folklore, Sacrifice, and Danger in the Jaiminīya Brāhmaṇa* (Chicago: University of Chicago Press, 1985), 19–21.
77. Patton, "Telling Stories about Harm."

BIBLIOGRAPHY

Agarwal, Satya P. *The Social Role of the Gītā: How and Why*. Delhi: Motilal Banarsidass, 1993.

Allocco, Amy L. "Snake Goddesses and Anthills: Modern Challenges and Women's Ritual Responses in Contemporary South India." PhD diss., Emory University, 2009.

Appleby, R. Scott. *The Ambivalence of the Sacred: Religion, Violence, and Reconciliation*. Lanham, MD: Rowman and Littlefield, 2000.

Bauman, Chad M. "Reporting Violence: Media Accounts of Hindu-Christian Violence in Orissa and Beyond." Paper delivered at the annual meeting of the American Academy of Religion, November 3, 2008.

The Bhagavad Gita. Trans. Laurie L. Patton. London: Penguin, 2008.

Biardeau, Madeleine. "Ancient Brahmanism, or Impossible Non-violence." In *Violence/Non-violence: Some Hindu Perspectives*, ed. Denis Vidal, Gilles Tarabout, and Eric Meyer, 85–104. New Delhi: Manohar, 2003.

Bodewitz, Henk W. "Hindu Ahiṃsā and Its Roots." In *Violence Denied: Violence, Nonviolence and the Rationalization of Violence in South Asian Cultural History*, ed. Jan E. M. Houben and Karel R. van Kooij, 17–44. Brill's Indological Library 16. Leiden: Brill, 1999.

Bouillier, Véronique. "The Violence of the Non-violent, or, Ascetics in Combat." In *Violence/Non-violence: Some Hindu Perspectives*, ed. Denis Vidal, Gilles Tarabout, and Eric Meyer, 27–63. New Delhi: Manohar, 2003.

Brass, Paul. *Theft of an Idol: Text and Context in the Representation of Collective Violence*. Princeton, NJ: Princeton University Press, 1997.

Caldwell, Sarah. *Oh Terrifying Mother: Sexuality, Violence, and Worship of the Goddess Kali*. New Delhi: Oxford University Press, 1999.

Datta, Pradip Kumar. "VHP's Ram: The Hindutva Movement in Ayodhya." In *Hindus and Others: The Question of Identity in India Today*, ed. Gyanendra Pandey, 46–73. New York: Penguin, 1993.

Doniger, Wendy. *Tales of Sex and Violence: Folklore, Sacrifice, and Danger in the Jaiminīya Brāhmaṇa*. Chicago: University of Chicago Press, 1985.

Dundas, Paul. "The Non-violence of Violence: Jain Perspectives on Warfare, Asceticism, and Worship." In *Religion and Violence in South Asia: Theory and Practice*, ed. John R. Hinnells and Richard King, 41–61. London: Routledge, 2007.

Embree, Ainslee T. *Utopias in Conflict: Religion and Nationalism in Modern India*. Berkeley: University of California Press, 1990.

Engineer, Asghar Ali. "Communal Violence and the Role of Law Enforcement Agencies." In *Religion, Religiosity, and Communalism*, ed. Praful Bidwai, Harbans Mukhia, and Achin Vanaik, 127–42. New Delhi: Manohar, 1996.

Fox, Jonathan. *Ethnoreligious Conflict in the Late Twentieth Century: A General Theory*. Oxford: Lexington Books, 2002.

Gandhi, Mahatma. *The Bhagavad Gita According to Gandhi*. Trans. John Strohmeier. Albany, CA: Berkeley Hill Books, 2007.

Gold, Daniel. "Organized Hinduisms: From Vedic Truth to Hindu Nation." In *Fundamentalisms Observed*, ed. Martin E. Marty and R. Scott Appleby, 531–93. Fundamentalism Project, vol. 1. Chicago: University of Chicago Press, 1991.

———. "Rational Action and Uncontrolled Violence: Explaining Hindu Communalism." *Religion* 21 (1991): 357–70.

Gommans, Jos. "The Embarrassment of Violence in Europe and South Asia, c. 1100–1800." In *Violence Denied: Violence, Nonviolence and the Rationalization of Violence in South Asian Cultural History*, ed. Jan E. M. Houben and Karel R. van Kooij, 287–315. Brill's Indological Library 16. Leiden: Brill, 1999.

Hansen, Thomas Blom. *The Saffron Wave: Democracy and Hindu Nationalism in Modern India*. Princeton, NJ: Princeton University Press, 1999.

Harman, William P. "Negotiating Relationships with the Goddess." In *Dealing with Deities: The Ritual Vow in South Asia*, ed. William P. Harman and Selva J. Raj, 25–41. Albany: State University of New York Press, 2006.

Heesterman, J. C. *The Inner Conflict of Traditions: Essays in Indian Ritual, Kingship, and Society*. Chicago: University of Chicago Press, 1985.

Houben, Jan E. M. "To Kill or Not to Kill the Sacrificial Animal (Yajña-Paśu)? Arguments and Ethical Perspectives in Brahminical Ethical Philosophy." In *Violence Denied: Violence, Non-violence and the Rationalization of Violence in South Asian Cultural History*, ed. Jan E. M. Houben and Karel R. van Kooiji, 105–83. Brill's Indological Library 16. Leiden: Brill, 1999.

Houben, Jan E. M., and Karel R. van Kooij, eds. *Violence Denied: Violence, Non-violence and the Rationalization of Violence in South Asian Cultural History*. Brill's Indological Library 16. Leiden: Brill, 1999.

Jaffrelot, Christophe. "Opposing Gandhi: Hindu Nationalism and Political Violence." In *Violence/Non-violence: Some Hindu Perspectives*, ed. Denis Vidal, Gilles Tarabout, and Eric Meyer, 299–324. New Delhi: Manohar, 2003.

Jatavallabhula, Danielle Feller. "Raṇayajña: The Mahābhārata War as a Sacrifice." In *Violence Denied: Violence, Non-violence and the Rationalization of Violence in South Asian Cultural History*, ed. Jan E. M. Houben and Karel R. van Kooiji, 69–103. Brill's Indological Library 16. Leiden: Brill, 1999.

Jordaan, Roy E., and Robert Wessing, "Construction Sacrifice in India, 'Seen from the East.'" In *Violence Denied: Violence, Non-violence and the Rationalization of Violence in South Asian Cultural History*, ed. Jan E. M. Houben and Karel R. van Kooiji, 211–47. Brill's Indological Library 16. Leiden: Brill, 1999.

Juergensmeyer, Mark. *Terror in the Mind of God: The Global Rise of Religious Violence*. Berkeley: University of California Press, 2001.

Kak, Subhash. *The Aśvamedha: The Rite and Its Logic*. Delhi: Motilal Banarsidass, 2002.

Kakar, Sudhir. *The Colors of Violence: Cultural Identities, Religion, and Conflict*. Chicago: University of Chicago Press, 1996.

Kinsley, David R. *Hindu Goddesses: Visions of the Divine Feminine in the Hindu Religious Tradition*. Berkeley: University of California Press, 1985.

———. *Tantric Visions of the Divine Feminine: The Ten Mahavidyas*. Berkeley: University of California Press, 1997.

Lawrence, Patricia. "Kali in a Context of Terror: The Tasks of a Goddess in Sri Lanka's Civil War." In *Encountering Kali: In the Margins, at the Center, in the West*, ed. Rachel Fell McDermott and Jeffrey J. Kripal, 100–123. Berkeley: University of California Press, 2003.

Llewellyn, John, ed. *Defining Hinduism: A Reader*. New York: Routledge, 2006.

Lincoln, Bruce. *Death, War, and Sacrifice: Studies in the Ideology and Practice*. Chicago: University of Chicago Press, 1991.

Magno, Joseph A. "Hinduism on the Morality of Violence." *International Philosophical Quarterly* 28/1 (March 1988): 79–93.

Mahony, William K. *The Artful Universe: An Introduction to the Vedic Religious Imagination*. Albany: State University of New York Press, 1998.

McClymond, Kathryn. *Beyond Sacred Violence: A Comparative Study of Sacrifice*. Baltimore: Johns Hopkins University Press, 2008.

McCutcheon, Russell T. *Critics Not Caretakers: Redescribing the Public Study of Religion*. Albany: State University of New York Press, 2001.

Michaels, Axel. *Hinduism: Past and Present*. Trans. Barbara Harshav. Princeton, NJ: Princeton University Press, 2004.

Mines, Diane P. *Fierce Gods: Inequality, Ritual, and the Politics of Dignity in a South Indian Village*. Bloomington: Indiana University Press, 2005.

Mukhia, Harbans. "Communal Violence and the Transmutation of Identities." In *Religion, Religiosity and Communalism*, ed. Praful Bidwai, Harbans Mukhia, and Achin Vanaik, 25–36. New Delhi: Manohar, 1996.

Oguibénine, Boris. "On the Rhetoric of Violence." In *Violence/Non-violence: Some Hindu Perspectives*, ed. Denis Vidal, Gilles Tarabout, and Eric Meyer, 65–83. New Delhi: Manohar, 2003.

Patton, Laurie L. *Bringing the Gods to Mind: Mantra and Ritual in Early Indian Sacrifice*. Berkeley: University of California Press, 2005.

———. "Telling Stories about Harm: An Overview of Early Indian Narratives." In *Religion and Violence in South Asia: Theory and Practice*, ed. John R. Hinnells and Richard King, 11–40. London: Routledge, 2007.

Pennington, Brian K. *Was Hinduism Invented? Britons, Indians, and the Colonial Construction of Religion.* New York: Oxford University Press, 2005.

The Principal Upaniṣads. Trans. S. Radhakrishnan. London: George Allen and Unwin, 1953.

Reich, Tamar C. "Sacrificial Violence and Textual Battles: Inner Textual Interpretation in the Sanskrit *Mahābhārata.*" *History of Religions* 41/2 (November 2001): 142–69.

The Rig Veda. Trans. Wendy O'Doniger Flaherty. London: Penguin, 1981.

Shulman, David. *The Hungry God: Tales of Filicide and Devotion.* Chicago: University of Chicago Press, 1993.

Smith, Brian K., and Wendy Doniger. "Sacrifice and Substitution: Ritual Mystification and Mythical Demystification." *Numen* 36/2 (December 1989): 189–224.

Strenski, Ivan. "Legitimacy, Mythology, and Irrational Violence in Hindu India." In *Ethical and Political Dilemmas of Modern India,* ed. Ninian Smart and Shivesh Thakur, 1–14. New York: St. Martin's Press, 1993.

Tilak, Bal Gangadhar. *Śrīmad Bhagavad Gītā Rahasya; or, Karmayogaśāstra.* Trans. Bhalchandra Sitaram Sukthankar. 1935. Reprint, New Delhi: Asian Educational Services, 2007.

Urban, Hugh B. "The Power of the Impure: Transgressing, Violence, and Secrecy in Bengali Śakta Tantra and Modern Western Magic." *Numen* 50/3 (2003): 269–308.

Van Woerkens, Martine. *The Strangled Traveler: Colonial Imaginings and the Thugs of India.* Trans. Catherine Tihanyi. Chicago: University of Chicago Press, 2002.

Varadarajan, Siddharth, ed. *Gujarat: The Making of a Tragedy.* New York: Penguin, 2002.

Vidal, Denis, Gilles Tarabout, and Éric Meyer. "On the Concepts of Violence and Nonviolence in Hinduism and Indian Society." In *Violence/Non-violence: Some Hindu Perspectives,* ed. Denis Vidal, Gilles Tarabout, and Éric Meyer, 11–26. New Delhi: Manohar, 2003.

Waghorne, Joanne Punzo. *Diaspora of the Gods: Modern Hindu Temples in an Urban, Middle-Class World.* New York: Oxford University Press, 2004.

Witzel, Michael. "Vedas and Upaniṣads." In *The Blackwell Companion to Hinduism,* ed. Gavin Flood, 68–101. Oxford: Blackwell, 2003.

Younger, Paul D. *Playing Host to Deity: Festival Religion in the South Indian Tradition.* New York: Oxford University Press, 2002.

CHAPTER 2

⤔

"A Time for War and a Time for Peace"[.]

Teaching Religion and Violence in the Jewish Tradition

MICHAEL DOBKOWSKI

INTRODUCTION

Judaism, like the other great religious traditions of long standing, contains a rich and multivocal set of texts, traditions, ideas, and historical experiences susceptible to being used for good or ill, for restraint or for violence. Elsie Boulding, the distinguished sociologist and peace activist, refers to an essential duality in religious life as two contrasting cultures, which she calls the "holy war" and "peaceable garden" cultures found in all religions. Religions face an enduring and systemic tension between encouraging religiously motivated violence, self-righteousness, and hegemonic thinking on the one hand and advocating tolerance, dialogue, respect for difference, and peaceful compromise as represented by the notion of a peaceable garden on the other.[1] Every religion is caught in this sacred dilemma, establishing, by force if necessary, its particular view of the right and holy based on its understanding of divinely revealed truth and an openness and tolerance for those individuals and groups that do not fit into the sacred consensus. Religions preach love and respect for all people but they also, at the same time, often support a sacred view of the moral and social order they would like to be binding on all humanity. Religions can instruct us that it is ultimately important to try to love our neighbors, but they are also faced with how to respond when those neighbors refuse to accept a particularistic view of the "sacred canopy."

This chapter examines the issues of violence, war, and power in the study of Judaism and suggests a general approach to how they can be presented in a religious studies context. It assumes that Judaism has a perspective on these issues, albeit not speaking with one voice, but it also recognizes and demonstrates that Judaism exists—like the other great world religions—both as an ideal system of values and morals and as a social construct that is affected by history, human creativity, interactivity, and cultural synthesis. It is both a product and a creation of society.[2] It exists in its idealized state, but as the ancient rabbis noted in the classical Rabbinic period, the Torah, the sacred text, was not revealed in heaven and given to angels, but on earth to human beings, on a modest mountain in the Sinai wilderness where the air was hot and dusty, not rarefied. Torah was not given to angels because they do not suffer poverty or oppression, need not heal the sick or raise up those who are bowed down. Human beings do. Teachers, scholars, and students alike need to appreciate that religions exist both as concepts and as forces that motivated people in the past, as well as those living today, with all the limitations and imperfections that make us human.

THE PARADOX OF CREATION

Having said this, does Judaism have an ethos that informs how the tradition approaches the issue of violence? The author of the Book of Ecclesiastes wrote that there is "a season set for everything, a time for every experience under heaven; . . . a time for war and a time for peace" (Eccles. 3:1–3, 7–8). There is a fascinating midrash (rabbinic legend) that provides some insight into Judaism's perspective on this book. The legend says that when God created the first human, he took him around the Garden of Eden and said: "Behold my works, how beautiful, how splendid they are. All that I have created, I created for you. Take care, therefore, that you do not destroy my world, for if you do, there will be no one left to repair what you have destroyed" (Midrash, Eccles. Rabbah).[3] Judaism was among the first religions to insist on the dignity of the person, the sanctity of human life, and humanity's responsibility to nature. Murder became not just a crime against a person but a sin against God.[4] "Whoever shed the blood of man shall his blood be shed, for in the image of God has God made man" (Gen. 9:6). For Judaism, and certainly not only for Judaism, the religious voice is above all a moral voice. Abraham was chosen as the first monotheist so that he would instruct his children "to do what is right and just" (Gen. 18:19). A young Moses came to the defense of a Hebrew slave being beaten by an Egyptian, resorting to violence to protect the innocent (Exod. 2:11–14). He saw a Hebrew slave attacking another Hebrew slave and he intervened. He witnessed Midianite shepherds preventing Jethro's daughters from watering their flock, and he intervened. Moses later told the Israelites, "Justice, justice shall you pursue" (Deut. 16:20). Isaiah began his prophetic mission with a most powerful speech made against the idea that you can serve God in the house of prayer while ignoring him in the marketplace and the public square (Isa. 1:2–31). Micah summed up Judaism's ethos: "To do justly, and to love mercy, and to walk humbly with your God" (Mic. 6:8).[5]

But as stated earlier, Judaism emphasizes that the Torah was given on Mt. Sinai, not in heaven. These principles need to be applied to the world, with all of its imperfections and inequities.

Society is a moral enterprise. The crucial insight of the Hebrew Bible as interpreted by many great modern thinkers, including Abraham Joshua Heschel, Martin Buber, and Rabbi Jonathan Sacks, the chief rabbi of Britain and the Commonwealth, is that human beings need God and God needs human beings. It is a reciprocal relationship.[6] We cannot live alone, but we cannot live together without conflicts. It was Judaism's great contribution to see the human arena as something other than a state of ongoing war in which power reigned supreme. Most cultures in the ancient world valued victory and conquest. Their heroes were military leaders and mighty kings; their ethic was one of power and empire. The prophets of Israel, in contrast, were among the first to conceive of peace, not victory, as an ideal.[7] They linked Israel's potency to its moral strength. Jews would be protected from aggressors if they lived up to the terms of the covenant with God; God and only God, they claimed, would be the guarantor of Jewish power as long as they obeyed her laws.[8]

Biblical faith, with its emphasis on responsibility and its appreciation of the need to contextualize the spiritual, constantly holds before us the paradox and cunning of human history. There are times when human beings are able to scale the heights of goodness and might. There are other occasions, far too numerous, when they descend to the depths of cruelty and violence.[9] Given this reality, the rabbis were perplexed. Why did God create human beings? In an ancient midrash, the rabbis have the angels query God on this decision. The text says, "Let us make man in our image" (Gen. 1:26). The extraordinary use of the first person plural evokes the image of a heavenly court in which God is surrounded by angels. The midrash envisions God consulting with them, perhaps hinting at a measure of divine ambivalence. Truth and peace oppose creating humans on the grounds that such creatures would surely be deceitful and violent. Love and righteousness favor their creation, for without humanity how can there be love and righteousness in the world? God ultimately sides with those favoring creation (Gen. Rabbah, 8:5). It is one thing to believe that God in her goodness created the natural order. It is quite another to believe that God in her goodness created a form of life capable of inflicting unspeakable harm and violence on its members. The Torah says that before the Flood, contemplating the violence that filled the world, "God regretted that He had made man on earth, and His heart was saddened" (Gen. 6:6). Why did God create humankind? The rabbis assert that creation testifies not merely to God's power, but also to her belief in humanity.[10]

POWER FROM A DIASPORIC PERSPECTIVE

While Judaism abhors war, as we shall see, and anticipates a messianic era in which war will cease to exist, it recognizes that the world of history is not messianic. It provides guidelines for determining when it is indeed a time for war and when it is not, and it establishes rules for the just conduct of wars—all the while seeking to avoid war and to work for peace.[11] Most of the relevant rabbinic literature on the status of war was generated from a position of exile, in the absence of a sovereign Jewish state in which Jewish communities had no political or military impact on international society. It is only in three, or possibly four, relatively short periods of Jewish history that Jews have held political or military autonomy or exercised military authority—namely, from Moses to the destruction of the first temple (c. 1250–586 B.C.E.), during the Hasmonean dynasty (168–63 B.C.E.), for several hundred years in the tenth to twelfth centuries in southern Spain, and from the Balfour Declaration period to the establishment of the state of Israel to the present (1917–).[12] The historicity of the conquest of Canaan is somewhat in dispute, but we know that whatever form it took, it led to the establishment of a united kingdom under kings David and Solomon, who ruled it for seventy years, 1000–922 B.C.E. Soon after Solomon's death, however, the country split into northern and southern kingdoms. Northern Israel disappeared with the fall of Samaria in 721 B.C.E.; southern Judah fell to the Babylonians 135 years later. King Nebuchadnezzar razed the Temple, put the city to the torch, and sent a choice section of the population—thousands of elites, intellectuals, and skilled workers—into exile. When the Persians conquered the Babylonians fifty years later, they allowed a vanguard of the Jews to return home to build the second Temple and eventually to establish a second commonwealth. Several hundred years later, the Maccabean-Hasmonean period unfolded, a century of military exploits and expansionism that ended with Roman rule and ultimately Roman hegemony and the destruction of Jerusalem and the Temple.

In 70 C.E. many pious and disaffected Jews in Jerusalem revolted against Rome. After some internal successes, the Romans diverted enough legions to defeat them and the Jewish state was eliminated, not to appear again until the twentieth century. Almost a thousand Jews killed themselves and their families at Masada, a fortress in the Judean desert, rather than surrender to the Romans. Outraged by this obstinacy and resistance, the Romans destroyed the Temple. In 135 C.E. there was a final revolt, the Bar Kochba Revolt, and after it the Romans forbade the Jews to enter the newly renamed city of Jerusalem, Aelia Capitolina. Most Jews were in diaspora by then. Judaism entered its Rabbinic period: it became a text-centered faith with the synagogue replacing the Temple, and Torah study and prayer replacing sacrifice. The religion became more insular and contemplative.

Nevertheless, Jews, on occasion, continued to have experience with power and war.[13] During the early centuries of Muslim conquest in Spain in the ninth and tenth centuries, many Jews were active in assisting the Muslim conquerors and later served as a home guard. Some of them bore arms and were involved in wars to protect their cities. A few rose to very high authority. The best-known example is Samuel Ha-Nagid, the commander of the army of the kingdom of Granada in the early eleventh century.

It was primarily the biblical and Hasmonean experiences with war, however, that produced precedents and legal decisions, which were generated from a position of exile and were interpreted and applied throughout the ages. It must be emphasized that Jewish history, identity, and consciousness were forged primarily away from Israel and with limited experiences with autonomy and power. Jews have been away from "home" more than they have been at "home." As a result, waging war is not a significant part of the long-term Jewish historical memory and did not become an ideal filled with honor and glory as it did in many other cultures. Jewish heroes historically have predominantly been scholars and cultural icons, not fighters.[14] There is a reluctance to idealize force—only people who were learned in Torah, who were models of morality and reconciliation, were worthy of respect. This has changed somewhat since the Holocaust and with the establishment of the state of Israel and its need to have a strong military and defense in a very hostile region of the world.[15] Violence, however, remains a tool of last resort used only to defend life and human rights.

JEWISH PERSPECTIVES ON MARTYRDOM

An examination of the Jewish view on martyrdom is instructive in light of this, and may provide useful pedagogical entry into the discussion of Judaism and violence. The Akeda, the binding of Isaac described in Genesis 22, serves as the quintessential example of the Jewish embrace of sacrifice, even to the point of spending human life, and became the model for Jewish martyrdom throughout the ages.[16] The Akeda has come to mean that God in her mystery can demand the death of the innocent and that God, at times, will expect that the faithful sacrifice their lives to sanctify God's name. In this story, one of the most interpreted stories in the Bible, God called upon Abraham to take his son Isaac up to an altar and offer him as a burnt sacrifice. Abraham got up early in the morning, walked three days with his son, reached the destination, bound him, and lifted the knife, when he was stopped just in time by an angel. This story, reflected in the story of Jesus in the New Testament (carrying the cross as Isaac carried the wood up the mountain, each about to be sacrificed) and retold (with changes) in the Koran, is central to all Western monotheistic traditions. The lesson learned from Abraham's willingness to sacrifice his beloved son is that life is not the ultimate value; rather, obedience and complete faith may trump it. Jewish legend and subsequent interpretations made a paradigm of the Akeda.

The message of the Akeda is that martyrdom is readily accepted in times of crisis and communal tragedies. Although Judaism greatly values life, it has also made an important place for martyrdom as a legitimate response to forced conversions or other significant threats to Jewish existence. Relying on the biblical verse, "You shall not profane my holy name, that I may be sanctified in the midst of the children of Israel" (Lev. 22:32), many Jews allowed themselves to be killed, to die, as the expression says, al Kiddush HaShem, for the sanctification of God's name. Martyrdom is enshrined in the central liturgical statement in Judaism, the Sh'ma Yisrael prayer, which contains an affirmation of the absolute oneness of God followed by a commitment to love God and be willing to offer one's body, soul, and property to God (Deut. 6:4–9).[17]

Only in three situations are Jews obligated to accept death rather than acquiesce (although they retain the right of self-defense). These situations are idolatry, adultery, and murder (Babylonian Talmud, Tractate Sanhedrin, 74a).[18] If ordered to publicly transgress these commandments in any way, a Jew is expected to accept *Kiddush HaShem* rather than commit these acts. However, if the times are particularly oppressive and the coercion happens in private, Jews should try to avoid being killed. Murder clearly is never countenanced. This concept of sanctification does not devalue innocent life—on the contrary, it expresses the value of the innocent life the Jew refuses to take. Certainly there is no analogy between letting oneself be killed to prevent one's own forced sin of idolatry, sexual immorality, or murder, and killing someone else because they threaten your religion or for the sake of attaining personal reward in the hereafter. More generally, authorities have held that a Jew is considered to have died in the spirit of *Kiddush HaShem* if, like the victims of Nazism, he is killed only because he is a Jew; the sanctification is achieved through submission, not aggression.[19]

The operating principle is, however, that only when there is no other alternative are Jews obligated to submit to martyrdom. Whenever possible the Jew is to try to find a way to survive. This is the argument that Rabbi Leo Baeck, the leader of German Jewry in the 1930s, presented to Gandhi when Gandhi suggested that the German Jews allow themselves to be killed to draw the world's attention to the Nazi oppression. There were rabbis in the ghettos of Nazi-occupied Eastern Europe who urged the Jews to sanctify God's name by trying to live, *Kiddush Hachaim*, the sanctification of life, rather than *Kiddush HaShem* through death. When the oppressor wants to murder body and soul, the obligation is to do everything to live.[20] The aim of the Torah is "to live by it and not die" by it (Babylonian Talmud, Sanhedrin, 74a). Similarly, Maimonides, perhaps the greatest Jewish philosopher and Talmudist, argued in the twelfth century that anyone who becomes a martyr when it is not mandatory has sinned, transgressing the strong prohibition against suicide.

Judaism teaches that life is good and must be embraced and celebrated; it is opposed to ascetic denial. Yet it also speaks about the power of pain and suffering as a way of expiating sin. Collective suffering of the Jewish people is not seen as arbitrary but is viewed by the tradition as having a purpose and, by the rabbis in the Talmud, as "ye su rim shel a ha va," literally, afflictions of love brought by God for the spiritual improvement of Israel.[21] Pain and suffering, horrible as they may appear, are also for Judaism an occasion for service and dedication. Deuteronomy presents a seemingly uncomplicated religious calculus: the good are rewarded, the wicked punished. The Book of Job, of course, probes and challenges this approach. God here, as in the Akeda, tests the faithfulness of Job, a pious, wealthy, and highly esteemed man. Job is made to suffer greatly, losing his wealth, health, family, and social standing. But when urged to denounce and reject God for his fate, he refuses. "Naked I came from my mother's womb, and naked I shall return. . . . May the name of God be blessed forever" (Job 1:20).

The rabbis problematize the whole calculus further. The fact is that we do not always know why the good suffer and the wicked prosper. And just as the righteous are not always blameless, the wicked may have redeeming features, and suffering itself may have a purpose in God's design. The Mishnah in the fourth century teaches that when a criminal is put to death for his crime, the divine presence, the

Shechinah, suffers with him (Babylonian Talmud, Sanhedrin, 46a). Rabbi Meir (second century C.E.) taught that a hanged criminal's body must be immediately and respectfully buried, because to disgrace it is an offense against God, in whose image all humans are made (Sanhedrin, 46b).

THE HANUKKAH MYTH

Suffering has a purpose, even if it is not apparent, and one should be prepared to endure and live through suffering, as epitomized by Job and the Akeda. These notions of unwavering faith and self-sacrifice in suffering were central to one of those moments of Jewish sovereignty mentioned earlier, the Maccabean revolt, and to some degree the Maccabees and their scribes attempted to mainstream martyrdom as integral to Judaism. They were only partially successful. The Maccabees took their name from Judah, son of Mattathias, who came to be called the Hammer, Ma'qūbah in Aramaic.[22] Judah Maccabeus and his brothers took the land of Israel back from its occupiers, the Seleucid Greeks. After Alexander the Great died in 332 B.C.E., his empire was divided between the Seleucid and Ptolemaic empires. Judea had the misfortune of being in the middle of these empires. When it was not a battleground, it was a stomping ground. Roughly from 332 to 200 B.C.E., the Jews were ruled by the Ptolemies from the south. Their rule was not particularly intrusive. From 200 to 164, control was passed to the more aggressive Seleucids up north, who were interested in spreading, even imposing, Greek culture. Matters came to a head under King Antiochus IV (175–164), when Greek symbols and practices were brought even to the Temple Mount. The crisis came in 171 B.C.E. when Antiochus dismissed the high priest, Jason, and chose a new high priest, Manelaus, who was very sympathetic to the Greek cultural approach and the financial needs of Antiochus. Manelaus began channeling some of the money that had once gone to the Temple directly to the king. In 168 B.C.E. an altar to Zeus was built upon the Temple altar and sacrifice was made. This decision violated the very core of Judaism: to worship no idols, to avoid even casual human images; to bow before no god other than the Jewish God.

The Maccaebean movement produced a rich literature of resistance and martyrdom, particularly expressed by the court historians of the Hasmonean dynasty who followed the successful revolt and who wrote Maccabees I and II (not included in the Jewish canon, but in the Roman Catholic Bible). The texts describe this response. One of the leaders in the Jewish reaction was a priest named Mattathias. When the king's agents came into the town of Modein for the sacrifices, Mattathias appeared with five militant sons and a number of other followers and put on a display of refusal. Maccabees I describes a Jew who came forward in the presence of all to offer a sacrifice upon the altar in Modein, following the king's command. When Mattathias saw this, "he burned with zeal and his heart was stirred. He gave vent to righteous anger."[23] He killed the offending Jew and killed the king's officer overseeing the sacrifices. Thus the great revolt of traditionalist Jews began. Mattathias and his sons fled to the mountains. They were joined by many zealots and soon a guerrilla war began in earnest. When Mattathias died in 166 B.C.E., the leadership passed to his son Judah, called Maccabeus (Hammer). He defeated an expedition sent from Syria to squash his revolt, then occupied Jerusalem, cleansed the Temple, took Israel back from its occupiers, and then extended its boundaries to cover more territory than ever before, even under King Solomon. Judah and his brothers, Simon and Jonathan, reconsecrated the Temple in 165 B.C.E., and the Jewish holiday of Hanukkah celebrates this event.[24]

The Maccabees and their scribes and interpreters constructed their ideal of martyrdom in direct response to the politics of their period. A martyr was to be a "witness," an '*êyd* in Hebrew, whose faith was so deep he would even willingly accept death in his resistance to the surrounding culture.[25] According to Maccabean theology, there was no middle ground between true belief and the threatening influence of the surrounding world. The choice was not between remaining faithful and compromise but between martyrdom and collaboration with the enemies of Israel. This history is primarily told in their texts in support of martyrdom. The story of Chana and her seven sons is emblematic and a favorite that emerges from this literature. Antiochus asked each of Chana's sons to bow to an idol. One after another, from the eldest down to a boy of two years, they refused and went out to die before their mother's eyes. As the little one was being escorted off to be killed, Chana is supposed to have shouted: "Go to Abraham and tell him that he bound one son to the altar, I bound seven, and mine paid the ultimate price" (Maccabees II, 7:20–23).

These themes of resistance and martyrdom are emphasized in the version of the story that was penned by their followers. They want us to believe that Hanukkah is the celebration of the revolt that reclaimed the Temple and that it should be remembered as marking a clash between powerful pagan oppressors and determined Jewish victims. The rabbis in the Talmudic period (second–seventh centuries), however, have a very different take on the events and the lessons to be learned from them. In a religious studies context, these divergent interpretive traditions afford teachers a highly fruitful pedagogical opportunity to focus on the very different ways the Maccabees and Hanukkah are appropriated in the Jewish tradition and what can be learned from that divergence. Religious belief effectively remains abstract until taken up into the lives of individuals and communities. Why would the Hasmoneans want the story to emphasize military heroism and the rabbis take a very different tack? What does this tell us about the experiences and values of the two cultures? In religious studies courses, we urge our students to read below the surface of the texts. We want them to query what is apparently known already or can be discovered through a probing of the historical situations of the writers and ask why certain stories and approaches rise to the surface, why certain "myths" develop. We want our students to take interest in the context of the writing of these texts and in the function of the creation of the texts for the writers who craft them for the purpose of projecting their vision of the community for posterity. The creation of the Hanukkah "myth" provides us with a rich teaching opportunity.

Were the Maccabees true Jewish heroes? While there is certainly a legitimate place for war in most Jewish traditions, there is generally much less toleration for deriving personal glory from military victory.[26] The effort to focus on the

Maccabees as military heroes is a modern development. Unlike the court historians of Maccabees I and II, the rabbinic rendering of Hanukkah focuses instead on God's redemptive power. It is evident from the Talmudic account discussing the basic historical narrative of Hanukkah that the Maccabees, played only a minor role in achieving political power. There was no such power, nor were there any warriors who were central in achieving victory (Babylonian Talmud, Tractate Shabbat, 21b).[27] Whereas the Hasmonean texts remember Hanukkah for the Maccabean reconquest of Jerusalem, the rabbis virtually ignored the family's role in the holiday. Instead, rabbinic texts focus exclusively on God's deliverance of the Jews and on the miracle of the Temple itself.[28] According to the Talmud, the celebration of Hanukkah commemorates the miracle of one flask of pure oil that was able to burn in the Temple menorah for eight days (Babylonian Talmud, Tractate Shabbat, 21b). That miracle and not the military victory formed the basis of the Hanukkah festival in rabbinic literature. With miracles there is no need for heroes. Therefore, the *gi bo rim*, the powerful ones, that are mentioned in the Jewish liturgy for Hanukkah, the Al Ha'nisim prayer (the miracles), were the Greeks, while the Jews were characterized as a weak people.[29] The new hero emerging from the rabbinic interpretations, moreover, is a person of self-discipline and a strict observer of rabbinic law, not a warrior. The rabbis were most uncomfortable and critical of the Maccabees and the Hasmoneans who followed because they were zealots, men of extreme behavior, undisciplined and unpredictable. Rabbinic Judaism, if nothing else, was a religion of order, predictability, and moderation. So a story of war—even a defensive one, even a war of religion—becomes for the rabbis a tale of a miracle of lights, a conquest of spirit over might, of faith over power. The hero of Hanukkah is not Chana, Judah, or his brothers, but God. The Haftarah portion that the rabbis selected to be read on the Sabbath of Hanukkah from the prophet Zechariah, chapters 2–4, clearly emphasizes this point as well. It ends with the refrain, "not by might, not by power, but by My spirit, says the Lord of Hosts" (Zech. 4:6). Teaching these texts and their competing interpretations and purposes in a religious studies context not only may help reveal how and why texts are created the way they are, but may also direct student attention to myth formation and to the projected version of a tradition that ultimately becomes normative. It may give students some insight into how the grand narratives of a tradition emerge as opposed to alternative ones and what functions they may serve.

THE PURSUIT OF PEACE (SHALOM)

Certainly, as we have seen, Judaism places a high premium on the value and the sanctity of life. The Deuteronomist proclaims: "I call heaven and earth to witness against you this day, that I have put before you life and death, blessing and curse; therefore choose life that you and your children may live" (Deut. 30:19). Jewish sources from the Bible onward, however, acknowledge war as a given of human existence. War is viewed as a historical phenomenon—undesirable but nevertheless tolerable, even necessary under certain circumstances. That is why the tradition rejects the extreme pacifism of a Gandhi: Judaism sees war as a reflection of the real yet fallen human condition in history as opposed to the metahistorical era of the Messianic days.[30] There are occasions in which Jews have understood their tradition as commanding them to go to war—under Joshua to occupy the land of Israel, in general to defend themselves—even though loss of life will certainly result. The Book of Esther (Megillat Esther), the source for the holiday of Purim, describes how the Jews of ancient Sushan (Persia) turned the tables on King Ahasuerus's minister Haman and their enemies on the very day of their scheduled massacre, in an early example of anticipatory self-defense. "Throughout the provinces of King Ahasuerus, the Jews mustered in their cities to attack those who sought their hurt; and no one could withstand them, for the fear of them had fallen upon all the peoples. . . . So the Jews struck at their enemies with the sword, slaying and destroying; they wreaked their will upon their enemies" (Esther 9:2–5). The festival of Purim celebrates the world turned upside down: the victims become the victors; the day of death becomes the day of victory and celebration. We have already seen that rather than publicly perform idolatry, adultery, or murder, a Jew is to accept death as martyrdom, again asserting that certain values transcend the value of life.[31] There may be few values more precious than life but they do exist. Life is not of infinite value for Judaism, since it asserts that life derives its finite value from God, the source of infinite value. Therefore it is to be treasured highly, but not as highly as godliness itself.[32]

There is a sense of the tradition that can be derived from the spirit and style of the biblical and rabbinic literature. That sense does not support pacifism but rather elevates the cause of peace or *shalom*, a term that appears over 200 times in scripture alone, and in almost every major prayer.[33] The Hebrew word *shalom* is derived from a root denoting wholeness or completeness, and its frame of reference is bound up with the notion of *shlemut*, perfection. As the word suggests, peace is not the normal state of the world.[34] In its ultimate sense, *shalom* anticipates the perfect peace that can only be ushered in by the messiah. It is obviously a much-desired condition but one difficult to attain. The prophets of Israel were concerned not only with orphans and widows but with the morality of treaties and alliances, and issues of economic and social equality. Judaism was from very early on forced to live not only with abstract ideals, with the relationship between God and people, but with problems of competition and power. The prophets preached peace when there was no peace (Jer. 6:14). They denounced those who cried "peace" when there was war. The greatest desire for peace cannot, by itself, avert conflict. "The watchman," Ezekiel exhorts, "who sees the sword come; and does not blow the horn so that the people are not warned, and the sword comes and destroys one of them in the vain hope for peace; . . . I will demand a reckoning for his blood from the watchman" (Ezek. 33:6).[35]

A plethora of biblical, Talmudic, and midrashic sources extol the virtues of peace. It is an ideal. The Talmud views the promotion of peace as the purpose of the entire Torah (Babylonian Talmud, Tractate Gittin, 59b).[36] The rabbis refused to allow people to walk outside on the Sabbath wearing their weapons as "they are nothing but a disgrace" (Babylonian Talmud, Tractate Shabbat, 63a).[37] The medieval biblical commentators Rabbi Shlomo Yitzhaki, known as Rashi (eleventh century) and Nachmonides, known as the Ramban (thirteenth century) explain that the prohibition of using hewn stones for the altar in the Temple reflects an aversion to associating a supreme holy site with the implements of warfare, swords. King Solomon, whose name means peace, was given the privilege of building the Temple, not his father, King David, because according to the accounts in Chronicles (1 Chron. 22:8), "he shed much blood and fought great battles . . . in My sight." "Seek peace and pursue it," says the psalmist. (Ps. 34:15). The rabbis, noting the apparent redundancy of the verbs *seek* and *pursue*, enjoined the Jewish people to work for peace not only for themselves but for others as well. The tradition does not require people to seek and pursue the other commandments, but only to fulfill them in the proper manner. "But peace you must seek in your own place and pursue it even to another place as well (Jerusalem Talmud, Tractate Pe'ah, 1:1).[38] Rashi, commenting on the apparent redundancy in the passage in Genesis 32:8 describing Jacob's encounter with his brother Esau where the text says in Hebrew, "Va'yira . . . va'yeitzer" (he was frightened and anxious), explains that Jacob was frightened that he and his family might be harmed but was anxious and distressed that he might have to harm his brother in self-defense.

So while Judaism advocated the pursuit of peace and rejected pacifism as an ideal, it supported, on the national level, what might be called selective pacifism.[39] It developed criteria for judging the legitimacy of war and it established rules for the conduct of war while simultaneously seeking to avoid conflict and working for peace. It recognized that sometimes justice requires violence not only in self-defense but also in pursuit of limited and circumvented national aims. A careful analysis and discussion of Judaism's understanding of war, particularly commanded war, or holy war, is an invaluable way for instructors and students alike to contextualize Judaism's approach to this central issue. To that I now turn.

CATEGORIES OF JEWISH WARFARE

Generally speaking, the practitioners of holy war conceive and interpret their behavior through a theological prism—these religious battles, involving violence and killing, are redefined as religious undertakings under divine sanction, which cannot be explained through normal logic and secular reasoning. The violence in holy war is not conventional human violence where individuals confront each other for secular goals such as power, wealth, revenge, or status; they are sacred events being fought for God or God's honor. Indeed, in this theological view they are not violent at all. They may look like violence, but these are conflicts to bring truth and redemption, to inspire faith and establish justice. Scripture does not describe these wars as events of violence; rather, they are battles for justice, even peace. The God of the Hebrew Bible, though portrayed as a warrior God, is above all understood as a God of mercy and justice who uses war to achieve a peaceful and just world.[40]

The Jewish ethics of war focus on two issues: its legitimation and its conduct—when it is permissible to go to war and how warfare is to be conducted.[41] The Bible describes many wars, but the primary biblical source on the laws of war is chapter 20 of Deuteronomy.[42] There Moses spoke to the Israelites who were about to enter the land of Canaan promised to Abraham by God, and he exhorted them, in the name of God, not to fear their enemies because God was with them. He described the encouragement that the "warrior" priest would offer. He then listed several categories of people who were exempt from battle, including a new bridegroom and the person who is "afraid and disheartened." Then Moses stated, "when you approach a town to attack it, you should offer it terms of peace" (Deut. 20:10). He described what the Israelites were to do if the offer was acceptable and how they were to conduct the battle if it were not. The chapter concludes with the commandment prohibiting the cutting down of fruit-bearing trees for the purpose of building siege works (20:19–20). The Mishnah and the Talmud, the central oral traditions of Judaism (c. 200–650 C.E.), then classify wars according to their sources of legitimation. Biblically mandated wars are termed mandatory (*Mil he met Mitzvah* or *Mil he met Hovah*). Wars undertaken at the discretion of the Sanhedrin, the great court of seventy-one of ancient times, or possibly its modern equivalent, the Israeli Knesset, are termed discretionary (*Mil he met r'shut*).[43]

Which specific wars fall into the category of mandatory wars? Although some points are at issue, it is widely agreed among rabbinic authorities that mandatory wars obtained in only two or possibly three instances: Joshua's war of conquest against the seven Canaanite nations directly command by God; the war against Amalek, also commanded by God; and a war of clear and pressing defense against an attack already launched.[44] Discretionary wars are understood as expansionary efforts to strengthen one's strategic position or to secure economic gains and prestige, like the wars engaged in by King David against the Philistines or the Hasmonean kings expanding the borders of Israel. As discussed earlier, these are the wars that disqualified David from building the Temple but not from remaining king. If he fought he could not build, but he could fight without religious sanction. Also, as discussed earlier, the rabbis do not interpret the Maccabean revolt as a commanded war to defend the land and oppose idolatry within it. They stress God's miraculous intervention.[45]

The first type of mandatory war is only of historical interest since the Canaanite nations lost their national identity through either war or absorption in ancient times. *Mil he met Mitzvah* was Israel's longest war, stretching from its beginnings under Moses through the campaigns under Joshua and Judges and ending finally under the leadership of King Saul, a span of about 200 years. To this day, Jewish national memory and identity are rooted in both the liberation from Egypt and the settlement of the land of Israel.[46]

BIBLICALLY MANDATED WARS—HISTORY OR MYTH?

In assessing the impact of the Conquest, we are considering a complicated model. We are not, however, looking at history. The chroniclers of these events were not primarily interested in recording what happened in detail. The texts—Deuteronomy,

Joshua, and Judges—are mainly interested in understanding God's will and in the establishment of a community dedicated to the ideals of justice and charity. So the record of the events is not the same as the events themselves. In fact, there has been a rather lively debate for some time among biblical scholars and archaeologists on the historicity of the biblical descriptions.[47] As history they may be suspect; but as sacred symbolic history they were and remain very important.[48] Jewish law on *Mil he met Mitzvah* teaches a dual message—that the horrors of war must be strictly limited and that it is a commandment for the Jewish people to settle the land of Israel.

Viewing the biblical version of the Conquest as sacred history (rather than narrative history) implies that what is significant about the Conquest is what the "authors" of the texts want to convey in their grand narrative and what the community of believers chooses to learn from it.[49]

One reading of the event, the one that is so troubling, is that the battles in the books of Joshua and Judges, as well as the Pentateuch itself, provide a model for crusades and even genocide; that God's people may utilize any means to achieve the sought-after end.[50] As one representative scholar noted, the Hebrew Bible certainly expresses love for the stranger and advocates for widows and orphans and calls forth justice.[51] But these are all eclipsed by an enormous reservoir of God's violence. "There are," he says, "many portraits of a violent, seemingly pathological God and of violent human conduct justified in relation to God."[52] In *The God Delusion*, Richard Dawkins, the noted British scientist, argues that the Bible is a positively immoral document. To buttress his position, Dawkins takes on God, who orders Abraham to murder his son, and the Torah itself, which, on his reading, sanctions ethnic cleansing, from Moses's massacre of the Midianites to Joshua's slaughter of the Canaanites. On the Akeda he writes, "this disgraceful story is an example simultaneously of child abuse, bullying in two asymmetrical power relationships, and the first recorded use of the Nuremburg defense 'I was only obeying orders.'" The fact that, according to Dawkins, none of this probably ever happened is immaterial: "The point is that, whether true or not, the Bible is held up as a source of our morality. And the Bible story of Joshua's destruction of Jericho and the invasion of the Promised Land in general, is morally indistinguishable from . . . . Saddam Hussein's massacres of the Kurds and Marsh Arabs."[53] Similar arguments can be found in a spate of recent books by people like R. D. Gold, Sam Harris, and Christopher Hitchens.[54]

The normative Jewish tradition, however, chose to limit the application of the Conquest to one series of biblical battles against specific nations and during a particular period of time. No other wars were to utilize the justification or the methods of this war, and Jewish tradition coalesced around the idea that even that biblical war had certain limits beyond which the conquering Israelites dared not venture.[55]

The main prose description of the Conquest is found in the Deuteronomic books: Deuteronomy, Joshua, Judges, 1 and 2 Samuel, and 1 and 2 Kings. These books begin with Moses's valedictory, delivered as he turned the leadership over to Joshua, and are referred to by scholars as the Deuteronomistic history because it has long been thought that they were written by an author or authors who accepted the basic perspective found in Deuteronomy and allowed this perspective to guide their accounts of Israelite history in the centuries following Moses (1250 B.C.E.). These books narrate how the people conquered the Promised Land (Joshua); how the tribes of Israel lived as separate communities before a king was appointed (Judges); how the kings (Saul, David, and Solomon) came to rule over all of Israel (1 and 2 Samuel, 1 Kings); and then how the kingdom was divided after Solomon's death until the destruction of the Northern Kingdom by the Assyrians (722 B.C.E.) and the Southern Kingdom by the Babylonians in 586 B.C.E. (1 and 2 Kings). These books cover some 700 years of Israel's history.[56]

In Deuteronomy, Moses instructs the people about their obligation both to take the land and to settle it in accordance with their covenant with God. A clear and persistent line is drawn connecting right behavior to their ability to successfully dwell in the Promised Land. Contrast is drawn to the seven Canaanite nations. It is due to their persistent moral and religious transgressions, even abominations, such as idolatry, child sacrifice, and ritual prostitution that the Canaanites have forfeited their claim to the land. An additional concern was that if allowed to interact freely with Jews, they would corrupt them (Exod. 23:32–33, Lev. 18:24–25, Deut. 7:3–5).

Joshua, like Moses before him, is merely an agent of God, carrying out God's commands. All the Deuteronomic books are united in their theological conception of the Conquest, viewing the event as a demonstration of God's involvement in human history as an active, historical God, particularly through the act of liberating the Jews from Egypt and helping them control the land. They emphasize the sins of the Canaanites and, later in the Book of Joshua and elsewhere, that many Israelites also abandoned the covenant so central to the Deuteronomic view of history. God fights for Israel as an *Ish Mil cha ma*, a warrior God as described in the Song of the Sea in Exodus (Exod. 15:1–18), as the sole liberator to the exclusion of any human intermediaries.[57] Later the song moves ahead to God's establishment of the people in their new land. "In Your strength You guide them to Your holy abode. . . . All the dwellers in Canaan are aghast. Terror and dread descend upon them. Through the might of Your arm they are still as stone—Till Your people cross over" (Exod. 15:13, 15, 17–18).[58]

The Book of Joshua goes on to describe in great detail the various battles of the Conquest and the necessary and obligatory nature of the extermination of the seven nations decreed by God as a war to root out the evil and idolatrous culture of the local peoples. Israel's periodic losses of will and lapses into compassion are criticized by God and Joshua and are seen as only leading to greater evil. Throughout the Book of Joshua, the armies of Israel succeed whenever they obey God's law. When they deviate from these directions in even minor ways, God punishes them with defeat.[59] As mentioned earlier, scholars have long wrangled over the historicity of these accounts—there is no archaeological evidence, for example, to support the claim of the complete destruction of Jericho in the thirteenth century B.C.E. What we are interested in, however, is how the Deuteronomistic historians thought of these events.[60]

In later Jewish understanding, the Conquest was viewed not as a source of military strategy or even as bestowing divine approval on religious war. Rather, it was to teach about Israel's provenance and how it was demonstrated in a specific histor-ical moment and in one special place.[61] The two central postulates of the Conquest are its divine origin and its strict limits. A Jewish consensus developed around the insistence that this war and the war against the Amalekites are the only wars in human history that were explicitly commanded by God.

Because the war was initiated by special permission, most commentators believed it could occur only once. The Talmud asserted, after the destruction of the second Temple, "Israel shall not go up by a wall [not return to Israel en masse] and shall not rebel against the nations of the world" (Babylonian Talmud, Tractate Ketubbot, 3a). The assumption here is that there could be no organized national conquest of Israel. Jews as individuals could return, but an organized movement to take back the land by force was precluded. Maimonides excluded the possibility of any new conquest of the land since there was no king, no Temple, and no Sanhe-drin to sanction it. He put *Mil he met Hovah* beyond history in a category of its own.[62]

Rabbinic interpreters as well as medieval commentators have ruled consistently that since the Canaanite nations and the Amalekites lost their national identity in ancient times and all trace of them has vanished—as the Mishnah states, "Sannach-erib came and put all nations in confusion" (Yada'im, 4:4)—the first two categories of mandatory wars are no longer valid and cannot serve as a precedent for current situations in the Middle East between Israelis and Palestinians, for example.[63] The rabbinic source recognized that the original Conquest was incomplete, that mem-bers of the seven nations and Amalekites survived, but insisted that after 586 B.C.E. the commandment was no longer operable. After the forced deportations it was sim-ply impossible to identify a person's national origin with complete confidence. It is clear that rabbinic commentators developed an approach to this law, the thrust of which is that it applies only in a highly limited way in concrete situations and its primary relevance is symbolic. Lacking a clearly defined divine instruction, with no standing Temple and priests, later Jewish thinkers removed the entire category of *Mil he met Hovah* (mandatory war) from the realm of practical action. Thus Mai-monides, reflecting Talmudic sources, severely limited the commandment's applica-bility, saying even these specific nations are not to be destroyed if they make peace with Israel and choose to accept the Noahide laws (Mishnah Torah, Law of Kings, 6:1,4).[64] *Mil he met Hovah* was no longer a part of policy and politics; it reverted to history and theology.

Only the two remaining categories, reactive defensive wars (which are gener-ally classified as mandatory) and expansionary wars (which are classified as dis-cretionary, *Mil he met r'shut*), remain intact and operative to some degree.[65] The category of *Mil he met r'shut* was developed to account for the later wars of the kings, particularly King David, both to render them permissible and to limit their occurrence in the future.[66] So, for example, Kind David's response to the Philistine attack is termed mandatory while his wars of territorial aggrandizement are called discretionary.[67] In the language of the Babylonian Talmud, King David's wars were wars *le-re va hah*, for territorial expansion (Babylonian Talmud Tractate, Sotah, 44b).[68]

RABBINIC HERMENEUTICS AS A PEDAGOGICAL MODEL

These categories essentially emerge out of an extensive discussion of a Mishnaic text that very generally outlines them.[69] By doing a careful analysis of this text in the classroom, students can be introduced to some of the hermeneutical assumptions and techniques of the rabbinic mind as expressed in the Mishnah and the Talmud. The rabbis referred to the Talmud as a *yam*, a sea that is vast and intricate. "Turn its pages for everything is in it," a Talmudic sage declared (Pirkei Avos, *The Ethics of the Fathers*, chapter 5, 21). Vastness and an uncategorizable nature was what defined it. When Maimonides wanted to extract from the Talmud's peculiar blend of folklore, legalistic arguments, biblical exegesis, and intergenerational rabbinic discussions some basic categories and legal assumptions, he was denounced as a heretic for attempting to replace the creative chaos of the Talmud with order and system. Its very chaos was seen as its link to divine inspiration. Within the text, rabbis who lived generations apart participate and give the appearance of speaking and arguing directly to each other. The premise of the Talmud is that it is not a book in the normal sense—it has no beginning, middle, or end. Going back to the sea metaphor, it is a sort of drift net for catching God, stretching out through time and space. The reality is that just about everything swims into the net—legal questions, stories, pieces of myth and folklore, rabbinic conversations, and epistemological questions. And as a net meant to catch God, it also ensnares and traps people, particularly students, in the process. It draws them in.[70]

Engaging with this difficult and strange literature in the classroom is challenging but can be facilitated by incorporating a collaborative approach to teaching and learning. I borrow assumptions about the benefits of collaborative learning from feminist pedagogy, which developed methods to ameliorate the inhibiting effects on women students of highly competitive, often male-dominated classes. Feminist pedagogy encouraged all students to feel confident about articulating their views while showing respect for and acknowledging the importance of other views for their own critical thinking. This collaborative approach to learning was also the preferred method of the rabbis. People are meant to study the Talmud in pairs—*hevruta*, the Aramaic word for a Talmudic study partner, has the same root as the word *haver*, or friend. Out of these study pairs a community is born and out of that community a society of collaborative learners.

Returning now to that Mishnaic text in Tractate Sotah, I will try to show how the rabbis and later interpreters attempted to derive broad principles from some textual anomalies and ambiguities contained within it. Once the text is introduced, it might be useful to divide the class into *hevruta* (pairs) for collaborative learning and interaction.

In discussing the biblical exemptions from military service listed in Deuteronomy 20, the Mishnah in Tractate Sotah (44b) states: "To what does this apply? To discretionary wars, but in wars commanded by the Torah (*Mil he met Mitzvah*) all go forth, even a bridegroom from his chamber and a bride from her canopy. Rabbi Judah says: To what do these verses apply? To wars commanded by the

Torah (*Mil he met Mitzvah*), but in obligatory wars (*Mil he met Hovah*) all go forth."

The plain meaning of the Mishnah seems to be that Rabbi Judah and the sages, the majority of the rabbis, disagreed about exemptions from commanded wars. But it is not clear from the text what the precise definitions of these categories are and what are the distinctions between *Mil he met Mitzvah* and *Hovah* as subsets of commanded wars.[71] This text and subsequent Talmudic discussions, as understood both by Rashi (eleventh century) and by Maimonides (twelfth century) in their commentaries, do not point to a fundamental disagreement between Rabbi Judah and the sages on the basic definition and scope of commanded wars. Both maintain that the biblical exemptions apply only to discretionary wars. Furthermore, they agree that the wars waged by the kings for territorial expansion were discretionary and those engaged in by Joshua for the Conquest were required by God.

The Talmud introduces a new category of war, however, and claims that Rabbi Judah and the sages disagreed about that. The category consists of wars "to diminish the heathens so that they shall not march against them" (Mishnah Sotah 8:7, 44b).[72] The disagreement is over this new situation. The sages included such defensive wars in the general category of discretionary wars because they are not specifically mandated by God in scripture. Rabbi Judah maintained that even though that was the case, preemptive strikes of the sort described fulfill a commandment because they are necessary for self-defense. In other words, even though the Bible does not specifically require such wars, it indirectly commands that we engage in them as part of the general biblical obligation to defend yourself based on Exodus 22:1, which exonerates an individual who kills an intruder.[73] Rabbi Judah, therefore, described wars of anticipatory self-defense as commanded wars, *Mil he met Mitzvah*, and invented a new term, "obligatory wars" (*Mil he met Hovah*) to describe wars required by God in the Torah such as the wars of the Conquest.[74]

To summarize, the conceptual structure of the Mishnah and subsequent Talmudic commentary and interpretation distinguish two or perhaps three types of war: specifically biblically commanded wars; discretionary wars, including the expansionary wars of the kings; and, according to Rabbi Judah, indirectly commanded wars, including preemptive defensive wars. For the sages, the last of these is simply another example of discretionary wars, but for Rabbi Judah they constituted a separate category of commanded (*Hovah*) wars.[75]

Medieval commentators further nuance Rabbi Judah's interpretive category. The thirteenth-century Franco-Provençal scholar Meiri (1249–1316) believes a preemptive strike, which he describes as a military response against an enemy who it is feared might attack or who is already preparing for war, is judged to be mandatory by the majority of the sages but deemed discretionary by Rabbi Judah. According to this reading, Rabbi Judah defines as mandatory only wars in response to an already launched attack.[76] In any case, Meiri seems to set the rather stringent requirement of a factual threat, not a perceived threat. Maimonides also limits the mandatory classification to a defensive war launched in response to an attack (Maimonides, Hilchot Melachim, 5:1).

As a category, discretionary wars (*Mil he met r'shut*) stand somewhere between defensive and offensive wars. The rabbis made a clear effort, continuing throughout the medieval period, to link *Mil he met r'shut* more closely to defensive wars. They restricted the legal disputes over *Mil he met r'shut* to various kinds of preemptive and defensive measures. The rabbis were also able to limit the utility of this type of warfare by imposing on it several stringent requirements.[77]

The easier it is to initiate a war, the more likely it is that governments will resort to war. The rabbis ruled that discretionary wars cannot be initiated by the king, or modern equivalent, without the advice and consent of the Sanhedrin and the "approval" of God as demonstrated by the Urim and Thummim (oracle worn by the high priest), thus further limiting its applicability (Babylonian Talmud, Tractate Sanhedrin, 16a; Eruvin, 45a).[78] Before going to war, the Sanhedrin must weigh the probable losses, consider the chances of success, and assess the will of the people and the support of God.[79] The initiative of the king and the approval of the Sanhedrin are not required for wars that God has expressly commanded, nor for defensive wars (Babylonian Talmud, Tractate Eruvin, 45a). The implication here is that consensus would be rare for discretionary wars and that if it were reached, then the war would be just. Each institution—king, Sanhedrin, and Urim and Thummim—served a specific purpose in ensuring the justice of the war. The king alone had the power to call forth an army. The Sanhedrin was in a unique position to assess whether the proposed war was necessary and whether it could meet the king's objectives. And the oracle was required to legitimize the war based on God's wishes.[80] Subsequent opinions tended to reduce severely the range of discretion in discretionary wars. Thus, Maimonides (twelfth century) forbade the waging of war against any nation before peace offers were made and insisted that even in the case of mandatory war, if the enemy sued for peace and accepted the seven Noahide commandments, they were not to be harmed (Mishnah Torah Hilchot Melochim, 6:1). These conditions applied even to nations living within Israel's borders. Rashi (eleventh century) believed it applied only to cities outside the borders of Israel. Both scholars maintained that peace always takes priority over war.[81] One may be flexible in interpreting these requirements to substitute the Jewish governing authority in Israel in modern times or heads of the Jewish community and prominent rabbis in the Middle Ages to stand in for the king and Sanhedrin, but there certainly is no substitute for the approval of God through the Urim and Thummim. Therefore, it is the opinion of most commentators that with these three requirements the rabbis basically made the category of *Mil he met r'shut* irrelevant. Since *Mil he met Hovah* is also moot because we can no longer identify the seven Canaanite nations and the Amalekites, the consensus is that the only war that Jews may wage legally, according to the Halachah (Jewish law), is a defensive war. As noted earlier, there is some difference of opinion over whether a preemptive strike against an enemy who may attack or is preparing to attack is to be considered mandatory (according to Meiri), or discretionary (according to Rashi). All, however, justify preemptive war for defensive purposes only. Revenge is not accepted as a motive for a preemptive strike. Initiating a war is justified only to save lives, not to punish an enemy.

ETHICAL CONDUCT OF WAR

Judaism also developed guidelines for the ethical conduct of war. An important contextual feature is the long-standing concern within Judaism of the inherently dehumanizing effects of war.[82] Beginning with Deuteronomy 20 and extending through much of rabbinic literature and later commentators, the Jewish tradition established rules to preserve as much moral sensitivity as possible in the practice of war. War is permitted only when it is clear that the lives saved by waging war are likely to be significantly greater in number than those lost through the war itself.[83] Before laying siege to a city, for example, it must be determined that it can be captured without destroying it. There is no license to destroy a city, or a nation, for the purpose of "saving" it. Scorched-earth tactics are forbidden. Similarly, war is permitted only when there is sound military reason to assume victory and only after overtures of peace have been offered. This approach developed into a generally accepted matter of Halachah that all warfare had to be preceded by an offer of peace, even for *Mil he met Hovah*.[84] This instruction was first expressed in Deuteronomy 20:10, "When you approach a town to attack it you shall offer it terms of peace." Maimonides expanded this, saying, "no war is declared against any nation before peace offers are made to it" (Mishneh Torah, Kings VI, 1). Peace must be offered at least three times before hostilities may commence (Kings VI, 5). This prerequisite applies to the laying of a siege as well.[85] If the terms are not accepted, the siege is not to begin until the enemy has opened hostilities. Even after a siege or its modern equivalent is initiated, no direct cruelties may be inflicted on noncombatants, and an escape route must be left open for them.[86] Access to escape became a principle of Jewish law to guarantee that no one was held involuntarily within the town walls. If there was constant access to escape, then civilians who remained inside the town were choosing to do so, in effect electing to become soldiers, thereby waiving their noncombatant protection (Maimonides, Mishnah Torah, Kings and Wars, VI, 7).[87]

National vendettas are not justifications for wars. Although victory is the goal, indeed victory with all due haste to minimize human suffering, peace without total victory is preferable to war, and wanton destruction is to be avoided.[88] Nachmonides (thirteenth century) emphasizes that acts of destruction are acceptable only if they advance the goal of victory (Nachmonides, Commentary on Deuteronomy 20:19–20). Since Deuteronomy 20:19–20 prohibits the destruction of fruit-bearing trees, Maimonides expands this directive to include also those who "smash household goods, tear clothes, demolish a building, stop up a spring, or destroy articles of food with destructive intent." They all transgress the command: "Thou shalt not destroy" (Mishnah Torah, Kings and Wars, 6:10).[89] Since the prohibition against destroying trees is formulated in a rhetorical manner, "are trees in the field human to withdraw before you into the besieged city?" (Deut. 20:19), so it is deduced that just as a tree, had it fled, would not be destroyed, so a person and his possessions, were he to flee, should not be damaged as well.[90] These ethical constraints in the waging of war underscore that Judaism is interested in safeguarding the moral character of the soldier and preserving the human image of the enemy, and that it is with reluctance that the Jewish tradition justifies war, which, in our time, it does almost exclusively for self-defense. In the thirteenth century, Nachmonides, who expressed an apprehension that "the most refined of people become possessed with ferocity and cruelty when advancing upon the enemy," also noted that the Torah wants the soldier to "learn to act compassionately with all enemies even during wartime" (Commentary on Deuteronomy 23:10).[91] The modern Israeli army, the IDF, notwithstanding ample criticism of its actions, tries to reflect these values in the doctrine articulated by former Prime Minister David Ben Gurion as the "purity of arms." This doctrine enjoins that great care must be exercised to limit the damage to human life and property during warfare and that civilian lives must be protected as much as possible, even at the cost of the lives of Israeli soldiers.[92] This code of conduct required Israeli soldiers to maintain their humanity even during combat.

Some believe that the Jewish relationship to power and even to violence may be changing since the Holocaust and its aftermath.[93] The Holocaust epitomizes the state of Jewish powerlessness, vulnerability to destruction, and victimization. Trapped in Europe and made the target of a campaign of extermination, the Jews were truly impotent victims during the war years, 1939–45. The Jews of Europe, especially in those countries ruled directly by the Nazis such as Poland, the conquered areas of Soviet Russia and Holland, and Germany itself, were exposed to the genocidal system and intent of the Nazis, which allowed very few escape systems. There also was the sense that the enemies of Nazism, particularly the United States, Great Britain, and the Soviet Union, did far too little to stop the genocidal killing. Their responses were limited, tentative, and tied to winning the war. The victims of the Holocaust and the survivors felt abandoned and impotent. In the wake of the Holocaust, Jewish victimization and powerlessness became the central justification for Jewish power. The prevailing sentiment emerged that Jews needed to embrace power and never allow themselves to be powerless and defenseless again.[94] Powerlessness, in this view, is tantamount to national self-destruction and is a sin. This view asserted that Jews were victims because they did not make survival their cardinal commandment; they did not pursue power with the single-mindedness necessary for survival. For the proponents of this ideology, which soon became normative, survival meant the survival of the Jewish state.[95] In the words of the late Emil Fackenheim, one of the most important twentieth-century Jewish philosophers and one of the foremost exponents of the ideology of survival, Auschwitz presents the Jews with a "614th commandment: not to render to Hitler a posthumous victory."[96] As the embodiment of the divine commandment of collective Jewish survival, the state of Israel assumes profound religious meaning.

In this context, examples of Jewish heroism from ancient history, such as the zealots at Masada or the biblical Samson, were given new resonance. The final defeat of the zealots at Masada where, according to the Roman-Jewish historian Josephus, the rebels took their own lives rather than surrender to the Romans at the end of the Great Revolt, became a metaphor for the modern Jewish state surrounded by determined enemies and prepared, possibly, to commit national suicide rather than surrender.[97] Dictators and terrorists delight in parading their military might—note the military displays of Iran, North Korea, and Hezbollah. Israel, in contrast, invites visiting foreign dignitaries to tour its Holocaust Memorial, Yad

Vashem, and initiates new IDF officers at Masada. The symbolic message is clear. Another historical metaphor that has emerged is the biblical Samson. The state of Israel, possessing, most believe, nuclear weapons, might choose the "Samson Option" if seriously threatened, dying with the "Philistines" rather than surrendering to its enemies. In this new political climate in the Middle East, the Jew remains a victim, but now a victim with an army and nuclear weapons at its disposal.[98]

Judaism and the contemporary state of Israel are divided between those who are moved by the imperative to pursue peace and those who warn, like the prophet Jeremiah, against saying "peace, peace, when there is no peace." The Tanach tells of how Jacob prepared to meet his brother Esau, who had earlier tried to kill him (Gen. 32:4–33). Like the state of Israel today, he planned for three possibilities: for diplomacy, for prayer, and for war. And like Israel today, that encounter involved Jacob in an intense inner struggle: "A man-angel wrestled with him until the break of dawn" (Gen. 32:5). Jacob, like Israel and Judaism, has to wrestle between contending forces and conflicting tendencies. It is from that struggle that Jews, as a people, get their name Israel, "for you have struggled with beings divine and human, and have prevailed" (Gen. 32:29).

MORALITY AND WAR

As a school of thought, the moral war tradition is rooted in Christian theology, but its ultimate roots are in Jewish monotheism. As described throughout this chapter, the Jewish concept of war as a human activity that must be informed by moral constrictions first appears in Deuteronomy, chapter 20, which regulates how the army should prepare for battle, how to lay siege and negotiate lifting it, and the obligations to prisoners of war.

The crucial distinction in the discussion of morality and war is that between *jus ad bellum*, or justice in going to war, and *jus in bello*, or justice in waging war (see also chapter 12, William French's essay in this volume). The first asks whether one is ever justified in going to war in the first place, and we have seen that Judaism's basic answer is that the nation must protect itself against aggression and thereby ensure its continued existence. Another point is the price of ending the war, be it by surrender, negotiated settlement, or victory. *Jus in bello* is the attempt to wage war according to a code, lest the nation nullify whatever justification there may have been for the original decision to fight. This is a separate issue from *jus ad bellum* and reaches down to the individual behavior of soldiers in the field, irrespective of whether the war they are engaged in is just. A just war can be waged unjustly and an unjust war could conceivably be justly waged. Judaism mandates the protection of civilians and captured soldier who are never legitimate targets.

Israel has mostly tried to be moral. Sometimes it has made mistakes, even serious ones, but it has mostly owned up to them. Judaism does not sanction murder, wanton brutality, or revenge. Of course, some Jews do commit these crimes because individuals are flawed and fallible. But when Jews do murder, or torture, or take revenge, they do so against the values of the normative tradition and they face sanctions and criticisms from coreligionists and their leaders. My claim here should not be misunderstood. Judaism celebrates peace but it recognizes that there are occasions when wars cannot be avoided. There are many more sources that can be cited about Judaism and peace than there are about Judaism and war, and that certainly is laudatory. But the centrality of peace in Judaism does not mean that there is something profoundly "un-Jewish" about war: no thinking person can deny the harmful nature of war. But that does not make the conduct of war contrary to Jewish principles if the conditions of *jus ad bellum* and *jus in bello* are met. Indeed, an unwillingness to fight for survival would be a departure from what the Jewish tradition has always advocated. Yes, the tradition urges Jews to be sensitive, even appalled, at the suffering of their enemies. "If your enemy falls, do not exult," urges Proverbs 24:7. But Jews are still permitted, indeed commanded, to defend themselves and to defeat their enemies.

CONCLUSION

Peace is a paradox. Many religions and cultures praise it and decry conflict and war, yet they engage in war and often find themselves in conflict. "Seek peace and pursue it," the Psalmist said (Ps. 34:15). *Z ai' a Mentsh*, live up to your potential as a human being, many Jewish parents have exhorted their children in Yiddish. Every major prayer in Jewish liturgy concludes with the plea for peace, including the grace after meals, the Amidah silent prayer, the priestly blessing, and the Kaddish, the memorial prayer for the dead.[99] The Book of Psalms states that the Lord "hates him that loves violence" (Ps. 11:5).[100] The compilers of the Mishnah end that monumental work with a prayer for peace, "the Lord will give strength to His people; the Lord will bless His people with peace" (Mishnah Uktsin, 3:12).[101] No major Jewish holiday or festival celebrates the waging of a war. Hanukkah celebrates the rededication of the Temple and the miracle of the oil, not the war that preceded it.[102] The Hebrew word for peace, *shalom*, derives from a root that signifies wholeness and completion.[103] *Shalom*, more than just an absence of war, represents a state of fulfillment, a time when all people are able to meet their daily physical and spiritual needs. As the word suggests, peace, sadly, is not the normal state of the world. In its ultimate sense, it describes the achievement of the messiah. From the time that Isaiah revealed his vision of a future when even the wolf will lie down with the lamb, peace has been a cornerstone of Jewish messianism.[104]

Shalom also means a state of not being at war, as in the biblical command to "proclaim peace," to offer peace to one's enemy. Judaism formulated the idea of *dar chei shalom*, the ways of peace. This is not just a sentimental idea but a concept that found its way into Jewish law. *Dar chei shalom* asserts that the basic duties that I owe to members of my faith, I owe to those outside as well, because I share a space with my neighbors, a common humanity derived from a singular creator, and we must be able to live together if we are to live at all.[105] The Torah enjoins Jews to remember, *zachor*. The verb "to remember" appears over 160 times in the Hebrew Bible.[106] Jews are commanded to remember that they were once strangers in the land of Egypt. They are to remember this so that they will not oppress the stranger because they know the heart of the stranger.[107] There is a moment of moral drama in the Passover Seder when Jews spill drops of wine at the mention of the plagues as symbolic tears for their Egyptian oppressors who suffered. Traditional Jews do not say the Hallel (praise) prayer during the last days of Passover, some authorities say, to mourn for the Egyptians who drowned at the Red Sea pursuing the Israelites.[108] In the biblical account, just as the Egyptians who had followed them into the sea were about to reach them, the waters closed in on the pursuers. The Israelites, safe on the other side, saw their former taskmasters and Pharaoh's army destroyed. They were finally free and in the biblical rendering celebrated by singing the famous Song at the Sea (Ex. 15:1–18). But later Jewish tradition was apparently uncomfortable with the Jews celebrating their freedom if it came at the expense of other lives. According to a rabbinic midrash, as the Israelites were singing, praising God for their salvation, the heavenly angels also sought to join the song and the praise. But instead of being pleased, God chastened them, asking, "the work of My hands is being drowned in the sea, and you would chant hymns?" (Babylonian Talmud, Megillah, 10b). Even at the moment of victory that had saved the people, the Jewish tradition was discomfited by the violence and death that victory itself necessitated. Compassion must be felt even for one's enemies. *Dar chei shalom* is a recognition that we live in a world of complex interdependencies.

"Seek peace and pursue it." The rabbis, noting the duplication of the verbs *seek* and *pursue*, emphasize how important yet elusive the concept of peace is and suggested that this means we are required to work for peace not only for ourselves but for the "strangers" as well.[109] People are not commanded to run after or pursue the other commandments, just to fulfill them appropriately. "But peace you must seek in your own place and pursue it even to another place as well" (Jerusalem Talmud, Pe'ah, 1:1).[110] *Dar chei shalom* may be a blueprint for peace in a complex, unredeemed world.

NOTES

1. Elsie Boulding, "Two Cultures of Religion," *Zygon* 21/4 (1986): 501–16; Charles Selengut, *Sacred Fury: Understanding Religious Violence* (Walnut Creek, CA: Altamira Press, 2003), 2–3.
2. See Peter L. Berger, *The Sacred Canopy* (New York: Anchor, 1967), 3–51.
3. See Jonathan Sacks, *The Dignity of Difference* (New York: Continuum, 2002), 1–3.
4. See Jonathan Sacks, *A Letter in the Scroll* (New York: Free Press, 2000), 75.
5. See Jonathan Sacks, *Faith in the Future* (London: Darton, Longman and Todd, 1995), 11.
6. See Abraham Heschel, *God in Search of Man* (New York: Farrar, Straus and Giroux, 1996); Abraham Heschel, *Man Is Not Alone* (New York: Farrar, Straus and Giroux, 1995); Martin Buber, *Good and Evil* (New York: Scribner's, 1953); Martin Buber, *Israel and the World* (New York: Schocken, 1978).
7. Sacks, *A Letter in the Scroll*, 96.
8. See Ruth R. Wisse, *Jews and Power* (New York: Schocken, 2007), 12–13. I use feminine pronouns to refer to God whenever possible to balance the dominance of masculine representational language for God.

9. See Sacks, *Faith in the Future*, 73.
10. Ibid.
11. Elliot N. Dorff, *To Do the Right and the Good* (Philadelphia: Jewish Publication Society, 2002), 161.
12. See Wisse, *Jews and Power*.
13. Ibid.
14. Dorff, *To Do the Right*, 178.
15. Ibid.
16. Selengut, *Sacred Fury*, 201–2.
17. Ibid., 183.
18. Bradley Shavit Artson, *Love Peace* (New York: United Synagogue of America, 1988), 42–43.
19. Ibid., 43.
20. See Leonard Baker, *Days of Sorrow and Pain: Leo Baeck and the Berlin Jews* (New York: Macmillan, 1978), xiii; Shimon Huberband, *Kiddush Hashem: Jewish Religious and Cultural Life in Poland During the Holocaust* (New York: Yeshiva University Press, 1987).
21. Selengut, *Sacred Fury*, 188.
22. Bruce Chilton, *Abraham's Curse* (New York: Doubleday, 2008), 46–48.
23. I Maccabees 2:24.
24. See Chilton, *Abraham's Curse*, 49–57, for a discussion of this history.
25. Ibid., 49.
26. Artson, *Love Peace*, 87.
27. Meir Bar-Ilan, "Jewish Violence in Antiquity: Three Dimensions," in *Jewish Studies in Violence*, ed. Roberta Rosenberg Farber and Simcha Fishbane (Lanham, MD: University Press of America, 2007), 75.
28. Artson, *Love Peace*, 89.
29. Bar-Ilan, "Jewish Violence in Antiquity," 75.
30. Aviezer Ravitzky, "Peace," in *Contemporary Jewish Religious Thought*, ed. Arthur A. Cohen and Paul Mendes-Flohr (New York: Charles Scribner's Sons, 1987), 690.
31. Artson, *Love Peace*, 45.
32. Ibid.
33. Maurice Lamm, "After the War—Another Look at Pacifism and Selective Conscientious Objection," in *Contemporary Jewish Ethics*, ed. Menachem Marc Kellner (New York: Sanhedrin, 1978), 223.
34. Michael Walzer, "Commanded and Permitted Wars," in *Law, Politics, and Morality in Judaism*, ed. Michael Walzer (Princeton, NJ: Princeton University Press, 2006), 150–51.
35. Lamm, "After the War," 223.
36. Yitzchak Blau, "Ploughshares into Swords: Contemporary Religious Zionists and Moral Constraints," in *Jewish Studies in Violence*, ed. Farber and Fishbane, 179–80.
37. Ibid., 177.
38. Dorff, *To Do the Right*, 179.
39. Lamm, "After the War," 166.
40. Selengut, *Sacred Fury*, 20.
41. Reuven Kimelman, "War," in *Frontiers of Jewish Thought*, ed. Steven T. Katz (Washington, DC: B'nai B'rith Books, 1992), 309.
42. Dorff, *To Do the Right*, 166.
43. Kimelman, "War," 309.
44. Everette E. Gendler, "War and the Jewish Tradition," in *Contemporary Jewish Ethics*, ed. Kellner, 198–99.

45. Walzer, "Commanded and Permitted Wars," 157.
46. Artson, *Love Peace*, 103.
47. See Israel Finkelstein and Neil Asher Silberman, *The Bible Unearthed* (New York: Free Press, 2001), for a lively and informed discussion of this issue, as well as Robert Eisen, *The Peace and Violence of Judaism* (New York: Oxford University Press, 2011), 15–64.
48. Artson, *Love Peace*, 103.
49. Ibid., 105.
50. Ibid., 106.
51. Jack Nelson-Pallmeyer, *Is Religion Killing Us?* (New York: Continuum, 2003), xi–xiii.
52. Ibid., xiii.
53. Richard Dawkins, *The God Delusion* (New York: Houghton Mifflin, 2006), 242–47.
54. See R. D. Gold, *Bondage of the Mind* (Menlo Park, CA: Aldus Books, 2008); Christopher Hitchens, *God Is Not Great* (New York: Twelve, 2007); and Sam Harris, *The End of Faith* (New York: Norton, 2005).
55. Artson, *Love Peace*, 106.
56. Bart D. Ehrman, *God's Problem* (New York: HarperOne, 2008), 69.
57. Artson, *Love Peace*, 113.
58. Ibid., 115.
59. Selengut, *Sacred Fury*, 23–24.
60. Ehrman, *God's Problem*, 71.
61. Artson, *Love Peace*, 106, 116.
62. Ibid., 117.
63. Walzer, "Commanded and Permitted Wars," 161.
64. Artson, *Love Peace*, 182.
65. Kimelman, "War," 309.
66. Artson, *Love Peace*, 162.
67. Kimelman, "War," 309.
68. Artson, *Love Peace*, 169.
69. Dorff, *To Do the Right*, 166.
70. See Jonathan Rosen, *The Talmud and the Internet* (New York: Farrar, Straus and Giroux, 2000), for a fascinating analysis of the richness and complexity of the Talmud.
71. Dorff, *To Do the Right*, 166.
72. Ibid.
73. Ibid., 167.
74. Ibid.
75. Ibid., 168.
76. Kimelman, "War," 312–13.
77. Artson, *Love Peace*, 171–72.
78. Ibid.
79. Kimelman, "War," 312–13.
80. Artson, *Love Peace*, 175.
81. Aviezer Ravitsky, "Prohibited Wars," in *Law, Politics, and Morality in Judaism*, ed. Walzer, 170–71. See also Eisen, *The Peace and Violence*, 65–128.
82. Dorff, *To Do the Right*, 179.
83. Kimelman, "War," 314.
84. Artson, *Love Peace*, 132.
85. Kimelman, "War," 314.
86. Artson, *Love Peace*, 154–55.
87. Ibid., 156.
88. Kimelman, "War," 314.

89. Artson, *Love Peace*, 158.

90. Kimelman, "War," 316.

91. Ibid., 317.

92. David Biale, *Power and Powerlessness in Jewish History* (New York: Schocken, 1986), 157, 164.

93. Ibid., 157, 164.

94. Ibid., 161; and Yaacov Lozowick, *Right to Exist: A Moral Defense of Israel's Wars* (New York: Doubleday, 2003), 29, 74–75, 118–19, 260–62; and Eisen, *The Peace and Violence*, 141–203.

95. Biale, *Power and Powerlessness*, 141–44.

96. Emil Fackenheim, *God's Presence in History* (New York: Harper, 1970), 84. See also Emil Fackenheim, *The Jewish Return into History* (New York: Schocken, 1978).

97. Biale, *Power and Powerlessness*, 161.

98. Ibid., 148, 161; and Lozowick, *Right to Exist*, 74–75, 118–19, 260–62.

99. Dorff, *To Do the Right*, 164.

100. Artson, *Love Peace*, 60.

101. Ibid., 61.

102. Dorff, *To Do the Right*, 164.

103. Walzer, "Commanded and Permitted Wars," 150.

104. Artson, *Love Peace*, 60.

105. Sacks, *Faith in the Future*, 80.

106. Yosef Hayim Yerushalmi, *Zakhor* (New York: Schocken, 1989), 5–6.

107. Sacks, *Faith in the Future*, 84.

108. Ibid., 102.

109. Dorff, *To Do the Right*, 179.

110. Ibid.

BIBLIOGRAPHY

Artson, Bradley Shavit. *Love Peace and Pursue Peace*. New York: United Synagogue of America, 1988.

Baile, David. *Power and Powerlessness in Jewish History*. New York: Schocken, 1986.

Baker, Leonard. *Days of Sorrow and Pain: Leo Baeck and the Berlin Jews*. New York: Macmillan, 1978.

Bar-Ilan, Meir. "Jewish Violence in Antiquity: Three Dimensions." In *Jewish Studies in Violence*, ed. Roberta Rosenberg Faber and Simcha Fishbane. Lanham, MD: University Press of America, 2007.

Berger, Peter. *The Sacred Canopy*. New York: Anchor, 1987.

Blau, Yitzchak. "Ploughshares into Swords: Contemporary Religious Zionists and Moral Constraints." In *Jewish Studies in Violence*, ed. Roberta Rosenberg Faber and Simcha Fishbane. Lanham, MD: University Press of America, 2007.

Boulding, Elsie. "Two Cultures of Religion." *Zygon* 21/4 (1958): 501–16.

Buber, Martin. *Good and Evil*. New York: Scribner's, 1953.

———. *Israel and the World*. New York: Scribner, 1978.

Chilton, Bruce. *Abraham's Curse*. New York: Doubleday, 2008.

Dawkins, Richard. *The God Delusion*. New York: Houghton Mifflin, 2006.

Dorff, Elliot N. *To Do the Right and the Good*. Philadelphia: Jewish Publication Society, 2002.

Ehrman, Bart D. *God's Problem*. New York: Harper One, 2008.

Eisen, Robert. *The Peace and Violence of Judaism: From the Bible to Modern Zionism*. New York: Oxford University Press, 2011.

Eller, Jack David. *Cruel Creeds, Virtuous Violence: Religious Violence across Culture and History*. Amherst, NY: Prometheus, 2010.

Fackenheim, Emil. *God's Presence in History*. New York: Harper, 1970.

———. *The Jewish Return into History*. New York: Schocken, 1978.

Finkelstein, Israel, and Neil Asher Silberman. *The Bible Unearthed*. New York: Free Press, 2001.

Gendler, Everette E. "War and the Jewish Tradition." In *Contemporary Jewish Ethics*, ed. Menachem Marc Kellner. New York: Sanhedrin, 1978.

Gold, R. D. *Bondage of the Mind*. Menlo Park, CA: Aldus, 2008.

Harris, Sam. *The End of Faith*. New York: Norton, 2005.

Heschel, Abraham Joshua. *God in Search of Man*. New York: Farrar, Straus and Giroux, 1996.

———. *Man Is Not Alone*. New York: Farrar, Straus and Giroux, 1995.

Hitchens, Christopher. *God Is Not Great*. New York: Twelve, 2007.

Huberband, Shimon. *Kiddush Hasheim: Jewish Religious and Cultural Life in Poland*. New York: Yeshiva University Press, 1987.

Kimelman, Reuven. "War." In *Frontiers of Jewish Thought*, ed. Steven T. Katz. Washington, DC: B'nai B'rith Books, 1992.

Lamm, Maurice. "After the War—Another Look at Pacifism and Selective Conscientious Objection." In *Contemporary Jewish Ethics*, ed. Menachem Marc Kellner. New York: Sanhedrin, 1978.

Lozowick, Yoacov. *Right to Exist: A Moral Defense of Israel's Wars*. New York: Doubleday, 2003.

Nelson-Pallmeyer, Jack. *Is Religion Killing Us?* New York: Continuum, 2003.

Ravitzky, Aviezer. "Peace." In *Contemporary Religious Thought*, ed. Arthur A. Cohen and Paul Mendes-Flohr. New York: Scribner's Sons, 1987.

Rosen, Jonathan. *The Talmud and the Internet*. New York: Farrar, Straus and Giroux, 2000.

Sacks, Jonathan. *The Dignity of Difference*. New York: Continuum, 2002.

———. *Faith in the Future*. London: Darton, Longman, and Todd, 1995.

———. *A Letter in the Scroll*. New York: Free Press, 2000.

Selengut, Charles. *Sacred Fury: Understanding Religious Violence*. Walnut Creek, CA: Altamira Press, 2003.

Walzer, Michael. "Commanded and Permitted Wars." In *Law, Politics, and Morality in Judaism*, ed. Michael Walzer. Princeton, NJ: Princeton University Press, 2006.

———. *Just and Unjust Wars*. New York: Basic Books, 1977.

Wisse, Ruth R. *Jews and Power*. New York: Schocken, 2007.

Yerushalmi, Yosef Hayum. *Zakhor*. New York: Schocken, 1989.

CHAPTER 3

Teaching Buddhism and Violence

BRIAN DAIZEN VICTORIA

INTRODUCTION

Perhaps the greatest challenge the instructor faces in teaching the topic of Buddhism and violence may be convincing students (and possibly a few instructors) that there is anything to teach about. That is to say, it has been my experience that many in the West, Buddhists and non-Buddhists alike, continue to believe that Buddhism is the one religion, perhaps the only one, that has not been connected to violence, at least other than being the victim of violence, for example, the current oppression of Buddhism in Tibet at the hands of the Chinese government.

On the surface there appears to be ample support for this belief, for Buddhism's founder, Buddha, Śākyamuni is recorded in chapter 10, stanza 129 of the Dhammapada as having taught: "All persons tremble at being harmed, all persons fear death; remembering that you are like unto them, neither strike nor slay."

Furthermore, regardless of sectarian affiliation, the very first precept that both Buddhist clerics and laity pledge to follow is: "Do not kill." How then could someone claiming to be an adherent of the Buddhist faith, that is, the Buddha Dharma, justify the use of violence in the name of that faith? Isn't the current Dalai Lama, Tenzin Gyatso, winner of the 1989 Nobel Peace Prize, the very embodiment of Buddhist nonviolence?

Given this situation, the first thing the instructor may have to do is invite students to entertain the possibility that Buddhism's connection to violence and warfare not only may exist but may be far deeper than they suspect given Buddhism's more than 2,500 years of history that is only now becoming known in the West. And once students are willing to entertain this possibility, the next step is to introduce them to some historical examples where the connection of Buddhism to violence is clear and unmistakable. For example, soon after establishing the Sui dynasty in China in 581 C.E., Emperor Wen wrote:

> With the armed might of a *Cakravartin* King [universal monarch], We spread the ideals of the ultimately benevolent one [the Buddha]. With a hundred victories and a hundred battles, We promote the practice of the ten Buddhist virtues. Therefore, *We regard weapons of war as having become like incense and flowers* [presented as offerings to the Buddha] and the fields of this visible world as becoming forever identical with the Buddha land.[1]

Should students think this is merely one isolated incident, or no longer relevant since it occurred so long ago, one could introduce a more recent example that occurred shortly prior to the outbreak of the Russo-Japanese War in 1904. It was then that the Japanese True Pure Land (Shin) scholar-priest Inoue Enryō wrote:

> In Russia state and religion are one, and there is no religious freedom. Thus, religion is used as a chain in order to unify the [Russian] people. Therefore, when they [the Russian people] see Orientals, they are told that the latter are the bitter enemies of their religion. It is for this reason that on the one hand this is a war of politics and on the other hand it is a war of religion. . . . If theirs is the army of God, then ours is the army of the Buddha. It is in this way that Russia is not only the enemy of our country but of the Buddha as well.[2]

As these two widely disparate remarks reveal, Buddhism, past and present, is anything but free from the scourge of religion-sanctioned violence. Once Buddhism's connection to violence has been raised as a possibility in students' minds, an instructor is ready to move on to the next and critically important topic, that is, what were the mechanisms whereby this came about?

Before addressing this question, however, it is only proper that I share with instructors the theoretical construct that I employ in seeking to respond. In particular, how does Buddhist-related violence fit into the larger question of religiously sanctioned violence across the board?

I suggest the answer is to be found in various enabling mechanisms that can be shown to exist in all of the world's major religions, numerous malleable doctrines and associated praxis that, in certain situations and circumstances, can be reconfigured or transformed into instruments that at least countenance, if not actively condone, the use of violence. What makes these doctrines and praxis so difficult to identify for both those inside and outside of a particular faith tradition is that on the surface, that is, their "bright sides," these entities appear to have little or nothing to do with sanctioning violence. Thus, to assert, for example, that this or that doctrine has a violence-condoning "dark side," that is, one such enabling mechanism, immediately provokes a strong denial from those within that faith, that is, "defenders of the faith," who immediately point to the standard interpretation or bright side of the doctrine or praxis in question.

For example, Christian believers are typically promised eternal life in heaven as their reward for having lived a pious life on earth. On the surface this teaching would seem to have no connection whatsoever to religiously sanctioned violence. How could this article of faith possibly become an enabling mechanism condoning the use of violence?

The answer is no further away than the daily newspaper, as, for example, in an article that appeared in the July 17, 2004, issue of the *Cleveland Plain Dealer*. The Rev. James R. McGonegal, pastor of Saint Ignatius of Antioch Church in Cleveland, Ohio, gave the eulogy for a fallen U.S. soldier in Iraq:

> Sgt. Joseph Martin Garmback was killed last week in Samarra, Iraq. . . . "Joey loved being a soldier. He was so self-sacrificing," said the Rev. James R. McGonegal. "This man knew something about living and dying, and giving his life for someone else." Many dried their eyes when McGonegal assured them Garmback was going to a better place, a safer place. "He is safe at home, at last, at peace," McGonegal said.

Needless to say, Rev. McGonegal, a Roman Catholic, did not discuss how many Iraqi combatants (or noncombatants) Sgt. Garmback may have killed prior to "giving his life for someone else." What was beyond doubt was that eternal life was the sergeant's reward for sacrificing himself for his country, no matter how much killing of the other was required in the process.

In modern warfare the one certainty is that there will be massive loss of life, both military and, increasingly, civilian. How could this carnage be sustained if not for the military chaplains and religious figures on all sides who bestow a transcendent meaning on the lives and possible deaths of soldiers on the battlefield? Something they (or their peers) subsequently repeat to the soldiers' loved ones at home. And what greater ultimate reward could there be than eternal life?

Inasmuch as I have given many examples of such enabling mechanisms in multiple faiths in a recent Web-based journal article, I will not belabor the point here.[3] Further, let me make it very clear that pointing to the existence of violence-affirming elements in other faiths is not meant as an apologetic, let alone an excuse, for the existence of similar elements in Buddhism. Each faith deserves to be judged on its own merits (and demerits), especially as manifested in historical praxis.

Let me also note that my own field of expertise is focused on the Mahāyāna school of Buddhism as found in Japan. Thus many of the historical examples I will use to illuminate uniquely Buddhist enabling mechanisms are taken from my research on Buddhism in this country. Nonetheless, broader research in the field makes it clear that the connection of such Buddhist doctrines as selflessness and karma to violence and warfare are not the exclusive preserve of any one Buddhist school or nation. That, of course, is a contentious point, one deserving further exploration. Note, too, that the following is neither an exhaustive nor comprehensive list of all the violence-enabling mechanisms within Buddhism, but, taken as a whole, they do provide students with a good introduction to the topic.

BUDDHIST ENABLING MECHANISMS
Violence as a Product of Karma

A good place for the instructor to begin an introduction to Buddhism's violence-enabling mechanisms is the doctrine of karma, inasmuch as it is one of Buddhism's core concepts. As in the case of Christian eternal life, on the surface karma appears to have no connection to violence for, in its simplest formulation, it simply states that human actions inevitably have consequences, good or bad, determined primarily, but not exclusively, by the intent of the actor.

Nevertheless, the concluding chapter of one of the most famous and influential Mahāyāna scriptures in East Asia, the Lotus Sūtra, contains the following passage:

> Whoever in future ages shall receive and keep, read and recite this sūtra, such persons will no longer be greedily attached to clothes, bed things, drink, food, and things for the support of life; whatever they wish will never be in vain, and in the present life they will obtain their blessed reward. Suppose anyone slights and slanders them, saying "You are only madmen, pursuing this course in vain with never a thing to be gained." The doom for such a sin as this is blindness generation after generation. . . . . If anyone sees those who receive and keep this sūtra, and proclaims their errors and sins, whether true or false, such a one in the present life will be smitten with leprosy. If he ridicules them, generation after generation his teeth will be sparse and missing, his lips vile, his nose flat, his hands and feet contorted, his eyes squint, his body stinking and filthy with evil scabs and bloody pus, dropsical and short of breath, and [with] every evil disease.[4]

Such is the karmic fate awaiting those who dare to criticize followers of the Lotus Sūtra. And since their blindness and so on lasts "generation after generation," it is clear that the blind, the lepers, the physically deformed of this world have only themselves to blame for their afflictions. In short, they had it coming.

In light of this understanding of karma, it is no wonder that when wedded to the strong, Confucian-influenced familialism of East Asian countries, physical impairment has long been a source of great shame not only for impaired individuals but for their entire family. Over the centuries thousands upon thousands of such individuals and their families have had to endure discrimination, ridicule, isolation, harsh treatment, and worse because of the alleged evil they committed in past lives. (Note that at this point the instructor may wish to introduce some of the basic tenets of Confucian social ethics and outline, if only briefly, the process by which these ethics became incorporated into Buddhism in East Asian countries.)

Karma in Japan

Building on this understanding, institutional Buddhist leaders of all sects have, since the middle of the Meiji period (1868–1912), employed the doctrine of karma in their ideological struggle against Western liberalism and individualism, not to mention anarchism, socialism, and communism. As early as 1879, for example, the noted Shin sect scholar-priest Shimaji Mokurai (1838–1911) wrote an essay titled "Differentiation [Is] Equality" (J., *Sabetsu Byōdō*). Shimaji asserted that distinctions in social standing and wealth are as permanent as differences in age, sex, and language. Thus, those struggling for social equality, most especially socialists, are fatally flawed because they place emphasis solely on social and economic equality. That is to say, socialists fail to understand the basic Mahāyāna Buddhist teaching that due to the working of karma, "differentiation is identical with equality" (J., *sabetsu soku byōdō*).[5]

Socialism and its like were regarded as imports from a West that threatened Japan's existence not only externally, through force of arms, but internally, through ideological subversion. Another outspoken proponent of this viewpoint was Lt. General (and Viscount) Torio Tokuan (1847–1905). General Torio was the founder of the Yuima-kai (Skt., Vimalakīrti), a lay society established in 1881 to promote Zen practice among Japan's military leaders. Headquartered at the Rinzai Zen monastery of Shōkokuji in Kyoto, this society actively pursued its nationalist and militarist mission on an ever-expanding scale up through Japan's defeat in 1945.

Torio's ideological orientation is well illustrated by the following excerpt from a newspaper editorial he wrote for Japan's *Daily Mail* in 1890:

> The adoption of the [Occidental] principles of liberty and equality in Japan would vitiate the good and peaceful customs of our country, render the general disposition of the people harsh and unfeeling, and prove finally a source of calamity to the masses. . . . Though at first sight Occidental civilization presents an attractive appearance, adapted as it is to the gratification of selfish desires, yet, since its basis is the hypothesis that men's wishes constitute natural laws, it must ultimately end in disappointment and demoralization. . . .
>
> Occidental nations have become what they are after passing through conflicts and vicissitudes of the most serious kind. . . . Perpetual disturbance is their doom. Peaceful equality can never be attained until built up among the ruins of annihilated Western States and the ashes of extinct Western peoples.[6]

I doubt this author is alone in his perception that Gen. Tokuan appears to be predicting the outbreak of World War II (typically referred to in Japan as the Asia-Pacific War) a full half century before it occurred. Be that as it may, the instructor may wish to pause here to discuss the validity (or otherwise) of the general's assertions.

Military Usage

Given this background, it was not difficult for Buddhist chaplains, who had accompanied Japanese troops to the battlefield as early as the Sino-Japanese War of 1894–95, to incorporate karma into their morale-building talks given to soldiers as well as in funerals for those who fell in battle. The Nishi (West) Honganji branch of the True Pure Land sect (Jōdo-Shinshū), for example, recognized the need for chaplains as early as 1902, when forty-six priests were dispatched to more than forty military bases throughout Japan.[7]

In the same year, Nishi Honganji produced a booklet titled *Bushidō* (Way of the Warrior) as part of a series called *Seishin Kōwa* (Lectures on Spirit). The connection between the two events is clear in that it was Ōtani Kōen (1850–1903), an aristocrat and the branch's administrative head, who both dispatched the military chaplains and contributed a foreword to the booklet. Kōen explained that the booklet's purpose was "to clarify the spirit of military evangelization."[8]

As its title suggests, Nishi Honganji intended this booklet to provide the doctrinal basis for its outreach to the military. That this outreach had a broader focus than the soldiers themselves can be seen from the inclusion of a concluding chapter titled "To the Parents and Family of Military Men." Although Japan was at peace in 1902, there was an increasing awareness of the possibility of war with Russia. Thus, sectarian leaders like Kōen realized that soldiers' parents and family members would be concerned that their loved ones might die in battle.

The booklet's author was Satō Gan'ei (1847–1905), a military chaplain as well as clerical head of the lay-oriented Yuima-kai associated with Nishi Honganji. The military character of this association is clear in that three high-ranking imperial army officers were members, each contributing a calligraphic endorsement to the booklet. One of the three, Lt. General Ōshima Ken'ichi (1858–1947), later served as minister of war in two cabinets and privy counselor during the Asia-Pacific War.

In his introduction, Gan'ei explained that the purpose of religion in Japan was "to be an instrument of the state and an instrument of the imperial household." More specifically, the government had granted Buddhism permission to propagate itself "to ensure that citizens fulfill their duties [to the state] while at the same time preserving social order and stability."[9] Gan'ei claimed that religionists like him had been charged with making sure this important task was accomplished.

Yet what connection did karma have with this? Gan'ei explained the military relevance of this doctrine:

> Everything depends on karma. There are those who, victorious in battle, return home strong and fit only to die soon afterwards. On the other hand, there are those who are scheduled to enter the military yet die before they do so. If it is their karmic destiny, bullets will not strike them, and they will not die. Conversely, should it be their karmic destiny, even if they are not in the military, they may still die from gunfire. Therefore there is definitely no point in worrying about this. Or expressed differently, even if you do worry about it, nothing will change.[10]

There can be no question here of soldiers dying because of the mistaken decisions made by their political or military leaders. As Gan'ei tirelessly pointed out, the imperial military was under the direct control of its commander in chief, his majesty the emperor, whose "bountiful benevolence cannot fail but bring tears of gratitude to the eyes of all parents and family members."[11]

Thus, a soldier's death is attributable solely to the karma of that particular soldier. In short, like the physically impaired in the Lotus Sūtra, he had it coming, and there was nothing that the soldier or his loved ones, let alone his military superiors or even the emperor, could do to change that. And equally important, none of the soldier's superiors could be held responsible for his death in the event he were to fall on the battlefield.

Violence as a Product of Rebirth

In introducing this topic, the instructor should begin by explaining the Buddhist understanding of the doctrine of rebirth: upon death, the consciousness of a person becomes one of the causes contributing to the emergence of a new group of the five constituent elements (Skt., *skandhas*) that compose personhood. For this reason the new grouping may once again be conventionally regarded as a person.[12] It should be noted, however, that the consciousness arising in the new person is considered to be neither identical to, nor different from, the old consciousness. Instead, it forms part of a causal continuum or stream with it. Further, the basic cause for this persistent re-arising of the person is the abiding of consciousness in ignorance (*avidjā*). Thus, when ignorance is uprooted and nirvāṇa realized, rebirth will cease.

While the preceding doctrinal understanding of rebirth clearly shows that Buddhism does not embrace reincarnation (i.e., the rebirth of a soul in a new body), at the level of popular belief the distinction between rebirth and reincarnation has been muted, if not effectively erased. In the first instance, this can be said to be the result of a popular understanding of karma that questions why some appear to escape punishment for evil deeds in their present lives, while, conversely, some who do good receive no reward. Thus, without future lives in which to even the score, karma would appear unfair if not totally capricious.

While the popular understanding of rebirth among Buddhists does not condone violence as such, it has, nevertheless, aided in reducing the significance of death on the battlefield to the point that it is but one more phase in the broader cycle of life and death. In fact, as is discussed below in more detail, there is scriptural justification for the claim that killing an evil person can bring about a better rebirth for the killer if the motive is sufficiently pure.

We see a Japanese expression of the connection between rebirth and violence as early as the fourteenth century in the person of the famous warrior Kusunoki Masashige (1294–1336). Although today Kusunoki is regarded as a Shinto *kami* (god) and enshrined at Minatogawa Shrine in Kobe city, his early education took place at the Buddhist temple of Kanshinji where he studied under the priest Ryukaku. His abiding faith in Buddhism is demonstrated by, among other things, the fact that he wrote a commentary on the Lotus Sūtra, a copy of which is on display at Minatogawa Shrine. Nevertheless Kusunoki did not become a priest but elected to become a warrior and then a general, retained by Emperor Go-Daigo in the latter's bid to regain political power through defeating the Kamakura shōgunate (military government).

Kusunoki was a brilliant tactician and strategist as well as the embodiment of the samurai ideal of loyalty to one's sovereign. Thanks to his cunning defense of two key loyalist fortresses at Akasaka and Chihaya, he successfully helped Go-Daigo return to power. However, the emperor's rule was brief, for another of his loyalist generals, Ashikaga Takauji, had ambitions of his own to rule and betrayed Go-Daigo, leading his army against the emperor.

Although the forces he led were greatly outnumbered, Kusunoki remained loyal to Go-Daigo even though this meant certain death. With his army completely surrounded, Kusunoki and his remaining followers chose to commit suicide rather than suffer the disgrace of being killed by the rebel forces. According to legend, Kusunoki's last words were: "[I vow to be] reborn seven times over to punish the brigands [who rebelled against the emperor]." Later, with the rise of an expansionist nationalism in nineteenth-century Japan, this pledge was changed to: "I vow to be reborn seven times over to repay the debt of gratitude I owe my country." This pledge, enduring as it did over multiple lifetimes, came to be regarded as epitomizing the essence of loyalty. Not surprisingly, during the Asia-Pacific War Kusunoki became an inspiration to kamikaze pilots and others who saw themselves as his spiritual heirs in sacrificing themselves for the sake of the emperor.

During the war years, Buddhist priests also used the doctrine of rebirth as one method of reducing the grief (and anger) of family members at the death of a loved one on the battlefield. For example, in 1942 the Sōtō Zen scholar-priest Yamada Reirin (1889–1979) included the following in his book *Zengaku Yawa* (Evening Talks on Zen Studies):

> The true form of the heroic spirits [of the dead] is the good karmic power that has resulted from their loyalty, bravery, and nobility of character. This cannot disappear. . . . .
> The body and mind produced by this karmic power cannot be other than what has existed up to the present. . . . . The loyal, brave, noble, and heroic spirits of those officers and men who have died shouting, "May the emperor live for ten thousand years!" will be reborn right here in this country. It is only natural that this should occur.[13]

On the surface, the Christian belief in eternal life in heaven as a reward for the faithful seems far removed from, if not the very antithesis of, the Buddhist belief in rebirth. Yet, when it comes to consoling the bereaved families of fallen soldiers the question must be asked (even if it cannot be answered here), is there, psychologically speaking, a significant difference between the two beliefs? That is to say, both equally hold out the prospect of life after death. In fact, as Yamada suggests, it would hardly be surprising should many of the bereaved (not to mention the fallen soldiers themselves) prefer to have their loved ones "be reborn right here in this country."

Violence as "Skillful Means" *(Upāya)*

Once again, the instructor should first introduce the Sanskrit word *upāya* to students, pointing out that it refers to temporary or provisional teachings that are regarded as a means to lead sentient beings to the final or ultimate truth. This concept is so well-known in Japan that one popular maxim is *uso mo hōben*, that is, even lies are *upāya*, or skillful means.

The Lotus Sūtra contains a famous example of *upāya* in which a man comes home to find his house on fire and his children inside entertaining themselves with their favorite playthings. He calls out to his children to leave the house, but they don't believe it's on fire and continue playing with their toys. Thinking about how he may use skillful or expedient means, the man tells his children that he has arranged for them to receive gilded carts and toy oxen to play with. However, they will have to come outside since these entertainments await just outside the gate of the house. Hearing this, the children run from the burning house and are saved.

What makes such means skillful is the use, guided by wisdom and compassion, of a specific teaching (means) geared to the abilities of the audience being taught. That is to say, skillful means seek to bring out the spiritual potentialities of people at different levels of spiritual attainment and understanding through speech or actions that are adjusted to their individual needs and adapted to their capacity for comprehension.

The concept of skillful means plays a particularly important role in Mahāyāna Buddhism in regard to the actions of Bodhisattvas, that is, "wisdom [seeking] beings" ever ready to sacrifice their own well-being to benefit others. The claim is made that a Bodhisattva or practitioner may use expedient methods to help ease the suffering of people, introduce them to the Dharma, or help them on the road to nirvāṇa. This doctrine is sometimes used to explain some of the otherwise strange or unorthodox behavior engaged in by Buddhist practitioners, especially Zen masters, in extreme cases. It thereby becomes theoretically possible for many normally proscribed practices, such as theft, sexual encounters, and even violence to be regarded as acceptable uses of skillful means.

The doctrinal justification for violence-affirming skillful means can be seen in the Upaya-kaushalya Sūtra (Skillful Means Sūtra). Included in this sūtra is a story about Buddha Śākyamuni in a previous life when he was still a Bodhisattva. While on board a ship, Śākyamuni discovers that there is a robber intent on killing all 500 passengers. Śākyamuni ultimately decides to kill the robber, not only for the sake of the passengers but also to save the robber himself from the karmic consequences of his horrendous act. The negative karma from killing the robber should have accrued to Śākyamuni but it did not, for, as he explained:

> Good man, because I used ingenuity out of great compassion at that time, I was able to avoid the suffering of one hundred thousand *kalpas* of *samsāra* [the ordinary world of form and desire] and that wicked man was reborn in heaven, a good plane of existence, after death.[14]

Should there be any doubt as to whether skillful means remain operative in contemporary Buddhism, one need look no further than the present Dalai Lama. While he today claims to be a man of peace, this was not always so. In the 1950s and 1960s, at the time the CIA supplied weapons to Tibetan guerillas in support of their armed rebellion against the Chinese, the Dalai Lama defended his followers' actions in a filmed interview as follows: "It is a basic Buddhist belief that if the motivation is good, and the goal is good, then the method, even apparently of a violent kind, is permissible. But then, in our situation, in our case, whether it is practical or not, that is the question."[15] Although the Dalai Lama does not specifically use the term "skillful means" in his defense of the acts of violence on the part of the CIA-backed Tibetan guerillas, his reference to the importance of their good motives (and goals) places him squarely in accord with the preceding sūtra inasmuch as its central teaching is that "taking life is not reprehensible 'when it develops from a virtuous thought.'"[16] Further, it should be noted that the current Dalai Lama's position is by no means idiosyncratic for, as Peter Harvey has noted, "In Tibet, at the highest level of tantric practice, acts of violence or killing are sometimes permissible to destroy a person or evil spirit that is causing great harm to many or to Buddhism."[17]

Ironically, if the doctrine of skillful means can be used to justify violence, it can be used as readily to justify peaceful actions. Once again, the Dalai Lama serves as a case in point, for following the CIA's cessation of support for Tibetan guerillas in 1974, it was left to the Dalai Lama to convince the remaining guerillas to finally lay down their weapons. He did this by sending an audiotape to the guerilla base in Mustang, Nepal, in which he said: "You have, with great dedication and sincerity, risked your lives over many years in the struggle for our just cause. However, there has now been a change in our situation that, while very disappointing, means that from this point onwards we must struggle to reach our goal by peaceful means."[18] In light of these words it can be said that skillful means is truly a doctrine for all seasons, one that can be equally used to justify violence or peace as Buddhist leaders deem appropriate. Its use depends on no more than what is most advantageous to the goals these leaders seek to attain.

Violence as the Expression of Compassion

Closely aligned to the doctrine of skillful means is the belief that Buddhism condones killing when it is a manifestation of compassion for the victim. As the instructor will recall, when the Buddha killed the robber he did so "out of great compassion." Further, it must be stressed that the Upaya-kaushalya Sūtra is but one of many Mahāyāna sūtras that excuse, if not actually condone, killing when done out of compassion. The Sanskrit Mahāparinirvāṇa Sūtra, for example, tells how Buddha Śākyamuni killed several high-caste Brahmins in a previous life to prevent them from slandering the Dharma. The compassion here is said to have originated out of Śākyamuni's desire to save the Brahmins from the karmic consequences of their slander.

And what of Buddhist compassionate killing in the modern period? During the Asia-Pacific War, the Zen-trained layman Lt. Col. Sugimoto Gorō wrote: "The wars of the empire are sacred wars. They are holy wars. They are the [Buddhist] practice (*gyō*) of great compassion (*daijihishin*). Therefore the Imperial military must consist of holy officers and holy soldiers."[19] If Sugimoto is correct, it must be said that seldom if ever has the world witnessed such massive acts of "compassion," for the imperial Japanese military is generally regarded as having killed somewhere between 10 to 20 million Chinese and other Asians, not to mention Allied soldiers, in the course of its attempted conquest of Asia. Nonetheless, in 1937 two Sōtō Zen scholars claimed that Japan was motivated by the highest ideals of Buddhism:

> Were the level of wisdom of the world's people to increase, the causes of war would disappear and war cease. However, in an age when the situation is such that it is impossible for humanity to stop wars, there is no choice but to wage compassionate wars which give life to both oneself and one's enemy. Through a compassionate war, the warring nations are able to improve themselves, and war is able to exterminate itself.[20]

As the instructor may wish to point out to students, these scholars completely failed to address the question of just how much death and destruction would occur during the process of "giv[ing] life to both oneself and one's enemy."

Violence in Defense of the Dharma

For instructors already familiar with one or more of the world's other religions, especially the Abrahamic faiths, violence as a defense should be a relatively straight-forward section to teach. Many if not most students will already be aware that one of the most common and universal religious justifications for the use of violence is that such violence is undertaken "in defense of the faith." In this Buddhism is no different, for as indicated, for example, in chapter 5 of the Sanskrit Mahāparinirvāṇa Sūtra, Mahāyāna followers are admonished to protect the Dharma at all costs, even if this means using weapons to do so and breaking the prohibition against taking life. Similarly, in the Gandavyuha Sūtra an Indian king by the name of Anala is singled out for praise because he is "said to have made killing into a divine service in order to reform people through punishment."[21]

As for Theravāda Buddhism, the contemporary Sinhalese monk Uduwe Dhammaloka has been the leader of a campaign urging monks to enter politics as part of the ongoing revival of Buddhism in Sri Lanka. "There is no bar in Buddhism to prevent monks entering politics," he told the AFP news service in an interview in 2004, "for when there were threats to the nation, monks even went to the battlefield."[22]

BBC correspondent Priyath Liyanage noted in his 1998 article, "Popular Buddhism, Politics and the Ethnic Problem," that one of the key features of this revival has been the popularization of many of the historic chronicles of Sri Lanka, notably the Mahavamsa, written in the sixth century C.E. The Mahavamsa details three separate occasions in which it is claimed that the Buddha visited Sri Lanka. It also lauds the piety of the second-century B.C.E. Sinhalese Buddhist King Duttugamunu, whose army, accompanied by monks, placed Buddhist relics on their spears as they drove Tamil rivals out of Sri Lanka and united the whole of the island under the king's leadership.

Although, technically, the Mahavamsa is not canonical, it is widely venerated, not least of all for having successfully fused national identity, territorial integrity, and religious duty into one even though that was accomplished at the point of a spear. As the modern Sinhala Buddhist scholar-priest Walpola Rahula noted:

> From this time the patriotism and the religion of the Sinhalese became inseparably linked. The religio-patriotism at that time assumed such overpowering proportions that both *bhikkhus* [monks] and laymen considered that even killing people in order to liberate the religion and the country was not a heinous crime.[23]

Given this background, it is hardly surprising that the violence-affirming ideology of the Mahavamsa would find its way into modern Sinhalese politics in the course of that country's recently concluded, bitter, and lengthy civil war with its non-Buddhist Tamil minority. Nor is it surprising that Priyath Liyanage would describe the contemporary situation in Sri Lanka as follows: "to committed Sinhala Buddhist ideologues, however, violence can be justified to counter the threat posed . . . to the unity of land, race and religion."[24]

Violence as Nonviolence Due to Selflessness

Students who are at all familiar with Buddhism will recognize the doctrine of *anātman* as yet another one of Buddhism's core teachings. This Sanskrit term is composed of the negative prefix *an* (no) plus *ātman*, referring to an eternal, unchanging self or soul. Through this doctrine, Buddha Śākyamuni sought to deny the belief that the self was in any way eternal.

> What we call "I," or "being" is only a combination of physical and mental aggregates, which are working together interdependently in a flux of momentary change within the law of cause and effect. . . . There is nothing permanent, everlasting, unchanging and eternal in the whole of existence. . . . According to the Buddha's teaching, it is as wrong to hold the opinion "I have no self" (which is the annihilationist theory) as to hold the opinion "I have a self."[25]

That Walpola Rahula felt the need to warn against an annihilationist interpretation of *anātman* is no accident, for there are numerous examples throughout Asian history in which Buddhists have used the doctrine of the "no-self" and its derivatives to discount the notion that the killing of such a no-self amounts to killing at all. The most dramatic (or extreme) example of this sophistry is to be found in the Zen school in Japan where, as early as the seventeenth century, the famous Rinzai Zen Master Takuan (1573–1645) wrote the following to his warrior patron, the highly accomplished swordsman Yagyū Tajima no Kami Munenori (1571–1646):

> The uplifted sword has no will of its own, it is all of emptiness. It is like a flash of lightning. The man who is about to be struck down is also of emptiness, and so is the one who wields the sword. None of them are possessed of a mind that has any

substantiality. As each of them is of emptiness and has no "mind" (*kokoro*), the striking man is not a man, the sword in his hands is not a sword, and the "I" who is about to be struck down is like the splitting of the spring breeze in a flash of lightning.[26]

In Takuan we have a priest, who even in today's Japan epitomizes Zen "enlightenment," telling us that the killing of a human being is of no more consequence than "the splitting of the spring breeze in a flash of lightning." Furthermore, many noted Zen masters and scholars, including D. T. Suzuki in more recent years, have given their unqualified support for what has been traditionally expressed as the "unity of Zen and the sword" (J., *zenken ichinyo*).

In his famous book *Zen and Japanese Culture*, first published in 1938, Suzuki wrote:

> Zen discipline is simple, direct, self-reliant, *self-denying*; its ascetic tendency goes well with the fighting spirit. The fighter is to be always single-minded with one object in view: to fight, looking neither backward nor sidewise. To go straight forward in order to crush the enemy is all that is necessary for him. . . . . A good fighter is generally an ascetic or stoic which means he has an iron will. This, when needed, Zen can supply.[27]

And, of course, a close (and deadly) corollary is the Zen teaching of the "unity of life and death" (*shōji ichinyo*).

The Zen school, as is well known, has been deeply influenced by the Mādhyānika school of Mahāyāna Buddhism, with its teaching of two levels of truth, conventional and ultimate. By placing an exclusive emphasis on ultimate truth (Skt., *paramartha-satya*), Takuan and his like devalued and delegitimized conventional truth to the point that human life effectively became worthless. In so doing they were able to provide *Bushidō* with a metaphysical foundation that not only sanctioned killing but eulogized the Zen-trained warrior's willingness to die in the process of taking life in loyal service to his feudal lord (and the emperor in the modern period) as the antinomian expression of full enlightenment.

Should there be any doubt that Takuan's teachings were subsequently incorporated into Zen support for Japanese militarism, we need look no further than wartime Sōtō Zen leader Ishihara Shunmyō, who said in March 1937:

> Zen master Takuan taught that in essence Zen and *Bushidō* were one. . . . I believe that if one is called upon to die, one should not be the least bit agitated. On the contrary, one should be in a realm where something called "oneself" does not intrude even slightly. Such a realm is no different from that derived from the practice of Zen.[28]

Imperial army Major Ōkubo Kōichi responded to Ishihara's comments:

> The soldier must become one with his superior. He must actually become his superior. Similarly, he must become the order he receives. That is to say, *his self must disappear*. In so doing, when he eventually goes onto the battlefield, he will

advance when told to advance. . . . On the other hand, should he believe that he is going to die and act accordingly; he will be unable to fight well. What is necessary, then, is that he be able to act freely and without [mental] hindrance.[29]

Given this mandate, it is hardly surprising that a so-called god of war (J., *gunshin*) like Lt. Col. Sugimoto Gorō would find inspiration for his "selfless" service to the emperor during the war years in the doctrine of no-self (*muga*), often translated as egolessness.

Nor was Sugimoto content with using his practice of Zen merely to rid himself of his ego. He further strived to embrace the state of egolessness. Sugimoto asserted: "The essence of the unity of the sovereign and the people is egolessness. Egolessness and self-extinction are most definitely not separate states. On the contrary, one comes to realize that they are identical with one other."[30]

During the Asia-Pacific War, all Japanese soldiers were indoctrinated during training with a program of *Bushidō*-promoting "spiritual education" (*seishin kyōiku*) based on the metaphysical foundation of the twin unities of Zen and the sword, life and death. Once trained, they were dispatched to the battlefield where nearly 3 million of them died "selflessly," even as they killed more than 10 million Chinese and other "selfless" enemies in the process. If the enlightened Zen Master Takuan is to be believed, all of these deaths were no more than "the splitting of the spring breeze in a flash of lightning."

Violence as a Manifestation of *Samādhi* Power

On the Battlefield

The instructor should first point out that in Buddhism, *samādhi* refers to the concentrated state of mind, that is, the mental "one pointedness," achieved through the practice of meditation. Prior to and during the Asia-Pacific War, Japanese Zen leaders, including D. T. Suzuki, often wrote about this meditation-derived power, emphasizing the effectiveness of samādhi-power on the battlefield. They all agreed that the Zen practice of seated, cross-legged meditation (i.e., *zazen*), was, as an allegedly value-neutral exercise, the fountainhead of this power, a power as available to wartime Japanese soldiers as it had been to samurai warriors in the past.

However, students also need to be made aware that the Pali *suttas* (sūtras) of the southern Theravāda school of Buddhism reject taking Buddhist meditation as value neutral and specifically warn against the misuse of samādhi (i.e., *miccha-samādhi*). In the Gopaka Moggallana Sutta, for example, Ananda, one of Buddha Śākyamuni's chief disciples, pointed out to Vassakara, the chief minister of the country of Magadha, that Śākyamuni did not praise every form of meditation:

What kind of meditation, Brahman, did the Lord [Śākyamuni] not praise? . . . .He [who] dwells with his thought obsessed by ill-will, and does not comprehend as it really is the escape from the ill-will that has arisen; he, having made ill-will the main thing, meditates on it, meditates absorbed, meditates more absorbed, meditates quite absorbed. . . . The Lord does not praise this kind of meditation, Brahman.[31]

Meditating "obsessed by ill-will" is not, of course, the only misuse to which meditation or samādhi can be put. Meditative obsession with "the pleasures of the senses," "sloth and torpor," "restlessness and doubt," and so on are also condemned. But, as anyone who has actually been to the battlefield will tell you, once the bullets start flying, and especially after one's fellow soldiers are wounded or killed, ill-will is inescapable.

Finally, there was the question of Sugimoto's death on the battlefield in 1937. Based on reports he had received, Rinzai Zen Master Yamazaki Ekjū—described how Sugimoto had been leading his troops into battle when an enemy hand grenade landed behind him and exploded:

> A grenade fragment hit him in the left shoulder. He seemed to have fallen down but then got up again. Although he was standing, one could not hear his commands. He was no longer able to issue commands with that husky voice of his. . . . Yet he was still standing, holding his sword in one hand as a prop. Both legs were slightly bent, and he was facing in an easterly direction [toward the Imperial Palace]. It appeared that he had saluted though his hand was now lowered to about the level of his mouth. The blood flowing from his mouth covered his watch.[32]

In Yamazaki's mind, at least, this was his lay disciple's finest moment—the moment when he most clearly displayed the power that was to be gained by Zen practitioners. That is to say, Sugimoto had died standing up. As the master explained:

> In the past it was considered to be the true appearance of a Zen priest to pass away while doing zazen. Those who were completely and thoroughly enlightened, however, ... could die calmly in a standing position. . . . The reason this was possible was due to samādhi power [J., jōriki].[33]

Yamazaki ended his eulogy for his lay disciple as follows:

> To the last second Sugimoto was a man whose speech and actions were at one with each other. When he saluted and faced the east, there is no doubt that he also shouted, "May His Majesty, the emperor, live for 10,000 years!" [Tennō-heika Banzai.] It is for this reason that his was the radiant ending of an Imperial soldier.
>
> Not only that, but his excellent appearance should be a model for future generations of someone who lived in Zen. . . .
>
> Although it can be said that his life of thirty-eight years was all too short, for someone who has truly obtained samādhi power, there is no question of a long or short period. The great, true appearance of Sugimoto Gorō was of someone who had united with emptiness, embodying total loyalty [to the

emperor] and service to the state. I am convinced he is one of those who should he be reborn seven times over, would reverently work to destroy the enemies of the emperor.[34]

In light of his unbounded loyalty, Sugimoto was celebrated in both the Rinzai and Sōtō sects as the model of a military figure thoroughly imbued with the Zen spirit, so much so that he was immortalized as a "god of war" (*gunshin*) through Japan's defeat in 1945.

Buddhist Terrorism

In light of the current concern about Islamic-related terrorism, students will be interested to learn that in Japan, meditation-derived samādhi power was also employed against domestic opponents. Thus in 1932 a band of ultranationalists, led by the Zen-trained layman Inoue Nisshō (1886–1967), assassinated two of Japan's most prominent financial and political leaders with plans to assassinate some twenty more.

The band's first victim was Inoue Junnosuke (1869–1932), a former finance minister, who was shot on the evening of February 9, 1932, as he entered Komamoto Elementary School in Tokyo to deliver an election speech. His assassin was twenty-two-year-old Ōnuma Shō (1911–78), a onetime baker's assistant and carpenter's apprentice. In subsequent court testimony Ōnuma explained that he had debated with himself over whether to strike before Junnosuke spoke or afterward. In the end he decided to strike before due to his concern that innocent well-wishers might be injured if he waited until Junnosuke's departure.

This, however, was not Ōnuma's only concern, for he was beset by anxiety over the act of assassination itself. Especially on the morning of the assassination day, he had been so upset he wondered whether he would be able to carry out his assignment. It was at this point that Ōnuma sought strength from the Buddhist training he had received from Inoue. First he quietly recited four sections of the Lotus Sūtra and then recited merely the title of the sūtra (i.e., *daimoku*), four or five times to calm down. Finally he began to practice zazen in the full lotus posture, as he later testified:

> After starting my practice of zazen I entered a state of samādhi the likes of which I had never experienced before. I felt my spirit become unified, really unified, and when I opened my eyes from their half-closed meditative position I noticed the smoke from the incense curling up and touching the ceiling. At this point it suddenly came to me—I would be able to carry out [the assassination] that night.[35]

As mentioned above, the purpose of samādhi power within Buddhism is the facilitation of true spiritual growth and understanding. Thus, the application of this power to either enhancing martial prowess on the battlefield or perpetrating acts of domestic terrorism must be considered as little less than astounding. Equally if not more astounding, however, is the September 1934 court testimony of the noted Rinzai Zen Master Yamamoto Gempō (1866–1961), abbot of Ryūtakuji, who defended these terrorist acts as follows:

> It is true that if, motivated by an evil mind, someone should kill so much as a single ant, as many as one hundred and thirty-nine hells await that person. This holds true not only in Japan but all the countries of the world. Yet, the Buddha, being absolute, has stated that when there are those who destroy social harmony and not a crime. . . . Thus, Buddhism, which has as its foundation the true perfection of humanity, has no choice but to cut down even good people in the event they seek to destroy social harmony.[36]

While "destroy[ing] social harmony" is the preeminent transgression within Confucianism, not Buddhism, in the heavily Chinese-influenced Zen school, the promotion of social harmony was long ago incorporated as a core value (together with such Taoist values as intuition and spontaneity). This history of syncretism, however, in no way lessens the responsibility of the Zen school and its leading representatives, who, for centuries in Japan, have consistently condoned the taking of human life as being in accord with the Buddha Dharma. Further, when Buddhist meditation is transmuted, as it has been in Zen, into a value-neutral technique, it, too, can readily become yet one more enabling mechanism for violence.

CONCLUSION

By this time students should realize that Buddhism, like all of the world's major faiths, does indeed have a long historical and doctrinal connection to violence. In Buddhism's case, such doctrines as karma, rebirth, skillful means, compassion, selflessness, and samādhi power, each a core Buddhist teaching, have long been used to justify violence and warfare. The myth of Buddhism as a religion of peace notwithstanding, down through the centuries and extending to the present day, those calling themselves Buddhists have frequently and willfully ignored the pacific aspect of their faith. Students will no doubt want to know more about why this happened but beyond the preliminary normative comments introduced above, the answers lie beyond the scope of this chapter.

There is, however, one final area of inquiry that cannot be overlooked. We cannot help but ask whether there are heroes of the faith, either individuals or organized groups, who have attempted to address, if not oppose, the enlistment of key Buddhist doctrines, as well as praxis, in support of various forms of violence?

The answer is that while not entirely unknown, there are very few, especially when compared with the many adherents of Christian denominations such as the Quakers, Amish, and Mennonites who have made pacifism a cornerstone of their faith. Yet Buddhism is not entirely without its heroes even if their numbers are relatively small. For example, the martyred Sōtō Zen priest Uchiyama Gudō (1874–1911) was the first in modern Japanese history to directly attack the emperor system, claiming, "There are three leaches who suck the people's blood: the emperor, the rich, and the big landowners. . . .. It should be readily obvious that the emperor is not a god if you but think about it for a moment."[37] As for Buddhism, Gudō also attacked, among other things, the socially reactionary use of karma:

> Is this [your poverty] the result, as Buddhists maintain, of the retribution due you because of your evil deeds in the past? Listen, friends, if, having now entered the twentieth century, you were to be deceived by superstitions like this, you would still be [no better than] oxen or horses. Would this please you?[38]

Thus, it can be seen that a few Buddhist leaders have sought to address socially reactionary interpretations of certain key Buddhist doctrines. The so-called engaged Buddhist movement, started by the activist Vietnamese monk Thich Nhat Hanh in 1963, should also be included in this category. Engaged Buddhists believe that they have a responsibility to address and reduce suffering in all of its forms, both physical and spiritual, including suffering resulting from social injustice, exploitation, and oppression. Nevertheless, this very amorphous movement attracts only a small fraction of Buddhists in Asia together with some Western adherents of Buddhism as well.

As hopeful as movements like that of the engaged Buddhists may be, it doesn't alter the fact that Buddhism, like the world's other major faiths, continues to harbor both doctrines and praxis that, as revealed above, can be used to condone and even promote violence. Judging from their writings, even those who identify themselves as engaged Buddhists have yet to admit or critique this dark side of their own tradition.[39] They tend to believe all that is required is taking Buddhist ethics and praxis out of traditional temples and monasteries and applying these things to the transformation of the greater society. Yet, as this chapter has made clear, until, and unless, the dark side of Buddhism is both admitted and directly addressed, Buddhism will remain a religion of both peace and violence.

NOTES

1. Quoted in Brain Daizen Victoria, *Zen at War*, 2nd ed. (New York: Rowman and Littlefield, 2006), 201, emphasis added.
2. Ibid., 30.
3. For further examples, see "Holy War: Toward a Holistic Understanding," in the inaugural issue of *Journal of Religion, Conflict and Peace* (2007): http://www.plowsharesproject. org/journal/php/article.php?issu_list_id=8&article_list_id=17.
4. Quoted in Bunno Kato, *The Threefold Lotus Sutra* (Tokyo: Kōsei, 1989), 343, emphasis added.
5. Quoted in Victoria, *Zen at War*, 42. J., Japanese; Skt., Sanskrit.
6. Ibid., 237 n. 34.
7. For further details concerning Japanese institutional Buddhism's attitude toward the Sino-Japanese War, see ibid., 19–21. For a more general discussion of

the role of Buddhist military chaplains within the Imperial Japanese Army, see Brian Daizen Victoria, *Zen War Stories* (New York: RoutledgeCurzon, 2003), 150–62.

8. Quoted in Victoria, *Zen War Stories*, 150.
9. Ibid., 151.
10. Ibid., 153.
11. Ibid., 153.
12. The five constituent elements, a.k.a. aggregates, are as follows: (1) physical form; (2) feelings, including both physical and emotional; (3) perceptions, including thoughts, sights, sounds, etc.; (4) will or volition, and (5) consciousness or states of mind.
13. Quoted in Victoria, *Zen at War*, 132.
14. Quoted in Garma C. C. Chang, ed., *A Treasury of Mahayana Sutras* (University Park: Pennsylvania State University Press, 1964), 456–57.
15. Interviewed in the BBC documentary film *Shadow Circus: The CIA in Tibet* (1998).
16. Quoted in Peter Harvey, *An Introduction to Buddhist Ethics* (Cambridge, UK: Cambridge University Press, 2000), 135.
17. Ibid., 137.
18. Quoted in the BBC documentary film *Shadow Circus: The CIA in Tibet*.
19. Quoted in Victoria, *Zen at War*, 119.
20. Ibid., 91.
21. Quoted in Paul William, *Mahayana Buddhism* (London: Routledge, 1989), 161.
22. Quoted in Buddhist Channel, "Monks Should Stay Out of Sri Lanka Politics, Says Monk Legislator," October 24, 2005. http://www.buddhistchannel.tv/index. php?id=1,1858,0,0,1,0.
23. Quoted in Harvey, *An Introduction to Buddhist Ethics*, 257.
24. Priyath Liyanage, "Popular Buddhism, Politics and the Ethnic Problem," 1998, http://www.c-r.org/our-work/accord/sri-lanka/buddhism-politics.php.
25. Walpola Rahula, *What the Buddha Taught*, 2nd ed. (New York: Grove Press, 1974), 66.
26. Quoted in D. T. Suzuki, *Zen and Japanese Culture* (Princeton, NJ: Princeton University Press, 1959), 114.
27. Ibid., 62, emphasis added.
28. Quoted in Victoria, *Zen at War*, 103. Note that Ishihara Shummyō was the editor in chief of the pan-Buddhist magazine *Daihōrin* (Great Dharma Wheel), and therefore exerted influence well beyond the Sōtō Zen sect to which he was affiliated.
29. Ibid., 103, emphasis added.
30. Ibid., 123.
31. Maurice Walshe, trans., *Thus Have I Heard: The Long Discourses of the Buddha* (London: Wisdom Publications, 1987), 63–64.
32. Quoted in Victoria, *Zen at War*, 125.
33. Ibid., 127.
34. Ibid., 126.
35. Quoted in Onuma Hiroaki, *Ketsumeidan Jiken Kōhan Sokki-roku*, vol. 3 (Tokyo: Ketsumeidan Jiken Kōhan Sokki-roku Kankō-kai, 1963), 403.
36. Ibid., 737.
37. Quoted in Victoria, *Zen at War*, 44.
38. Ibid., 43.
39. See, for example, my critique of the dark side of engaged Buddhism: Brian Victoria, "Engaged Buddhism: A Skeleton in the Closet?" *Journal of Global Buddhism*, http://www.globalbuddhism.org/2/victoria011.html.

BIBLIOGRAPHY

British Broadcasting Corporation. *Shadow Circus: The CIA in Tibet.* 1998.

Buddhist Channel. "Monks Should Stay Out of Sri Lanka Politics, Says Monk Legislator." October 24, 2005. http://www.buddhistchannel.tv/index.php?id=1,1858,0,0,1,0.

Chang, C. C., ed. *A Treasury of Mahayana Sutras.* University Park: Pennsylvania State University Press, 1983.

Harvey, Peter. *An Introduction to Buddhist Ethics.* Cambridge: Cambridge University Press, 2000.

Inoue Enryō. *Enryō Kōwa-shū.* Tokyo: Kōmeisha, 1904.

Kato, Bunno. *The Threefold Lotus Sutra.* Tokyo: Kosei, 1989.

Liyanage, Priyath. "Popular Buddhism, Politics and the Ethnic Problem." 1998. http://www.c-r.org/our-work/accord/sri-lanka/buddhism-politics.php.

Onuma Hiroaki. *Ketsumeidan Jiken Kōhan Sokki-roku* [The Stenographic Record of the Public Trial of the Blood Oath Corps Incident]. 3 vols. Tokyo: Ketsumeidan Jiken Kōhan Sokki-roku Kankō-kai, 1963.

Rahula, Walpola. *What the Buddha Taught.* New York: Grove Press, 1974.

Suzuki, Daisetz. *Zen and Japanese Culture.* Princeton, NJ: Princeton University Press, 1959. Originally published in 1938 as *Zen Buddhism and Its Influence on Japanese Culture.* Kyoto, Japan: Eastern Buddhist Society.

Victoria, Brian Daizen. *Zen at War.* Boulder, CO: Rowman and Littlefield, 2006.

———. *Zen War Stories.* New York: RoutledgeCurzon, 2003.

Walshe, Maurice, trans. *Thus Have I Heard: The Long Discourses of the Buddha.* London: Wisdom Publications, 1987.

William, Paul. *Mahayana Buddhism.* London: Routledge, 1989.

CHAPTER 4

⌀

Violence and Religion in
the Christian Tradition

WILLIAM MORROW

Newspapers and other media are fond of describing acts of violence as "sense-less" and "irrational." One of my major pedagogical goals, however, is to sug-gest the opposite. Along with many others, I assume that actions perpetrated by religiously motivated agents are the results of interpretative processes that can be analyzed and understood.[1] A survey of academic calendars in North American universities will show that there are relatively few courses devoted specifically to the subject of violence and Christianity. It is more typical to find cases of Chris-tian violence contextualized in broader surveys on religion and violence or addressed in topical courses devoted to themes such as war, racism, or violence against women. My own experience is drawn from teaching a course called Reli-gion and Violence. The majority of the course's examples are drawn from Christi-anity, Hinduism, and aboriginal cultures in North America (roughly a third each). A comparative approach makes it possible to discover that religious symbol systems have both similarities and differences. The focus of this essay, however, is on phenomena in Christianity.

The pedagogical approach to religiously motivated violence presented here rec-ommends the metaphor of problem solving. Recent literature on postsecondary education emphasizes empowering student learning. A pedagogy based on problem solving can address such concerns. Among the benefits of problem-based learning (PBL) are the following:[2]

- PBL is based on real-world problems. The messy complex problems encountered in the real world act as a stimulus for finding, organizing, and integrating information that will ensure its recall and application to future problems.

- PBL is a motivating way to learn. Students are involved in active learning, working with real problems; what they have to learn and study is seen as important and relevant to their own lives.

Particularly in the North American context, many (if not most) students will be familiar with a Christian rhetoric that emphasizes the religion's concern for peace and justice. The problem-based approach is useful because these students will enter the course perceiving the nexus between Christianity and violence as puzzling, and one that calls for explanation. Within the context of PBL, the purpose of a course on violence and Christianity would be to examine representative texts, rituals, and incidents and provide interpretative models for analyzing them. Nevertheless, a perspective that focuses on analyzing the religious motivations of perpetrators of violence is not without pitfalls. There is a valid concern that the quest for understanding may lead to condoning horrendous actions;[3] this needs to be recognized and addressed.

The wide range of possible examples and the lengthy history of Christianity are amenable to a case study or incident-based approach. By attempting to map the relationship between symbols, commitments, and conflicts, students may come to understand why certain historical agents made the choices they did, even if these are choices that they do not approve of. Engagement with particular cases of religiously motivated violence is stimulated by studying various models of violent processes. Students in the life sciences are familiar with taxonomies because they are helpful tools for classifying individual specimens into larger groups of related flora and fauna. Similar approaches are also used in the social sciences.[4] I find a classificatory approach useful because it helps students identify the characteristics of a "specimen" of religiously contextualized violence, while also providing an efficient way of discussing a family or group of related incidents in a course that (at least in my case) only runs for a single semester.

After making some general observations related to teaching about violence and religion, a second section illustrates their application to Christianity. One obvious inadequacy of the following discussion, however, needs to be highlighted at the outset. My experience is drawn from teaching a course in which problems involved in understanding the relationship between religious symbol systems and violent occurrences constitute its main focus. I am well aware that there is an extensive literature on nonviolence and peace making in Christianity, but these important topics are not given prominence here.

SOME METHODOLOGICAL PERSPECTIVES

On Violence

While most will agree that violence implies harm and injury directed toward others, it is possible to refine this definition in a number of ways.[5] The following aspects of violence are of particular importance in understanding its nexus with religion:

- Violence is relational: it entails the exercise of power and control to establish, maintain, or alter personal and social relationships that favor the perpetrator.[6]
- Violence is justified in the eyes of those who use it to obtain their goals.
- Violence involves perceptions of victims as deserving the harm that comes upon them (othering).

The analysis of violence deals, therefore, with constructions of identity and self, key considerations in the interpretation of harmful incidents quite apart from any religious context.[7] Of course, concerns for identity dovetail with discourse about religion.[8] As human institutions, religions are important means for creating, sustaining, and transforming a sense of self in the world (whether collective or individual). Consequently, religions are implicated in processes of forming or defending identities that can lead to violence against others.

The theme of identity can create a helpful reference point in the classroom for an investigation of violence in Christianity. Issues of identity are particularly vital to college and university students, who typically enter postsecondary education in adolescence. Since students frequently struggle with forming their own self-conceptions and sense of agency, highlighting the challenges involved in negotiating various claims on the construction of an effective self, the need to belong, and challenges posed by the choices of others can create useful bridges between times and cultures that seem foreign to students and their own experiences.

Various perspectives are available for understanding the motivations of agents in contexts of conflict. Methodologically, I mainly draw on approaches informed by depth psychology, feminism, and sociology. It is important that students be familiar with a variety of explanations for three reasons: the complexity of the subject, the nature of scholarship, and the variety of student learning patterns.

First, exposure to different theoretical approaches and analytical grids conveys the fact that the topic of violence and religion is very complex. In this respect, as I teach the course, I find myself reacting to a sort of unstated assumption in popular culture that religious violence is sui generis. But one need not be a religiously identified person to engage in the kinds of interpretative processes that lead to violent actions. For example, academic work on othering has observed similar characteristics in a wide variety of situations, including Stanley Milgram's famous experiments on obedience and authority and incidents of mass murder and genocide.[9] Many forms of criminal assault and abuse also involve rationalizations that justify a violent response to the other.[10] Moreover, the capacity to symbolize one's own commitments in a situation of conflict to the detriment of the other party is not confined to religious actors (think about phrases such as "the war on drugs" or the characterization of the former Soviet Union as an "evil empire"). It is important, therefore, not to drive too firm a wedge between religious and nonreligious violence. Clashes over natural resources, wealth, the means of (re)production, and status comprehend both religious and nonreligious forms of social organization. Whether or not a propensity for violence is inherent in the human condition remains debatable,[11] and similar ambiguities apply to an assessment of the relationship between religion and violence because religion is also a human activity.

Second, using a variety of interpretative models provides instructive insights into the nature of scholarship, which involves ongoing debate and disagreement as to how to weigh various factors and approaches. A good illustration of this is found in the differing perspectives of René Girard and Mark Juergensmeyer, with the former favoring sacrifice as the lens for interpreting acts of religious violence while the latter prefers the metaphor of war.[12] One could envisage building a course around the works of these two thinkers with the goal of investigating which concept has the most explanatory power. Finally, students themselves are different, and using a variety of explanations increases the chances that some part of the course accords with their own modes of thinking and learning.

Above, I underscored the relationship between religion, violence, and the construction of identity. This connection has a therapeutic concern as well. Studies on the effects of violence recognize the phenomenon of secondary trauma as well as primary experiences of physical and psychological violation. Persons in the helping professions are well acquainted with the fact that trauma can accompany the act of witnessing the effects of violence.[13] Inasmuch as reading about violence is also an act of witness, even the university classroom is not entirely safe.

To study violence and religion is to undertake personal risk. When students report that something they have read upsets them, when they have to put an article down because they "just couldn't read any more," when particular material is "depressing" or makes them wonder about the meaningfulness of life, they are experiencing the effects of violence. These are (milder) forms of what can be called "the disruption of the assumptive world," a common experience of victims of trauma.[14] Even reading about violence can disturb one's confidence in the predictable patterns of life, its goodness, and its purposefulness.

In my opinion, there is no such thing as a completely safe level of exposure to images or accounts of violence. What ninety-nine people may be able to encounter with equanimity can viscerally disturb the hundredth. Usually I face classes of around eighty to one hundred students, the majority of whom are young women. Statistically, it is almost certain that some of them bring to class personal histories as victims of violence. Since I do not know the personal histories of my students, I have no way of knowing what material may trigger a strong reaction. For this reason, I prefer to deal with historical phenomena rather than recent events. Time and space give one a kind of protective distance that facilitates questions about the motivations of perpetrators and aggressors. In my experience, exposure to visual images of violence carries a greater risk than written materials. Consequently, I tend not to use a lot of visual images. Even so, I always make sure that students are aware that resources on campus are available to help them process difficult feelings that may legitimately arise from encountering material in the course.

On Religion

I use a modified version of Melford Spiro's well-known definition of religion: "An institution consisting of culturally patterned interactions with culturally postulated superhuman beings,"[15] *which symbolize ultimate concerns.* The portion in italics is not from Spiro, but it brings out the fact that religions are symbol systems that often address those elements of a sense of self or worldview that a group or individual hold most dear.[16] I assume that the Christian tradition has at its center the deified Jesus (although I am not sure whether "Christianity" represents a single religion or a family of related systems of belief and ritual). In practice, because I prefer to use historical incidents for the reasons stated above, my examples tend to come from Western Christianity in Europe and North America.

From the point of view of giving tools for PBL, two general principles can inform an approach to teaching religion and violence. These entail the "myth of redemptive violence" and the concept of "economies of sacrifice." In addition, it is useful to recognize how Christianity fits into a taxonomy of monotheism.

At the heart of what theologian Walter Wink calls the myth of redemptive violence is the belief that order can be legitimately imposed on chaos by violence.[17] The use of violence to transform a chaotic situation into an ordered one has proven extremely attractive in human history. Transformation is a key interest in religious mythologies and rituals, and this commitment leads to an ambivalent relationship between religions and violence. Although its disruptive effects may be criticized, the possibility of effecting changes in states of cognition and social relationships through violent means is often alluring to religiously motivated agents.

Within Christianity, an ambivalent attitude toward violence finds a particular focus in attempts to understand the necessity for the crucifixion of Jesus and its redemptive value. Recent literature has wrestled with the potential of Christian atonement theories to legitimate social violence.[18] It would be possible to construct an entire course on conflicting and competing theories of the cross in terms of their potential for legitimating or opposing human violence. Not only is there room for examining the role of atonement theology in creating an "opiate for the people" as described by Marxism, but Christianity has arguably justified various forms of social harm through an exaltation of suffering, including the oppression of women and children.[19]

Connected to the myth of redemptive violence is the concept of economies of sacrifice. Human societies organize themselves in ways that typically privilege certain social agents to the disadvantage of others. The idea of a sacrificial economy underscores the fact that, historically, a great deal of violence has not been considered as deviant behavior nor has prompted disapproval. On the contrary, it has been defined as virtuous activity in the service of generally esteemed social, economic, and political principles.[20]

Julia Kristeva's concept of abjection is useful in describing the dynamics of an economy of sacrifice. In her formulation, abjection is the visceral abhorrence that human beings feel toward experiences that compromise their sense of self. It is experienced as an intrusion of unwanted ambiguities that threaten a sense of social competence and cultural agency. Another term for abjection is "boundary failure."[21] The need to defend against the intrusion of unwanted ambiguities leads to the creation of a sacrificial economy, characterized by sets of actions and prohibitions meant to guard against the intrusion of boundary-threatening experiences by separating the cultural agent from them. Othering is fundamental to economies of sacrifice, as the other always offers a challenge to the boundaries of the self. Violence is predicated on the need to eliminate the other as a threat to the self. This dynamic is common to many kinds of human organizations, including religions.[22]

An approach to Christianity as a sacrificial economy could entail the consideration of a number of boundary issues, including relationships between church and state, the significance of embodied reality, and dealings between insiders and outsiders. In fact, each one of these themes could become the center of a course on Christianity and violence. Conflict or collusion between allegiances fostered by the church and those required by the state have frequently resulted in bloodshed. Extreme ascetic practices, the valorization of martyrdom, and systemic sexism can be rooted in the ambivalence with which Christianity has regarded physical embodiment. Finally, the quest to identify the "true" community of faith has often caused conflicted relationships between insiders and outsiders. Illustrative topics include the concern to define and root out "heresy" (e.g., the Inquisition) and institutions of systemic racism (e.g., apartheid).

While common in Christian cultures, economies of sacrifice can be combated by a symbol system that calls for the ethics Kristeva describes as welcoming the stranger.[23] Inclusive community and hospitality to the outsider are deeply engrained values in Christian ethics. A course based on boundary issues in the Christian tradition could also consider under which sorts of conditions its capacity for promoting boundary violations and social inclusion might be activated.

Taxonomically, monotheisms, whether Jewish, Christian, or Muslim, share traits in terms of their proneness to violence. These characteristics include supersessionism and teachings of contempt.[24] With respect to supersessionism, each monotheism purports to originate in a divine revelation that surpasses any other. All three are also prone to disparage those who do not adhere to their beliefs and practices. The impulse toward teachings of contempt is less pronounced in Judaism because it ordinarily regards membership in the group as a result of birth. But Christianity and Islam both place emphasis on willing submission to the truth; consequently those who refuse their revealed doctrines are not only outside the fold but also rebels. As a result, monotheistic symbol systems lend themselves to dynamics that are often visible in religiously motivated conflicts:[25]

- Assuring combatants of the rightness of their cause and the evil of the enemy's
- Sacralizing the identity of one party and demonizing the other's

MODELS OF RELIGIOUS VIOLENCE IN THE CONTEXT OF CHRISTIANITY

In this section, it will be possible to see the factors described above operative in various forms of violence sanctioned and perpetrated by Christian agents. While not all categories of religiously motivated violence can be readily illustrated from Christianity (e.g., ritual suicide, terrorism), the examples below are representative of what might be attempted using PBL. In each case, a real-life example is identified that constitutes the problem requiring investigation. Following is a mode of explanation useful in analyzing it. The subsections are arranged in roughly chronological order, according to the cases they refer to.

Martyrdom

The "Passion of Saints Perpetua and Felicity" is often cited in discussions of Christian martyrdom.[26] In 203 Perpetua, a young noblewoman still nursing her child, converted to Christianity, although this was against the laws of Emperor Septimus. Arrested with four others, including her pregnant maid Felicity, the five were condemned to death in the arena. Determined to maintain her Christian confession, Perpetua was unswayed by the pleas of her father and even forcible separation from her baby. She entered the arena having dreamed that she had taken the form of a male warrior and defeated the devil. Felicity was afraid her pregnancy would prevent her from joining her companions because pregnant women were not subject to the extreme penalty. But, in answer to prayer, she gave birth two days prior to the day of execution. Both women were put to death after facing violence from a mad cow.

At first glance, a discussion of martyrdom in an essay devoted to religiously motivated violence may seem out of place, since the women in this story were not perpetrators but victims. It was the Roman state that instigated their deaths on a charge that was tantamount to treason: their Christian confession did not permit them to burn incense to the genius of the emperor, which would have demonstrated their loyalty to Rome. Nevertheless, here one encounters a phenomenon that has many examples in various religions. What would inspire a religiously identified person to choose to become a victim of violence even when there was a clear way to avoid this fate?

There are different ways of discussing the choices that these two women and their companions made. The desire to imitate Christ, of course, has an important place. Since the beginning of the Christian era, the deaths of martyrs were compared to the sacrificial death of Jesus. Corresponding to their sufferings and ignominious end was the heavenly reward already prefigured by the risen Christ. Martyrdom, therefore, represents a kind of self-sacrificial activity. Similar dynamics are visible in a panoply of extreme forms of religious and political dedication that Eric Hoffer describes using a taxonomy of fanaticism. Hoffer lists the following factors that promote self-sacrifice to a larger cause:[27]

- Identification with a collective whole
- Make-believe (dying and killing are made easier when they are part of a ritual, ceremonial, or dramatic performance)
- Deprecation of the present (the assurance of a better future)
- Things that are not (commitment to things and hopes not realized)
- Doctrine (the imposition of a "fact-proof" screen between the faithful agents and reality by the claim to ultimate and absolute truth)

Each of these factors is visible in the martyrdoms of Perpetua and Felicity. Their identification with the church and its ultimate claims entailed a belief in a better future that was yet unrealized. Moreover, the public nature of their execution gave their deaths a dramatic quality.

Rodney Stark's rational choice theory is also helpful in explaining why someone might prefer martyrdom as the most rewarding choice under certain circumstances. Stark indicates that in addition to the desire to imitate Christ there was a social reward system that valorized martyrdom. His model points to a nexus between personal commitments and social validation.[28] While the number of martyrs in the pre-Constantinian era should not be exaggerated, martyrs were assured not simply of a place in heaven but also of a place of honor in the memory of the community, who treasured their remains. Fame and honor, of course, have long been considered compensators for death. In the case of Perpetua and Felicity, their martyr stories indicate that death would also give them a status normally reserved for males: they were able to die as champions for the faith.

But why make such an extreme choice if many of the rewards for doing so were, from a social perspective, only available within this life? The decisions of Perpetua and Felicity also rest on a worldview that was very different from that of Western (post)modernity. Supposed to stand over and judge the human condition was a much higher, more righteous, holy, and transcendent reality. It is often difficult for students to imagine such a worldview and an important pedagogical goal consists in helping them to understand that, historically, many people have thought in such terms. To translate this insight into the idiom of the story of Perpetua and Felicity: their Christian belief system made the world in which they lived "other." Martyrdom, therefore, fits into an economy of sacrifice. Paradoxically, for some religiously motivated actors, choosing death is a way of maintaining the integrity of a self that would otherwise be compromised.

War

The conquest of Jerusalem in 1099 was the culminating event of the First Crusade.[29] Contemporary accounts record that the crusaders massacred the majority of the city's inhabitants (Muslims and Jews) and sold the survivors into slavery.[30] Although the extravagance of these descriptions has been disputed by some modern historians,[31] many readers will be repelled by triumphant accounts of the siege which boast that the conquerors waded knee deep in the blood of the enemy. By the same token, visions of blood-stained victors, laden with booty, singing hymns of praise to Christ in the aftermath of the battle strike an incongruous note to modern sensibilities.

Within the ambit of a course on religion and violence, war is one of the more difficult topics to approach. This is due to the fact that military conflicts usually depend on a complex nexus of causes involving political, geographical, and economic determinants as well as ideological or religious motivations. But it is also a theme on which the work of significant theorists converges. Above, I noted the disagreement between Girard and Juergensmeyer as to whether sacrifice or war best represents a controlling metaphor for analyzing the connection between religion and violence. In fact, the insights of both of these thinkers are useful in approaching the topic of war and Christianity.

On the one hand, Juergensmeyer helpfully observes that warfare is a major symbol in many of the world's religions: "One can argue that the task of creating a vicarious experience of warfare—albeit one usually imagined as residing on a spiritual plane— is one of the main businesses of religion."[32] On the other hand, Girard provides a model of human rivalry that explains why conflict can lead to violence. Both of these perspectives are useful in approaching an event such as the crusaders' conquest of Jerusalem. The attackers and the defenders of the city thought of themselves as involved in a struggle sanctioned by God. Each side also regarded the other as an enemy who needed to be destroyed in order to secure possession of a mutually desired object.

Girard's relevance to this discussion may surprise some readers, as his thinking is usually associated with scapegoating (see below). But scapegoating is only one way in which a potentially violent rivalry between two parties can be resolved. Mimetic rivalry can also lead to the elimination of one party in the conflict. The diagram in Figure 4.1 illustrates a variant of Girard's principle of mimetic rivalry. The most basic model assumes that a subject learns what to desire (the object) from observing a model, that is, a person who already possesses what the subject thinks he or she lacks. On this level, the mimetic triangle can represent a rather benign process, which involves various forms of social learning (external mediation). But human conflict involves a reciprocal process in which social rivals play the roles of both model and subject in the mimetic triangle (internal mediation). This reciprocal process becomes more and more conflicted as the rivals approach each other in terms of relatively equal strength and desire for the object that they both want to possess. At this point, the rival may come to represent an obstacle to the desired object, which can only be obtained by eliminating one of the competing parties or discharging the conflict in some other way (e.g., scapegoating).[33]

Girard is useful, as students can relate to the mimetic triangle because they themselves are social learners. For example, they will be quite aware of the mimetic dynamics in advertising, which promotes the acquisition of a desirable object by presenting models for emulation and consumption. Sports also involve mimetic desire because similarly equipped teams compete for the same object; and students are familiar with the fact that rivalries in sports can lead to violence, such as bench-clearing brawls in baseball and fights in hockey.

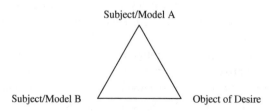

Figure 4.1 Girard's Mimetic Triangle

How is crusader violence to be explained? While political and economic factors (e.g., the expansion of Islam toward Constantinople) have their place, they will not explain the intense focus on Jerusalem. If one analyzes the conquest of Jerusalem from the perspective of mimetic rivalry, ideologies of supersessionism are implicated in that violence. As monotheisms, both Christianity and Islam were competing for acquisition of the same object. Possession of Jerusalem was the physical symbol of legitimacy as the religion that superseded its rivals. In addition, the crusaders and Muslims both belonged to religious organizations that valued the symbol of warfare, which they were able to realize in a literal fashion by enlisting the coercive power of the state.

As Rodney Stark points out, a single religion would not be able to impose itself on a society if it were not able to rely on political sponsorship and resources.[34] Actually, it is quite possible to have a fairly violent mythology and not engage in violent actions. A good example can be found in the genocidal program that occurs in the Hebrew Bible (cf. Deuteronomy 7 and Joshua 10). Critical scholarship regards this program as a historical fiction. Ancient Judaism never realized this genocidal myth literally. Even if it had wanted to (which is far from certain) it lacked the political resources to do so. The nexus between war and religion, therefore, depends on the relationship between a faith community and its structures of social support.

Stark's description of monotheism is also helpful in addressing the fate of Jerusalem's Jewish population in 1099. A climate of religious intolerance tends to increase when a few powerful particularistic religions are in conflict for social control.[35] The destruction of the Jewish community in Jerusalem by the crusaders matches these conditions, because the bloody struggle for domination of the city by the Christians would have exacerbated their intolerance for any other religious community. Of course, Christianity's supersessionist belief system also predisposed it to hostility toward Judaism, and this factor has been prominent in the violent history of Christian persecutions of Jews.[36]

Heroic Asceticism

A number of Christian medieval mystics engaged in rigorous forms of bodily discipline including sleep deprivation, starvation, and self-inflicted injury (e.g., flagellation). These extreme techniques can be described as forms of "heroic asceticism."[37] Their goal was to induce a change in consciousness. Beatrice of Nazareth (1200–68) is a case in point. In her teens, she was in the habit of beating her body with twigs and sharp yew leaves, which she also spread upon her bed to sleep on. During the day she wore sharp leaves next to her skin as well as a thick rope of thorns that she wound tightly around her body. As a result, she was unable to move or bend without experiencing fierce pain. Later she seems to have abandoned these violent measures, although ascetic practice remained important in her quest for mystical communion with God.[38]

Asceticism, of course, is a well-documented practice in many religions and it would be contentious to describe all sorts of fasting and other practices of self-denial as forms of violence. This is one of the reasons for choosing the epithet "heroic" to describe the kinds of extreme asceticism that merit discussion here. A second reason for using this epithet is that it calls into question the value of "heroism" itself. The ideology of heroism merits critical scrutiny in a course on violence and religion, because the category of "hero" is often associated with great religious figures.

Although Joseph Campbell's "monomyth" of the hero has been subject to critique,[39] his categories remain a useful point of departure for discussing the violent dynamics of heroism. To introduce the topic, I ask students to map their careers as university students on Campbell's paradigm of the heroic journey.[40] They know of separation (often from home), tests and helpers on the way to initiation (graduation), and the idea that they will return to their home with a boon (knowledge, a degree).

Students also readily appreciate the fact that the heroic mythos often valorizes transformation by means of violent processes (the myth of redemptive violence). Numerous examples are available through cartoons, television dramas, and other media such as video games. Often at the heart of the heroic mythos is a conflict involving three parties: the perpetrator, the victim, and a rescuer.[41] The perpetrator is in many ways the monstrous counterpart of the hero, who has the right to use legitimate violence against the illegitimate violence of the villain. From another perspective, the dynamics of heroism depend on the distinction between a good self and a bad self, with the assumption that the good self must prevail over the bad self. In Western Christian thought, the good self is often associated with the mind and the bad self with the body.[42]

Another aspect of violence, the effects of trauma, can also be located in the heroic mythos. While the separation of the hero from profane or ordinary reality might seem benign (Campbell's "call to adventure"), it may mask a pattern of psychological transformation that can be compared to the effects of traumatization. Victims of violence, such as combat veterans or rape victims, often report experiencing dissociative states to cope with threatening situations. To avoid being overwhelmed by fear and terror, they cut themselves off from various feeling functions.[43] While students may recognize this kind of psychological reaction as understandable and often unavoidable, they may not be prepared for the fact that cultures can employ intentional forms of traumatization to induce new forms of identity and consciousness.[44] The kind of initiatory hazing that characterizes heroic military organizations such as the Marines is a case in point. A dramatic and disturbing example of religiously sanctioned trauma involves female genital mutilation as a form of initiation into adulthood. In both instances, forms of violence are used to split off (dissociate) a person from previous identifications and forge a new social relationship.

Heroic asceticism can be viewed as deliberately induced bodily trauma to produce an alternate form of consciousness distinct (dissociated) from ordinary patterns of human thought. As in Campbell's heroic journey, ascetic procedures involve separation from ordinary reality to engage in a series of confrontations (tests) with human consciousness. The goal of extreme forms of self-harm was to induce a radical shift in cognition that allowed for mystical union with the deity (atonement with the Father). As a result, it was thought, the ascetic could return to the community from which he or she came with blessings either in the nature of new insights into the divine reality or unusual powers of healing and intercessory prayer. Nevertheless, ecclesiastical authorities were in general highly skeptical about the value of extreme penances and critical of those who practiced them.

Jerome Kroll and Bernard Bachrach advance two hypotheses to explain the prevalence of heroic asceticism in the late Middle Ages. First, there emerged a focus on identifying with the human aspects of the suffering Jesus. Second, heroic asceticism appealed to persons who sought mystical union with Christ but who were not able to employ, or lacked access to, a more traditional form of meditation and contemplation.[45] In this second case, the violence of extreme asceticism was related to the distance perceived between the beginning state of the practitioner and the idealized end state. The more radical the transformation from ordinary perception to the desired cognition, the more acceptable violence became as a means to an end.

The social effects of valorizing the violence of the crucifixion has become a matter of concern for Christians who are critical of a doctrine of Christ's death that represents it as an act of divinely authorized violence.[46] Contemporary theologians have argued that making God the author of the violence of the cross helps to sanction the concept of legitimate violence in the pursuit of socially valued goals.[47] The heroic asceticism of someone like Beatrice of Nazareth illustrates this concern. By taking the suffering Christ as a model, the violence she did to herself had divine sanction.

Collective Persecution

During the mid-fifteenth to the mid-eighteenth centuries, thousands of persons were tried for witchcraft—most of them women. Modern historians estimate that about 60,000 witches were executed during this period, roughly half the number tried for this offense.[48] There is no doubt that the vast majority of these persons were innocent of the crimes that they were accused of: they did not intend commerce with the devil. On the other hand, one must be careful in making such a statement, because it risks exculpating their persecutors under the assumption that the judicial authorities were simply deluded. This is decidedly not the case for the authorities at the time, who were convinced of the reality and gravity of their victims' crimes—the more so for having obtained their confession under torture. In fact, the witch hunts presuppose a culture constituted by myth and prone to control violence through a sacrificial economy. At the heart of the witch hunts was a crisis, in which a traditional worldview was undergoing immense change.[49]

Documentation for witch trials is quite rich for many regions in Western Europe, including collections of contemporary source materials.[50] I focus on the Scottish witch hunt for a couple of reasons. First, because it was conducted under the aegis of Protestantism, this phenomenon can be discussed without the complicating factor of the role and nature of the Inquisition. Second, the Scottish witch hunt is arguably one of the major witch hunts of Europe.[51]

As victims of collective persecution, witches may be regarded as scapegoats. Students readily grasp the four stereotypes of collective persecution that Girard claims are present in the dynamics of scapegoating:[52]

- Persecutions generally take place in times of crisis, which weaken normal institutions and favor mob formation.
- Dissolution of the social organization is analyzed as a crime. Often the crime is one considered to attack the very foundations of cultural order, including the family and those hierarchical differences without which there would be no social order.
- Someone is identified as the criminal. Ultimately, the persecutors always convince themselves that a small number of people or even a single individual, despite their relative weakness, is extremely harmful to the whole of society. The crowd's choice of victim may be random, but not necessarily. Often the persecutors choose their victims because they belong to a class that is particularly susceptible to persecution, rather than because of any particular act.
- Violence is used to eliminate or expel the criminal threat to the social order.

Fundamental to Girard's description is the disintegration of the prevailing social order. The collapse of existing hierarchies weakens cultural institutions that hold in check dangerous rivalries between social agents. Left unchecked, these social rivalries risk turning on each other unless an agreed-upon substitute can become the object on which both parties may discharge some of their mutual aggression.

While there is no single cause for the witch hunts, a combination of factors predisposed various areas in Europe to the elimination of witches at different times during the fifteenth to eighteenth centuries.[53] Rapid changes created considerable social instabilities as a result of new wealth (e.g., from exploration in the East and the Americas), new technology (e.g., the printing press), the rise of nationalism, new knowledge (e.g., the Renaissance), and new forms of religious organization and thought (the Reformation and Counter-Reformation). These changes threatened existing modes of social organization and often exacerbated long-standing rivalries between ecclesiastical and secular powers for domination. Throughout this period, church and state managed to blunt some of their mutual rivalries and gain at least symbolic control over social change by agreeing on the eradication of a class of persons thought to be exacerbating social unrest.

That most victims of this persecutory violence (lower-class females) were marked as different from the persecutors (elite males) fits in well with Girard's stereotypes.[54] But one must also reckon with the fact that regulation of women's bodies is a symbolic locus for ideologies of social control.[55] There is a close relationship between the fear of witchcraft in early modern Europe and the fear of rebellion, sedition, and public disorder.[56] Demonic imagery recommended itself because the social changes seemed fundamentally threatening to established order. An economy of sacrifice recognized the utility of eliminating those thought to have intercourse with demonic agencies: the witches. Consequently, church and state collaborated on the elimination of witches through legitimate violence (trials and inquisitions).

The scapegoating process can also be illustrated by considering certain forms of nonviolent resistance. Good examples are available in the American civil rights movement. The tactics of Martin Luther King Jr. and his associates were calculated to dramatize the injustice of segregation by unmasking the state-sanctioned violence that legitimated race laws and demonstrating that the victims of racism were not deserving of the violence to which they were subjected.[57]

Colonialism

During the nineteenth and twentieth centuries, aboriginal peoples in the United States, Canada, Australia, New Zealand, and Scandinavia were subjected to processes of enforced assimilation by state-sponsored educational systems, often managed with the cooperation of the church. Splitting children off from their parents, their native language, and culture, as well as banning native religious ceremonies (e.g., potlatches and the Sun Dance), was thought to be an exercise in benevolence. Given my context, I focus on the Canadian Indian residential school system, which had its heyday from the late 1880s through the 1960s.[58] Its violent subtext makes for hard reading when students encounter the memoirs of survivors of the residential schools.[59]

The relationship between colonizer and colonized can be described as one between a dominated and dominating society.[60] The colonizer requires that the colonial subject adopt the outward forms and internalize the values and norms of the occupying power.[61] One of the major metaphors for the colonial experience is "displacement." A valid and active sense of agency can be eroded by migrations and processes of indenture, but it may also be destroyed by cultural denigration: conscious and unconscious oppression of the indigenous personality by a supposedly superior racial and cultural model.[62] Alfred Memmi sees the idea of privilege at the heart of the colonial relationship.[63] As such, slavery is the ultimate expression of the colonial process. While I do not deal with them here, the experience of African American slavery and the conflicts between those who justified it and those who opposed it are excellent subjects for a course on Christianity and violence.

Two forms of colonial violence meet in the phenomenon of the Indian residential schools. One of these involves the assertion of Christian superiority through its supersessionist belief system. The other involves an educational method that Alice Miller describes as "poisonous pedagogy." The goal of poisonous pedagogy is domination of the child by the adult. It sanctions techniques which suppose that adults are masters of the dependent child and that the child's will must be "broken" as quickly as possible. Methods used for this purpose include manipulation, scare tactics, withdrawal of love, isolation, shaming, and coercion to the point of physical violence. Many of these techniques were sanctioned in child-rearing manuals published in the nineteenth and twentieth centuries.[64] Not surprisingly, these punitive practices are well documented in accounts of the residential school experience.

In the case of the residential schools, violence was considered appropriate because native children were doubly placed in the role of subordination to Christian adults: both because they were children and because they were natives, and therefore without the benefits of the presumed superiority of Western civilization. A typical sentiment expressed by an advocate of the residential school system: "In the industrial school the children are withdrawn for long periods—and the longer the better—from the degrading surroundings of their pagan homes, and placed under the direct influence of all that is noblest and best in our Christian civilization."[65] Though often well intentioned, Christian promoters of residential schools were unaware of the damage they would do to generations of children as they sought to convert them to the values of the dominant culture. Many lost not only their language and religion, but also the opportunity to learn the necessary social skills that would allow them to successfully parent their own children. The disastrous effects of this social experiment are still being lived out on the reservations and in cities where native people now live.

Sacrifice

The Tridentine Mass was the standard ritual for the rite of Holy Communion (the Eucharist) in the Roman Catholic church from 1570–1962. It is a rite in which the sacrificial action of Christ's death on the cross is re-represented to God by the church.[66] This religious action is presided over by a male priesthood that traces an unbroken line of succession from the present day to Christ's original apostles. Exponents of the Tridentine rite categorically oppose the suggestion that women be ordained to the priesthood. Their opposition is related to the sacrificial character of the Mass.

All branches of Christianity have traditionally restricted the exercise of the public offices of preaching and presiding over Holy Communion to authorized males (i.e., ordination). In various forms of Protestantism, this restriction is often supported by appeal to scriptural passages that seem to justify the subordination of women to men in the social order (cf. 1 Corinthians 14:34 and 1 Timothy 2:12). Nevertheless, scriptural interpretation on this issue has proven to be somewhat elastic. In the 19th century, several movements began to authorize women to engage in public ministries once limited to males (an important influence was the prominence of female leadership in missionary work, both at home and abroad). These included some forms of Methodism and Pentecostalism and the Salvation Army. During the 20th century a number of denominations in Western Christianity gradually followed this trend. The theological reasoning undergirding the Tridentine Mass, however, represents a different approach to the definition of ministerial offices in the church. Both the ritual and theological understandings of the Mass have been subject to changes and debate since the second Vatican council (1962–1965). While the magisterium of the Roman Catholic church continues to resist calls for ordination of women to the priesthood, it remains to be seen if post-Vatican II developments carry the same import for female ordination as the Tridentine rite.[67]

Sacrifice is a concept that is important in the study of Christianity. On the one hand, it affords some useful linkages with other religions (e.g., those of India, ancient Greece, and Mesoamerica); on the other, it is a feature that serves to distinguish Christianity among various forms of monotheism. While there are related phenomena in Judaism and Islam, sacrificial ritual and doctrine hold a more prominent place in Christianity because of the need to explain the significance of the crucifixion of Jesus in the divine economy.

There is a large debate in scholarly literature about what counts as sacrifice and how such rituals work.[68] Feminist sociologist Nancy Jay's use of the concept of "indexing," however, is helpful for discussing the social significance of various forms of sacrifices involving meals (alimentary sacrifice). Often the social value of the ritual is to be found in its capacities to mark social hierarchies (a type of indexing). A common goal of alimentary sacrifices in many societies is to index patrilineal (male-dominated) patterns of descent.[69]

Jay describes the logic of sacrifice in binary terms:[70]

Communion		Expiation
Joining		Separation
Conjunction	\<SACRIFICE\>	Disjunction
At-one-ment		Atonement
Integration		Differentiation

In this schema, the term *sacrifice* stands for a large number of actions in which animals (sometimes plants or people) are ritually killed. Often the victims are eaten, but this is not true of all forms of sacrifice. The ceremonies accompanying the act of killing and the consumption of the animal are rich in symbolic value. In many ways they express the dynamics of economies of sacrifice described in the introduction to this essay. In other words, while sacrificial rituals have many different forms and purposes, problems of boundary maintenance and boundary failure are often bound up with these symbolic actions. On the one hand, they may seek to strengthen a certain group of social agents by eliminating or controlling the intrusion of symbolically problematic factors (e.g., death, sin, sickness, weakness) that would compromise the integrity of the group. This motivation is represented in the chart by terms such as *expiation, separation,* and *disjunction*. On the other hand, they may serve to strengthen the group by creating a new sense of cohesion and solidarity. This motivation is represented in the chart by terms such as *communion, joining* and conjunction. Frequently, a sacrificial ritual will correspond to both of these motivations.[71] Sacrificial rituals, therefore, are ways of creating and maintaining a human society in symbolic terms.[72] By putting control of such rites in the hands of males, the power to create and sustain the society over time is marked as the province of men rather than women.[73]

The Tridentine Eucharist can be analyzed as a form of alimentary sacrifice that legitimates male lineage systems in the church. The ordination of men to the exclusion of women reflects a concept of apostolic succession in which bishops stand in a direct line with the original (male) apostles as inheritors of their ministry; priests are ordained as coworkers with bishops. In the Mass the priest presides over the sacrificial rite and feeds the people with the consecrated host. The priest's dominant role is marked by the fact that there are aspects of the virtual sacrifice of Christ in the Mass that he alone is permitted to perform (such as the consecration of the wine and bread), There is a connection between the sacrificial aspect of the Eucharist, therefore, and the organization of social hierarchies in the church. Maintaining a sacrificial understanding of the eucharistic event cements hierarchical relationships of priest over laity as well as male over female.[74] Thereby, the Tridentine rite indexes the male priesthood as the institution that both maintains and ensures the continuity of the mystical society that is the church through time.

Defenders of the male priesthood in the Tridentine tradition would protest that the Christian symbol system does not value men more than women. They would argue, however, that they are constrained by the conditions of the Christian revelation: Jesus only called males to be apostles and the Son of God was incarnated as a man; therefore, those best suited to re-present his sacrifice in the Mass are also males.[75] Nevertheless, by limiting the sacrificial ritual to male actors, women are systematically excluded from exercising many high offices in the church. Does this represent a form of violence? Obviously, an answer to this question depends on one's definition of violence.

Sacrificial economies typically project signifiers of abjection onto groups other than those who hold the balance of social power. For example, sex and ethnic differences are both implicated in sacrificial processes.[76] In the logic of sacrifice, violence is permitted in order to maintain socially valorized hierarchies. This pertains to the whole question of boundary maintenance, not only between clergy and laity, but also between males and females (cf. the scapegoating of women during the witchhunts) and the transcendent order and the ordinary world (cf. the logic of heroic asceticism). For these reasons, liturgical actions do not take place in a vacuum but have important social consequences and corollaries. A religion that limits the access of women to holy offices has to reckon with the possibility that such a restriction may justify the disempowerment of women in other spheres of life, whether this be intended by its theology or not.

SUMMARY

I make no claim that either the examples or classificatory schemes I have mentioned are comprehensive. I hope, however, that they are illustrative of some useful approaches to teaching Christianity and violence. Pedagogically, students are animated by grappling with real-life situations. They appreciate being exposed to a variety of examples and a variety of techniques for examining them. Problembased learning is also useful for exploring the ability of a religion such as Christianity to resist violence, although I have not discussed that here. Another aspect of religion and violence that I have neglected is the capacity of violent experiences to transform religious traditions in unexpected or unanticipated ways. For example, Joyce Salisbury appeals to the concept of "blowback" (a term used to connote the unintended consequences of violence) to show how the experience of martyrdom affected Christian theology and Roman society in ways that neither Christians nor government officials could foresee.[77]

No doubt a balanced approach to Christianity would take its interests in resisting violence and the concept of blowback into much greater consideration than I have attempted here. Nevertheless, the focus on aspects of harm and violation is deliberate and reflects a pedagogical agenda that, I believe, is vital in the present situation. Violence may be "unspeakable," but it is not unthinkable. On the contrary, the dynamics that lead to acts of violence are perhaps all too understandable. To leave violence without explanation is to mystify it and grant it a numinous power that it does not deserve. We have everything to gain and nothing to lose by demystifying violence. I believe that this commitment ought to be fundamental to any course on religion and violence.

NOTES

1. See, e.g., Leo D. Lefebure, *Revelation, the Religions, and Violence* (Maryknoll, NY: Orbis, 2000); Charles Kimball, *When Religion Becomes Evil* (New York: HarperSanFrancisco, 2002); Lloyd Stefan, *The Demonic Turn: The Power of Religion to Inspire or Restrain Violence* (Cleveland, OH: Pilgrim, 2003).

2. Queen's University Centre for Teaching and Learning, "Good Practice: Problem Based Learning," June 30, 2008, http://www.queensu.ca/ctl/goodpractice/problem/index/html.

3. Julia Leslie, "Suttee or *Satī*: Victim or Victor?" in *Roles and Rituals for Hindu Women,* ed. Julia Leslie (London: Pinter, 1991), 176–77.

4. For example, the various criteria set out in American Psychiatric Association, *Diagnostic and Statistical Manual of Mental Disorders*, 4th ed. (Washington, DC: American Psychiatric Association, 1994).

5. John R. Hinnells and Richard King, *Religion and Violence in South Asia: Theory and Practice* (London: Routledge, 2007), 3–5.

6. Cheryl A. Kirk-Duggan, *Violence and Theology* (Nashville, TN: Abingdon Press, 2006), 2–3.

7. See, e.g., J. Jeffrey Means, *Trauma and Evil: Healing the Wounded Soul* (Minneapolis: Fortress, 2000), 92–94; Willard Gaylin, *Hatred: The Psychological Descent into Violence* (New York: Public Affairs, 2003), 151–92.

8. See, e.g., Regina Schwartz, *The Curse of Cain: The Violent Legacy of Monotheism* (Chicago: University of Chicago Press, 1997), 4–5; Kirk-Duggan, *Violence and Theology*, 5.

9. James Waller, *Becoming Evil: How Ordinary People Commit Genocide and Mass Killing* (New York: Oxford University Press, 2002), 236–57.

10. See, e.g., Curt A. Bartol, *Criminal Behavior: A Psychological Approach*, 3rd ed. (Englewood Cliffs, NJ: Prentice Hall, 1991), 244–46; Donald G. Dutton, *The Abusive Personality: Violence and Control in Intimate Relationships* (New York: Guilford Press, 2003), 89–93.

11. A classic example is the contrasting descriptions of human nature advanced by Ashley Montagu, *Man and Aggression* (New York: Oxford University Press, 1968); and Konrad Lorenz, *On Aggression* (New York: Bantam Books, 1969).

12. René Girard, *Violence and the Sacred* (Baltimore, MD: Johns Hopkins University Press, 1977), 297; Mark Juergensmeyer, *Terror in the Mind of God: The Global Rise of Religious Violence* (Berkeley: University of California Press, 2000), 168–69.

13. This phenomenon is called "secondary" or "vicarious trauma." For a helpful overview of its impact on persons in helping professions, see Jan I. Richardson, *Guidebook on Vicarious Trauma: Recommended Solutions for Anti-Violence Workers* (Ottawa: Public Health Agency of Canada, 2001), 14.

14. I. Lisa McCann and Laurie Anne Pearlman, *Psychological Trauma and the Adult Survivor: Theory, Therapy, and Transformation* (New York: Brunner/Mazel, 1990), 57–62.

15. Melford E. Spiro, "Religion: Problems of Definition and Explanation," in *Anthropological Approaches to the Study of Religion,* ed. M. Banton (London: Tavistock, 1966), 96.

16. For the connection between religion and ultimacy, see Stefan, *Demonic Turn,* 14–19.

17. Walter Wink, *Engaging the Powers: Discernment and Resistance in a World of Domination* (Minneapolis: Fortress, 1992), 16.

18. See J. Denny Weaver, *The Non-violent Atonement* (Grand Rapids, MI: Eerdmans, 2001), 86–92.

19. See Joanne Carlson Brown and Rebecca Parker, "For God So Loved the World?" in *Christianity, Patriarchy, and Abuse: A Feminist Critique,* ed. Joanne Carlson Brown and Carole R. Bohn (New York: Pilgrim Press, 1989), 1–30.

20. Nancy Scheper-Hughes and Phillippe Bourgois, *Violence in War and Peace: An Anthology* (Oxford: Blackwell, 2004), 5.

21. Martha J. Reineke, *Sacrificed Lives: Kristeva on Women and Violence* (Bloomington: Indiana University Press, 1997), 26–32.

22. Julia Kristeva, *Powers of Horror: An Essay on Abjection* (New York: Columbia University, 1982), 110–12; Reineke, *Sacrificed Lives,* 67–73.

23. Reineke, *Sacrificed Lives,* 187–90.

24. This connection was articulated with respect to Christian anti-Semitism by Jules Isaac, *The Teaching of Contempt: Christian Roots of Anti-Semitism* (New York: Holt, Rinehart and Winston, 1964). I have broadened it here, however, because I think that all three of the major monotheisms possess their own brands of supersessionism with a corresponding suspicion of other creeds.

25. Miroslav Volf, "Forgiveness, Reconciliation, and Justice," in *Stricken by God? Nonviolent Identification and the Victory of Christ,* ed. Brad Jersak and Michael Hardin (Abbotsford, BC: Fresh Wind Press, 2007), 274.

26. Paul Halsall, ed., "The Passion of Saints Perpetua and Felicity," in *Internet Medieval Sourcebook,* April 1996, http://www.fordham.edu/halsall/source/perpetua.asp. This account is analyzed in Aideen Hartney, *Gruesome Deaths and Celibate Lives: Christian Martyrs and Ascetics* (Exeter: Bristol Phoenix, 2005), 33–50; and Joyce E. Salisbury, *The Blood of Martyrs: Unintended Consequences of Ancient Violence* (New York: Routledge, 2004), 118–22.

27. Eric Hoffer, *The True Believer: Thoughts on the Nature of Mass Movements* (New York: Mentor, 1958), 60–79.

28. Rodney Stark, *The Rise of Christianity: A Sociologist Reconsiders History* (Princeton, NJ: Princeton University Press, 1996), 163–89.

29. This well-known event is described in many books. A recent detailed account can be found in Thomas Asbridge, *The First Crusade: A New History* (Oxford: Oxford University Press, 2004), 295–319.

30. Eyewitness accounts of the conquest of Jerusalem by the crusaders make interesting reading for students. See Paul Halsall, ed., "The Fall of Jerusalem; The Frankish Victory," in *Internet Medieval Sourcebook,* December 1997, http://www.fordham.edu/halsall/source/cde-jlem.html.

31. See, e.g., Thomas F. Madden, *The New Concise History of the Crusades,* 2nd ed. (Lanham, MD: Rowman and Littlefield, 2006), 34.

32. Juergensmeyer, *Terror in the Mind of God*, 156.
33. Mack C. Stirling, "Violent Religion: René Girard's Theory of Culture," in *The Destructive Power of Religion: Violence in Judaism, Christianity, and Islam, Vol. 2, Religion, Psychology, and Violence*, ed. J. H. Ellens (Westport, CT: Praeger, 2004), 12–21. I use Girard's ideas because of their heuristic value for interpreting historical phenomena. I do not advocate Girard's theories about the origin of culture to students, because human culture seems far too complex to posit a single cause at its beginnings.
34. Rodney Stark, *One True God: Historical Consequences of Monotheism* (Princeton, NJ: Princeton University Press, 2001), 119–20.
35. Ibid., 122–24.
36. James Parkes, *The Conflict of the Church and the Synagogue: A Study in the Origins of Antisemitism* (New York: Atheneum, 1977), 373–75.
37. Jerome Kroll and Bernard Bachrach, *The Mystic Mind: The Psychology of Medieval Mystics and Ascetics* (New York: Routledge, 2005), 1–10.
38. Ibid., 150–60.
39. For example, Robert A. Segal, *Joseph Campbell: An Introduction*, rev. ed. (New York: Signet, 1990); Tamar Frankiel, "New Age Mythology: A Jewish Response to Joseph Campbell," *Tikkun* 4/3 (1989): 23–26, 118–20.
40. Joseph Campbell, *The Hero with a Thousand Faces*, 2nd ed. (Princeton, NJ: Princeton University Press, 1968), 245–46.
41. Barbara Whitmer, *The Violence Mythos* (Albany: State University of New York Press, 1997), 145.
42. Ibid., 131–32.
43. Judith Herman, *Trauma and Recovery: The Aftermath of Violence—from Domestic Violence to Political Terror* (New York: BasicBooks, 1997), 33–35.
44. Whitmer, *Violence Mythos*, 150–51.
45. Kroll and Bachrach, *Mystic Mind*, 199.
46. See, e.g., the collection of essays in Brad Jersak and Michael Hardin, *Stricken by God? Nonviolent Identification and the Victory of Christ* (Abbotsford, BC: Fresh Wind Press, 2007).
47. See, e.g., Emmanuel Charles McCarthy, "The Nonviolent Eucharistic Jesus: A Pastoral Approach," Center for Christian Non-Violence January 30, 2009, http://centerforchristiannonviolence.org/index.php.
48. Brian P. Levack, *The Witch-Hunt in Early Modern Europe*, 2nd ed. (London: Longman, 1995), 24–25.
49. Reineke, *Sacrificed Lives*, 140–50.
50. See, e.g., Alan C. Kors and Edward Peters, *Witchcraft in Europe 1100–1700: A Documentary History* (Philadelphia: University of Pennsylvania Press, 1972).
51. Christine Larner, *Enemies of God: The Witchhunt in Scotland* (London: Chatto and Windus, 1981), 197.
52. René Girard, *The Scapegoat* (Baltimore, MD: Johns Hopkins University Press, 1986), 12–23.
53. Levack, *Witch-Hunt*, 230–32.
54. This analysis is based on Larner, *Enemies of God*; and Lauren Martin, "The Devil and the Domestic: Witchcraft, Quarrels and Women's Work in Scotland," in *The Scottish Witch-Hunt in Context*, ed. Julian Goodare (Manchester: Manchester University Press, 2002), 73–89.
55. Reineke, *Sacrificed Lives*, 41.
56. Levack, *Witch-Hunt*, 64–67.

57. See Theophus H. Smith, "King and the Black Religious Quest to Cure Racism," in *Curing Violence*, ed. M. I. Wallace and T. H. Smith (Sonoma, CA: Polebridge Press, 1994), 230–51.

58. For detailed histories, see James R. Miller, *Shingwauk's Vision: A History of Native Residential Schools* (Toronto: University of Toronto Press, 1996); John S. Milloy, *A National Crime: The Canadian Government and the Residential School System, 1879–1986* (Winnipeg: University of Manitoba Press, 1999).

59. For example, Isabelle Knockwood, *Out of the Depths: The Experiences of Mi'kmaw Children at the Indian Residential School at Schubenacadie, Nova Scotia* (Lockeport, NS: Roseway, 1992); Nuu-Chah-Nulth Tribal Council, *Indian Residential Schools: The Nuu-chah-nulth Experience* (Port Alberni, BC: Nuu-Chah-Nulth Tribal Council, 1996).

60. Bill Ashcroft, Gareth Griffiths, and Helen Tiffin, *The Empire Writes Back: Theory and Practice in Post-colonial Literatures,* 2nd ed. (London: Routledge, 2002), 31.

61. Bart Moore-Gilbert, *Postcolonial Theory: Contexts, Practices, Politics* (London: Verso, 1997), 120.

62. Ashcroft et al., *The Empire Writes Back*, 9.

63. Albert Memmi, *The Colonizer and the Colonized* (Boston: Beacon Press, 1967), xii.

64. Alice Miller, *For Your Own Good: Hidden Cruelty in Child-Rearing and the Roots of Violence*, 3rd ed. (New York: Farrar, Straus and Giroux, 1990), 58–60.

65. Quote from Andrew Baird of the Presbyterian Church in Canada, general supervisor for work among the Indians (1889), cited in J. W. Grant, *Moon of Wintertime* (Toronto: University of Toronto Press, 1984), 178.

66. Franz Schmidberger, "The Theology and Spirituality of the Holy Sacrifice of the Mass," *The Angelus* (December 2002). October 21, 2011, www.angelusonline.org.

67. Controversy over the ordination of women in the Roman Catholic Church continues. For a survey of the current situation and theological arguments being used by both sides, see Phyllis Zagana, *Women & Catholicism: Gender, Communion, and Authority* (New York: Palgrave Macmillan, 2011), 89–135.

68. See, e.g., Maurice Bloch, *Prey into Hunter: The Politics of Religious Experience* (Cambridge: Cambridge University Press, 1992), 25–30.

69. Nancy Jay, *Throughout Your Generations Forever: Sacrifice, Religion, and Paternity* (Chicago: University of Chicago Press, 1992), 41–60.

70. Ibid., 17–29.

71. William Beers, *Women and Sacrifice: Male Narcissism and the Psychology of Religion* (Detroit: Wayne State University Press, 1992), 137–47. Beers provides an object relations perspective on Jay's thesis. In my experience, students are more apt to understand Jay's sociology than Beers's psychology, although the two are complementary.

72. Bloch, *Prey into Hunter*, 24–45.

73. Jay, *Throughout Your Generations*, 30–40.

74. Ibid., 112–27. See also Beers discussion of the theology underlying Eucharistic practice in the Episcopal (Anglican) Church U.S.A. prior to its decision to ordain women to the priesthood in *Women and Sacrifice*, 163–79.

75. M. R. O'Brien, "Women and Papal Teaching," in *New Catholic Encyclopedia*, 2nd ed. (Washington, DC: Catholic University of America, 2003), 422.

76. See Beers, *Women and Sacrifice*, 178.

77. Salisbury, *Blood of Martyrs*, 204. The concept of unintended consequences of violence can be profitably applied to various religious situations. A good example in Hinduism would be the rise of the popularity of Rama after the Muslim conquests; see Zaheer Baber, "'Race,' Religion and Riots: The 'Racialization' of Communal Conflict in India," *Sociology* 38 (2004): 704.

BIBLIOGRAPHY

American Psychiatric Association. *Diagnostic and Statistical Manual of Mental Disorders.* 4th ed. Washington: American Psychiatric Association, 1994.

Asbridge, Thomas. *The First Crusade: A New History.* Oxford: Oxford University Press, 2004.

Ashcroft, Bill, and Gareth Griffiths, and Helen Tiffin. *The Empire Writes Back: Theory and Practice in Post-colonial Literatures.* 2nd ed. London: Routledge, 2002.

Baber, Zaheer. "'Race,' Religion and Riots: The 'Racialization' of Communal Conflict in India." *Sociology* 38 (2004): 701–18.

Bartol, Curt A. *Criminal Behavior: A Psychological Approach.* 3rd ed. Engelwood Cliffs, NJ: Prentice Hall, 1991.

Beers, William. *Women and Sacrifice: Male Narcissism and the Psychology of Religion.* Detroit: Wayne State University, 1992.

Bloch, Maurice. *Prey into Hunter: The Politics of Religious Experience.* Cambridge: Cambridge University Press, 1992.

Brown, Joanne Carlson, and Rebecca Parker. "For God So Loved the World?" In *Christianity, Patriarchy, and Abuse: A Feminist Critique,* ed. Joanne Carlson Brown and Carole R. Bohn, 1–30. New York: Pilgrim Press, 1989.

Campbell, Joseph. *The Hero with a Thousand Faces.* 2nd ed. Princeton, NJ: Princeton University Press, 1968.

Dutton, Donald G. *The Abusive Personality: Violence and Control in Intimate Relationships.* New York: Guilford Press, 2003.

Frankiel, Tamar. "New Age Mythology: A Jewish Response to Joseph Campbell." *Tikkun* 4/3 (1989): 23–26, 118–20.

Gaylin, Willard. *Hatred: The Psychological Descent into Violence.* New York: Public Affairs, 2003.

Girard, René. *The Scapegoat.* Baltimore, MD: Johns Hopkins University Press, 1986.

———. *Violence and the Sacred.* Baltimore, MD: Johns Hopkins University Press, 1977.

Grant, J. W. *Moon of Wintertime.* Toronto: University of Toronto Press, 1984.

Halsall, Paul, ed. "The Fall of Jerusalem; The Frankish Victory." In *Internet Medieval Sourcebook.* December 1997. http://www.fordham.edu/halsall/source/cde-jlem.asp.

———. "The Passion of Saints Perpetua and Felicity." In *Internet Medieval Sourcebook.* April 1996. http://www.fordham.edu/halsall/source/perpetua.asp.

Hartney, Aideen. *Gruesome Deaths and Celibate Lives: Christian Martyrs and Ascetics.* Exeter: Bristol Phoenix, 2005.

Herman, Judith. *Trauma and Recovery: The Aftermath of Violence—from Domestic Violence to Political Terror.* New York: Basic Books, 1997.

Hinnells, John R., and Richard King. *Religion and Violence in South Asia: Theory and Practice.* London: Routledge, 2007.

Hoffer, Eric. *The True Believer: Thoughts on the Nature of Mass Movements.* New York: Mentor, 1958.

Isaac, Jules. *The Teaching of Contempt: Christian Roots of Anti-Semitism.* New York: Holt, Rinehart and Winston, 1964.

Jay, Nancy. *Throughout Your Generations Forever: Sacrifice, Religion, and Paternity.* Chicago: University of Chicago Press, 1992.

Jersak, Brad, and Michael Hardin. *Stricken by God? Nonviolent Identification and the Victory of Christ.* Abbotsford, BC: Fresh Wind Press, 2007.

Juergensmeyer, Mark. *Terror in the Mind of God: The Global Rise of Religious Violence.* Berkeley: University of California Press, 2000.

Kimball, Charles. *When Religion Becomes Evil.* New York: HarperSanFrancisco, 2002.

Kirk-Duggan, Cheryl A. *Violence and Theology.* Nashville, TN: Abingdon Press, 2006.

Knockwood, Isabelle. *Out of the Depths: The Experiences of Mi'kmaw Children at the Indian Residential School at Schubenacadie, Nova Scotia.* Lockeport, NS: Roseway, 1992.

Kors, Alan C., and Edward Peters. *Witchcraft in Europe 1100–1700: A Documentary History.* Philadelphia: University of Pennsylvania Press, 1972.

Kristeva, Julia. *Powers of Horror: An Essay on Abjection.* New York: Columbia University, 1982.

Kroll, Jerome, and Bernard Bachrach. *The Mystic Mind: The Psychology of Medieval Mystics and Ascetics.* New York: Routledge, 2005.

Larner, Christine. *Enemies of God: The Witchhunt in Scotland.* London: Chatto and Windus, 1981.

Lefebure, Leo D. *Revelation, the Religions, and Violence.* Maryknoll, NY: Orbis, 2000.

Leslie, Julia. "Suttee or *Satī*: Victim or Victor?" In *Roles and Rituals for Hindu Women*, ed. Julia Leslie, 175–91. London: Pinter, 1991.

Levack, Brian P. *The Witch-Hunt in Early Modern Europe.* 2nd ed. London: Longman, 1995.

Lorenz, Konrad. *On Aggression.* New York: Bantam Books, 1969.

Madden, Thomas F. *The New Concise History of the Crusades.* 2nd ed. Lanham, MD: Rowman and Littlefield, 2006.

Martin, Lauren. "The Devil and the Domestic: Witchcraft, Quarrels and Women's Work in Scotland." In *The Scottish Witch-Hunt in Context*, ed. Julian Goodare, 73–86. Manchester: Manchester University Press, 2002.

McCann, I. Lisa, and Laurie Anne Pearlman. *Psychological Trauma and the Adult Survivor: Theory, Therapy, and Transformation.* New York: Brunner/Mazel, 1990.

McCarthy, Emmanuel Charles. "The Nonviolent Eucharistic Jesus: A Pastoral Approach." Center for Christian Nonviolence. January 30, 2009. http://centerforchristian-nonviolence.org/index.php.

Means, J. Jeffrey. *Trauma and Evil: Healing the Wounded Soul.* Minneapolis: Fortress, 2000.

Memmi, Albert. *The Colonizer and the Colonized.* Boston: Beacon Press, 1967.

Miller, Alice. *For Your Own Good: Hidden Cruelty in Child-Rearing and the Roots of Violence.* 3rd ed. New York: Farrar, Straus and Giroux, 1990.

Miller, James R. *Shingwauk's Vision: A History of Native Residential Schools.* Toronto: University of Toronto Press, 1996.

Milloy, John S. *A National Crime: The Canadian Government and the Residential School System, 1879–1986.* Winnipeg: University of Manitoba Press, 1999.

Montagu, Ashley. *Man and Aggression.* New York: Oxford University Press, 1968.

Moore-Gilbert, Bart. *Postcolonial Theory: Contexts, Practices, Politics.* London: Verso, 1997.

Nuu-Chah-Nulth Tribal Council. *Indian Residential Schools: The Nuu-chah-nulth Experience.* Port Alberni, BC: Nuu-Chah-Nulth Tribal Council, 1996.

O'Brien, M. R. "Women and Papal Teaching." *New Catholic Encyclopedia.* 2nd ed. 14: 823–28. Washington, DC: Catholic University of America, 2003.

Parkes, James. *The Conflict of the Church and the Synagogue: A Study in the Origins of Anti-semitism.* New York: Atheneum, 1977.

Queen's University Centre for Teaching and Learning. "Good Practice: Problem Based Learning." June 30, 2008. http://www.queensu.ca/ctl/goodpractice/problem/index.html.

Richardson, Jan I. *Guidebook on Vicarious Trauma: Recommended Solutions for Anti-Violence Workers.* Ottawa: Public Health Agency of Canada, 2001.

Reineke, Martha J. *Sacrificed Lives: Kristeva on Women and Violence.* Bloomington: Indiana University Press, 1997.

Salisbury, Joyce E. *The Blood of Martyrs: Unintended Consequences of Ancient Violence*. New York: Routledge, 2004.

Scheper-Hughes, Nancy, and Phillippe Bourgois. *Violence in War and Peace: An Anthology*. Oxford: Blackwell, 2004.

Schmidberger, Franz. "The Theology and Spirituality of the Holy Sacrifice of the Mass," *The Angelus* (December 2002). October 21, 2011. www.angelusonline.org.

Schwartz, Regina. *The Curse of Cain: The Violent Legacy of Monotheism*. Chicago: University of Chicago Press, 1997.

Segal, Robert A. *Joseph Campbell: An Introduction*. Rev. ed. New York: Signet, 1990.

Smith, Theophus H. "King and the Black Religious Quest to Cure Racism." In *Curing Violence*, ed. M. I. Wallace and T. H. Smith, 230–51. Sonoma, CA: Polebridge Press, 1994.

Spiro, Melford E. "Religion: Problems of Definition and Explanation." In *Anthropological Approaches to the Study of Religion*, ed. M. Banton, 85–126. London: Tavistock, 1966.

Stark, Rodney. *One True God: Historical Consequences of Monotheism*. Princeton, NJ: Princeton University Press, 2001.

————. *The Rise of Christianity: A Sociologist Reconsiders History*. Princeton, NJ: Princeton University Press, 1996.

Stefan, Lloyd. *The Demonic Turn: The Power of Religion to Inspire or Restrain Violence*. Cleveland, OH: Pilgrim, 2003.

Stirling, Mack C. "Violent Religion: René Girard's Theory of Culture." In *The Destructive Power of Religion: Violence in Judaism, Christianity, and Islam. Vol. 2. Religion, Psychology, and Violence*, ed. J. H. Ellens, 11–50. Westport, CT: Praeger, 2004.

Volf, Miroslav. "Forgiveness, Reconciliation, and Justice." In *Stricken by God? Nonviolent Identification and the Victory of Christ*, ed. Brad Jersak and Michael Hardin, 268–86. Abbotsford, BC: Fresh Wind Press, 2007.

Waller, James. *Becoming Evil: How Ordinary People Commit Genocide and Mass Killing*. New York: Oxford University Press, 2002.

Weaver, J. Denny. *The Non-violent Atonement*. Grand Rapids, MI: Eerdmans, 2001.

Whitmer, Barbara. *The Violence Mythos*. Albany: State University of New York Press, 1997.

Wink, Walter. *Engaging the Powers: Discernment and Resistance in a World of Domination*. Minneapolis: Fortress, 1992.

Zagana, Phyllis. *Women and Catholicism: Gender, Communion, and Authority*. New York: Palgrave Macmillan, 2011.

CHAPTER 5

Confronting Misoislamia

Teaching Religion and Violence in Courses on Islam

AMIR HUSSAIN

With the terrorist attacks in America on September 11, 2001, in Madrid on March 11, 2004, and in London on July 7, 2005, Islam and violence have become synonymous in the minds of many North Americans and Europeans. More than twenty years earlier, the Iranian Revolution (and its aftermath) first alerted some people to the role of violence in the contemporary Muslim world. While many around the world consider Islam to be a religion of violence, many Muslims consider it a religion of peace. Clearly, anyone teaching courses in Islam has to deal with issues of both peace and violence. What makes the study of Islam unique among the traditions covered in this section is the negative valence associated with Muslims. As Brian Victoria points out in chapter 4, students naively think of Buddhism, for example, as a religion of peace. They are usually surprised when they pick up a copy of *Buddhist Warfare* (2010), for both its title and its provocative cover image of a young novice, in robes, holding a handgun. The case of Islam is quite different. To take only one insidious example, look at the cover of the April 9, 2010, issue of *Commonweal*, a progressive Catholic magazine. In illustrating an otherwise excellent cover story on religion and violence by noted scholar R. Scott Appleby, both of the photographs accompanying the article, including the cover photo of someone wiping up blood from the floor of a mosque, are specifically Islamic. The pictorial message is clear: only Islam is a religion of violence. And this comes from a progressive voice of Catholicism in America.[1]

In North America, one has seen a shift from the rise of Islamophobia post-9/11 (discussed later in this chapter) to what I term *misoislamia*, a neologism that captures the move from a fear (*phobia*) to a hatred (*miso*) for Islam and Muslims. As of this writing in the summer of 2010, the hot-button issue (besides the usual debate on whether President Obama was a secret Muslim) was the "Ground Zero" mosque proposed for Manhattan.[2] There will, unfortunately, be other such issues in the future that can be discussed in courses on Islam.

This chapter examines the issues of violence in the study of Islam and is structured on the Introduction to Islam course that is taught at most universities that have courses in religious studies or theology. The issues raised, however, will be applicable to a wider range of courses on Islam. I have been teaching such courses on Islam for over fifteen years in departments of both religious studies and theological studies, and several of my publications have been about pedagogical issues.[3] I have also served as co-chair of the contemporary Islam group at the American Academy of Religion and as a member of the steering committee for the study of Islam section. Both positions have allowed me to understand the relevant issues of violence and pedagogy that arise in courses on Islam and discuss them with fellow instructors. In this chapter, I deal with the important issues of peace and violence that need to be addressed with respect to (a) the biography of Muhammad, (b) the Qur'an, (c) the spread and historical development of Islam, (d) the contemporary Muslim world, and (e) the self-understandings of Muslims.

While there is a growing literature on both pedagogy and Islam,[4] and Islam and violence,[5] there is relatively little on the specific issue of teaching about violence and Islam. As Brian K. Pennington and I observed in the original proposal for this volume, and following the work of my mentor, Wilfred Cantwell Smith,[6] this chapter takes as one of its aims the interrogation of the idea that traditions are cohesive, self-identifying entities about which one may make sweeping, general characterizations. If students can be brought to the realization that "Islam" is a conceptual construct whose apparent cohesiveness has only partial correspondence to observed reality, their ideas about the place of violence in Islam will certainly develop more complex shadings as well. Informed and responsible pedagogy will help students understand that this religious tradition is a site of contestation over issues such as the use of violence and that history bears witness to these internal, ongoing debates.

FOR STUDENTS AND INSTRUCTORS: SORTING OUT THE VOCABULARY

To begin to explore the place of violence in Islam, it is fitting to begin with a word that has made its way into our English vocabulary, but is almost always misunderstood. The word *jihad*, often mistranslated as "holy war," appears only four times in the Qur'an. The verb form of the word, *jahada*, occurs about twenty-five times, while *mujahid* (one who makes jihad) appears another four times. The verb means to strive or struggle in the path of God, and the noun refers to that same struggle. The term for war is *harb*; "holy war," therefore, would be *harb muqaddas*. Those who wage war against society or fight such a war would be *muharibun*, a word that is discussed below. The Muslim tradition has distinguished between two types of jihad, the inner and the outer struggle in the path of God. The inner jihad is the personal struggle to become a better Muslim, and has nothing to do with war and violence.

Sufis, the mystics of Islam, are especially good at understanding this inner struggle. The struggle is familiar to adherents of any religion who try to temper inclinations toward evil with an ongoing commitment to righteousness.

The outer jihad is the effort to make one's society reflect the principles of submission to God. In this way, it can be a violent struggle, but it is also what Christians refer to as bearing faithful witness, living your faith in such a way as to affect the structures of society. The Prophet Muhammad said that the greatest jihad is to speak the truth to an unjust ruler. Unfortunately, some Muslims have understood outer jihad to be a struggle against Jews and Christians, citing Jews and Christians as unbelievers. However, I think this misses the meanings of the terms *belief* and *unbelief*. When the Qur'an addresses itself to believers, it is not speaking only to Muslims. The Qur'an is explicit here: "whoever believes in God and the Day of Judgment and does good, they shall have no fear, neither shall they grieve" (5:69). A believer is one who believes in the one true God and is thankful to God, whether Muslim, Jew, or Christian. Unbelievers, by definition, are not non-Muslims, but those who are not thankful to God.

Muslims commonly use the term *jihadists* for those who engage in this outer struggle with violence. In the 1980s, North American Christians, who have their own definitions of a "just war," did not necessarily consider this a bad thing. That was when the American government helped to arm the Afghan *mujahideen* (the plural of *mujahid*, or one who makes jihad) against the Soviet Union, which had invaded Afghanistan in 1979. The mujahideen at that time were famously described by President Ronald Reagan as "freedom fighters." Tragically, with the help of American military and economic support, many of these same people would become the Taliban who, two decades later, would be ousted by their former supporters.

Many North Americans today confuse the mujahideen with "terrorists." The latter are described by a term that Muslim legal scholars use: *muharibun* (those who make war against society). Khaled Abou El Fadl, one of the most brilliant Muslim legal scholars in North America, explores the muharibun in his book *The Great Theft: Wrestling Islam from the Extremists*. "The classical jurists, nearly without exception," he writes, "argued that those who attack by stealth, while targeting noncombatants in order to terrorize the resident and wayfarer, are corrupters of the earth . . . .; those guilty of this crime were considered enemies of humankind and were not to be given quarter or sanctuary anywhere."[7] It is clear, therefore, that the Muslim tradition itself distinguishes between those who struggle to make their society more Islamic, including those who engage in a "just war," and those who destroy society through terrorism and violence.

VIOLENCE AND ISLAMIC ORIGINS

War and Violence in the Life of Muhammad and in the Qur'an

Let us move to the issues of violence in the biography of Muhammad. Anyone teaching this biography in a course on Islam (or for that matter, an introductory course on world religion) must be aware that he or she cannot criticize, promote, or be objective about Muhammad without taking a political stand. Among the events that need particular attention in terms of how they are taught are the establishment of a Muslim community in Medina; the battles between Muhammad's community in Medina and the Meccans; the treatment of the Jews of Medina; and the conquest of Mecca. All of these events are discussed below. Here, I make no prescriptions about how they should be taught. One of the great pleasures of being a university instructor is the autonomy one has (or should have) in the content of one's courses. However people choose to frame these incidents in their classes, these are the events that need to be discussed.

Muhammad was born into a tribal and polytheistic world. Gross inequalities among people defined the society, and slavery was an accepted part of the historical milieu (as it was in Christian and Jewish settings at the time). In the prevailing patriarchal ethos, being a man meant protecting the tribe's honor, often entering into feuds with those who had done wrong. Justice was meted out not by judges but by tribal retribution. It was an age of the blood vendetta, familiar in modern times to those who know *The Godfather* trilogy of films. Pre-Islamic Arabia was also fairly isolated from the empires on its borders, being surrounded with water on three sides and desert to the north. The Byzantine Empire lay to the west, while the Sassanian Persian Empire was on the east. These empires had battled each other and were in decline by the time of Muhammad's birth.

When Muhammad began to preach, his message was not well received. This is not surprising, since he was challenging the society of his time. In a time of polytheism, he was preaching monotheism. In a world of drastic social inequality, he was preaching that everyone was equal before God, and that all people were slaves to God. In many ways, his message was similar to the one that Jesus preached some 600 years earlier in Palestine, and like Jesus's followers, Muhammad's disciples were persecuted. Bilal, the Ethiopian slave who later became a religious leader in Medina, was tortured by his owner for converting to Islam. Muhammad sent some of his most vulnerable followers to Ethiopia, where they were protected from persecution by Christians. The persecutions increased after the death of Muhammad's uncle, Abu Talib, who had provided protection to Muhammad. Soon Muhammad and his followers were forced to migrate to Medina, leaving most of their property behind in Mecca.

Permission to Fight in Islam

In Medina, Muhammad brought unity to the two rival Arab tribes and their Jewish allies who were all trying to control the city. In the Constitution of Medina, Muslims, the polytheistic Arabs, and the Jews were referred to as a single community (*ummah*). Here we see the interactions of religion and politics in early Islam. While the polytheistic Arabs and the Jews accepted Muhammad as their political leader, they were not required to embrace Islam, but they did have to obey Muhammad's political judgments. For the Muslim community, Muhammad was both a religious and political figure, a prophet and a statesman. It was in this context that Muslims believe that the first revelations allowing for war were sent down.

To this point, there was no sanction in the Qur'an for any kind of violent response to the persecution that the Muslims had endured. Then came the following verses of the Qur'an:

Permission is given to fight to those upon whom war is made, who were wronged. Truly God is well able to help them, those who were driven out of their homes unjustly, simply because they said our Lord is God. Did not God use some people to repel others, or else monasteries and churches and synagogues and mosques where the name of God is constantly mentioned would have been pulled down? Truly God will help those who help God. Surely God is Almighty. (22:39–40)

There also came these verses about the reward to those killed in fighting:

O you who have faith! be not like those who disbelieve and say of their brethren when they travel in the earth or engage in fighting: Had they been with us, they would not have died and they would not have been slain; so God makes this to be an intense regret in their hearts; and God gives life and causes death and God sees what you do. And if you are slain in the way of God or you die, certainly forgiveness from God and mercy is better than what they amass. And if indeed you die or you are slain, certainly to God shall you be gathered together. (3:156–58)

Muhammad and his followers felt justified, therefore, in raiding Meccan caravans that were selling goods that the Muslims had left behind during their emigration. In 624, the Meccans learned that Muhammad was going to raid one of their caravans at a watering station named Badr. The Meccans sent their army to that spot, and it was there that the first battle was fought. The Muslims were outnumbered but were able to defeat the Meccans. In the Muslim understanding, they were victorious because God had helped them (Qur'an 8:17). Later verses also spoke of the battle:

God had helped you at Badr, when you were a contemptible little band. So observe your duties toward God, and thereby show your gratitude. Remember when you [Muhammad] said to the believers: "Is it not enough that your Lord helped you with 3,000 angels sent down? If you remain steadfast and act aright, even if the enemy should come rushing headlong, your Lord would help you with 5,000 attacking angels." (Qur'an 3:123–25)

At the Battle of Badr, Muhammad took a number of Meccan captives. The fact that he did not kill his prisoners was out of character in the culture and is thus instructive for Muslim attitudes to war and vengeance. "Oh Prophet!" says the Qur'an in another revelation about the battle, "Say to those of the captives who are in your hands: If God knows anything good in your hearts, God will give to you better than that which has been taken away from you and will forgive you, and God is Forgiving, Merciful" (8:70). Chapter 8 of the Qur'an ("The Spoils of War") was revealed after the Battle of Badr, and makes further points about how the Muslims should fight against the polytheists of Mecca. It opens with the line that the spoils of war belong to God and God's Messenger. The implication is clear: One does not fight war for gain, since the rewards belong to God. The chapter also states clearly that while Muslims should prepare for war, they should also prepare for peace with the Meccans: "And if they incline to peace, then incline to it and trust in God; surely God is the Hearing, the Knowing" (8:61).

The Meccans achieved their revenge a year after the Battle of Badr, when they launched the Battle of Uhud (a hill not far from Medina). Among the Muslim casualties were Muhammad's beloved uncle Hamzah, and Muhammad himself was injured in the fighting. It was after Uhud that the following verses were revealed, which need to be discussed in relevant classes.

> Certainly God conferred a benefit upon the believers when God raised among them a Messenger from among themselves, reciting to them God's communications and purifying them, and teaching them the Book and the wisdom, although before that they were surely in manifest error. What! when a misfortune befell you, and you had certainly afflicted [the unbelievers] with twice as much, you began to say: Whence is this? Say: It is from yourselves; surely God has power over all things. And what befell you on the day when the two armies met was with God's knowledge, and that God might know the believers. And that God might know the hypocrites; and it was said to them: Come, fight in God's way, or defend yourselves. They said: If we knew fighting, we would certainly have followed you. They were on that day much nearer to unbelief than to belief. They say with their mouths what is not in their hearts, and God best knows what they conceal. Those who said of their brethren whilst they [themselves] held back: Had they obeyed us, they would not have been killed. Say: Then avert death from yourselves if you speak the truth. And reckon not those who are killed in God's way as dead; nay, they are alive and are provided sustenance from their Lord; Rejoicing in what God has given them out of God's grace and they rejoice for the sake of those who, [left] behind them, have not yet joined them, that they shall have no fear, nor shall they grieve. They rejoice on account of favour from God and grace, and that God will not waste the reward of the believers. For those who responded to the call of God and the Messenger after the wound had befallen them, those among them who do good and guard [against evil] shall have a great reward. Those to whom the people said: Surely men have gathered against you, therefore fear them, but this increased their faith, and they said: God is sufficient for us and most excellent is the Protector. So they returned with favour from God and grace, no evil touched them and they followed the pleasure of God; and God is the Lord of mighty grace. (3:164–74)

There are also these verses about those who do not fight when asked to fight:

> Those who were left behind were glad on account of their sitting behind God's Messenger and they were averse from striving in God's way with their property

and their persons, and said: Do not go forth in the heat. Say: The fire of hell is much severe in heat. Would that they understood. Therefore they shall laugh little and weep much as a recompense for what they earned. Therefore if God brings you back to a party of them and then they ask your permission to go forth, say: By no means shall you ever go forth with me and by no means shall you fight an enemy with me; surely you chose to sit the first time, therefore sit with those who remain behind. (9:81–83)

These verses continue:

And whenever a chapter is revealed, saying: Believe in God and strive hard along with God's Messenger, those having ampleness of means ask permission of you and say: Leave us [behind], that we may be with those who sit. They preferred to be with those who remained behind, and a seal is set on their hearts so they do not understand. But the Messenger and those who believe with him strive hard with their property and their persons; and these it is who shall have the good things and these it is who shall be successful. God has prepared for them gardens beneath which rivers flow, to abide in them; that is the great achievement. (9:86–89)

There are also these verses about fighting those who fight against you:

And fight in the way of God with those who fight with you, and do not exceed the limits, surely God does not love those who exceed the limits. And kill them wherever you find them, and drive them out whence they drove you out, and persecution is severer than slaughter, and do not fight with them at the Sacred Mosque until they fight with you in it, but if they do fight you, then slay them; such is the recompense of the unbelievers. But if they desist, then surely God is Forgiving, Merciful. And fight with them until there is no persecution, and religion should be only for God, but if they desist, then there should be no hostility except against the oppressors. (2:190–93)

Finally, there are these verses about those exempt from fighting:

It shall be no crime in the weak, nor in the sick, nor in those who do not find what they should spend [to stay behind], so long as they are sincere to God and God's Messenger; there is no way [to blame] against the doers of good; and God is Forgiving, Merciful; Nor in those who when they came to you that you might carry them, you said: I cannot find that on which to carry you; they went back while their eyes overflowed with tears on account of grief for not finding that which they should spend. The way [to blame] is only against those who ask permission of you though they are rich; they have chosen to be with those who remained behind, and God has set a seal upon their hearts so they do not know. (9:91–93)

It was in the wake of the battle of Uhud that Muhammad was forced to deal with one of the Jewish groups in Medina. According to Muslim tradition, one of the Jewish clans, sensing the weakness of the Muslims after the defeat at Uhud, attempted to kill the Prophet. As a result, this clan was banished from Medina. A similar situation had occurred following the Battle of Badr, when a different Jewish clan was accused of breaking a pact with the Muslims.

Two years after their victory at Uhud, the Meccans sought to complete their triumph by completely destroying the Muslims. In 627, they marched on Medina, joined by some of the Jews whom Muhammad had exiled. On the advice of a Muslim supporter, Salman the Persian, the Medinans created a trench around their city. As a result, the Meccan cavalry could not advance into Medina. The Meccans laid siege to the city, but ultimately they could gain no victory. The confederation that the Meccans had created began to break down, and they had to give up the siege and return to Mecca.

During the siege, another of the Jewish groups in Medina was accused of breaking their treaty with Muhammad and aiding the Meccans. As a result, the men of that tribe were ordered to be executed on the judgment of one of the Arab tribes in Medina. However, it is clear that Jews who were killed in the wake of these battles were executed for treachery and treason, for breaking their treaty with Muhammad, and for working toward the destruction of the Muslim community. They were not executed simply because they were Jews.

Muhammad negotiated a peace treaty with the Meccans in 628. Although it was designed to last ten years, it was violated by one of the allies of the Meccans after only two years. As a result, Muhammad and his forces marched on Mecca in 630 and entered the city in triumph, but largely without violence. Muhammad ordered that his army give sanctuary to those who sought it, and to fight only those who fought against them. According to Muslim tradition, only four opponents were killed because of their enmity toward Muhammad. While some may think of this number as four too many, this conquest clearly did not involve the tremendous casualties that warfare in Arabia normally entailed.

Having taken Mecca, Muhammad did something radical. He gathered the leaders of Mecca who had driven him out of the city of his birth and waged war against him for the past five years, and offered them amnesty. By tribal custom, he had every right to execute them, but he chose not to do so. Here Muhammad showed the magnanimity for which he is famous in the Muslim tradition. In freeing his persecutors, he quoted from the words that the Qur'an has Joseph (the son of Jacob) speak when he is reunited with the brothers who sold him into slavery: "This day there shall be no upbraiding of you nor reproach. God forgives you, and God is the Most Merciful of those who show mercy" (12:92). As a result of this generosity, even more people converted to Islam. In forgiving the Meccans, Muhammad did one of the hardest things for humans: he forgave his enemies. Love for enemies had long been the teaching of Jesus, but as many Christians admit, the fulfillment of the teaching is nearly impossible, and it is rarely seen to be practical in situations of military conflict. But for Muhammad, forgiveness was the only way forward, and the only way to break the cycle of vengeance and retribution.

Following the conquest of Mecca, Muslims believe, chapter 9 of the Qur'an was revealed. This chapter marked the final break between Muhammad and the polytheists of Arabia. This chapter is unusual in being the only one that does not begin with the standard opening, "In the name of God, the Beneficent, the Merciful." The chapter is titled "Repentance," and the fifth verse is known as the Verse of the Sword. It is often quoted by anti-Muslim polemicists, but not usually in its entirety. Verses 5 and 6 read:

> So when the sacred months have passed away, then slay the polytheists wherever you find them, and take them captive and besiege them and lie in wait for them in every ambush of war, but if they repent and keep up prayer and contribute to charity, leave their way free to them; surely God is Forgiving, Merciful. If any one of the polytheists ask you for asylum, grant it to them, so that they may hear the word of God; and then escort them to a place of safety. That is because they are a people who do not know. (9:5–6)

Clearly, this part of the Qur'an sanctions killing polytheists who do not denounce their polytheism. In this respect, one could compare the Muslim campaign against polytheists in Arabia to Israel's conquest of pagan peoples in Canaan in the biblical book of Joshua. While there is violence in the Qur'an, it is not an indiscriminate violence. Moreover, it is a violence that is contextualized, meaning it occurs in the context of warfare between Muslims and polytheists. Finally, it is a violence that is tempered, as the following verse indicates: "Fight in the cause of God those who fight you, but do not transgress limits. Surely God does not love the transgressors" (2:190). In teaching about Islamic history and the spread of Islam, one has to deal with issues of peace and violence. The next section discusses these issues, beginning with the spread of Islam outside of the Arabian peninsula and the violence associated with conversion.

The Spread and Historical Development of Islam

In the last two years of Muhammad's life, a number of tribes converted from polytheism to Islam, perhaps for a number of reasons: a fear of being killed if they did not convert; an acceptance of Muhammad's message; the personal charisma of the Prophet himself; or a desire to be included in the Muslim community. This last point is particularly important. At the time of Muhammad's death, he was not simply a religious leader but a political figure as well. Much of the Arabian peninsula had converted to Islam by this time, so Muhammad's political power encompassed an entire region. The early history of Christianity, by contrast, saw the political and the religious spheres united more than three centuries after Jesus, as the Armenians, then the Ethiopians, and finally the Romans adopted Christianity as a state religion. It is for this reason that there is relatively little violence and warfare in the New Testament; the development of principles for a "just war" coincided with the development of a state church. Moreover, unlike Islam, Christianity has free-church streams that regard the shift to an imperial Christianity as a corruption of the ideals of the earliest followers of Jesus. Muslims generally regard the convergence of religious and political power as a good thing.

There is a popular misconception among students that Islam was spread primarily by the sword with forced conversions. The historical record does not bear this out. While there certainly were forced conversions in the history of Islam, the majority of people converted by their own choice. Take for example the Persian kingdom, which was one of the first to be conquered by the early Muslims. According to historian Richard Bulliet of Columbia University, the conversions in that region happened over many generations. The state religion in Persia before Islam was Zoroastrianism. From the detailed tax records of the Sassanian Empire, one can trace how Zoroastrian surnames gave way to Muslim ones over time. Thus, over a period of almost 200 years, Persia evolved from a country with no Muslims to a country that was more than 80 percent Muslim.[8] This is a far cry from the image of Arab Muslims on horseback with swords in hand telling people to "convert or die."

Some of the primary agents of conversion were the Sufi mystics. Living among the non-Muslim population, their example and teaching slowly attracted people to Islam.[9] Muslim traders also helped in the spread of Islam, particularly in South and Southeast Asia. In many ways, this is no different from the less invasive ways that Christian missionaries spread Christianity. It is also worth remembering that after the Babylonian Exile (that is, after the sixth century B.C.E.) Judaism encouraged the conversion of non-Jews; the biblical books of Ruth and Jonah, in particular, seem to reflect such a vision of inclusion of non-Jewish people in God's salvation plan. Later, with the development of Christianity, Jewish proselytizers also sought to force Gentile Christians to become Jews.

It is true that Islam expanded rapidly, due to the success of the message preached, the superiority of Muslim military leaders and their tactics, and the historical weakness of both the Byzantine and Persian kingdoms. Over time, people under Muslim rulers gradually converted to Islam. Often, economic factors played a role in the conversion. Christian, Jewish, and Zoroastrian subjects did not have to convert to Islam, since they were considered People of the Book. They did not have to pay the *zakat*, the charity incumbent upon all Muslims, and they did not have to serve in the army. However, they were required to pay a special tax in recognition of their non-Muslim status. Here, it is important to note that some people converted to Islam to avoid paying this tax, indicating that economic reasons sometimes are a factor in decisions about religion.

In 638, Muslims conquered Jerusalem under the second caliph, Umar. According to Muslim tradition, Umar entered Jerusalem on foot because he and his servant shared a single mount, and it was his servant's turn to ride. This gives one an idea of both the humanity and humility of Umar. The conquest involved no bloodshed, and all of the inhabitants who wanted to leave were allowed to do so without incident. Umar was escorted around the city by the Greek Orthodox patriarch. When it came time for one of the daily prayers, Umar was in the Church of the Holy Sepulchre, one of the most important Christian sites in Jerusalem. When he asked for a place to say his prayers, the patriarch told him to pray where he stood. Umar refused, saying that his later followers, in their zeal, would want to commemorate the spot where Muslims first offered prayer in Jerusalem. This would mean converting the church into a mosque, which was not something Umar was willing to do. Instead, he prayed outside the church. Sure enough, that spot was eventually marked with the Mosque of Umar. Umar's actions show a spirit of interfaith dialogue and cooperation. To this day, in fact, the keys to the church gate are kept by a Muslim family, so that various Christian groups do not have to struggle with each other for that honor.

For the most part, Christians were allowed to practice their faith in Jerusalem, unhindered by Muslims. Sadly, the Caliph Al-Hakim destroyed the Church of the Holy Sepulchre in 1009, but he suffered from mental illness and persecuted Muslims as well as Jews and Christians. The church was rebuilt by the Byzantine emperor in 1048. In 1095, Pope Urban the Second called for a Crusade to regain Christian control of the Holy Land. His rationale was religious—that Muslims were not allowing Christians to worship freely. However, this was not entirely the case. There were also underlying economic causes, including a rising class of landless knights in Europe who were increasingly restless and poor. In Palestine, they could either acquire their own land or be killed trying, thereby eliminating them as a threat to the aristocracy of Europe. It is a fascinating exercise to read Muslim accounts of the Crusades, which reveal the economic and religious motivations of the crusaders. A fascinating study of how the Crusades affected the ways in which Muslims and Christians subsequently understood each other is Norman Daniel's magnificent book *Islam and the West: The Making of an Image.*

After the Crusades, the Ottoman Turks became the great rival for European Christians. The Ottomans adopted the crescent as their symbol in opposition to the Christian cross, and the crescent has remained as an important Muslim symbol. (The Red Cross, for example, is known as the Red Crescent in the Muslim world, and the crescent adorns the flags of Turkey, Pakistan, Algeria, and Tunisia.) The Ottoman Empire was in power as Europe began to regain its supremacy, with European expansionism beginning in the sixteenth century with the exploration of America. By the nineteenth century, most of the Muslim world was under the colonial domination of Europeans. This colonialism was sometimes described as the "white man's burden" (after Rudyard Kipling's poem on the occasion of the American conquest of the Philippines), or what the French called the *mission civilisatrice* (civilizing mission). As Robert D. Lee wrote in *Rethinking Islam*:

> The periphery became the centre, and the Islamic world found itself marginalised by European imperialism and universalism. Imperialism brought British and French troops, administrators, and merchants to the Middle East and imposed varying degrees of political, economic, and social subordination on the area. That process reached an apogee at Versailles after World War I, when the victors took it upon themselves to dismantle the defeated Ottoman Empire and establish a system of mandates for the governance of the Middle East. No Middle Easterner participated in the decisions.[10]

Much of today's violence in the Muslim world is rooted in the European colonial heritage. This of course does not excuse the violence; it simply situates the violence in its historical context.

MORE RECENT EVENTS IN THE MUSLIM WORLD
Iran and Afghanistan

Recently, especially with the occupation of Iraq, many in the West have been talk-ing about bringing democracy to the Muslim world. Seldom discussed is the fact that many Muslim countries resist democracy precisely because of their experi-ence of European and American colonialism, which is thoroughly explored in books such as John Esposito's *The Islamic Threat: Myth or Reality?* To take only two examples, I comment specifically on Iran and Afghanistan at the end of the twen-tieth century. In what follows, given the current political climate, I do not want to be perceived as anti-American. For fifteen years, I have chosen to live in Southern California. Because of my experience in the large, multicultural centers of Toronto, Vancouver, and Montreal, I feel at home in Los Angeles. As a Canadian, I under-stand how every nation wants to further its own best interests when it relates to the rest of the world. I have observed, however, that the American government has worked against the establishment of democratic reforms when they threaten American interests.

In the twentieth century, this has happened in a number of settings, including Guatemala, Brazil, Chile, and Haiti. It has also happened in the Muslim world, ulti-mately feeding the kind of violence we are seeing today. There is hope, however, in the "Arab Spring" of 2011 and subsequent events.

The Islamic Revolution in Iran

In 1953, the Shah of Iran was overthrown, and a nationalist government was estab-lished by Prime Minister Mohammad Mossadegh. This was to be an Iranian repub-lic, different from the military dictatorship of the shah. Before long, however, the CIA helped to engineer the shah's return to Iran and helped reestablish him in power. In return, the shah allowed American and British firms to run—and profit from—the Iranian oil industry. The United States supported the shah militarily and helped to train the shah's secret police.

Since Iranian democracy was not in the perceived best interests of the American government in 1953, they did not support it. As opposition to the shah's regime grew, one of the few places available to meet and discuss political issues was the mosque. The shah could shut down the bazaar where people gathered, fearing they might conspire to overthrow him. However, he could not shut down the mosques. In the years leading up to the 1979 revolution under Ayatollah Khomeini, a move-ment took shape that brought religious fervor together with a renewed desire for political change. Author Salman Rushdie himself, no fan of the Islamic Republic that Iran became, wrote in 1984: "We may not approve of Khomeini's Iran, but the revolution there was a genuine mass movement."[11]

The shah fled Iran in 1979, leaving power to Khomeini, who had been exiled over a decade earlier for his opposition to both the shah and the United States. Khomeini, a religious scholar, led the Shi'a clergy in giving shape to the revolution, establishing what would become a theocracy under shari'ah law. It was not surprising that the revolution was followed by a bitter war with Iraq that lasted for eight years. This war was not between religious factions, since both Iraq and Iran had Shi'a majority populations. Instead, it was a clash of dictatorships: Saddam Hussein's military dictatorship in Iraq versus Khomeini's theocratic dictatorship in Iran. Both wanted to preserve their own rule, as well as control the territory and resources—both human and economic—of the other.

The Iranian Revolution was crucial, however, to the aims of Muslim radicals the world over. It showed them that they could defeat a dictator, even one supported by the West, and that it was possible to establish an Islamic regime. This new confidence inspired other acts of violence in the name of religion. In November 1979, Sunnis seized control of the Grand Mosque in Mecca for two weeks. Subsequently, the Shi'as, who make up the majority in Arabia's Eastern Provinces, rioted against the Saudi government, which was Sunni. Both of these uprisings were quelled by the Saudis, but they signaled a willingness among Muslims to fight for what they thought was correct.

The Soviet Invasion of Afghanistan

The Soviet invasion of Afghanistan also occurred in 1979. In December, the Soviet Army assassinated President Hafizullah Amin and installed another president. The result was a decade-long war against the Soviets. Since this took place during the Cold War, the United States and its allies helped to fund and train the Afghan resistance, the mujahideen. As documented in Mahmood Mamdani's book *Good Muslim, Bad Muslim: America, the Cold War, and the Roots of Terror*, the U.S. Central Intelligence Agency was again instrumental in this intervention; the conflict was one of the largest and most expensive in the history of the CIA.

In some ways, one can regard this invasion as the beginning of a global movement for Muslim violence. Muslims were recruited from all over the world to fight the Soviets. Amazingly, they were able to defeat them. During this time, they were not seen as terrorists, but as freedom fighters, a portrayal that is supported by the movie *Rambo III*, in which a Green Beret goes to Afghanistan to help train the resistance after the Soviets capture his beloved mentor. Having armed the Afghanis to oust the Soviets, Americans were surprised to see these mujahideen turning their guns on each other in a brutal civil war, and then eventually on the United States after the Taliban government came to power.

Another surprise, seldom discussed today, is that in May 2001, four months before 9/11, the American government gave U.S. $43 million to the Taliban for their help in the War on Drugs. The aid was given in full knowledge that Osama bin Laden was active in anti-American terrorist camps in Afghanistan, and in the face of the Taliban's terrible record on human rights and the treatment of women. The American government's rationale for this grant was the Taliban's claim that the growing of opium was un-Islamic. I shudder to think what the Taliban did with that money.

TEACHING ABOUT ISLAM AND VIOLENCE POST-9/11: MEDIA
LITERACY AND ISLAMOPHOBIA

In the years before the terrorist attacks of 9/11, I would begin my courses on Islam with a standard historical introduction to the life of Muhammad and the beginnings of Islam.[12] I did this because my students—whether they were Muslim or not—often knew very little about Islam before they took my course. In the semester after 9/11, I found that this was no longer effective as the students came in with what they thought was a great deal of knowledge about Islam and the religious lives of Muslims. Unfortunately, most of their "knowledge" came from the popular media and was often at odds with the ways in which the majority of Muslims would understand their own faith. As a result, I began to use a book that described how television news works, where ratings and profit are much more important than the number of awards won for investigative journalism.[13] When what matters is ratings, the controversial and the provocative are privileged over the thoughtful and the accurate.

I mention this anecdote as it shows the power of the media in constructing our understandings of the world around us, including of course Muslims and Islam. Since most North Americans rely on television for their knowledge of world events, misleading information about Islam and Muslim lives is common. As a result, common perceptions are that Islam promotes violence, is more violent than any other religion, and oppresses women. Let us discuss the role of the media in shaping perceptions of Islam.

There is a growing amount of literature on religion and media. One thinks, for example, of the fine work of Stewart Hoover, Judith Buddenbaum and Debra Mason, Stewart Hoover and Lynn Clark, John Giggie and Diane Winston, and Claire Badaracco.[14] Their work has shown how religious groups use the media, as well as how the media understands, misunderstands, and covers religion. The Religion Newswriters Association (RNA), which Debra Mason directs, as well as the Religion and Media workshops at the American Academy of Religion arranged by S. Brent Plate, have been invaluable resources for both journalists and scholars. There have been good studies of how Muslims themselves are using the media. There are also excellent studies of how the media view and create representations of Islam. These views are often negative. For example, according to an online poll of RNA members, the top two religion news stories in 2006 were about Islam: reactions to the publication of cartoons about Muhammad in Denmark, and Pope Benedict XVI linking Islam and violence in a speech in Germany.[15]

Moving from the media in general to television in particular, the images of Muslims are also often negative. A useful exercise in an introductory class is to ask students about Muslim characters on television. At first, students are stumped as no immediate images come to mind. After some time, a student usually comes up with the cartoon character Apu from *The Simpsons*, but is quickly corrected by other students that Apu is a Hindu, not a Muslim. A loyal viewer might then recall the Muslim character of Bashir bin Laden on *The Simpsons*, who appeared in the episode "Mypods and Broomsticks." Dave Chapelle is perhaps the most famous Muslim on television, yet only a few of my students can identify him as such, and none of the major characters on *Chapelle's Show* are Muslim. Students do eventually come up with the characters of Sayid on *Lost*, Imam Kareem Said and the Black Muslims in *Oz*, or terrorists such as Marwan or Abu Fayed in *24*. Some mention characters from Showtime's *Sleeper Cell*. A select few mention professional wrestlers such as the Sheikh, Abdullah the Butcher ("the madman from Sudan"), the Iron Sheikh, Sabu ("homicidal, suicidal, and genocidal"), or Muhammad Hassan.

All of these characters are evil, violent men: the wrestlers are all villains ("heels"); Sayid is a former member of the Iraqi Republican Guard; Kareem Said and the Black Muslims are all prisoners; while the terrorists in *24* and *Sleeper Cell* are, well, terrorists. Only one major character, Darwyn Al-Sayeed from *Sleeper Cell*, is a good guy, an undercover FBI agent.[16] However, he too is heavily involved in violence and vengeance. These portrayals do not of course reflect the realities of American Muslim life, where American Muslims are a success story, equal in wealth and higher education to non-Muslims.

Newsweek did a cover story on Islam in America, highlighting a 2007 survey by the Pew Forum on Religion and Public Life which found that 26 percent of American Muslims had household incomes above $75,000 (as compared to 28 percent of non-Muslims) and 24 percent of American Muslims had graduated from university or had done graduate study (as compared to 25 percent of non-Muslims).[17] "The first-ever, nationwide, random sample survey of Muslim Americans finds them to be largely assimilated, happy with their lives, and moderate with respect to many of the issues that have divided Muslims and Westerners around the world."[18] The issue of representation is different in Canada, with the Canadian Broadcasting Corporation's sitcom *Little Mosque on the Prairie* (which has not as of this writing been picked up in the United States). In this show, one sees the poetry of ordinary Canadian Muslim lives enacted with humor on the small screen. Ironically, one of the major characters in the show, Canadian actor Carlo Rota, has had a role since 2006 in *24*.

Negative portrayals of American Muslims on television must have some correlation with the negative ways in which actual American Muslims are perceived and the Islamophobia that results. The violent actions of a tiny minority of Muslim terrorists are amplified when they are virtually the only images available on television. One sees this, for example, in a poll by the Pew Forum on Religion and Public Life following the terrorist attacks in London in July 2005. In that poll, 36 percent of Americans felt that Islam was more likely to encourage violence in its followers (which was down from 44 percent in 2003), while those holding unfavorable opinions of Islam increased slightly (from 34 percent to 36 percent between 2003 and 2005).[19] In 2006, the Council on American Islamic Relations (CAIR) recorded 1,972 civil rights complaints from American Muslims, up almost 30 percent from 2005 and the most ever recorded by CAIR in its twelve-year history.[20] Also in 2006, a poll by the *Washington Post*–ABC News showed that 46 percent of Americans had negative views of Islam, up from 39 percent after the 9/11 attacks.[21] This makes the task of the instructor for an Islam course different from that of other courses in religion, where students may come in ignorant but usually not with preconceived biases. It may be necessary to de-exoticize Buddhists or Hindus, but one almost has to convince students that Muslims also possess the full measure of humanity.

Muslims in American Films

The portrayal of American Muslims is not markedly different in film than in television. The classic study of Arabs in Hollywood films is *Reel Bad Arabs* by Jack Shaheen, which describes over 900 films that portray Arabs. Shaheen describes Hollywood's portrayal of Arabs as the "systematic, pervasive and unapologetic degradation and dehumanization of a people."[22] In 2006, Sut Jhally made a one-hour documentary film of the same name, which is available from the Media Education Foundation, and is a good introduction to Shaheen's thesis about the misrepresentations of Arabs.[23] After the collapse of the Soviet Union, the standard "bad guys" shifted from Communists to Arabs. Another excellent resource is the short film *Planet of the Arabs*, made by Jackie Salloum in the form of a trailer, which collects the most stereotypically violent portrayals of Muslims and Arabs.[24]

Rubina Ramji has written an excellent article expanding the misrepresentation of Arabs to include other Muslims. Her article, available in the online *Journal of Religion and Film*, is required reading for anyone interested in the topic.[25] The article pairs well with the documentary and the short film, and all three can be discussed in one week's class. Ramji notes that following the 9/11 terrorist attacks, rentals of videos such as *True Lies* (1994), *Air Force One* (1997), and *The Siege* (1998), all of which feature Muslim terrorists, increased dramatically. In the case of *Air Force One*, whose plot revolves around Muslim terrorists hijacking the president's plane, the film was renting ten times more in Canada than before the attacks. Clearly, people were turning to films in light of current events. Given both the negative portrayals of Muslims in films and the popularity of those films post-9/11, it is important for instructors to address this in courses on Islam.

Since most of our students get their information about Islam and Muslim lives from television, it is important to begin with how television news works. I also use a videotape of Bill Moyers on *NOW* interviewing Jon Stewart about *The Daily Show with Jon Stewart*. My students are admirers of Stewart's work and agree with me that the "fake" news that he presents is much better than the "real" news. I have also brought guests from local television stations into my class to talk about ratings and how important they are to the local news. It can be quite a useful exercise to bring in someone from a local news station to discuss how the news works.

In the introductory packet of readings for my Islam class, I include Edward R. Murrow's famous 1958 speech to the Radio and Television News Directors Association.[26] Among the most prophetic lines, more important a half-century after they were first spoken, are these:

> We are currently wealthy, fat, comfortable and complacent. We have currently a built-in allergy to unpleasant or disturbing information. Our mass media reflect this. But unless we get up off our fat surpluses and recognize that television in the main is being used to distract, delude, amuse and insulate us, then television and those who finance it, those who look at it and those who work at it, may see a totally different picture too late.

It is a version of this speech that begins the 2005 film *Good Night, and Good Luck* (directed by George Clooney), and so the first scene of this film, with David Strathairn as Murrow, can be quite useful in the classroom.

THE COMPLEXITIES OF "MUSLIM VIOLENCE"

It surprises many North Americans that most Muslims are opposed to violence and terrorism. Like all people, Muslims also want to live in peace and safety. That this has to be made explicit indicates the sorry state of understanding between Muslims and non-Muslims. I cannot remember the last time I gave a talk to a non-Muslim group in the past decade where someone did not ask me hostile questions about Islam and violence. I am reminded of a story by the American folk singer Arlo Guthrie. Knowing his work for social justice, someone asked him to join a group of artists and musicians against hunger, to which Guthrie replied incredulously, "You mean there are artists and musicians *for* hunger?"

A few Muslims are actively involved in peace and justice groups such as the Muslim Peace Fellowship, which has existed since 1994 in the United States and is affiliated with the Fellowship of Reconciliation. These groups have strenuously worked to contradict the claim, often repeated in the American media since 9/11, that Muslims have not condemned terrorism. One still encounters this disturbing perception repeatedly—in letters to the editor in local American newspapers, as well as in right-wing Web sites that are easily found on the Internet. But the record is clear: hours after the horrors of 9/11, the Muslim Public Affairs Council, the Council on American Islamic Relations, and the American Muslim Political Coordination Council all issued statements condemning the attacks and offering their resources to help the victims. On the following Friday, September 14, Muslim leaders around the world condemned the attacks in their Friday sermons. Shaykh al-Tantawi of Egypt's Al-Azhar University, one of the most respected Sunni institutions, declared: "It is not courageous to attack innocent children, women and civilians. It is courageous to protect freedom, it is courageous to defend oneself and not to attack." Significantly, both Iranian President Mohammed Khatami and Sheikh Fadlallah, the spiritual leader of Hizbullah, said that the attacks were barbaric and un-Islamic. At the end of this chapter is an appendix that lists these sources, as well as more recent Web sources about Muslims who have condemned terrorism and violence.

SUICIDE TERRORISM

Another common misconception among students is that Muslims value suicide bombing. As in other religious traditions, suicide is explicitly forbidden in Islam. It is seen as challenging the authority of God, who determines the span of human lives. So, for example, the Qur'an states: "Do not kill yourselves, truly God is Merciful to you" (4:29). It is true that the Qur'an promises a heavenly reward to those who die in defense of the faith (the relevant verses are cited earlier), but suicide is not part of that vision:

Oh you who believe! Be not like those who disbelieve and say of their brethren when they travel in the earth or engage in fighting: Had they been with us, they would not have died and they would not have been slain; so God makes this to be an intense regret in their hearts; and God gives life and causes death and God sees what you do. And if you are slain in the way of God or you die, certainly forgiveness from God and mercy is better than what they amass. And if indeed you die or you are slain, certainly to God you will be gathered together. (3:156–58)

Also contrary to popular belief, the Qur'an never specifies that martyrs will receive a certain number of virgins as part of their reward. So why do some Muslims conduct suicide bombings in the name of their faith? It is true that some see this as a legitimate opportunity for martyrdom, and a tiny minority of Muslim scholars have offered justification for these heinous acts. David Cook has written an excellent scholarly book on this issue, which can be discussed in upper-division classes.[27]

In discussions of martyrdom, an important resource is the Mardin Conference that took place in Turkey in March 2010. Mardin was a fortress where a thirteenth-century Muslim jurist, Ibn Taymiyyah, issued a series of famous fatwas justifying violence against unjust rulers. It is these fatwas that are used by many terrorists as religious justification for their attacks, and Osama bin Laden has often quoted from them in his sermons and writings.[28] The Mardin Conference brought fifteen senior Islamic scholars from across the Muslim world to the same fortress, where they discussed the context of Ibn Taymiyyah's rulings some 700 years earlier. Ibn Taymiyyah, writing in the aftermath of the Mongol conquest and devastation of Baghdad (the seat of Islamic authority at the time), went against the teachings of his own conservative Hanbali school to allow violence against authoritarian rulers to re-establish Islamic rule. Not only did the fifteen scholars contextualize Ibn Taymiyyah's fatwas, they concluded that "anyone who seeks support from this fatwa for killing Muslims or non-Muslims has erred in his interpretation." They also concluded, "It is not for a Muslim individual or a group to announce and declare war or engage in combative jihad . . . .on their own."[29] Clearly, there are complex issues here about Islamic authority and legality that need to be discussed.

If one looks beneath the surface, one often discovers economic and political motivations for suicide terrorism in addition to religious ones. The case of the Israeli-Palestinian conflict makes this clear. Palestinian terrorists do not attack Israelis because they are Jews but because of the political and economic ramifications of the Israeli occupation of Palestine. It is also understandable that a young Palestinian man who has no hope for a reasonable future in the Occupied Territories would volunteer to blow himself up if his family would receive financial support from a sponsoring organization.

Another bit of information that students in the West tend to forget is that suicide bombing is not only a Muslim phenomenon. In fact, Robert Pape, in his brilliant book *Dying to Win: The Strategic Logic of Suicide Terrorism*, indicates that from

1980 to 2004 the world leader in suicide terrorism was not a Muslim group but the Tamil Tigers (a separatist Hindu group) in Sri Lanka.[30]

THE DUPLICITY OF OUR GOVERNMENTS: STATE TERRORISM

As we examine the actions of individual terrorists, we cannot hide from a larger reality that often provides context for such acts: the violence and terror perpetrated by states. To return to the Israeli-Palestinian scene, when a Palestinian civilian kills an Israeli soldier, our media rightly call it an act of terrorism. However, when an Israeli soldier kills a Palestinian civilian, that is usually termed a security operation, not an act of terrorism. Again, let me be very clear: I condemn all terrorism and violence. On a personal note, I have been in a café in Jerusalem, afraid that I might be killed by a Palestinian suicide bomber. But in Israel I have also been afraid of being killed in a military operation or shot by an Israeli settler. None of those options, of course, is acceptable to me. But when I raise the larger issues among audiences who are both pro-Zionist and anti-Palestinian (and there is significant difference between those two terms), I am often accused of being unhelpful.

Many students find it difficult to examine complex roots of a problem; it is much simpler to treat the immediate symptoms. The late Brazilian Archbishop Dom Helder Camara once said: "When I give food to the poor, they call me a saint. When I ask why the poor have no food, they call me a communist." To apply that complaint to the terrorism discussion, some people rightly want to condemn terrorism but do not want to ask the deeper questions of why people resort to terrorism. But we must address the deeper questions if we want to put an end to terrorism.

In Israeli-Palestinian discussions in the classroom and on the campus, therefore, let us certainly bring to the table the violence of suicide bombers and other terrorists. But let us also bring larger inequities and prejudices, such as the following. First, automatic entitlement to Israeli citizenship based on religious identity: while there are Arabs (both Christian and Muslim) who have Israeli citizenship, they are a minority and they do not have rights equal to Jewish Israelis. Second, the extent of casualties: by conservative estimates, Israelis have killed three times more Palestinians than the number of Israelis killed by Palestinians. Third, simplistic understandings of complex communities: Although 15 percent of Palestinians are Christians with very deep historical roots, North Americans think of them almost entirely as Muslims. We think of Palestinian actions as being rooted in their Muslim faith. Ironically, we do not think of the actions of the Israeli Defense Forces—Jewish soldiers defending a Jewish state—as being Jewish.

When the state kills in our name, we tend not to think of that as violence. By the end of 2001, some three months after the war in Afghanistan began, U.S. armed forces with the help of coalition forces (including Canadian soldiers) had killed more than 3,000 Afghanis in our war with them. This was approximately equal to the number killed in the terrorist attacks of 9/11. Even more disturbing is that by conservative estimates, some 20,000 Iraqis had been killed by just the third anniversary of the invasion of Iraq, almost seven times the number who perished in 9/11. All this took place ostensibly as part of the "war on terrorism," even though no link was ever demonstrated between Saddam Hussein's dictatorship in Iraq and the terrorist attacks of 9/11. By comparing the numbers of victims, I am not advocating any calculus of suffering. The loss of one person is already a tragedy. Yet the losses among our enemies usually do not figure in our thinking.

OUR OWN VIOLENCE

Just as some of our students are blind to the violence of our governments, they may also ignore the violence in their own culture and in their own lives. Of course, this differs depending on the population of students that our universities serve. We may not think much about the history of violence in North America, particularly the violent impact of European colonialism on the indigenous peoples of the Americas. Christian students may similarly forget or downplay the Christian affiliations and commitments of the Nazis, whose religion failed to stop them from carrying out the Holocaust. They may be unaware of the violent atrocities committed by the Lord's Resistance Army in Uganda. They may forget the religious affiliation of those who perpetrated the Rwandan genocide in 1994, or the Srebrenica massacre in 1995. They may be ignorant of the death toll in the 1998–2002 civil war in the Congo, in which millions of Christians and practitioners of traditional African religions (and very few Muslims) have killed each other. Or closer to home, they may think that they abhor violence, yet blithely glorify it in hymns like "The Battle Hymn of the Republic" (one of the hymns that was sung at the first United Methodist Church service I ever attended when I began teaching at Cal State Northridge, where the guest preacher was my department chair).

Depending on our university, we may be isolated from the violence that is all around us. In contemporary America, some 10,000 people are murdered annually by handguns; almost the same number die in handgun suicides. Since the reinstatement of the death penalty in the United States in 1976, over 1,200 people have been executed by the state. One of the most serious issues faced by young people in our cities is gang life. Our movies, television shows, video games, and music all celebrate a culture of violence. In 2006, for example, the Academy Award for best original song went to "It's Hard Out Here for a Pimp," which glorifies the sexual and economic exploitation of women.

Violence is therefore integrated into the very structure of our society. We live in a complex web in which the violence "out there" is connected to our own violence in more ways than we may acknowledge. It is tempting to project our own violence onto someone else, preferably someone—a nation, an ethnic group, or a religion—that is markedly different from us. Without excusing any of the violence committed by Muslims, one can see how it is often connected to economic exploitation, military occupation, or the achievement of political goals. However, it is usually simply labeled as "Muslim violence," as if religion is the sole motivation for the violence. It is much simpler to blame 9/11 and other terrorist acts on Muslims in general than on specific Muslims who have departed from their coreligionists in their own religious ideals. This leads to misoislamia, which needs to be countered. Even to acknowledge that not all Muslims are terrorists, however, does not get at the root of the problem. While it takes a great deal of analysis, humility, and courage, the kind of acknowledgment we all need these days is that we and our society are, to a great extent, enmeshed in and part of the violence we decry. Insomuch as that enmeshment is primarily between Muslims and Christians, that is the very reason why we need to learn to dialogue more deeply together.

APPENDIX

American Muslim Reactions to the Attacks on September 11, 2001

From the Muslim Public Affairs Council

In response to the criminal attacks against targets in New York City and Washington, DC, the Muslim Public Affairs Council issued the following statement:

1. We feel that our country, the United States, is under attack
2. All Americans should stand together to bring the perpetrators to justice
3. We warn against any generalizations that will only serve to help the criminals and incriminate the innocent
4. We offer our resources and resolve to help the victims of these intolerable acts, and we pray to God to protect and bless America[31]

From the American Muslim Political Coordination Council

American Muslims utterly condemn what are apparently vicious and cowardly acts of terrorism against innocent civilians. We join with all Americans in calling for the swift apprehension and punishment of the perpetrators. No political cause could ever be assisted by such immoral acts.[32]

From CAIR

CAIR is calling on Muslims nationwide to offer whatever assistance they can to help the victims of today's terrorist attacks in New York and Washington, D.C.

Muslims in local communities should take the following IMMEDIATE ACTIONS:

> *Muslim medical professionals are asked to go to the scenes of the attacks to offer aid and comfort to the victims.
> *Muslim relief agencies should contact their counterparts to offer support in the recovery efforts.

*Individual Muslims should donate blood by contacting the local office of the Red Cross. (Call 1-800-GIVE-LIFE.) They should also send donations to those relief agencies that are on the scene of the attacks.[33]

Statements from Muslim Leaders Across the World on Friday, September 14

Leaders of Muslim communities around the Arab world today repeated their condemnation of the terror attacks on US trade and military landmarks as brutal and un-Islamic. Sheikh Mohammed Sayyed al-Tantawi of Al-Azhar, the highest institution in Sunni Islam, warned that those who attack innocent people will be punished by Allah, in his weekly sermon to thousands of worshippers in Cairo. "Attacking innocent people is not courageous, it is stupid and will be punished on the day of judgement," the moderate Sheikh Tantawi said at Al-Azhar mosque. "It's not courageous to attack innocent children, women and civilians. It is courageous to protect freedom, it is courageous to defend oneself and not to attack," he said.

In Lebanon the spiritual guide of pro-Iranian Shiite Muslim extremists, Sheikh Mohammed Hussein Fadlallah, said the "barbaric" attacks were un-Islamic. Sheikh Fadlallah said the attacks that destroyed the World Trade Center in New York and part of the Pentagon in Washington were "acts of suicide which are not rewarded [by Islam] because they are crimes. These are not operations of martyrdom which are carried out with the aim of jihad [struggle] with legitimate means and in circumstances which justify those means," he told the press.

Sheikh Fadlallah, who earlier said he was "horrified" by the attacks, said they would not serve the interests of Muslims and Arabs, particularly the Palestinians. "Beside the fact that they are forbidden by Islam, these acts do not serve those who carried them out but their victims, who will reap the sympathy of the whole world," he said. "Islamists who live according to the human values of Islam could not commit such crimes," said the sheikh, who is considered close to the liberal movement of moderate Iranian President Mohammed Khatami. "It's a horrible massacre on every level with no positive results for the basic causes of Islam, such as the Palestinian cause which now risks suffering a serious setback." He said that as Muslims and Islamists "we are opposed to the American government" because of its "absolute support for the Zionist enemy [Israel]." "But we want to be friends with the American people and we can by no means blame the American people and carry out such barbaric acts," he said.[34]

Palestinian Reactions: A Letter from a Methodist Minister in Jerusalem

[One of the images broadcast in the aftermath of 9/11 was of Palestinians celebrating the attacks. This letter was written by Rev. Sandra Olewine, who at the time was the Jerusalem liaison for the United Methodist Church. The letter was sent out to members of that denomination in response to those images.]

Dear Friends,

In these days when much of the world reels from the heinous actions of hijackers using passenger jets as "flying bombs" into major buildings in the US, likely killing thousands, certainly injuring tens of thousands and leaving families the world over grief stricken and lost, words and images should be carefully chosen, particularly by those in leadership and in the media.

These acts raise the term "terrorism" to an unprecedented level. Most acts ever given this designation pale in the face of the massive human loss and destruction. Never again will any of us step foot on a plane and not remember, at least for a fleeting moment, what happened in New York City, Washington DC and Pennsylvania. For many, and particularly for many Americans, the recognition of human vulnerability has never been as clear as it is in these days.

We humans often don't live well in the midst of such vulnerability. We try to create a sense of stability and security in our environment by whatever means necessary in order to cope with disruption, death and grief. Retreating to "safe spaces" and finding someone to blame, someone towards whom to direct our anger and despair, is not difficult to understand. But, sometimes such "retreating" can lead to a strong urge to "protect ourselves against them" whomever "them" might be.

As I watch the scenes which are displayed on television and listen to the words of some of the American leadership, I am dismayed by the careless and blanket statements concerning Muslims in particular and Arabs in general which are being expressed. The need to create "security" by blaming evil deeds on an entire tradition of people does not do justice to the lives of those killed. The work of 20, 50, 100, or 1,000 should not lead us to make blanket assumptions or statements about over a billion people. In every country, in every tradition, in every race, there are people who act out of malice and hatred to destroy others. Surely we Americans have not forgotten that the last horrible terrorist act carried out in our country was by ourselves.

I've had numerous emails from people asking me to help interpret the scenes they have watched of Palestinians "celebrating" after the event. Yes, there were some gatherings of people, particularly in Nablus, who were shown in the very early hours of the horrible attacks in the US on the street, dancing and cheering, and passing out chocolate. But, these expressions were few and certainly did not represent the feelings or mood of the general population. The deep shock and horror of the Palestinian people, the real sorrow for all the dead and wounded, was, and continues to be, unseen by the world, particularly in the USA. It is the story unheard.

Because those few scenes were disturbing, the easy response is to cast judgment on the participants, naming those "celebrating" as inhuman, despots, or despicable. The more difficult response, though, particularly in the midst of grief, is to ask the questions about what might drive people, men, women and children, to such actions. One might remember that the people who were seen "celebrating" are a people who for almost a year have been under a brutal siege, who due to the siege have been unable to feed their families and hover on the brink of poverty and despair, who have watched their children and their parents killed by bullets, tank shells and guided missiles, most of which are supplied to the Israeli Occupation

Army by the USA. One might remember such things as one watches those images. Attempting to understand motivations doesn't discount our feelings of anguish at such scenes, but does allow us to keep humanity a bit more intact in a time of such utter brokenness. But, more important to me is what has mostly gone unseen by the American public. I have to ask why these scenes of a few Palestinians have been shown again and again and again, as if they capture the "truth" of Palestine. How few cameras have caught the spontaneous sorrow, despair, tears and heartache of the vast majority of the Palestinian people. As the news unfolded here on Tuesday afternoon about the extent of the attacks, people gathered, as people did everywhere, in front of television screens to learn as much as possible. My phone rang and rang as Palestinians from around the West Bank called to express their horror and their condolences.

Yesterday following a prayer service held at St. George's Anglican Cathedral, I talked briefly to the US Consul General in Jerusalem. We talked about the scenes from here which were most prevalent on the TV. He told me that his office had received a stack of faxes of condolences from Palestinians and Palestinian Organizations "this high" (indicating a stack of about 12 inches). He asked his staff to fax a copy of every last one of them to CNN to give a different visual image from Palestine.

When we left the cathedral after the service, we drove by the American Consulate in East Jerusalem. Gathered there were about 30 Palestinian Muslim schoolgirls with their teachers. Looking grief-stricken, they held their bouquets of dark flowers and stood behind their row of candles. Silently, they kept vigil outside our Consulate. But no cameras captured their quiet sorrow.

When I got home, my neighbor explained that her son who is in 8th grade came home in the afternoon and talked to her about the students' reactions at school. He told her that everyone was talking about what had happened. He said that many were asking "how could someone do that?" "Is someone human who can carry out such acts?" He went on to tell her that many of the girls were crying. Friends, then, began stopping by my home. Palestinian Christian and Muslim came together, visiting me to express their sorrow and to ask what they could do. Again, the phone rang incessantly with Palestinians asking if everyone I knew was okay and asking if they could do anything to help.

As we talked many went on to tell of stories of their loved ones who are in the States—relatives they were worried about having been injured or killed or who had been subject to harassment in the last couple of days. Others talked of having received emails from people who had been supporters of their work who wrote saying "I can never again support the Palestinian people," as if somehow Palestinians everywhere were suddenly responsible for the attacks in the States.

The remarkable thing to me, though, was that despite such messages, these same people still wrote letters of condolences, made phone calls to friends, and asked what they could do to help. Despite the world, and particularly the American world, not seeing them or seeing them only as "terrorists," Palestinians continued to express their common humanity with people everywhere as they shared in the heartache and dismay.

In a separate message I will forward to you some of the condolences which have gone out. I pray you will share them widely in order to share the sorrow, in order that this part of the story also might be heard.

Lastly, I also want to express my gratitude to the many of you who have written notes of concern, expressing your prayers, for the people here, worrying about how this situation will impact the lives of all living in this region. In the midst of your own suffering and anxiety, your own horror what has happened, your heart was large enough, your vision wide enough, to still see the suffering and anxiety of others. This is no small gift and is a true mark of the grace of God.

Trusting in God's everlasting presence,

Sandra

Rev. Sandra Olewine

United Methodist Liaison—Jerusalem[35]

Statement from Scholars of Islam

Monday, September 17, 2001

On behalf of our membership, drawn from the U.S., Canada and several other countries, we are grief-stricken at the horrifying events of this past week. Yet as scholars of the Islamic religion, we must take time from our grief, and the counselling of our students, to help prevent the continuing persecution of Muslims on American soil.

The attacks on the Pentagon and the World Trade Center are nothing short of murder. Those office workers did nothing wrong, nothing to deserve such a terrible fate, and the murder of innocents can never be justified and must not be tolerated. Anger and frustration at the death of these men and women are completely understandable and shared by us all, yet that anger must not be directed at individuals utterly innocent of these terrible crimes. We have heard and witnessed many reports of verbal and physical attacks against Muslims (and people who were thought to be Muslims) throughout the U.S., and Muslims have been warned to stay home or to avoid wearing traditional dress. Our own Muslim students, many of whom come from South Asia, Africa or the Middle East, are fearful of what may happen to them in the days to come.

Particularly distressing is the fact that many American Muslims have fled to the United States, seeking a haven from intolerant regimes in Kosovo, Afghanistan or Iraq. For them now to face intolerance and violence here is an abuse of our Nation's most deeply cherished beliefs. Likewise, many of our Muslim students have only just arrived in this country, seeking here new hope and solutions for the poverty and violence they face at home.

Statements of hate or racial slurs are not a part of the American way, and we join President Bush and others calling on all Americans to respect the rights of Muslim Americans. Further, we urge people of good faith everywhere to reach out to Muslim neighbors. Churches, synagogues and temples should hold interfaith services of mourning, arrange for pot luck dinners together and work to heal the rifts that recent events have caused. Muslims from overseas should be invited to tell their stories. We should learn about the poverty and authoritarian regimes that they have fled, not to increase our pride in the United States, but to learn ways we can help alleviate the social and political diseases that cause disaffected young men to see Muslim extremists as leaders. We believe that education is the antidote to further violence on both sides. American Muslims are good neighbors, devoted to their families and to following God's commands to do good works.

There are now some eight million Muslims in the United States, and mosques are to be found in most every major city. The overwhelming majority are peace-loving human beings who share the shock and despair of all Americans. They know that terrorist acts in the name of Islam are a perversion of their most sacred beliefs, and the actions of a few should not characterize the whole.

With over 1 billion adherents, Islam is the second-largest religion in the world after Christianity. Like Christians and Jews, Muslims believe in one God who has sent a series of prophets into the world "to command the good and forbid the evil." Jesus is revered in the Qur'an, the scripture of Islam, as are Abraham, Moses and the Virgin Mary. According to Muslims, the Qur'an was revealed to the Prophet Muhammad some 600 years after Jesus' birth. It was written in Arabic, and Arabic is still the religious language of Islam.

But only 20% of all Muslims are Arabs (and about 50% of all Arab-Americans are Christian). Most are from the Indian subcontinent, Southeast Asia or Africa. Although many Muslims might differ with Israeli policy, Muslims do not hate Jews; rather Muslims honor Jews and Christians as fellow recipients of "the book," God's revelation to all humankind. In fact, the Qur'an commands all Muslims "If they incline toward peace, then you should too!" Suicide is utterly forbidden in Islam, and war must be declared by the State, not by individuals.

These injunctions explain clear statements by the governments of Syria, Saudi Arabia and Libya denouncing Tuesday's attacks. Radical groups like Hamas have also denounced it, along with the Palestinian leadership. Such political statements must be taken seriously as they are backed up by all major religious authorities, from the Rector of al-Azhar University to the Grand Mufti of Saudi Arabia, who forbid suicide missions, especially terrorist attacks against civilians. Just this past Friday, Sheikh Mohammed Sayyed al-Tantawi of Al-Azhar, the highest institution in Sunni Islam, denounced the attack on the World Trade Center and the Pentagon. In his weekly sermon to thousands of worshippers in Cairo, he said: "Attacking innocent people is not courageous; it is stupid and will be punished on the day of judgment." Sheikh Tantawi added "It's not courageous to attack innocent children, women and civilians. It is courageous to protect freedom, it is courageous to defend oneself and not to attack." Likewise, President Mohammad Khatami of Iran in an official statement said: "On behalf of the Iranian government and the nation, I condemn the hijacking attempts and terrorist attacks on public centers in American cities which have killed a large number of innocent people."

As scholars of religious traditions, we observe that religious symbols are used for political motives all over the world in Hindu, Christian, Jewish, and Muslim traditions. However, we must critically distinguish between politically motivated deployment of religious symbols and the highest ideals that these traditions embody. Just as most would regard bombers of abortion clinics to be outside the pale of Christianity, so the actions of these terrorists should not be accepted as representing Islam in any way.

As Tuesday's events gradually shift into the past, the horror of what has occurred becomes even clearer. Many of us have been hit personally by these attacks; we grieve, we cry and we search for answers. Let us now join together as Americans and respond to this act of hatred with compassion and understanding, reaching out to our Muslim neighbors and stopping the cycle of violence.[36]

Fatwa (Legal Opinion) from Spanish Muslims on March 11, 2005

Muslim clerics in Spain have issued what they called the world's first fatwa, or Islamic edict, against Osama bin Laden as the country marked the first anniversary of the Madrid train bombings that killed 191 people. They accused him of abandoning his religion and urged others of their faith to denounce the al Qaeda leader, who is believed to be hiding out near the Pakistan-Afghanistan border. The ruling was issued by the Islamic Commission of Spain, the main body representing the country's 1 million-member Muslim community. The commission invited imams to condemn terrorism at Friday prayers. The fatwa said that according to the Koran "the terrorist acts of Osama bin Laden and his organization al Qaeda . . . are totally banned and must be roundly condemned as part of Islam."[37]

Web Resources

Islamophobia: Excellent discussions of Islamophobia can be found on Tabsir, the Web Site run by Hofstra University anthropologist Daniel Martin Varisco, and on the Religion Dispatches site: http://tabsir.net/?cat=24; http://www.religiondispatches. org/tags/islamophobia/.

Smear Casting: How Islamophobes Spread Fear, Bigotry and Misinformation (a report by Fairness and Accuracy in Reporting about Islamophobia in the media): http://smearcasting.com/pdf/FAIR_Smearcasting_Final.pdf.

One often hears the line that Muslims have not condemned terrorism and violence. This Web site documents examples of various Muslim voices against terrorism. Muslim Voices Against Terrorism: http://www.theamericanmuslim.org/tam.php/ features/articles/muslim_voices_again st_extremism_and_terrorism_2/.

The Muslim Public Affairs Council has a national grassroots campaign to fight terrorism, with the following brochure that encourages "co-operation with all levels of law enforcement": http://www.mpac.org/publications/campaign-to-fight-terrorism/campaign-to-fight-terrorism-brochure.pdf.

NOTES

1. I sent in a letter to the editor asking for more information about the choice of photographs. That letter was never answered.
2. Keith Olbermann is to be singled out among journalists for his willingness to address the serious issues of misoislamia. See for example the "final comment" segment of his daily television show on August 16, 2010, available on the Web: http://www.youtube.com/watch?v=QZpT2Muxoo0.
3. Amir Hussain, "Teaching about Hindus and Muslims in the USA: 'And All They Will Call You Will Be Deportee,'" in *Teaching about Asian-Pacific Islanders: Effective Activities, Strategies, and Assignments for Classrooms and Communities*, ed. Edith Chen and Glenn Omatsu (Lanham, MD: Rowman and Littlefield, 2006), 139–52; Amir Hussain, "Teaching Inside-Out: On Teaching Islam," *Method and Theory in the Study of Religion* 17/3 (2005): 248–63; Amir Hussain, "Site Visit to a Mosque," *Spotlight on Teaching, Religious Studies News—AAR Edition* 19/4 (October 2004): xviii.
4. For example, see Brannon Wheeler, ed., *Teaching Islam* (New York: Oxford University Press, 2002); Mark Berkson, "A Non-Muslim Teaching Islam: Pedagogical and Ethical Challenges," *Teaching Theology and Religion* 8/2 (2005): 86–88; Khaldoun Samman, "Towards a Non-essentialist Pedagogy of 'Islam,'" *Teaching Theology and Religion* 8/3 (2005): 164–71; Amir al-Islam, "Educating American Muslim Leadership (Men and Women) for the Twenty-First Century," *Teaching Theology and Religion* 9/2 (2006): 73–78.
5. For example, see Eliza Griswold, *The Tenth Parallel* (New York: Farrar, Straus and Giroux, 2010); Khaled Abou El Fadl, *The Great Theft: Wrestling Islam from the Extremists* (New York: HarperCollins, 2005); Roxanne Euben, *Enemy in the Mirror: Islamic Fundamentalism and the Limits of Modern Rationalism* (Princeton, NJ: Princeton University Press, 1999); Reuven Firestone, *Jihad: The Origin of Holy War in Islam* (New York: Oxford University Press, 1999); Bruce Lawrence, *Shattering the Myth: Islam Beyond Violence* (Princeton, NJ: Princeton University Press, 1998).
6. See for example his *Towards a World Theology* (Philadelphia: Westminster Press, 1981); or *Islam in Modern History* (Princeton, NJ: Princeton University Press, 1957).
7. Abou El Fadl, *The Great Theft*, 242.
8. Richard W. Bulliet, *Islam: The View from the Edge* (New York: Columbia University Press, 1994), 37–44.
9. An excellent example for use in class is Anna Bigelow, *Sharing the Sacred: Practicing Pluralism in Muslim North India* (New York: Oxford University Press, 2009).
10. Mohammed Arkoun, *Rethinking Islam: Common Questions, Uncommon Answers*, trans. Robert D. Lee (Boulder, CO: Westview Press, 1994), vii.
11. Salman Rushdie, "Outside the Whale," *Granta* 11 (1984), 136.
12. F. E. Peters, *Muhammad and the Origins of Islam* (Albany: State University of New York Press, 1994).
13. Neil Postman and Steve Powers, *How to Watch TV News*, 3rd ed. (New York: Penguin, 2008).
14. See the bibliography for references to these works.
15. As noted in *Religious Studies News*, 22/3 (May 2007): 11.
16. It is interesting to note that all three characters are named some variant of *sayyid*, a title given to a descendent of the Prophet Muhammad.
17. "Islam in America," *Newsweek*, July 30, 2007, 27.

18. Pew Forum on Religion and Public Life, "Muslim Americans: Middle Class and Mostly Mainstream," May 22, 2007, http://pewforum.org/surveys/muslim-american/.

19. Pew Forum on Religion and Public Life, http://www.pewforum.org/uploadedfiles/ Topics/Religious_Affiliation/Muslim/muslims-survey-2005.pdf.

20. Council on American-Islamic Relations, "The Struggle for Equality," http://www. cair.com/PDF/2006-CAIR-Civil-Rights-Report.pdf.

21. Claudia Deane and Darryl Fears, "Negative Perception of Islam Increasing," *Washington Post*, March 9, 2006, http://www.washingtonpost.com/wp-dyn/content/article/2006/03/08/AR2006030802221_pf.html.

22. Jack Shaheen, *Reel Bad Arabs: How Hollywood Vilifies a People* (Brooklyn: Interlink Publishing, 2001), 1.

23. *Reel Bad Arabs* [film], http://www.mediaed.org/videos/MediaRaceAndRepresentation/ReelBadArabs.

24. Jackie Salloum, *Planet of the Arabs* [film], http://www.youtube.com/ watch?v=Mi1ZNEjEarw.

25. Rubina Ramji, "From *Navy Seals* to *The Siege*: Getting to Know the Muslim Terrorist, Hollywood Style," *Journal of Religion and Film* 9/2 (October 2005), http://www. unomaha.edu/jrf/Vol9No2/RamjiIslam.htm.

26. Radio Television Digital News Association, http://www.rtdna.org/pages/media_ items/edward-r.-murrow1106.php?id=1106.

27. David Cook, *Martyrdom in Islam* (Cambridge: Cambridge University Press, 2007).

28. For Osama bin Laden's own statements, see Bruce Lawrence, ed., *Messages to the World: The Statements of Osama bin Laden* (New York: Verso, 2005).

29. Quoted in Asghar Ali Engineer, "Ibn Taymiyyah and His Fatwa on Terrorism," *Alternate Voice* 23 (August/September 2010): 5.

30. Robert Pape, *Dying to Win: The Strategic Logic of Suicide Terrorism* (New York: Random House, 2005), 139.

31. Muslim Public Affairs Committee, "MPACnews—Statement on Terrorist Attacks," September11,2001,http://www.islamicity.com/articles/articles.asp?ref=MP0109-337.

32. "American Muslims Condemn Terror Attacks, IslamiCity, September 11, 2001, http://www.islamicity.com/articles/articles.asp?ref=am0109-335.

33. "Muslims Asked to Offer Help for Victims of Terrorist Attacks," IslamiCity, September 11, 2001, http://www.islamicity.com/articles/articles.asp?ref=am0109-335.

34. " Attacks on US Are Un-Islamic, Say Clerics," IOL News, September 14, 2001, http:// www.iol.co.za/news/world/attacks-on-us-are-un-islamic-say-clerics-1.69136.

35. Sandra Olewine, "The Sorry Unseen, the Story Unheard," September 13, 2001, http://groups.colgate.edu/aarislam/olewine.htm.

36. Study of Islam Section, American Academy of Religion, http://groups.colgate.edu/ aarislam/response.htm.

37. "Bin Laden Fatwa as Spain Remembers from CNN.com," March 11, 2005, http:// ics01.ds.leeds.ac.uk/papers/vp01.cfm?outfit=pmt&requesttimeout=500&folder =2053&paper=2199.

BIBLIOGRAPHY

Abou El Fadl, Khaled. *The Great Theft: Wrestling Islam from the Extremists*. New York: HarperCollins, 2005.

Arkoun, Mohammed. *Rethinking Islam: Common Questions, Uncommon Answers*. Trans. Robert D. Lee. Boulder, CO: Westview Press, 1994.

Badaracco, Claire, ed. *Quoting God: How Media Shape Ideas about Religion*. Waco, TX: Baylor University Press, 2005.

Buddenbaum, Judith, and Debra Mason, eds. *Readings on Religion as News*. Ames: Iowa State University Press, 2000.

Bulliet, Richard W. *Islam: The View from the Edge*. New York: Columbia University Press, 1994.

Daniel, Norman. *Islam and the West: The Making of an Image*. Edinburgh: Edinburgh University Press, 1989.

Eickelman, Dale, and Jon Anderson, eds. *New Media in the Muslim World: The Emerging Public Sphere*, 2nd ed. Bloomington: Indiana University Press, 2003.

Esposito, John. *The Islamic Threat: Myth or Reality?* 3rd ed. New York: Oxford University Press, 1999.

Euben, Roxanne. *Enemy in the Mirror: Islamic Fundamentalism and the Limits of Modern Rationalism*. Princeton, NJ: Princeton University Press, 1999.

Firestone, Reuven. *Jihad: The Origin of Holy War in Islam*. New York: Oxford University Press, 1999.

Giggie, John, and Diane Winston, eds. *Faith in the Market: Religion and the Rise of Urban Commercial Culture*. New Brunswick, NJ: Rutgers University Press, 2002.

Griswold, Eliza. *The Tenth Parallel: Dispatches from the Fault Line Between Christianity and Islam*. New York: Farrar, Straus and Giroux, 2010.

Hoover, Stewart. *Religion in the Media Age*. London: Routledge, 2006.

———. *Religion in the News: Faith and Journalism in American Public Discourse*. Thousand Oaks, CA: Sage, 1998.

Hoover, Stewart, and Lynn Clark, eds. *Practicing Religion in the Age of Media: Explorations in Media, Religion, and Culture*. New York: Columbia University Press, 2002.

Jerryson, Michael K., and Mark Juergensmeyer, eds. *Buddhist Warfare*. New York: Oxford University Press, 2010.

Karim, Karim. *Islamic Peril: Media and Global Violence*. Updated ed. Montreal: Black Rose Books, 2003.

Keshavarz, Fatemeh. *Jasmine and Stars: Reading More Than Lolita in Tehran*. Chapel Hill: University of North Carolina Press, 2007.

Lawrence, Bruce. *Shattering the Myth: Islam Beyond Violence*. Princeton, NJ: Princeton University Press, 1998.

Mamdani, Mahmood. *Good Muslim, Bad Muslim: America, the Cold War, and the Roots of Terror*. New York: Pantheon, 2004.

Mottahedeh, Roy. *The Mantle of the Prophet: Religion and Politics in Iran*. Oxford: Oneworld Publications, 2002.

Pape, Robert. *Dying to Win: The Strategic Logic of Suicide Terrorism*. New York: Random House, 2005.

Peters, F. E. *Muhammad and the Origins of Islam*. Albany: State University of New York Press, 1994.

Postman, Neil, and Steve Powers. *How to Watch TV News*, 3rd ed. New York: Penguin, 2008.

Qureshi, Emran, and Michael A. Sells, eds. *The New Crusades: Constructing the Muslim Enemy*. New York: Columbia University Press, 2003.

Ramji, Rubina. "From Navy Seals to *The Siege*: Getting to Know the Muslim Terrorist, Hollywood Style." *Journal of Religion and Film* 9/2 (October 2005).

Said, Edward. *Covering Islam: How the Media and the Experts Determine How We See the Rest of the World*, updated ed. New York: Vintage, 1997.

Shaheen, Jack. *Reel Bad Arabs: How Hollywood Vilifies a People*. Brooklyn: Interlink Publishing, 2001.

————. *The TV Arab*. Bowling Green, OH: Bowling Green State University Press, 1984.

Smith-Christopher, Daniel L., ed. *Subverting Hatred: The Challenge of Nonviolence in Religious Traditions*, 10th anniv. ed. Maryknoll, NY: Orbis Books, 2007.

Wheeler, Brannon, ed. *Teaching Islam*. New York: Oxford University Press, 2003.

CHAPTER 6

The Specter of Violence in Sikh Pasts

ANNE MURPHY

INTRODUCTION

I first began this essay in 2005, in the tragic days after Hurricane Katrina laid waste to large sections of New Orleans. As reports filled the airwaves and television screens with the scenes of devastation and the mismanagement of the rescue and then cleanup and reconstruction efforts, we saw vividly some of the multiple forms of violence perpetrated by the state, in this case through willful neglect. The diffuse and elusive nature of such almost-but-not-quite-disinterested destruction sobers the attempt to characterize or explain the particularity of any kind of violence. This difficulty is perhaps even more striking in the case of violence that is "religious": defining a realm of violence in such terms assumes that this form of violence is of a fundamentally different order than that which is secular. As Richard King has noted in an insightful discussion of the problematic of the religious with reference to violence, not only is what constitutes the "religious" unclear, but the framing of violence in such terms "distracts us from asking deeper, structural questions about violence as a condition of modern, 'everyday' life" and "insulates the institutional forms, organizations and ideologies that govern modern ('secular') life from critical interrogation."[1]

To understand alternative and sometimes competing definitions of violence, the *representation* of violence must take center stage in analysis. Foregrounding representation allows investigation of how connections between religion and violence are made and how our understanding of the terms involved—the religious, the secular, and the forms of violence associated with each—are constructed.

Such attention to representations and the political work they do is particularly valuable when teaching about the history of the Sikh tradition, a religious tradition born in the fifteenth century in the Punjab, a cultural and linguistic region now split between the modern nation-states of India and Pakistan, but with an influential diaspora community. Imagining the relationship between the Sikh tradition and violence is a complicated matter, particularly so perhaps because of this diaspora community, the 2 million or so Sikhs who live outside of Punjab. This essay presents an overview of selected instances and related representations of violence associated with Sikh tradition and this diaspora community, and discusses issues that shape these representations of the Sikh past. In doing so I will call attention to the multiplicity of representations and historical realities of violence with reference to the Sikh tradition and suggest strategies for analyzing representations of the tradition such that violence is visible as multidimensional and complex, and fundamentally related to the forms of violence of the secular.

VIOLENCE AND THE SIKH TRADITION?

Questions regarding violence, both religious and secular, as well as its representation, were particularly salient in 2005, the same year that Katrina struck New Orleans, in the wake of the official "apology" to the Sikh community rendered by India's prime minister, Manmohan Singh—himself a Sikh. Singh did so in response to the disclosure of the findings of a state-sponsored investigative commission that named representatives of the state as having actively participated in the 1984 anti-Sikh "riots" in New Delhi and elsewhere after the assassination of Indira Gandhi, then prime minister, by her Sikh bodyguards.[2] In the days following the prime minister's demise, thousands of Sikhs were injured and killed, hunted down by organized groups of assailants. Dr. Singh issued his apology as a representative of the Congress Party, the same party that Indira Gandhi once represented. Indira Gandhi's assassination had been committed in retaliation for her ordering the Indian army to enter the interior complex of the Darbar Sahib or Golden Temple in Amritsar, causing the destruction of key buildings and the killing of pilgrims and militants alike. That government offensive was part of an ongoing struggle to quell a Sikh separatist movement in the Indian state of Punjab, elements of which sought an independent Sikh state of Khalistan.

The forms and figures of violence toward and by the state are complex here, as is the idea of "Sikh violence." It should also be noted that the commission report that inspired the prime minister's apology was the eleventh committee or commission set up by the government to investigate the violence of the "riots."[3] Prior commissions had offered inconclusive and incomplete results (as, it must be noted, this one did as well—as I write this, efforts are still ongoing to bring those named to some kind of justice).[4] This form of violence—that perpetrated with the encouragement and/or assistance of members of government—seems to evade easy delineation. Yet violence perpetrated by Sikhs has, on the other hand, received far more attention, such that, as Balbinder Singh Bhogal recently put it, "the image of a bearded, turban-wearing Sikh male with sword [acts] as a negative icon symbolizing religious violence and separatism."[5] Violence, then, haunts representation of Sikhs today, and the form it most often takes positions Sikhs as perpretrators.[6]

Lest these issues seem to relate to South Asia alone, let us consider two North American examples of how violence has haunted the representation of the Sikh community, one in a way related to these issues, and the other in somewhat different terms. This is important for two reasons, first because of the teaching contexts this book addresses in North America, and second because South Asian and North American contexts are materially connected. The first of these two examples is the June 1985 bombing of Air India Flight 182, which originated in Vancouver, Canada. The plane went down with 329 passengers and crew.[7] To date only one person has been convicted in the case through the Canadian courts: Inderjit Singh Reyat, who pleaded guilty to manslaughter in 2003. The alleged leader in the bombing, Talwinder Singh Parmar, died in India over a decade ago, and other suspects were acquitted in 2005. In 2008 the annual Vaisakhi parade in Surrey, a suburb of Vancouver, Canada, brought the case general public notice again. Vaisakhi is a harvest festival, but, more important, it also celebrates the founding of the Khalsa, a definition of Sikh identity initiated by the tenth and final human Guru, Guru Gobind Singh (1666–1708, Guru 1675–1708), in 1699, before Guruship was invested in the Sikh canon, the Adi Granth or Guru Granth Sahib, at the death of Guru Gobind Singh. One aspect of membership in the Khalsa is the maintenance of the "5Ks" or five symbolic markers, one of which is the well-known uncut hair associated with Sikhs. Controversy had previously erupted in Surrey, in 2007, because Parmar's picture was included on a parade float.[8] In 2008, most important local political leaders declined to participate in the parade in protest, garnering considerable media attention. Parmar's picture did not reappear that year, but photos of members of groups considered by the Canadian government to be terrorist organizations did. In 2009 and 2010 controversy erupted again and Ujjal Dosanjh, former member of parliament and premier of British Columbia, was threatened with violence if he attended the 2010 parade because of his comments critical of the use of such representations; most political leaders subsequently boycotted the parade.[9] The Khalistan movement and its representation, therefore, are continuing contentious issues in western Canada.

A second North American example is of quite a different order. It involves an instance of violence against a Sikh: Balbir Singh Sodhi, who was killed in Arizona on Saturday, September 15, 2001. This act was committed because an aspect of the distinctive clothing of the Sikhs—the turban, which is associated with one of the 5Ks, the *kes* or uncut hair—was mistaken for dress seen on members of al Qaeda.[10] Sodhi's death was quickly followed by the killing of a Pakistani Muslim in Dallas, Texas. These were the first two bias crimes committed after the 9/11 attacks on Washington, DC, and New York City,[11] and violence of this kind has continued to be an ongoing problem for Muslims as well as Sikhs across the United States.[12] What is crucial to note here is that while the issue of Khalistani separatism is something that many associate with the Sikhs as an example of "religious violence," discussion of violence in relation to the Sikhs rarely foregrounds this kind of violence, against Sikhs.

These two examples demonstrate several things when considered alongside the violence against Sikhs in 1984. First, while academic classes that cover the Sikh tradition might be more likely to highlight violence in the Sikh past (as discussed below), it also lives in the present and takes myriad forms that are often related in subtle ways. Some are more visible than others, and this varying visibility bears scrutiny. Second, the designation of violence as religious requires careful attention and at times skepticism. Are the instances mentioned above—of violence against a Sikh after 9/11, of violence by Sikhs associated with the Khalistan movement (and against them), of violence against Sikhs during the 1984 "riots" —examples of religious violence? The multiple kinds of violence thus far described, directed against Sikhs and perpetrated by them, make it difficult for us to easily describe the usability, as well as limits, of religion as an explanatory factor. Thus Khalistan is ostensibly about religion, in that it is about a homeland for the Sikhs, a religious community (although this designation itself requires further thought). This movement is, however, more centrally about India's national identity and minority rights within the postcolonial state—and also fundamentally about the rise of the Hindu Right in India at the same time the Sikh movement gained power. In the case of the Surrey parade, we see how issues around national identity and minority rights resonate both in Canada and in South Asia. This gives these representations great power in the diaspora context. Post-9/11 bias crimes are acts of religious as well as racial bias, in the sense that both Muslims and Sikhs are targeted specifically for their real or assumed religious identities; yet most would not name the perpetrators of such violence as committing "Christian violence." Indeed, in some senses this is justified: the specifically religious aspects of the violence and its justification are not immediately apparent. Specifically religious motivations are, however, generally too readily accepted for Sikh actors in media and other accounts.

The naming of religious versus secular violence, therefore, is problematic. Violence associated with Sikh pasts interfaces with, complicates, and in some cases directly mirrors secular violence. The violence associated with the Khalistan movement implicates the state of India, both in how violence has been directed in rhetorical and material terms against the state and in the role of the Indian state in the *production* of violence itself (such as that which was orchestrated against Sikhs in New Delhi and elsewhere in 1984 after the assassination of Prime Minister Indira Gandhi, and in the repression and extrajudicial killings in Punjab before and after that). The role of the state in relation to the violence associated with recent Sikh pasts has been described ably by a diverse set of commentators on South Asian forms of collective violence from Stanley Tambiah to Paul Brass. In the words of Joyce Pettigrew, for many Sikhs in the early 1990s, "Delhi, the central government and oppression . . . [were] interchangeable."[13] It is the seeming unrepresentativity of this violence of the state—since it has eluded full description, and legal prosecution of the guilty remains grossly incomplete—in contrast to the overrepresentation of violence perpetrated by Sikhs that demands that we consider the representation of violence itself as a phenomenon worthy of scholarly and pedagogical attention. While allowing us to address the meaning and lives of violence in religious traditions, such attention also allows us to examine the processes and contradictions that normalize violence in some contexts—often but not exclusively in the hands of the state—but deem it aberrant and particularistic, outside of universal values and the rational, in the hands of religious actors and communities. This is not to excuse such violence: as J. Z. Smith's famous article on Jonestown—and more recently, Saba Mahmood's fine work on Islamic piety in Egypt—makes clear, understanding is not advocacy.[14] Understanding representations of violence provides for a further goal, relevant to our task in this volume: that of obtaining concrete ways of teaching about religious violence. It is in this regard that the case of violence in Sikh contexts is particularly relevant for a comparative understanding of the representation of violence and the politics of such representations. In these days when violence is so generally associated with Islam, the Sikhs provide a useful comparative case for thinking about how and why the religious does—and doesn't—relate to violence, and how and why representations of such violence can become so problematic, in themselves.

A DIALOGIC NOTION OF VIOLENCE

It is a somewhat obvious point, but one that nonetheless bears repeating, that contrary to some perceptions of the tradition from the outside, violence does constitute an aspect of Sikh history but should not be seen as fundamental to it. This is not to say that there are not strong ethics and practices around notions of defense and the valorization of military strength within core Sikh texts and practices. It is to say that conflict and associated violence are generally represented as important in specific, historical terms, and Sikh responses are seen as just that: responsive. When representing the tradition it is crucial that one take this stance seriously and recognize the degree to which persecution creates the frame for violence-as-response in Sikh tradition and how a dialogic notion of violence must inform our understanding of its presence now and in the past.

The normative historiography on the tradition reveals this dialogic nature of violence. A distinction is often drawn (and overdrawn) between the period of the first five Sikh Gurus and the latter five. Guru Nanak (1469–1539) founded a tradition focused on the divine experience of the sacred *nām* or name; this feature of Sikh thought and practice has retained its place at the center of the tradition since that time. Community formation was also an important part of Nanak's vision, and the Sikhs were notably well organized early on. By the time of the fifth Guru, Guru Arjan Dev (1563–1606, Guru 1581–1606), the community of Sikhs (the term literally means student, derived from the Punjabi verb *sikhnā*, to learn, and related to the Sanskrit *shishya*, student) had grown significantly and was a powerful political as well as religious presence in Punjab. The growth of the community brought it to the attention of Mughal forces, leading to the martyrdom of Guru Arjan. Although the degree to which the martyrdom of Guru Arjan was immediately described as such has been debated—and along with this, the degree to which the culture of *shaheedi* or martyrdom was developed at that time—this event had a profound impact on the community.[15] Later Sikh historiography tells us that Guru Hargobind (1595–1644, Guru 1606–44) took up the arms of *miri-piri* in this period. *Miri* in this context represents secular rule, and *piri* religious preceptorship. The

Guru thus embraced more fully the political elements of his role, in response to the death of Guru Arjan Dev.

Violence would shape the Sikh tradition further in coming centuries, but a larger pattern of political and religious mobilization is established here. The need to defend the growing Sikh community became urgent in subsequent decades, after the martyrdom of the ninth Guru, Guru Tegh Bahadur (1621–75, Guru 1664–75). Not only Mughal forces but also rival claimants to power in the nearby Punjab hills kept the Sikh community under pressure. The formation of the Khalsa by the tenth and final human living Guru (the Sikh canon, the Guru Granth Sahib is considered the living Guru now), Guru Gobind Singh, reflects this need to bring the community together along clearer lines and to define its relationship to outside groups and authorities. Although the exact shape of the Khalsa in the early years is not definitive from the historical record, earliest descriptions of the Khalsa do emphasize its role as the continuing authority of the Guru in the world and in bringing the community together.[16] Martial symbols animate the Khalsa and its ethics, and the final Guru is usually portrayed with the attributes associated with kingship—the regal hawk, bejeweled turban, and throne.[17]

It is the eighteenth century that W. H. McLeod rightly calls "the heroic period of Sikh tradition," and it is to this period that reference is often later made when describing the ways in which Sikhs have suffered—and triumphed—in violent circumstances, and how the Sikh response to violence has been shaped.[18] A visit to the Central Sikh Museum in Amritsar vividly reveals the violence of the past; the museum's contents are dominated by historical paintings that portray instances of this violence.[19] The eighteenth century is the period of the *ghallūghāre*, or holocausts, when large numbers of Sikhs were hunted down by Mughal and other regional forces.[20] Memorials to the persecution of Sikhs in the past, such as those found in this and other similar museums, are often presented alongside memorials to more recent—and more controversial, in our current moment—victims of violence. It is these representations that are so vividly a part of Sikh cultural life today, and cause some of the controversies mentioned earlier. As Brian Axel has noted, the Internet has provided a particularly rich ground for such representations: "Websites circulate images of corpses of Sikh men alongside testimonies of torture survivors and updates on present conflicts; chatrooms and email listserves provide opportunities for debate regarding the utility of violent or non-violent tactics."[21] They are, therefore, a part of our students' public culture, no matter what their background.

THE NEED FOR REPRESENTATION

What do we do with such images of the violent past in relation to the Sikh tradition? As Jeffrey Olick has noted in his discussion of collective memory of traumatic pasts and the politics of regret that memory can entail, "one prerequisite for that unflinching acceptance of the burden of history" that some might identify in the post–World War II German acceptance of responsibility for the Holocaust and other German atrocities in the war "is that it was just that: a historical burden rather than a present accusation."[22] Later generations of Germans were ready to face their past, and the role of Germans as perpetrators of violence, because it was indeed past. The violence that confronts Sikhs, however, is not so easily faced, because it is so very much a part of the present. Violence in the more distant Sikh past is portrayed with less urgency than that related to the more recent past and present, but it is related to the production of Sikh subjectivity today in subtle ways, through analogies that are made between past and present. This is because the representation of violence and conflict in Sikh contexts in recent periods is generally perceived as mimicking prior historical instances of violence against Sikhs. This, indeed, was observed by many commentators on the Khalistan movement in the 1980s and 1990s—Robin Jeffreys, Mark Juergensmeyer, Harjot Oberoi, and Veena Das, to name a few—the ways in which history served as a central locus for representing violence against Sikhs.[23] In this way, as Veena Das has noted, temporal differences have been submerged, and the present seems to embody the past.[24]

Second- and third-generation Sikhs in North America fashion their own relationship with the forms of violence associated with the recent Sikh past through this historical past to narrativize and understand these forms of violence in relation to the present. As Olick suggests, we must remember that the ability and need to remember changes from generation to generation. This need is expressed in the October 2005 issue of the *Sikh Review*, a moderate and popular publication based in India, with an international editorial board and audience. While the articles in this issue—dedicated to the theme "1984: A Requiem?"—overwhelmingly concern the Nanavati Commission report, a number of them also focus on history. "The Sikhs must not forget or ignore [the] Sikh Holocaust" writes one author;[25] another article is titled "Forgetting the 1984 Killings Would Be Immoral: A Massacre Is a Massacre!"[26]

It is in this sense that discussion and representation of violence is of vital importance. Unfortunately, this too is a matter of controversy. Indian Prime Minister Manmohan Singh was quoted in June 2010, during a small memorial service to the victims of the Air India bombing in Canada, as saying that "'constant reminders' of the period are not helpful to Sikhs or the wider Indian community" and that the community should "move ahead from crimes of the past." At the same meeting, Ujjal Dosanjh was quoted as saying, "There are elements both in India and abroad that continue to undermine both the unity and integrity of India and in fact the fabric of the community abroad" through the mobilization of the memory of the 1984 violence against Sikhs.[27] This violence should not be remembered, in this argument, because such memories destabilize both the Indian state and the diasporic community.

Yet memory need not destabilize; indeed, it can be an essential part of a nation's or community's constitution as it moves beyond a violent past, as the German example demonstrates. South Africa, Northern Ireland, and elsewhere provide even more compelling examples.[28] Along such lines, Pradip Datta has suggested a "truth and reconciliation" approach to the past in South Asia, noting recent work on partition that has sought to "dismantle the strategies of forgetting that had hidden the public memory of partition and to recover the traumas of partition along with the identities that it produced."[29] Balpreet Singh Boparai, a spokesperson for the World Sikh Organization (or WSO), is said to have asserted—in response to Manmohan Singh's statement—"You can't move forward as a democracy unless you address past wrongdoings."[30] But the WSO is a controversial organization, making this call to memory similary controversial. Remembering, however, need not be interpreted as a separatist act. Indeed, as one British Columbia media personality, Bhupinder Hundal, asked, "Why does standing up for justice for either cause [Air India, or the persecution of Sikhs in 1984] automatically categorize you as Pro–Indian government or Pro–Khalistani?" The political positions entailed by memory, he suggests, need to be more complicated.[31] Only memory and a commitment to its representation can allow Sikhs to move past the impossible choice they have forced to face, as identified by Arvind Mandair: to distance themselves from the right to resist the state (or even to critique it) or to be perceived as separatists.[32]

Thus although one must respect Dosanjh's commitment to his position in western Canada today and abhor the threats he received, what is missing in the critique of memory is acknowledgement of the need to rememberitself. Recognition and remembrance are not so easily dismissed. Interestingly, as Sikhs were enjoined to forget, a *Globe and Mail* columnist at the same time bemoaned the Canadian failure to remember the Air India bombing.[33] Whose memory matters? How can the victims of the Air India bombing and the violence against Sikhs both find a place in the field of memory? Representation and violence are fundamentally tied to one another, and remembrance—the act of calling the past into the present, while asserting its place in the past—is key to healing, not to a single political agenda.

The narration of violence in history is multivalent in Sikh tradition—we see this in the range of positions held by Manmohan Singh, Ujjal Dosanjh, Bhupinder Hundal, and Balpreet Singh Boparai, above. So too are its effects. It is in this vein that we might consider the earlier words of India's prime minister, Manmohan Singh, commenting upon the Nanavati Report—when he provided the first apology for the "riots": "The past is with us. We cannot rewrite it. We cannot undo the past, but we have an option, today, to build a better future."[34] Such a statement may certainly allow for the avoidance of blame and the question of compensation for the victims—and thus many further battles will need to be fought for justice for those killed and injured during the violence against Sikhs in 1984 and for their families—but it also suggests how the representation of the violence of the past as a historical fact in the past, and its recognition, can allow for the simultaneous suggestion of a future.

There is thus another temporal aspect to many Sikh representations of the violence of the past—in addition to the past/present aspect highlighted by Veena Das—that iterates something prior and also suggests what might follow. The work done to construct a present and future as well as a past in relation to violence is something we must consider when attempting to understand the representation of religion and violence in both the past and present—and when we hope to understand the work that representations of violence do. Allowing for the engaged remembering of such violence must be a part of the process.

THE WORK OF REPRESENTATION

Active pursuit of an independent Khalistan has waned in recent years, although there is no guarantee it will not become important again, and it certainly persists in places in British Columbia. In such a context, the key question goes beyond "what is religious violence in Sikh contexts?"—that is, what has constituted it and what are the historical circumstances of its becoming?—to "what comes after?" in fulfillment, one might say, of mourning and memory itself. What comes after is only possible if memory is allowed for. Memory in itself is not enough to make dissent irrelevant—most of the grievances in Punjab in the 1980s still exist, and, as I have noted, civil rights for Sikhs in diaspora are a pressing issue as well.[35] Memory is accompanied by material concerns of urgency.

But importantly, Sikhs have adapted wide-ranging tactics and approaches to dealing with the inequities and sometimes violence of the state. The rhetoric of human rights is thus central to Sikh discourse in India and in diaspora and is a primary form of engagement with the Sikh past among young Sikhs.[36] Other forms of engagement with being Sikh and constructing community have also taken center stage. Some of these collapse temporal and other distinctions in the experience of the crisis of the present (as was characteristic in Khalistani rhetoric), but violence is not the only form of articulation of this collapse. One such alternative mode of engagement is philanthropy. This is not new for Sikhs—*seva* or service is a central tenet of the tradition, as it is among other South Asian religious traditions. But today, *seva* is mobilized among Sikhs in diaspora as an opportunity to engage actively with India and to make a difference in the lives of Sikhs there, without a direct link to violence; it is also a major force among Sikhs within India. One Delhi-based organization, the Nishkam Sikh Welfare Council, began specifically to help the victims of the Delhi violence in 1984 and prove to fellow Indians that Sikhs are not inherently violent.[37] Sikhs have described this mode of action as getting beyond the binary of violence or nonviolence, support or denial of Khalistan. Somewhat amazingly, service also constituted a major component of the local Sikh response to 9/11: many Sikh taxi drivers in New York mobilized to provide free taxi services for victims and family of victims after 9/11, even while members of the community were under attack. Comparative analysis of this mode of action in relation to religious communities at other moments in a larger history of violence (both religious and not) might bear fruit. In the Sikh case, it is one way to get beyond the binaries that haunt the representation of violence and gesture toward a future. As teachers, we can thus call attention to how religious actors and communities construct their present in relation to the pasts of violence—and through them, to what comes next.

The representation of the Sikh past is always a work in progress, always open to possibility. To understand and teach about violence in relation to Sikh—or any religious—tradition we must examine the work that representations of violence do, both within the tradition and from outside. When I spoke with Sikhs in New York City after 9/11, many made direct parallels between the 1984 anti-Sikh violence and the persecution of Sikhs in the United States in 2001 (and since).

The imagination of the forms of violence within the Sikh past thus connects the North American context with a larger history and makes this past local. This simultaneously global and local case offers an opportunity to consider the representation of violence and the responses it allows. Axel has emphasized the discursive effect of the Internet-mediated image of the deceased Sikh militant/martyr: "what is at stake is not the resolution of the conflict but the incitement to discourse prompted by the visual image of the corpse's mutilated body."[38] The martyr's body reaches out to that which cannot actually be experienced—the sublime—and brings it into the mediated world.[39] Axel has suggested, "Names like Khalistan and Bhindranwale [a major Sikh separatist leader], . . . do not represent or stand in for the identities of already-existing communities or localities. In contrast, the performative act of naming conjures a world of changing significations and relations."[40] It has been argued here that the remembrance and representation of violence can, if recognized and allowed, reconfigure relations in multiple ways, not just those that adhere to one set of political claims. By examining such representations and their complexity—and the multiplicity of their significations—students understand not only a particular religious tradition but something more essential about how communities respond to the ongoing violence of our lives today. And why it is so important to remember.

NOTES

1. Richard King, "The Association of 'Religion' with Violence: Reflections on a Modern Trope," in *Religion and Violence in South Asia: Theory and* Practice, ed. John R. Hinnells and Richard King (London: Routledge, 2007), 227.
2. On the apology: "Prime Minister Manmohan Singh said in Parliament that he had no hesitation in admitting that the anti-Sikh riots of 1984 were a shameful episode in the country's history. He went on to apologise 'not only to the Sikh community but the whole Indian nation' with the assertion that 'what took place in 1984 was the negation of the concept of nationhood . . . enshrined in our Constitution.' He said: 'On behalf of our government, on behalf of the entire people of this country, I bow my head in shame that such a thing took place.'" Venkitesh Ramakrishnan, "Nanavati Commission Report: 1984—the Untold Story," *Frontline* 22/18 (2005), http://www.flonnet.com/fl2218/stories/20050909005201900.htm, accessed November 7, 2005.
3. The others are described in: "Nanavati Commission Report: The Probe Series," *Frontline* 22/18 (2005), http://www.flonnet.com/fl2218/stories/20050909004902400.htm, accessed November 7, 2005.
4. See for example the news item by Amnesty International: "Sikh Massacre Victims Await Justice in India, 25 Years On," April 9, 2009, http://www.amnesty.org/en/news-and-updates/sikh-massacre-victims-await-justice-india-25-years-20090409, accessed October 22, 2011. For a sense of efforts within the Sikh community, see Sikhs for Justice, http://www.sikhsforjustice.org/.
5. Balbinder Singh Bhogal, "Text as Sword: Sikh Religious Violence Taken for Wonder," in *Religion and Violence in South Asia: Theory and Practice*, ed. John R. Hinnells and Richard King (London: Routledge, 2007), 107.

6. See Brian K. Axel, *The Nation's Tortured Body: Violence, Representation, and the Formation of a Sikh "Diaspora"* (Durham, NC: Duke University Press, 2001).

7. CBC News, "Air India Flight 182," http://www.cbc.ca/news/airindia/, accessed July 21, 2008.

8. CBC News, "Controversial Photos Displayed at Surrey's Vaisakhi Parade," April 12, 2008, http://www.cbc.ca/canada/british-columbia/story/2008/04/12/sikh-parade.html, accessed July 21, 2008.

9. CBC News, "B.C. Premier Demands Apology," April 16, 2010, http://www.cbc.ca/news/canada/british-columbia/story/2010/04/16/bc-vaisakhi-parade-threats-dosanjh-hayer.html, accessed October 21, 2011.

10. Some versions of the list of 5Ks includes the turban itself as a member of the set, with the term *keskī*.

11. Laurie Goodstein, "National Briefing Southwest: Arizona: Immigrant's Killing May Bring Death Penalty," *New York Times*, November 8, 2001, A18; Michael Janofsky, "National Briefing Southwest: Arizona: Indictment in Killing of Sikh," *New York Times*, September 27, 2001, A16; Tamar Lewin, "Sikh Owner of Gas Station Is Fatally Shot in Rampage," *New York Times*, September 17, 2001, B16. For discussion of these events and Sikh responses, see Anne Murphy, "Mobilizing *Seva* (Service): Modes of Sikh Diasporic Action," in *South Asians in the Diaspora: Histories and Religious Tradition*, ed. Knut Axel Jacobsen and Pratap Kumar (Leiden: Brill, 2004), 367–402.

12. See United Sikhs, *First Global Sikh Civil Rights Report 2008*, http://www.unitedsikhs.org/rtt/sikhconf/FirstGlobalSikhCivilRightsReport.pdf. The House of Representatives passed "Resolution Condemning Bigotry and Violence Against Arab-Americans, American Muslims, and Americans from South Asia" on September 14 (H. Con. Res 227); discussion of the resolution openly addressed the bias some South Asian and Arab Americans were experiencing. See "Text of H. Con. Res. 227 [107th]," http://www.govtrack.us/congress/billtext.xpd?bill=hc107-227, accessed October 21, 2011.

13. Joyce Pettigrew, *Sikhs of the Punjab: Unheard Voices of State and Guerilla Violence* (London: Zed Books, 1995), 10. Stanley Tambiah, *Leveling Crowds: Ethnonationalist Conflicts and Collective Violence in South Asia* (Berkeley: University of California Press, 1996); Paul Brass, *The Production of Hindu-Muslim Violence in Contemporary India* (Seattle: University of Washington Press, 2003). Brass is well known for defining with subtlety the institutionalized riot systems (both as aspects of the state and beyond), which provide the structural conditions for mass violence in South Asia more generally As Brass notes, "riots . . . are unacknowledged and illegitimate but well-known and accepted transgressions of routine political behavior in India" (356). Ashutosh Varshney has also produced work of interest on violence among religious groups in South Asia, although he focuses on what maintains peace, rather than what destroys it; as Brass noted in a posting on the H-ASIA listserv, this focus allows him to elide much of the violence of the state. Ashutosh Varshney, *Ethnic Conflict and Civic Life: Hindus and Muslims in India* (New Haven, CT: Yale University Press, 2002).

14. Saba Mahmood attempts to understand and not valorize the particular modes of being associated with Islamic pietistic forms of ethics and action. Jonathan Z. Smith, "The Devil in Mr. Jones," in *Imagining Religion: From Babylon to Jonestown* (Chicago: University of Chicago Press, 1982), 102–20; Saba Mahmood, "Feminist Theory, Embodiment, and the Docile Agent: Some Reflections on the Egyptian Islamic Revival," *Cultural Anthropology* 16/2 (2001): 202–36.

15. See Louis Fenech, "Martyrdom and the Sikh Tradition," *Journal of American Oriental Society* 117/4 (1997); Lou Fenech, *Martyrdom in the Sikh Tradition: Playing the "Game of Love"* (Delhi: Oxford University Press, 2000).

16. See Anne Murphy, "History in the Sikh Past," *History and Theory* 46/2 (October 2007): 345–65. On the historical formation of the Khalsa, see W. H. McLeod, *Sikhs of the Khalsa: A History of the Khalsa Rahit* (Delhi: Oxford University Press, 2003).

17. See Bhogal for discussion of how the figures of Guru Nanak and Guru Gobind Singh are seen to symbolize the passive/spiritual and militant/political aspects of the tradition.

18. W. H. McLeod, "The Sikh Struggle in the Eighteenth Century and Its Relevance for Today," in *Exploring Sikhism: Aspects of Sikh Identity, Culture, and Thought* (Delhi: Oxford University Press, 2000), 71.

19. The museum recently installed a portrait of Sant Jarnail Singh Bhindranwale, causing controversy; see Varinder Walia, "Portrait of Bhindranwale Installed at SGPC's Sikh Museum," November 29, 2007, http://www.tribuneindia.com/2007/20071130/main4.htm, accessed July 24, 2008.

20. On the period of the eighteenth century in Punjab and the trials faced by the Sikh community in the century, see J. S. Grewal, *The Sikhs of the Punjab* (Cambridge: Cambridge University Press, 1990), 82–98.

21. Brian Axel, "Digital Figurings of the Unimaginable: Visual Media, Death, and Formations of the Sikh Diaspora," *Journal of Ethnic and Migration Studies* 34/7 (September 2008): 1145–59. For quote, see 1146.

22. Jeffrey Olick, *The Politics of Regret: Collective Memory and Historical Responsibility in the Age of Atrocity* (London: Routledge, 2007), 143.

23. Robin Jeffrey, "Grappling with the Past: Sikh Politicians and the Past," *Pacific Affairs* 60 (1987): 59–72; Harjot Oberoi, "Sikh Fundamentalism: Translating History into Theory," in *Fundamentalisms and the State: Remaking Polities, Economies, and Militance*, ed. Martin E. Marty and Scott Appleby (Chicago: University of Chicago Press, 1993), 278; Mark Juergensmeyer, "The Logic of Religious Violence," *Journal of Strategic Studies* 10 (1987): 176ff.; Veena Das, *Critical Events: An Anthropological Perspective on Contemporary India* (Delhi: Oxford University Press, 1995), 121.

24. Das, *Critical Events*, 118–36.

25. Sajjan Singh Bajwa, "Prevention of Future Holocausts," *Sikh Review* (October 2005): 67.

26. Vir Sanghvi, "Forgetting the 1984 Killings Would be Immoral: A Massacre Is a Massacre!" *Sikh Review* (October 2005): 58–60.

27. Bill Curry and Anthony Reinhart, "Singh Meets Air India Families; Indian PM Calls on Indo-Canadians to 'Move Ahead' from Crimes of the Past," *Globe and Mail*, June 29, 2010, A4.

28. This comparison is explored further in my as yet unpublished paper, "The Politics of Possibility and the Commemoration of Trauma," delivered at the After 1984 conference in Berkeley, California, in September 2009.

29. Pradip Datta, "Historic Trauma and the Politics of the Present in India," *interventions* 7/3: 317.

30. Curry and Reinhart, "Singh Meets Air India Families."

31. Bhupinder Hundal, "The Community's Image Tarnished Again," Omni News, April 19, 2010, http://www.omnibc.ca/news/webstories.php?language=18&id=2350, accessed October 21, 2011.

32. Arvind Mandair, "The Global Fiduciary: Mediating the Violence of Religion," in *Religion and Violence in South Asia: Theory and Practice*, ed. John R. Hinnells and Richard King (London: Routledge, 2007), 220.

33. Patrick Brethour, "Why Canada Chose to Unremember Air India and Disown Its Victims," *Globe and Mail*, June 25, 2010, http://www.theglobeandmail.com/news/opinions/why-canada-chose-to-unremember-air-india-and-disown-its-victims/article1618762/.

34. Speech of Manmohan Singh, as printed in *Sikh Review* (October 2005): 81–83.
35. Prior grievances include control over water rights and the continued deferral of the assignment of Chandigarh as the capital of Punjab (at present, the two Indian states of Haryana and Punjab share this capital).
36. As Axel discusses, the diaspora in the Sikh case, as in so many others (Ireland, etc.) has played an incredibly important role within political violence around the Sikh separatist issue. See Axel, *The Nation's Tortured Body*.
37. For the material drawn on in this paragraph, see Murphy, "Mobilizing *Seva*."
38. Brian Axel, "Diasporic Sublime: Sikh Martyrs, Internet Mediations, and the Question of the Unimaginable," *Sikh Formations: Religion, Culture, Theory* 1/1 (2005): 140; and Axel, "Digital Figurings," 1151.
39. Axel, "Digital Figurings," 1153–54.
40. Ibid., 1157.

BIBLIOGRAPHY

Asad, Talal. "Reading a Modern Classic: W.C. Smith's *The Meaning and End of Religion*." *History of Religions* 40/3 (2001): 204–22.

Axel, Brian. "Diasporic Sublime: Sikh Martyrs, Internet Mediations, and the Question of the Unimaginable." *Sikh Formations: Religion, Culture, Theory* 1/1 (2005): 127–54.

———. "Digital Figurings of the Unimaginable: Visual Media, Death, and Formations of the Sikh Diaspora." *Journal of Ethnic and Migration Studies* 34/7 (September 2008): 1145–59.

———. *The Nation's Tortured Body: Violence, Representation, and the Formation of a Sikh "Diaspora."* Durham, NC: Duke University Press, 2001.

Bajwa, Sajjan Singh. "Prevention of Future Holocausts." *Sikh Review* (October 2005): 67.

Bhogal, Balbinder Singh. "Text as Sword: Sikh Religious Violence Taken for Wonder." In *Religion and Violence in South Asia: Theory and Practice*, ed. John R. Hinnells and Richard King, 107–35. London: Routledge, 2007.

Brass, Paul. *The Production of Hindu-Muslim Violence in Contemporary India*. Seattle: University of Washington Press, 2003.

CBC News. "Air India Flight 182," http://www.cbc.ca/news/airindia/, accessed July 21, 2008.

———. "B.C. Premier Demands Apology," April 16, 2010, http://www.cbc.ca/news/canada/british-columbia/story/2010/04/16/bc-vaisakhi-parade-threats-dosanjh-hayer.html, accessed October 21, 2011.

———"Controversial Photos Displayed at Surrey's Vaisakhi Parade," April 12, 2008, http://www.cbc.ca/canada/british-columbia/story/2008/04/12/sikhparade.html, accessed July 21, 2008.

Das, Veena. *Critical Events: An Anthropological Perspective on Contemporary India*. Delhi: Oxford University Press, 1995.

Datta, Pradip. "Historic Trauma and the Politics of the Present in India." *interventions* 7/3 (2005): 316–20.

Fenech, Louis. "Martyrdom and the Sikh Tradition." *Journal of American Oriental Society* 117/4 (1997): 623–43.

———. *Martyrdom in the Sikh Tradition: Playing the "Game of Love."* Delhi: Oxford University Press, 2000.

Goodstein, Laurie. "National Briefing Southwest: Arizona: Immigrant's Killing May Bring Death Penalty." *New York Times*, November 8, 2001, A18.

Grewal, J. S. *The Sikhs of the Punjab*. Cambridge: Cambridge University Press, 1990.

Janofsky, Michael. "National Briefing Southwest: Arizona: Indictment in Killing of Sikh." *New York Times*, September 27, 2001, A16.

Jeffrey, Robin. "Grappling with the Past: Sikh Politicians and the Past." *Pacific Affairs* 60 (1987): 59–72.

Juergensmeyer, Mark. "The Logic of Religious Violence." *Journal of Strategic Studies* 10 (1987): 479–99.

———. "Teaching about Religious Violence without Trivializing It," *Spotlight on Teaching* 18, 4 (October 2003): ii.

King, Richard. "The Association of 'Religion' with Violence: Reflections on a Modern Trope." In *Religion and Violence in South Asia: Theory and Practice*, ed. John R. Hinnells and Richard King, 226–57. London: Routledge, 2007.

Lewin, Tamar. "Sikh Owner of Gas Station Is Fatally Shot in Rampage." *New York Times*, September 17, 2001, B16.

Mahmood, Saba. "Feminist Theory, Embodiment, and the Docile Agent: Some Reflections on the Egyptian Islamic Revival." *Cultural Anthropology* 16/2 (2001): 202–36.

Mandair, Arvind S. "The Emergence of Modern 'Sikh Theology': Reassessing the Passage of Ideas from Trumpp to Bhai Vir Singh." *Bulletin of the School of Oriental and African Studies* 68/2 (2005): 253–75.

McLeod, W. H. "The Sikh Struggle in the Eighteenth Century and Its Relevance for Today." In *Exploring Sikhism: Aspects of Sikh Identity, Culture, and Thought*, 70–90. Delhi: Oxford University Press, 2000. Originally published 1992.

———. *Sikhs of the Khalsa: A History of the Khalsa Rahit*. Delhi: Oxford University Press, 2003.

Murphy, Anne. "History in the Sikh Past." *History and Theory* 46/2 (October 2007): 345–65.

———. "Mobilizing *Seva* (Service): Modes of Sikh Diasporic Action." In *South Asians in the Diaspora: Histories and Religious Traditions*, ed. Knut Axel Jacobsen and Pratap Kumar, 367–402. Leiden: Brill, 2004.

"Nanavati Commission Report: The Probe Series." *Frontline* 22/18 (2005), http://www.flonnet.com/fl2218/stories/20050909004902400.htm, accessed November 7, 2005.

Oberoi, Harjot. "Sikh Fundamentalism: Translating History into Theory." In *Fundamentalisms and the State: Remaking Polities, Economies, and Militance*, ed. Martin E. Marty and Scott Appleby. Chicago: University of Chicago Press, 1993.

Pettigrew, Joyce. *Sikhs of the Punjab: Unheard Voices of State and Guerilla Violence*. London: Zed Books, 1995.

Ramakrishnan, Venkitesh. "Nanavati Commission Report: 1984—the Untold Story." *Frontline* 22/18 (2005), http://www.flonnet.com/fl2218/stories/20050909005201900.htm, accessed November 7, 2005.

Sanghvi, Vir. "Forgetting the 1984 Killings Would Be Immoral: A Massacre Is a Massacre!" *Sikh Review* (October 2005): 58–60.

Singh, Manmohan. Speech, in *Sikh Review* (October 2005): 81–83.

Singh, Nikky Guninder Kaur. *The Feminine Principle in the Sikh Vision of the Transcendent*. Cambridge: Cambridge University Press, 1993.

Smith, Jonathan Z. "The Devil in Mr. Jones." In *Imagining Religion: From Babylon to Jonestown*. Chicago: University of Chicago Press, 1982.

Tambiah, Stanley. *Leveling Crowds: Ethnonationalist Conflicts and Collective Violence in South Asia*. Berkeley: University of California Press, 1996.

Tatla, Darshan Singh. *The Sikh Diaspora: The Search for Statehood*. London: UCL Press, 1999.

"Text of H. Con. Res. 227 [107th]." http://www.govtrack.us/congress/billtext.xpd?bill=
   hc107-227, accessed October 21, 2011. accessed October 21, 2011.
Varshney, Ashutosh. *Ethnic Conflict and Civic Life: Hindus and Muslims in India*. New Haven,
   CT: Yale University Press, 2002.
Walia, Varinder"Portrait of Bhindranwale Installed at SGPC's Sikh Museum." November
   29, 2007, http://www.tribuneindia.com/2007/20071130/main4.htm, accessed July
   24, 2008.

PART TWO

Approaches

CHAPTER 7

Cities of Gold

*Teaching Religion and Violence
through "Sacred" Space*

AARON W. HUGHES

INTRODUCTION

The single greatest threat to what it is that we do or think we do in the classroom is
the slogan that religions are all about peace and that it is power-hungry or politically
motivated individuals that somehow hijack an inner core or essence that is perceived
to be incorruptible or beyond the pale of the quotidian. This model of religious
studies so common among our students, the larger community, the media, and, dare
I say it, our colleagues would reduce us to multicultural supporters, interfaith dialogue facilitators, or peace builders. Although there is nothing inherently wrong
with any of these roles,[1] inside of the religious studies classroom they risk leaving a
false impression of what religious studies is or should be. It is an understanding of
the discipline, moreover, that is based on the rhetoric of faith and authenticity, a
rhetoric that necessarily masks the manifold ways that religions further contribute
to ambiguous meanings and unstable identities, and all of the banal and low-minded
repercussions that emerge from such ambiguity and instability.

My assumptions on teaching and writing about religion (admittedly, like any
set of assumptions, they are nothing more or less than that) revolve around critical
discourses that engage seriously reductionist and social-scientific approaches. The
academic study of religion, according to this understanding, is about the messiness
of explanation over the safety of understanding, about cultural production not
faith, about external forms as opposed to interiority, and about sociorhetorical
legitimation rather than the murky inner realms of spirituality.[2]

What follows is based on a series of theoretical reflections developed from a junior-level course that I regularly taught on religion and violence at the University of Calgary. (I have since changed institutions and my new administrative responsibilities mean that I do not often teach this course anymore—however, for the sake of convenience, I will leave this essay's verbs in the present tense.) Ideally (which of course means "rarely" in practice), students who sign up for this course should have taken in a previous semester a freshman course in which they are introduced to the critical tools necessary for approaching religion analytically as opposed to religiously. Moreover, in the best of all possible worlds, the Religious Space and Violence course will function as a gateway into my senior-level course on theory and method, where students will further explore the issues revolving around the constructed and contested nature of religion. The religion and violence course, for me, plays, quite literally, a central role within a three-course sequence wherein I expect students to explore the critical tools necessary for understanding the complexity that the term *religion* so easily masks.

As a segue into the broader issue of religion and violence, I have opted to focus on the theme of space that is constructed as "sacred" by religious practitioners. I find the theme of religious space and violence more manageable because it enables me to explore the more general rubric of religion and violence through a particular prism, which makes the selection of data and other examples much easier, thereby enabling me to get at some of the root causes in ways that are easier than if I was exploring the more general rubric. Because my own area of expertise is in Jewish and Islamic studies, for obvious reasons I tend to focus on Jerusalem and environs. I do, however, also look at other contested spaces (e.g., Ayodhya, Kosovo) as a way to illumine Jerusalem and vice versa.

In my course called Religious Space and Violence, which I have taught three times, my goals are (1) to get students to think about critical theory in religion by using concrete examples; (2) to prod them to think about religion as a humanly constructed phenomenon as opposed to a divinely given one; and (3) to get them to reflect critically on how the "religious" intersects with phenomena from which it is customarily differentiated: the political, the ideological, the economic, and so on.

Everyone who teaches ultimately finds a personal niche based upon perceived lacunae in their departmental settings. Because I teach in a fairly conservative department that is resistant to theory and method, I have become the de facto "theory person." As a consequence, my Religious Space and Violence course becomes one of the main vehicles at my disposal to introduce students to theory and method practically. The advantage of this is that students "do theory" without ever quite being conscious of this activity, thereby providing them with the depth to think about religion critically in their other courses that might otherwise downplay or marginalize the theoretical.

In what follows, I address, in greater detail, these theoretical issues and their practical consequences as they revolve around this specific course, followed by a discussion of my goal in teaching it. Following this, the majority of the chapter discusses the logistics of the class: my syllabus, books I find useful (and why), comparative techniques, supplementary materials (including films) that I employ, and my methods of evaluation.

MY PATH TO TEACHING RELIGION AND VIOLENCE: THE IMPORTANCE OF
THEORY AND METHOD IN THE CLASSROOM

I teach in a department, like most departments of religion or religious studies, whose members pride themselves on the fact that they teach religious studies as opposed to theology. Such boasts usually take the form of spending the first week of every course called Introduction to Religion X or Advanced Studies in Religion X differentiating between the two disciplines. This differentiation usually turns on the outsider-insider dynamic,[3] the perceived objectivity and concomitant neutrality of a discipline called religious studies in ways that make its first principles inherently distinct from those of theology, and then demonstrating how the study of religion in general and religion X in particular helps us to better understand the world around us. After this first week, however, these first principles are often unconsciously forgotten or intentionally cast aside and students are frequently subjected to the customary barrage of color commentary, essentialisms, and an often-bland combination of historical dates and facts, central tenets, and ritual obligations. Within this understanding of the discipline, the greatest virtue to be instilled in students is a form of multicultural understanding or sensitivity toward a religion or religions that they previously knew nothing about.

On one level there is certainly nothing wrong with this, and we, undoubtedly, help thousands of students over our careers develop a better understanding of their neighbors, friends, and colleagues. However, despite the nod to multiculturalism, I have frequently asked myself: Is this it? Did I spend all that time in graduate school, learning languages, reading obscure texts, and generally thinking about religion and religions in manifold theoretical ways just to reproduce, or to listen to my colleagues reproduce, a generic set of slogans that any minister, rabbi, or imam could just as easily produce? The most difficult aspect of teaching, as I have found since leaving graduate school ten years ago, is how to communicate something of religion's human, cultural, political, economic, and ideological aspects. Framed more provocatively, is it our goal to teach religion as a form of color commentary? Or is it our job to show our students how religion, like any other human discourse, is constructed, contested, manipulated, and used to justify everything from the metaphysical to the banal, from the high-minded to the murderous?

It is questions such as this last one that led me to develop my course Religious Space and Violence. Such a course, I believed at the time and for the most part still do, is a way to get students to move beyond understanding to explanation, to think about religion in ways that they customarily have not and do not. Moreover, they do this using vocabularies and conceptual categories that refuse to envisage religion as animated by a stable and uniform identity or essence that moves unchanged throughout history.

For me, theory and method (hereafter T&M) is the sine qua non of our discipline and it is necessary that we, as scholars, reflect upon it and that we show our students what exactly T&M can and cannot do. T&M is frequently met with the critique that those who engage in it refuse to get their hands dirty, presumably by refusing to play in the muck of the linguistic, philological, and historical skills of a particular religious tradition. Teaching a course on religion and violence, often through the prism of a particular city (e.g., Jerusalem), permits me to respond to such claims because in this course I am able to introduce students not only to a complex set of theoretical questions but to ones that are grounded in a particular set of tangible and historical data.

The greatest practical benefit that I give to students—and this is based on student evaluations at the end of the semester—is that they feel like they develop an understanding of religion beyond the often-generic type of material that they learn in classes that deal with a particular religion (i.e., this what practitioners of religion X believe; this is what they do and think; this is how they move their bodies in prayer, conceptualize and act upon the world, and so on). A course devoted to religion and violence enables students to take a problem (e.g., why do people kill in the name of religion?) and attempt to unpack it with an eye to understanding real-life situations that are very relevant to the worlds that they inhabit.

Before I proceed to an analysis of my class, I think it worth mentioning the type of institution in which I teach and the general constituency of the student body in my classes. I teach at a large urban campus in western Canada (the equivalent of an American state university), with a student body that is roughly 65 percent Caucasian and roughly 35 percent that are from East Asia (Taiwan, China) and South Asia (India, Pakistan) or are first-generation Canadian. Most students that sign up for my Religious Space and Violence course do so either because they are religious studies majors or because they are interested in the topic. Departmental regulations stipulate that students must first have taken one of two freshman-level courses, either Religions of the West or what we infelicitously call Nature of Religion. The former is the generic color-commentary course where students are exposed to the three Abrahamic traditions, and the latter is an omnibus course that, depending upon who teaches it, introduces students to concepts such as critical theory of religion, philosophy of religion, sociology of religion, and so on.

My course, Religious Space and Violence, especially post-9/11, is always full (capped at thirty-five), especially with students who want to learn about what might have motivated the terrorists and what exactly it was that informed their worldviews and made them tick. The course is not always easy to teach for a number of reasons that must be negotiated each semester: any class that deals with the Middle East, whether or not it deals explicitly with the Israeli-Palestinian conflict, necessarily provokes strong emotional reactions in people. This is especially the case at a place like the University of Calgary, which has a sizable Muslim student population on campus. Moreover, these tensions in the Middle East can be (and often are) played out, locally, in the classroom, especially when students find out that I am Jewish, and, because of this, they automatically assume that I am pro-Israeli and anti-Palestinian. In the classroom I am neither, and rather than preach this overtly I prefer to let my neutrality come out as we begin to deal with real issues.

A second practical issue that can make the course difficult to teach is the fact that, as a large urban campus in a large ethnically diverse city, the possibility always exists that some of my students will have had firsthand exposure to the type of violence that I teach about in the classroom. Moreover, because it is often a raw connection, there is sometimes an unwillingness or perhaps even an inability on the part of these students to step back from it and think about the interconnections between religion and violence theoretically. This situation is considerably more difficult to negotiate. I once discovered that this was the case only when the student came to talk to me after she had dropped the class.

Regardless, and taking the aforementioned caveats in mind, I persevere with this course in the hope that I can get students to jettison some of their traditional assumptions about religion, much of which involve making use of distinctions such as good/bad, spiritual/fanatical, and even religious/political.[4] For the moment that we engage in such binary thinking, we automatically remove the second term of these pairs from serious engagement in the religious studies classroom. They become the foil from which the first terms are to be disembedded, differentiated, and ultimately defined. Teaching Religious Space and Violence is thus my attempt to address, on a local level, some of the ghosts in our disciplinary closet and, in the process, to correct some of the problematic assumptions that we continue to instill in our students.

Moreover, and framed on another level, such a course enables me to take a particular problem that is mentioned frequently in the news (e.g., Israel and the Palestinian-Israeli conflict) and provide students with the analytical and conceptual tools to unpack it, to step beyond the headlines and grapple with root causes. "Jew" and "Muslim," on one hand, so sexy and telltale, are in fact nothing but religious essentialisms (unfortunately the very essentialisms we so often peddle in our introductory courses) that are ultimately unhelpful. For me, the great paradox of teaching about religion and violence is that the term *religion* might not always be the most helpful in trying to understand the topic.

A SYLLABUS FOR RELIGIOUS SPACE AND VIOLENCE

Without reproducing my entire syllabus here, let me highlight what I do by dividing the (twelve- or thirteen-week) semester into a series of discrete but overlapping topics. According to week, I divide the class into the following components, detailed descriptions of which (including readings) follow below:

Week 1	Space, violence, and religion
Weeks 2–3	Jerusalem: from theory to practice
Week 4	Jerusalem: historical, geographical, and political
Weeks 5–6	Theoretical take on Jerusalem as a category
Weeks 7–9	Comparative studies
Week 10	What we learn about Jerusalem from this
Week 11	Jerusalem and violence in film
Weeks 12–13	What have we learned? Where do we go from here?

ESTABLISHING THE CONNECTION BETWEEN PLACE AND VIOLENCE

Let me now move from the general theme of religion and violence to the more specific topic of my chapter: space that is constructed to be religious or sacred in the minds of religious practitioners and violence.[5] To undertake this topic I find it useful to begin the semester by reading what I consider to be two classic works dealing with religious space broadly conceived and defined. The first is the introduction ("Approximations: The Structure and Morphology of the Sacred") and the chapter titled "Sacred Places: Temple, Palace, 'Centre of the World'" in Mircea Eliade's *Patterns in Comparative Religion*; the second is the critique of Eliade's notion of sacred space in Jonathan Z. Smith's "The Wobbling Pivot."[6] Although neither of these two pieces is devoted specifically to the theme of violence, both show fairly clearly what is at stake in dealing with so-called sacred space. Because they take radically different approaches to the notion of space, these two readings enable students to enter into the larger world of religious studies by examining some of its contested terms. In particular, my goal is that students will learn to use caution when employing terms such as *sacred* or *holy*, the latter adjective frequently being used to describe Jerusalem as the "holy land," by realizing such terms have distinct genealogies in the discipline.

Since my own operating academic assumptions about religions revolve around their active human constructions, their ideologies, and their ultimate instability, the first thing that I set out to do in my class is to dismantle the familiar, yet often meaningless, category of the "sacred." This involves subverting the Eliadian notion that the sacred is something extraordinary, something that manifests itself in any number of hierophanies or kratophanies on the level of human existence. For Eliade, "Every sacred space implies a hierophany, and irruption of the sacred that results in detaching a territory from the surrounding cosmic milieu and making it qualitatively different."[7]

The irruptions of the sacred subsequently become archetypes that are repeatable by religious practitioners on both temporal (i.e., sacred time) and spatial (i.e., sacred space) levels. For Eliade, these irruptions represent points of communication between god and humans, a "paradoxical point of passage from one mode of being to another."[8] Eliade's account of sacred space, perhaps unsurprisingly, tends to conform to the religious sensibilities of my students. Certainly, on one level, it might make sense to conceive of a place like Jerusalem as an omphalos, the *axis mundi*, or the place where heaven and earth intersect. On another level, however, is such terminology all that helpful or useful?

Juxtaposing Eliade's treatment of space with Smith's critique of Eliade enables my students to understand immediately the assumptions that are operative in the former's work. What, for example, is the relationship of a center to the periphery? Are all events regarded as "primordial" repeatable? Does "profane" space really represent chaos and the chaotic that must be overcome by religious practitioners?

Another unfortunate repercussion of Eliade's approach to the sacred more generally is his almost total disinterest in history and the historical record. In fact, for Eliade, history represents the profanation of the sacred, the movement away from the initial irruption, and the living in profane time and space as opposed to their sacred equivalents.[9] This, it seems to me, is emblematic of our discipline: we tend to use history when it suits us to make a particular point; however, at other times we are often content to try and make certain ahistorical comparisons under the guise of elucidating something problematically referred to as "the sacred."

My goal in using these two readings in the first week of the semester is to set the agenda for what is to come. Unlike Eliade, and more like Smith, we will not engage in theorizing about the sacred or some sort of sacred-profane binary. Likewise we will enter the realm of history (and politics and economics) to describe thickly a particular space that has been the site of various skirmishes that are often signed as "religious," whether by the media or those in the actual debates about Jerusalem.

It is worth mentioning that since I last taught this course, I have been thinking of employing the final chapter, titled "Snakes Alive: Religious Studies Between Heaven and Earth," found in Robert A. Orsi's *Between Heaven and Earth*.[10] This essay, although dealing primarily with lived religion in America, would nevertheless be very useful in helping students think about the various intellectual and religious motivations that have gone into the creation of a discourse of good and bad religions, including good and bad religious idioms both inside and outside of the academy.

Having hopefully cleared some terminological and conceptual ground in the first week with this exercise, I now move into the heart of the course.

TEXTBOOKS

One of the greatest difficulties I have when it comes to selecting books for a class devoted to the topic of religion and violence is to find ones that do not subscribe to the "violence as hijacking a normative tradition" thesis. The two primary books that I usually adopt for my course are Bruce Lincoln's *Holy Terrors* and Mark Juergensmeyer's *Terror in the Mind of God*.[11] These books, with radically different takes on the nature of religion and its relationship to violence, seem to balance each other nicely in the classroom.

Lincoln's *Holy Terrors* provides an excellent theoretical discussion on the theme of religion and violence, but not necessarily religious space and violence. I thus find it a useful exercise to get students to tease out the implications of Lincoln's work for our class (see my comments under Examinations and Term Papers below). The book itself begins with a critique of Clifford Geertz's classic definition of religion and subsequently goes on to problematize religion as something delimited and definable. Most useful for me in the classroom is Lincoln's broad-based, nontheological, and all-encompassing definition of religion as composed of four interrelated components:

1. A *discourse* whose concerns transcend the human, temporal, and contingent, and that claims for itself a similarly transcendent status.
2. A set of *practices* whose goal is to produce a proper world and/or proper human subjects, as defined by a religious discourse to which these practices are connected.

3. A *community* whose members construct their identity with reference to a religious discourse and its attendant practices.
4. An *institution* that regulates religious discourse, practices, and community, reproducing them over time and modifying them as necessary, while asserting their eternal validity and transcendent value.[12]

This four-pronged definition really sets the tenor of what is to follow in the semester. I find it so useful precisely because it facilitates students to consider further the fact that religion is not something that is simply internal or interior to the individual. Religion becomes, on Lincoln's reading, an ideology in which four domains—discourse, practices, community, and institution—configure and reconfigure in various permutations. Moreover, this definition enables students to understand that in any given religious tradition (e.g., Islam, Hinduism), there exist any number of possible varieties and subdivisions, "each of which undergoes its own historic process of development and change."[13] Very quickly, in other words, students are introduced to complexity within the category of religion and they also learn to avoid essentializing traditions.

I also find Lincoln's book useful in the classroom because of his taxonomic differentiation between *minimalist* and *maximalist* understandings of religion. The latter, more customarily called fundamentalist, argues that religion should permeate all aspects of human existence, whereas the former tends to restrict religion to a set of often-metaphysical concerns. Once again, within each religion, what Lincoln calls a "macro-entity," there exist various permutations of each of these categories. Such distinctions are useful in the classroom because they enable students to avoid characterizing Islam, simplistically and lazily as is so often done in the media and other public discourses, as essentially maximalist, and Judaism, based on popular television shows such as *Seinfeld*, as inherently minimalist. Each tradition, on the contrary, contains maximalist and minimalist trajectories, ones that are often antagonistic to one another within the same macro-entity.

Holy Terrors enables students to understand the complexity of religion in ways that do not simply restrict it to one part of a binary (e.g., religion-state, religion-politics). Moreover, Lincoln's subsequent discussion of the ways in which figures such as Osama bin Laden and George W. Bush construct their own discourse permits students to unpack further the role of discourse in relationship to the other three domains of Lincoln's definition. *Holy Terrors* also provides a good point of departure in the classroom for discussions of the interconnected relationship between religion and culture, and how religion is not simply a system of pure ideas but is intimately connected to series of social, political, and historical contexts. Indeed, as I argued at the beginning of this chapter, religion cannot be understood apart from these contexts.

Mention should also be made here that not all students like Lincoln's take on religion. Several of my better students have regarded it as too fraught with ideology and too materialist in its concerns. Several of the weaker students find Lincoln's discussion too complex to follow. It is a difficult and controversial work that requires much unpacking in the classroom. However, I have found the discussions that it gives rise to very stimulating. Most important, though, it gives the class a series of terms that we can refer to throughout the semester (e.g., minimalist, maximalist, macro-entity).

Mark Juergensmeyer's *Terror in the Mind of God* is also useful, though for completely different reasons. Unlike Lincoln's book, Juergensmeyer seeks to uncover the viewpoint of religious people who engage in violent actions. As such, the greatest utility of his book resides not in his theoretical apparatus (which, as I discuss in the following paragraph, I find problematic), but in the face-to-face interviews that he undertook with religious militants (e.g., Mahmud Abouhalima, who was involved in the 1993 World Trade Center blast, or Yoel Lerner, a messianic Zionist who lives in Jerusalem's Old City). Such interviews afford students a series of insights into the imaginations of these individuals that they would otherwise not have. The interviews are fascinating, lively, and always maintain the interest of students.

On a theoretical level, however, my main problem with Juergensmeyer's book is that it goes against the grain of my own take on religious violence. In particular, Juergensmeyer accepts the accounts of the people he interviews at face value. He does not, then, concern himself with the rhetorical or ideological valences of their language. People kill in the name of religion, according to him, because they say they do. In differentiating between "symbolic" violence (i.e., that which refers to something beyond the immediate target) and "strategic" violence (i.e., that which is part of a political strategy) Juergensmeyer ultimately subscribes to the "religion and—" binary that I am so interested in dismantling in the classroom.[14] All human actions are ultimately political and to say that 9/11 was more symbolic than practical, more ritualistic than political, needlessly separates reality into two essentially separate zones based on the sacred-secular.[15]

Students obviously like Juergensmeyer's work because it is highly readable and not nearly as theoretical in its orientation as Lincoln's book. They especially appreciate the firsthand descriptions of those who engage in violent activities in the name of religion. This asset, however, as I try to point out in the classroom, is also *Terror in the Mind of God*'s greatest liability.

HOW I UTILIZE THE READINGS

Given the different orientations and concerns of the two books, I try to get students to read them together, to cross-pollinate them. For example, in week 2 students are requested to read the introduction ("Terror and God") from Juergensmeyer combined with chapter 1 ("The Study of Religion in the Current Political Moment") from Lincoln. Again, in week 3 I combine Juergensmeyer's chapter 7 ("Theatre of Terror") with Lincoln's chapter 5 ("Religious Conflict and the Postcolonial State"). In this combination, students not only see two completely different academic takes on the topic of religion and violence but also are compelled to compare two of the most theoretical chapters from each book with an eye to understanding the inherent tensions between the secular character of the modern state and the often religious understanding of nation or nationhood. Although both Juergensmeyer and Lincoln only touch upon Jerusalem and the Israeli-Palestinian conflict, they both lay the groundwork for class discussion. Some questions that might guide such discussions include the following:

- What is the nature of the relationships between religious groups and state elites in Israel, Palestine, and even in North America?
- What are some of the ways that the tensions between these groups manifest themselves in terms of both violence and nonviolence?

BOOKS THAT HAVE NOT WORKED FOR ME

Since 9/11 a plethora of books have been published with the intention of trying to explain, understand, and interpret religious violence. Many of these books include the thesis that religion, or at least certain strands of religion, can make otherwise good people turn bad. Such books include, but are certainly not limited to, the rather sensationalist account found in Jessica Stern, the overly sociological account found in Almond et al., and the "violence as hijacking a normative tradition" account found in Charles Kimball.[16] Implicit in much of this literature is that violence happens when religious people turn to various acts of political defiance to make a point for their religion or religious worldview that they somehow feel is under threat. "Religion" is thus neatly bifurcated from "politics," as is "belief" from "action" and "good" from "bad." It is these binaries that, as mentioned above, Lincoln's book is so useful in trying to overturn.

I should also add that in a previous incarnation of this course I tried selections from René Girard's *Violence and the Sacred*,[17] but the students found this far too theoretical and opaque. This is not to say that I might not try it again in the future, only that I would have to rethink seriously how I introduced it.

SUPPLEMENTARY MATERIALS

Any class in religious studies necessarily demands primary sources. To this end, I try to incorporate a number of readings, including Web sites, that I think reflect both the dynamics and the difficulties of understanding the contestation that revolves around Jerusalem, while showing some of the historical depth that embodies this problematic.

The key, of course, is to get the primary sources to balance, supplement, or contradict the readings that students will encounter in both Lincoln and Juergensmeyer. Such primary sources, thus, function as a set of unmediated reflections by the players themselves about exactly what it is they are doing or, at least, think it is that they are doing.

Examples of such primary sources include the following:

- Proof texts from the Hebrew Bible (e.g., Joshua 23:1–13; Nehemiah 8:1–8) and the Qur'an (e.g., 17:1–3), especially its narrative expansions in the hadith and other literature describing the sanctity of Jerusalem[18]

- Historical materials dealing with the establishment of Jerusalem as the cultic center of ancient Israel
- Materials that show the importance of Jerusalem (now al-Quds) in the development of the political and religious rise of Islam
- Zionistic literature that predates the foundation of the state of Israel in 1948

Many of these historical documents are conveniently located in the sourcebook edited by F. E. Peters, which I either assign as the third textbook for the course or use various photocopies from.[19] This book presents a chronology of Jerusalem from biblical times through Muslim rule and the Crusades up to the nineteenth century. While some of these primary sources are on the dry side (especially when compared to the interviews with religious militants found in the Juergensmeyer book), they nonetheless provide a series of chronological eyewitness accounts of how exactly others have perceived and written about Jerusalem. In so doing, they show the depth of contestations that have revolved around this complicated city from a variety of Jewish, Christian, and Muslim perspectives. I also supplement these historical readings with a series of more up-to-date readings, such as readings from Western newspapers, in addition to Arab and Israeli English-language newspapers. This combination of the ancient and medieval with the contemporary nicely juxtaposes historical and modern accounts, thereby revealing something of the dynamics of space constructed as religious. Moreover, the fact that many of the more modern accounts are often filtered through a series of political and economic concerns shows that much more is at stake here than simply the so-called religious.

In addition to such materials, I also get my students to look at various Web sites that are relevant to the ideology of Jerusalem. Web sites, when regarded as primary sources as opposed to secondary ones (which, unfortunately students all too often mistake them for), play an important role in the classroom. Web sites that I have used include the following:

- The official Meir Kahane website (http://www.kahanetzadak.com), which provides a series of YouTube speeches, sermons, and debates about the sanctity of Jerusalem for Jews and the importance of removing its Arab presence
- Other pro-Jewish Jerusalem sites such as that of the Temple Mount Faithful (templemountfaithful.org) and the Jewish Defense League (jdl.org)
- Christian Zionist Web pages that speak of Jerusalem for Jews and that link this concept to the anticipated return of the Messiah, such as Christian Friends of Israel (cfijerusalem.org) and Christian action for Israel (christianactionforisrael.org)
- Selections from the sermons of Osama bin Laden concerning the plight of the Palestinians[20]

I introduce these Web pages and sermons at the beginning of the semester, immediately after the section on religion and space. This immediately takes us out of the theoretical domain of the academic study of religion and introduces us to the messiness of the situation on the ground. Here students encounter, many for the first time, hatred, racism, and hate speech in the name of religion. This is a far cry from the "religion equals peace" slogans that so many students are used to hearing. I certainly emphasize that many of these Web sites are of uncertain provenance and may be the creations of no more than one or two electronically savvy individuals. The goal, though, is not to get at who is creating these sites but to try to understand something of the rhetoric and ideology that motivate them.

After introducing students to these materials to show the stakes involved, I then move, diachronically, back to the historical record. This succeeds in framing the older materials through some of the concerns of the present and also gives students a glimpse at the way ideology functions in the earlier materials (as indeed it does in the contemporary material). I subsequently return to these sermons and pages again near the end of the semester to show how much of this historical material is filtered through the concerns of the present.

THE COMPARATIVE PERSPECTIVE

Because I frame my discussion of Jerusalem through the more general rubric of religion, violence, and space, it is necessary to have a comparative approach to the class. This is not just to pay homage to Müller's old adage that "to know one is to know none" but to get students to appreciate the utility of moving outside of their data to a number of other case studies and then return to their own data to see what has been learned in the process.[21]

Before beginning this section of the course, I always find it necessary to warn students about the shortcomings of comparison—in other words, how, on one level, it is false to compare and contrast different things from completely different cultural, geographical, and temporal contexts. Here I think it important to get students to realize that we do not compare in the sense that Joseph Campbell made famous, nor do we do so to flatten copious amounts of context-less data in the way that Eliade did. On the contrary, I try to emphasize that comparison works best when it is done thickly and contextually, and when it hinges on difference as opposed to similarity.

When I introduce the comparative component of the class, I want to focus not just on violence, but also on the more general rubric of religion and urban geography.[22] Here I assign students relatively short sections (twenty–twenty-five pages) from the writings of Paul Wheatley on the ancient Chinese city, Glen W. Bowersock on the Vatican, and Diana Eck on Banaras.[23]

Following these more general reflections on religion and space, we turn our attention to space and violence. Here, two examples we look at are Ayodhya and the former Yugoslavia. For Ayodhya, I usually assign the students a series of Web pages:

- For a brief and objective overview of the topic, I assign the BBC Web page dealing with the conflict (news.bbc.co.uk/2/hi/south_asia/1843879.stm), in addition to the internal links found there.[24]
- A Web page by militant Hindus that makes the case of religious, cultural, and legal claims to the area (www.ayodhya.com).

Following this, we discuss the relationship between peoplehood, memory, and soil. Implicit in the discussions is that what we have already encountered in our study of Jerusalem is not a unique phenomenon.

We also spend time looking at these relationships in the former Yugoslavia. In this regard I assign sections from Michael Sells's *The Bridge Betrayed*, which provides not only an excellent account of religion, space, and violence in the former Yugoslavia, but also supplements it with an important theoretical take on the data.[25] Finally, to round off the comparative component, I get students to read the chapter titled "The Sword of Sikhism" in Juergensmeyer's *Terror in the Mind of God*.

Once we look at all of these case studies, we return to Jerusalem and see if we can broaden our understanding of it. Students see, on the one hand, that Jerusalem is not unique. Yet, on the other, they realize how, in important ways, Jerusalem differs from some of the other sites given its own political, economic, and religious history.

MOVIES

Increasingly, an important feature of the religious studies classroom is showing movies or video clips to illustrate a point. To this end, I usually choose two movies that, in my opinion, adequately reflect the complexity of Jerusalem in the modern world. One of these is the Israeli-produced *Time of Favor* (*Ha-hesder*), and the other is the Palestinian-produced *Paradise Now*.[26] Both of these films, despite being produced on different sides of the contemporary conflict, are anything but polemic accounts of the situation on the ground. Indeed, if anything they show the complexity, frustration, and tragedy of the Palestinian-Israeli conflict as it revolves around key concepts such as space, memory, religion, politics, and economics. Moreover, both do so in ways that focus on particular individuals that can function as metonyms. Both movies, in other words, reinforce the larger theme of my course that the struggle over Jerusalem cannot simply be defined as a religious conflict.

"The land of Israel is bought with pain," says the female protagonist of *Time of Favor*. What follows is a narrative that combines a fundamentalist religious rabbi, a complicated (though fairly unbelievable) love triangle, and an attempt by some of the rabbi's pupils to blow up the Dome of the Rock when they find access to a series of underground tunnels running through Jerusalem's Old City. Despite the mixed reviews the film received, it nevertheless provides a good point of discussion for the intersection of charismatic religious leadership (in the character of Rabbi Meltzer and his West Bank Yeshiva) and veiled religious language (in Rabbi Meltzer's sermons) that can be taken in any numbers of ways, including the incitement to religious violence (as in the character of Pini).

The more critically acclaimed *Paradise Now* tells the story of two childhood friends in Nablus, Khalid and Said, who are about to undertake a suicide bombing in Israel. The film shows the relationship between the friends, their families (who know nothing of their plans), and their "handlers" (i.e., those who supply the bombs, lock them onto the friends, videotape their last statements, and give them their place to attack). As the movie proceeds, Said realizes that he cannot undertake the journey to Israel to carry out the attack and therefore cancels it. After a number of involved plot twists, Said tries to catch up to Khalid, who has slipped into Israel, to convince him to cancel his attack as well. The movie eerily ends with Khalid sitting on a bus full of Israeli soldiers, before the film cuts to white.

As with *Time of Favor*, the most interesting moments, at least from a pedagogical point of view, are in the various conversations that occur between the characters. Here, it is the anxiety-ridden conversations between Said and Khalid, as well as those that Said has with Suha, the woman he has fallen in love with, and who functions as the foil to the two friends' anger.

What is interesting about both movies is their almost total disregard of the other side. *Time of Favor* deals with religious violence by a militant group of Jews set on destroying the Dome of the Rock, whereas *Paradise Now* concerns itself solely with the struggles between two Palestinian friends. In *Time of Favor* we do not even encounter Arabs, and in *Paradise Now*, the only Israelis we encounter are silent and one-dimensional on buses. The first time, Khalid gets on a commercial bus and does not blow himself up is because he makes eye contact with a child onboard; and the second time, at the end of the movie, he is on the bus full of soldiers.

After watching both of these movies, I give students a small assignment, comprising 10 percent of their final grade, that includes a number of questions that they must answer:

- What motivates these individuals to plan their attacks? Is it simply religious?
- Why do each of these movies not deal with the other, except by way of indirect reference?
- How does religion intersect with other related phenomena in each movie (e.g., politics)?

EXAMINATIONS AND TERM PAPERS

I usually assign a take-home midterm, take-home final, and a term paper in my class. For the midterm (20 percent of the final grade), I ask students to reflect theoretically on the approaches found in the Lincoln and Juergensmeyer books. This usually involves getting students to read one of the interview chapters in the latter book and to supply a rhetorical analysis in light of the former. I list a series of questions and issues on the exam to help students structure their answers, such as these:

- In putting Lincoln and Juergensmeyer in conversation with one another, think about how their respective takes on or definitions of religion structure their concerns.
- Would Lincoln necessarily agree with how "person X" in Juergensmeyer would speak about religion? What hermeneutics of suspicion would he apply to his or her discourse?

- What would the interview look like if Lincoln were asking the questions? What kind of questions might Lincoln ask of these individuals?
- How might Juergensmeyer address some of the concerns raised by Lincoln?

For the take-home final exam (30 percent), I assign a series of broad-based and open-ended questions that get students to reflect on the topic, often encouraging them to articulate responses that nuance religion:

- Your Aunt Sally is over for Sunday dinner, and when she hears that you are taking this course, says something to the effect, "Well, we all know that religion is peaceful. . . . It is only crazy people who kill in its name!" How do you respond?

The term paper (40 percent) I leave open for whatever interests the students in terms of their disciplinary backgrounds and so on. They can write on any topic of religious space and violence that interests them as long as they clear the topic with me first. Topics can involve the economics of violence, writing on Kosovo or Ayodhya, comparing one aspect of Jerusalem with something similar in another place, and so on.

CONCLUSION

I find teaching a course devoted to the topic of religious space and violence very rewarding for several reasons. First, it gives me peace of mind that I am teaching students something useful about religion and not just repeating the slogans that religious people tell themselves when they are being religious. Such people certainly do this in the materials we read for this class, but the classroom now becomes the place where we are able to unpack and interrogate some of the political, ideological, sexist, and even machismo features that link up with what students are often more accustomed to when they speak about religion. I would be the last to argue that everything we do and teach has to have a practical value; however, this class lets me show something of the relevance of religion to the contemporary world. Moreover, it lets me do this in ways that avoid freeing religion from violence by saying that the root motives of such actions are not and cannot be religious because "all religions preach peace."

Teaching this course is also important to me because it lets me explore with students the embedded nature of religion. Religion, as a category or taxon, as others have well shown, is not something that exists out there in the world, easily accessible to the gaze of the expert in religious studies. Religion, on the contrary, is in many ways a modern construct that cannot be easily separated from a host of other social phenomena, in much the same manner that religious behavior or experience is ultimately an agglomeration of other social behaviors.

This brings me to the final reason why I teach a course on religious space and violence: the importance of introducing theory and method into the classroom in ways that are not separate from real data. This class enables me and my students to get our hands dirty, to avoid the charge that theory and method are impractical or devoid of relevance to religion as it is practiced in the real world. For the theme of religion and violence enables students to see how religious identities express themselves through violence, the way that even the most racist and murderous discourses can be coded as divine, and how religion couples with the political and the ideological in ways that question the very utility or basic assumptions of the term "religion".

NOTES

I would like to thank Jennifer M. Hall for reading a draft of this essay and making several suggestions.

1. I also have no intention of implying that the scholar of religious studies should not engage in such activities outside of the classroom.
2. I explore these issues in greater detail in Aaron W. Hughes, *Situating Islam: The Past and Future of an Academic Discipline* (London: Equinox Press, 2007), 49–56. A pedagogical approach that incorporates this may be found in Russell T. McCutcheon, *Studying Religion: An Introduction* (London: Equinox Press, 2007).
3. On this dynamic in the discipline, see the collection of essays: Russell T. McCutcheon, ed., *The Insider/Outsider Problem in the Study of Religion: A Reader* (London: Cassel, 1999).
4. There is of course a lengthy genealogy of such binaries in our discipline. Perhaps nowhere is this clearer than in William James, *The Varieties of Religious Experience: A Study in Human Nature*, centenary ed. (London: Routledge, 2002).
5. I prefer *space* to *sacred space* because I believe that no space is inherently sacred; it is conceived of as such only through a variety of political, ideological, economic, and historical reasons. The term *sacred* thus masks all of these much more complex factors and should, in my opinion, be avoided.
6. Mircea Eliade, *Patterns in Comparative Religion*, trans. Rosemary Sheed (New York: New American Library, 1958), 1–37, 367–87; Jonathan Z. Smith, "The Wobbling Pivot," in *Map Is Not Territory: Studies in History of Religions* (Chicago: University of Chicago Press, 1978): 88–103.
7. Mircea Eliade, *The Sacred and the Profane: The Nature of Religion*, trans. Willard R. Trask (New York: Harvest/HBJ, 1959): 26.
8. Ibid., 26.
9. Ibid., 110–13.
10. Robert A. Orsi, *Between Heaven and Earth: The Religious Worlds People Make and the Scholars Who Study Them* (Princeton, NJ: Princeton University Press, 2005).
11. Bruce Lincoln, *Holy Terrors: Thinking about Religion after 9/11* (Chicago: University of Chicago Press, 2003). This book underwent a second edition in 2006 that includes a section called "Theses on Religion and Violence." Mark Juergensmeyer, *Terror in the Mind of God: The Global Rise of Religious Violence*, 3rd ed. (Berkeley: University of California Press, 2003).
12. Lincoln, *Holy Terrors*, 5–7.
13. Ibid., 8.
14. Juergensmeyer, *Terror in the Mind of God*, 124–28.
15. Here I rely on the critique as set out in Russell T. McCutcheon, *The Discipline of Religion: Structure, Meaning, Rhetoric* (New York: Routledge, 2003), 269–71.
16. Jessica Stern, *Terror in the Name of God: Why Religious Militants Kill* (New York: Ecco, 2004); Gabriel A. Almond, R. Scott Appleby, and Immanuel Sivan, *Strong Religion:*

The Rise of Fundamentalisms Around the World (Chicago: University of Chicago Press, 2003); Charles Kimball, *When Religion Becomes Evil* (San Francisco: HarperSan Francisco, 2002).

17. René Girard, *Violence and the Sacred*, trans. Patrick Gregory (Baltimore, MD: Johns Hopkins University Press, 1977). Within this theoretical context, I make note of a newer book that includes a number of selections, including Girard, from classic texts (from Hegel to Benjamin to Taussig) dealing with this topic: Bruce B. Lawrence and Aisha Karim, eds., *On Violence: A Reader* (Durham, NC: Duke University Press, 2007).

18. On this literature, which can often be quite difficult for instructors not familiar with the canons of Islam, the most useful place to find it is in the Peters book, which I describe in the following paragraph.

19. F. E. Peters, *Jerusalem: The Holy City in the Eyes of Chroniclers, Visitors, Pilgrims, and Prophets from the Days of Abraham to the Beginnings of Modern Times* (Princeton, NJ: Princeton University Press, 1985).

20. In his speeches translated by James Howarth, *Messages to the World: The Statements of Osama bin Laden*, ed. and intro. Bruce Lawrence (London: Verso, 2005), 3–19.

21. Here I take as my point of departure Jonathan Z. Smith, *To Take Place: Toward Theory in Ritual* (Chicago: University of Chicago Press, 1987), 47–73.

22. In fact, I am currently thinking about offering a course on the topic of religion and urban geography.

23. Paul Wheatley, *The Pivot of the Four Quarters: A Preliminary Enquiry into the Origins and Character of the Ancient Chinese City* (Edinburgh: Edinburgh University Press, 1971); Glen W. Bowersock, "Peter and Constantine," in *St. Peter's in the Vatican*, ed. William Tronzo (Cambridge: Cambridge University Press, 2005), 5–16; Diana L. Eck, *Encountering God: A Spiritual Journey from Bozeman to Banaras* (Boston: Beacon Press, 2003).

24. As of 2007, one can now watch the destruction of the Babri Masjid on YouTube. I have not assigned this yet, but I might in a future incarnation of the class.

25. Michael A. Sells, *The Bridge Betrayed: Religion and Genocide in Bosnia* (Berkeley: University of California Press, 1998).

26. Joesph Cedar, *Time of Favor (Ha-hesder)* (Cinema Factory Production, 2000); Hany Abu-Assad, *Paradise Now* (Augustus Films, 2005).

BIBLIOGRAPHY

Abu-Assad, Hany. *Paradise Now*. Augustus Films, 2005.

Almond, Gabriel A., R. Scott Appleby, and Immanuel Sivan. *Strong Religion: The Rise of Fundamentalisms Around the World*. Chicago: University of Chicago Press, 2003.

Bin Laden, Osama. *Messages to the World: The Statements of Osama bin Laden*. Ed. and intro. Bruce Lawrence, trans. James Howarth. London: Verso, 2005.

Bowersock, Glen W. "Peter and Constantine." In *St. Peter's in the Vatican*, ed. William Tronzo, 5–16. Cambridge: Cambridge University Press, 2005.

Cedar, Joseph. *Time of Favor (Ha-hesder)*. Cinema Factory Production, 2000.

Eck, Diana L. *Encountering God: A Spiritual Journey from Bozeman to Banaras*. Boston: Beacon Press, 2003.

Eliade, Mircea. *Patterns in Comparative Religion*. Trans. Rosemary Sheed. New York: New American Library, 1958.

———. *The Sacred and the Profane: The Nature of Religion*. Trans. Willard R. Trask. New York: Harvest/HBJ, 1959.

Girard, René. *Violence and the Sacred*. Trans. Patrick Gregory. Baltimore, MD: Johns Hopkins University Press, 1977.

Hughes, Aaron W. *Situating Islam: The Past and Future of an Academic Discipline*. London: Equinox Press, 2007.

James, William. *The Varieties of Religious Experience: A Study in Human Nature*, centenary ed., foreword by Micky James, intro. Eugene Taylor and Jeremy Carrette. London: Routledge, 2002.

Juergensmeyer, Mark. *Terror in the Mind of God: The Global Rise of Religious Violence*, 3rd ed. Berkeley: University of California Press, 2003.

Kimball, Charles. *When Religion Becomes Evil*. San Francisco: HarperSan Francisco, 2002.

Lawrence, Bruce B., and Aisha Karim, eds. *On Violence: A Reader*. Durham, NC: Duke University Press, 2007.

Lincoln, Bruce. *Holy Terrors: Thinking about Religion after 9/11*. Chicago: University of Chicago Press, 2003.

McCutcheon, Russell T. *The Discipline of Religion: Structure, Meaning, Rhetoric*. New York: Routledge, 2003.

———. *Studying Religion: An Introduction*. London: Equinox Press, 2007.

———, ed. *The Insider/Outsider Problem in the Study of Religion: A Reader*. London: Cassel, 1999.

Orsi, Robert A. *Between Heaven and Earth: The Religious Worlds People Make and the Scholars Who Study Them*. Princeton, NJ: Princeton University Press, 2005.

Peters, F. E. *Jerusalem: The Holy City in the Eyes of Chroniclers, Visitors, Pilgrims, and Prophets from the Days of Abraham to the Beginnings of Modern Times*. Princeton, NJ: Princeton University Press, 1985.

Sells, Michael A. *The Bridge Betrayed: Religion and Genocide in Bosnia*. Berkeley: University of California Press, 1998.

Smith, Jonathan Z. *To Take Place: Toward Theory in Ritual*. Chicago: University of Chicago Press, 1987.

———. "The Wobbling Pivot." In *Map Is Not Territory: Studies in History of Religions*, 88–103. Chicago: University of Chicago Press, 1978.

Stern, Jessica. *Terror in the Name of God: Why Religious Militants Kill*. New York: Ecco, 2004.

Wheatley, Paul. *The Pivot of the Four Quarters: A Preliminary Enquiry into the Origins and Character of the Ancient Chinese City*. Edinburgh: Edinburgh University Press, 1971.

CHAPTER 8

Believing is Seeing

Teaching Religion and Violence in Film

KEN DERRY

INTRODUCTION: WHAT IS GOING ON

Sometimes truth defies reason.
—Fenton Meiks, *Frailty* (2001)

With teaching, as with religion, sometimes it can be hard to know exactly what is going on. One of my first students ever was a young man who spent each class staring out the window, eyes half-closed, never speaking. I assumed he was tired or bored, or both. I ignored him. When he finally did talk after many weeks, I discovered that he was, in fact, one of the most attentive students in the room. Clearly I had missed seeing him as he really was. As a result, I worked to become less quick to judge (and dismiss) students based on my own preconceptions.

I had a similar experience while coteaching the University of Toronto's Religion and Film course with a colleague, Tony S. L. Michael. Tony and I each selected half the films for the course, and Tony included Bill Paxton's *Frailty* on his list. In the story of a father who seems insane, brutally murdering several people because God tells him they are evil and must be destroyed, the movie's surprise ending reveals the father to have been right all along: the people he killed were, as he had been informed, monsters all.

I did not like it.

Aside from its trick finale, the film seemed to me rather one dimensional. Tony ignored my objections. He saw something in the film I did not and was convinced he could make good use out of it for a discussion of religion and violence. He had also come up with what he saw as an engaging preclass question: "Can you see connections between what happens in *Frailty* and what is going on currently in the world?" Although we typically used the weekly questions to encourage reflection on a specific (academic) topic, in this case Tony was simply trying to help students find a way to relate to what is, in many ways, an alienating film.

The results were both surprising and wonderfully instructive. Students, almost to a person, drew parallels between the movie's father and just about every vilified, violent political figure one could imagine. The big winners were George W. Bush and Osama bin Laden, although Hitler also scored well. In other words, to our surprise, the vast majority of students had completely missed the point of the film's ending. In their responses they consistently described the father as "deluded" into a "false belief," using his religion to "justify" murder. This is precisely the opposite of the understanding the movie clearly presents. But if it is so clear, why couldn't the students see what was going on?

With responses in hand, Tony threw out his most of his planned lecture and instead launched into an inspired discussion of what the students had seen in the film, and why. The discussion revealed and engaged the students' assumed position that God would never sanction the kind of violence depicted in the film. Whether or not the father's victims were evil, to our students these murders were unjustified and so, by definition, could not have been ordered by God—not even a fictional, cinematic version of God. The father was therefore insane, or self-justifying, or both. This stance was shared by the vast majority of our students, including those who self-identified as nonreligious, and it appeared that it was this stance that prevented them from even really seeing the film at all.

RELIGION AND VIOLENCE AND FILM

> Which one of these stories do you believe?
> —Commoner, *Rashomon* (1950)

Margaret Miles argues that in many ways films can function as religions, and in particular that they have a cumulative mythic effect upon us that shapes our worldviews. Seeing, in other words, often leads to believing.[1] In many ways I agree. However, my own experiences in the classroom suggest that the reverse may also at times be true, that what we believe has a very real effect on what we see.

Mary Bergen has written of her own interest in this dynamic, attempting to demonstrate in literature courses "that how one reads determines what one reads."[2] This interest developed out of her dissatisfaction with the Socratic method of teaching literature, the question-and-answer format traditionally designed to push or pull students toward a single "ideal" reading of the work at hand. Although as a student she found this method impressive (if also intimidating), as a teacher Bergen discovered that she was less interested in ideal readings than in opening up texts to diverse interpretations. Among other pedagogical benefits, this approach encourages and empowers students to really use the texts themselves, to derive understandings based on evidence and their own skills and knowledge rather than try to conjure up the elusive interpretation their instructor had already decided was the correct one. And it is the very diversity of these understandings of the same work that helps to demonstrate how each of us creates meaning in our own ways.

As Russell McCutcheon suggests, this process of interpretation is highly relevant to the study and teaching of both religion and film. In particular, he advises us "to see film—much like myth itself—as a contemporary medium whereby human communities construct and contest their ever-changing and emotionally charged social identities."[3] Instead of using movies as examples or manifestations of sacred phenomena, therefore, teachers of religion should instead take advantage of film's capacity to highlight the human process of (and tendency toward) creating meaning. To illustrate his point, McCutcheon discusses three films—*Rashomon* (1950), *Blow Up* (1966), and *Blow Out* (1981)—that explicitly dramatize this process.[4]

These films are also all explicitly violent, as each centers around attempts to understand a murder. Although McCutcheon himself does not mention this point, I believe it is worth highlighting. That is, I think that considerations of religion and violence are often particularly useful for discussing the ways in which people make sense of their world. Both terms are loaded, as it were, and many students have strong—at times intractable—opinions on the relations between them. But the very strength of these opinions can be used as a lever to uncover key preconceptions and shed some critical light on what supports them.

Certain films may facilitate this process, sometimes in surprising ways. Thus, the fact that *Frailty* is not a complicated movie in many respects actually makes it an effective pedagogical tool with which to raise some relatively complex questions. These include not simply whether, or in what ways, religions may promote violence, but also how assumptions about religion and violence affect the ways in which we literally and figuratively view the world.

In part films can work well in this regard because of their visceral power. They engage more senses, and do so more forcefully, than texts or lectures. There is a difference between discussing religion and violence in an abstract sense and discussing scenes in which Bill Paxton's god-conversant character kills people with an axe. Also, research has shown that the majority of people are visual learners (who understand and retain material better if it is presented through images), yet many of us continue to teach to the minority of students who are verbal learners (who prefer words or formulas).[5] Of course this fact does not mean that we should avoid texts and lectures, but simply that pictures can help us to address a fuller spectrum of learning styles.

Movies are also helpful in the classroom simply because visual culture is such a major component of students' experience. I have taught religion classes using literature as well as film. Both media certainly have their value, but in my experience students feel much more confident talking about movies, especially Hollywood movies. They rarely question anything I say about T. S. Eliot's *Four Quartets* but do not hesitate to challenge my interpretations of *Walking Tall* or *The Lion King*.[6] Not only is this kind of debate healthy on its own terms—keeping both instructors and students on their intellectual toes—but it also makes students active participants in their education rather than passive vessels for my ineffable wisdom.[7]

TEACHING PERSPECTIVES

I'm a god. I'm not *the* God . . .I don't think.
—Phil Connors, *Groundhog Day* (1993)

There are many, many ways in which one might use film in a classroom to consider questions of religion and violence.[8] My own approach is simply one that I have found reasonably successful in very particular respects, which is to say that I use films and academic theories that together help me to accomplish a number of specific pedagogical goals: engaging students in the subject matter; provoking reflection on the process of interpretation; increasing visual literacy; and encouraging a view of both films and academic theories as interpretations.

I usually begin a course by showing a movie that in my view is semantically rich and simply asking students to identify any aspects that may be considered religious or violent. I have found *Groundhog Day* works well for this exercise. It is possible to identify in this film a variety of Christian, Jewish, Buddhist, Hindu, and even Greek religious elements. The film also dramatizes what might be considered more generically religious themes and concepts including ritual, myth, prayer, and enlightenment.

The violence of *Groundhog Day* is similarly diverse. The main character, Phil, is both misogynistic and misanthropic. Also, in his quest to escape the eternal return of February 2, he commits acts of extreme harm against his own body. Such external violence arguably mirrors the internal violence he appears to have been doing to himself for years, putting his own interests ahead of others' and becoming lonely and miserable in the process. Finally, there is the violent snowstorm that strands Phil in Punxsutawney in the first place, initiating the dharmic cycle that ultimately leads to his awakening.

Reviewing all of these interpretations ideally accomplishes several goals. The exercise prepares students for a variety of unexpected ways of looking at films during the rest of the course, and at questions of religion and violence. In this regard it also suggests that a movie can "mean" many different things, that there is not necessarily a single, ideal interpretation that we are trying to find like a treasure hidden in a cave. And very often a student shows me a way of looking at *Groundhog Day* I had not seen before.

I then pose a question each week that connects a theoretical reading to a specific film; this reading will generally represent a particular understanding of religion, which will vary. One week we may be looking at Durkheim's understanding of ritual in connection to *Shall We Dance?* (1996), and the next, Freud's theory of religion as it relates to *Psycho* (1960). Students must submit their brief written response to the course's online discussion board before we actually talk about the material. This requirement means that most students come to class at least somewhat prepared, and also that I have a sense up front of how they have received both the film and the reading. I do not grade these submissions formally, but use them in determining participation marks.

The weekly questions often comprise a variation of, "Does this film fit this theory?" As such, they encourage the students to regard the movie from a certain

perspective, one they likely would not have considered before. With luck, responding to these questions will suggest that when we look at something we always do so
from a particular vantage point. We often only see what we are looking *for*, in other
words, a point that I try to emphasize in class by throwing in alternate ways of
considering the films not included in the readings. These other ways of seeing also
demonstrate that the readings themselves are not meant as course gospels, that
they too represent just one perspective.[9]

In a similar spirit, I tend not to impose a definition of either religion or violence,
but rather let possible meanings for both emerge from the readings and the films,
as well as from the students themselves. Thus the religion under consideration may
be both traditional and explicit, or unorthodox and implicit. Similarly, the violence
discussed can range from punching and shooting, to racism and sexism, to other
sorts of violence that may be less obviously related to moral considerations (like a
snowstorm, or having one's understanding of the world turned upside down).

I have, in fact, arranged the rest of this chapter along such categories of violence:
physical, structural, and mythic. For each, I consider two different approaches and
two different films. In making these selections, I have attempted to avoid repeating
material that has already received a good deal of attention elsewhere. It is partly for
this reason that I have not included any discussion of René Girard's notions of sacrifice and mimetic conflict, notions that seem highly relevant to an impressive array
of films.[10] It is also why I have omitted mention of what may be to some people the
most obvious "religion and violence" movie, Mel Gibson's *The Passion of the Christ*
(2004).[11] My hope in taking this approach is that readers will themselves discover in
what follows at least a few new ways of seeing religion, violence, and film.

PHYSICAL VIOLENCE

Jesus Christ, Action Hero

This is *my* town.
—Chris Vaughn, *Walking Tall* (2004)

One of the most common approaches in religion and film remains what I termed
many years ago "Christ-spotting."[12] It is certainly not difficult to do—by accident or
by design, movies are filled with literally hundreds of characters who fit at least
someone's idea of a Christ-figure—but it is not always easy to do well.[13] This is particularly true in the context of teaching. In my experience, most students have one
of two opposing responses to Christ-spotting: they either reject the approach as
meaningless ("What's the point if you can find Christ-figures everywhere?"), or else
they embrace it a bit too enthusiastically ("This is great: you can find Christ-figures
everywhere!").

Action movies complicate this exercise in pedagogically useful ways, however. A
hero that hits, shoots, or even kills the enemy and who also demonstrates a range
of Christlike qualities raises eyebrows, and questions. There are many such heroes
in Hollywood films, but one that I have especially enjoyed using in my classes is

Chris Vaughn from the 2004 remake of *Walking Tall*. The movie's basic plot is (very) loosely adapted from the real-life experiences of Sheriff Buford Pusser. It begins with Vaughn returning home after several years of service in the military to find his town in moral and economic ruin: the mill has been shut down and replaced with a casino by his old schoolmate Jay Hamilton, who also hooks kids on drugs, traps women in the sex trade, and has the corrupt sheriff in his pocket. In true action movie form, Vaughn turns vigilante and shuts Hamilton down.

In 1997 Lloyd Baugh provided what has become for many a classic outline of the cinematic Christ-figure;[14] when handed this outline students have no trouble ticking off the boxes that show how Vaughn fits it perfectly. He has mysterious origins; is committed to justice; performs miracles; has followers; fights authority; is sacrificed; prays; bleeds; suffers innocently; is crucified and resurrected; and saves people. Some students will also see that Vaughn's character shows many further parallels with conceptions of Jesus not highlighted by Baugh. He is a carpenter; he undergoes a baptism (in the rain after his crucifixion); he spends time with social outcasts (an ex-con and a stripper); he is tempted by "Satan" (Hamilton offers him money and power if Vaughn will submit to his authority); his first name is Chris (changed from Buford); he is arrested and tried and does not deny the charges against him; and he reenacts Jesus's temple outburst in Matthew 21:12–13 with an impressive attention to detail (going so far as to overturn a casino money changer's cart).

However, Vaughn displays other traits that seem less obviously Christlike, which is to say that he smashes his enemies (and their property) with a four-by-four, an enormous piece of wood that looks suspiciously like the beam of a cross—and although he initially decides not to use a gun, he is ultimately pushed to the point that he starts firing back. What to make, then, of this savior with a semiautomatic, a Jesus who literally beats his enemies with his cross? Even the most enthusiastic Christ-spotting students tend to balk at such a conception. Whether or not they are Christian, or know much about Christianity—and regardless of their views on capital punishment—students will generally agree that a character like Sister Helen Prejean in *Dead Man Walking* makes a more fitting Christ-figure than Chris Vaughn. A true model of Jesus would forgive, would turn the other cheek, would fight enemies with love.

But of course how do we really know what Jesus would do? Even if we only focus on the topic of peace and violence, and limit ourselves to the New Testament as source material, it does not take long to show that trying to understand the "real" Jesus is very difficult indeed. What are we to make, for example, of a figure who does indeed advocate love of enemies (Matt. 5:44) but who also uses a whip to drive animals and people out of the temple (John 2:15–16)? Who preaches forgiveness (Mark 11:25) but who condemns the scribes and Pharisees to hell (Matt. 23:33)? Who tells us to turn the other cheek (Luke 6:29) but whose apocalyptic wrath is terrifying (Rev. 6:16–17)?[15] To consider such dichotomies means that *Walking Tall*— a relatively simple action movie—has opened the door in critical ways to questions of religious history, ideology, and epistemology.[16]

It is not enough, in other words, to simply ask: "Is this character a Christ-figure?" Rather, we need to examine the kind of Christ-figure we are looking at, whose criteria we are using, and what those criteria are based on. Doing so encourages students not only to reflect on their own assumptions but, just as important, to question received scholarly wisdom. They might wonder, for example, why Lloyd Baugh's Christ-figure typology includes blood but not baptism, conflict with authority but not concern for the poor, and why it focuses more on actions and events than on teachings.

The final step, of course, is to ask what all this means in the context of the film. How do the Christ-related qualities that Chris Vaughn does and does not have tie into the larger framework of *Walking Tall*? This framework is essentially one in which a helpless community is overtaken by evil that cannot be dealt with by recourse to due process. Only a single champion who is greater than the average citizen, incorruptible, with the moral courage to take the law into his own hands, can deliver salvation; more specifically, salvation through violence. Casting Vaughn as a modern Christ, who lives by a higher code than the world does, who divides people into categories of us and them, saved and unsaved, and who ultimately destroys his enemies in an apocalyptic showdown, provides clear support to such a worldview.[17]

Superheroes, the Bible, and America

I believe in Harvey Dent.
—Bruce Wayne, *The Dark Knight* (2008)

As students can attest, the basic narrative structure of *Walking Tall* is one that is repeated over and over again in Hollywood action films. Often we need look no further than current or all-time box-office leaders for clear examples (see *Avatar, Star Wars*, etc.). However, in any list of such films one subcategory may stand out more than others: superhero movies.[18] In the past few years, *Spider-Man, Superman Returns*, and *Iron Man*—among many others—have all presented us with a world in which police or governments are powerless in the face of an evil threat, forcing a lone hero to operate outside the law to save the community using physical—and often lethal—violence. In response to such a threat, even Superman, it seems, cannot always avoid killing his enemies.[19]

According to Robert Jewett and John Shelton Lawrence, this perspective is both biblically based and quintessentially American. They have termed it "zealous nationalism" and argue that it is evident especially in biblical conquest narratives and apocalyptic literature in which good and evil are easily delimited and the enemies of God are destroyed.[20] Jewett and Lawrence trace the propagation of zealous nationalism throughout the history of America by forms of popular entertainment such as Indian captivity narratives in the seventeenth century, cowboy Westerns in the nineteenth and twentieth centuries, and (primarily) superhero comics in the past half-century. These stories reinforce the dangerous belief "that the world as a whole requires the services of American superheroism that destroys evildoers through selfless crusades."[21]

Movies make this link between America and the zealous (super)hero in many ways, most often through unsubtle placements of the national flag. When Vaughn steps off a ferry during the opening credits of *Walking Tall*, there is an American flag behind him; the endings of all three Raimi-directed *Spider-Man* films include a prominent shot of the hero with an enormous flag; *Superman 2* concludes with the Man of Steel replacing the flag on top of the White House;[22] and the penultimate image of a video tribute to the weapons-manufacturing protagonist in *Iron Man* is a flag-filled screen behind a cover of *Rolling Stone* that declares, "Tony Stark wants to save the world."

Stark in fact represents perhaps the most explicit embodiment of zealous nationalism in any superhero film, as exemplified by his comments at the demonstration of his new missile system:

> I humbly present the crown jewel in Stark Industries' Freedom line. They say the best weapon is one you never have to fire. I respectfully disagree. I prefer the weapon you only have to fire *once*. That's how Dad did it, that's how America does it, and it's worked out pretty well so far. Find an excuse to let one of these off the chain, and I personally guarantee you the bad guys won't even wanna come out of their caves. For your consideration: the Jericho.

Stark's speech hits all the right notes: freedom, weapon, America, bad guys. His weapon's name even references a biblical example of zealous nationalism, the Israelites' total, divinely mandated destruction of a Canaanite city (Josh. 6:20–21). He caps it all by raising a glass after the demonstration and making a toast: "To peace."[23]

Looking at superhero films in this way specifically links them to American government actions that righteously transgress domestic and international law. Many students are not entirely comfortable with this link, with putting *Iron Man* in the same category as the invasion of Iraq, the internment of prisoners at Guantanamo Bay, and the torture of suspected terrorists. For a few the discomfort is caused by the simple fact that they like superhero narratives and are pointedly opposed to these sorts of government actions; how can two things they feel so differently about be related? For most, the discomfort comes from seeing such narratives as simplistic fun, mere entertainment, and therefore not connected in any serious sense to— and certainly not responsible for—real-world events.

As Jane Mayer discusses in a 2007 *New Yorker* article, this latter point is exactly the one the producers of 24 made when faced with criticism that their show promoted violent behavior that absolutely fits the definition of zealous nationalism. Mayer recounts the opposition of several American military and FBI interrogators to Jack Bauer's torture of terrorists, opposition so strong that in November 2006 they met with the show's producers. The meeting included U.S. Army Brigadier General Patrick Finnegan, the dean of the U.S. Military Academy at West Point, who found that it had become increasingly difficult to convince cadets that torture was illegal, immoral, and ineffective; students would often respond, "If torture is wrong, what about 24?" Even more unnerving, Tony Lagouranis, a former army interrogator, describes soldiers in Iraq who would watch scenes from 24 of Bauer inflicting severe pain on suspects to gain information "and then walk into the interrogation booths and do the same things they've just seen."[24]

Opposing such a perspective is what Jewett and Lawrence have termed "pro-phetic realism," an approach to crisis concerned with making the world a better place by the impartial enforcement of laws, not by the righteous destruction of "evil." Prophetic realism is about recognizing the full, flawed humanity of every-one, including one's enemies, and attempting resolution through a democratic process. Jewett and Lawrence see this approach as having derived from Hebrew Bible prophetic writings (especially Jeremiah and Isaiah), as well as many New Testament teachings of both Jesus and Paul. Prophetic realism appears only as a minor note in American popular culture, however, and is notably absent, we are told, from superhero narratives.[25]

This is one reason why *The Dark Knight* is such a great film for class discussion, as it radically deviates from the standard superhero pattern of zealous nationalism.[26] The deviation may not be apparent at first glance, however. Like the recent cinematic versions of Spider-Man, Superman, and Iron Man, *The Dark Knight*'s Batman is an exceptional, heroic individual, willing both to endure and inflict violence to defend his community against a threat that has them terrorized. He is also forced to trans-gress the law when the police cannot solve a problem, kidnapping a criminal from Hong Kong and bringing him back to the United States, and tapping into every citizen's cell phone to track down the Joker.

Indeed, Batman is so good at being a hero—he is smarter and stronger than any-one else, and never loses a fight—that it is surprisingly easy to overlook how often he fails to actually save people. It is remarkable, in fact, how ineffective Batman is throughout the film in resisting the Joker's acts of terror. In addition to arriving too late to stop his enemy from blowing up a hospital or shooting at the mayor, Batman also fails to save the police commissioner, a judge, Rachel Dawes, and Harvey Dent. Such failures constitute one of the most important (and original) ways in which the film undermines the standard heroic position of zealous nationalism.[27]

The Dark Knight also gives us a more complicated moral world than the average superhero film does, a world not so easily divided into good and evil. For one thing, Wayne's motives for being Batman are not purely selfless; when he tells Rachel of his hope that the city will one day no longer need Batman, she replies: "I'm not sure the day will come when *you* no longer need Batman." Even the Joker, while mur-derous and horrifying, is not evil in any simplistic sense. He is mostly a force of chaos tearing apart the status quo, but the film itself suggests that the status quo is not always something to cheer for. As the Joker correctly points out, for example, a good portion of the people of Gotham value some lives (civic leaders, police) more than others (soldiers, criminals) and are also willing to offer up sacrifices to buy their own safety, including turning Batman over to a psychopathic killer.

But again the whole picture is more complex than this. The passengers on each of two ferries, for example, specifically refuse to detonate the bomb on the other ferry to save their own lives. Police and staff put themselves at risk to safely evacuate the hospital also primed by the Joker to explode. Lieutenant Gordon saves the mayor from assassination by leaping into the bullet's path. And District Attorney Harvey Dent makes himself a target of violence due to the fact that, as Wayne says, "He locked up half the city's criminals, and he did it without wearing a mask."

Perhaps most important, throughout the film Batman is determined to work with, not against, the forces of due process. He never executes his own judgment on criminals but hands them over to the police, and he stops other vigilantes who use lethal force to fight crime. He even prevents the Joker from falling to his death during their final battle, in pointed contrast to the ending of Tim Burton's *Batman* (1989). His explicit, primary motivation in fact becomes supporting and protecting Dent so that Batman can retire, because he believes that for the community to be healthy and functional it must have faith in the democratic rule of law, not in vigilantes. And so when Dent is driven into a homicidal rage by the murder of his fiancé and his own horrific scarring, wreaking vengeance on the corrupt police officers who executed these crimes, Batman takes the blame for the killings. In this way, the public image of Dent will remain meaningful in a way that specifically supports the notion of prophetic realism.

STRUCTURAL VIOLENCE

Canon Fodder

The king has returned.
—Rafiki, *The Lion King* (1994)

Ask students whether they notice any similarities among the top ten highest grossing films from the previous year (any year will work, but it's good to keep the discussion current). They will likely identify several patterns—including the persistence of physical violence—but they will also invariably find that one of the most glaring connections between these films is that in almost every case the protagonist is a straight white male.[28] To at least some of the students, this revelation will almost certainly come as a bit of a shock.

This informal study can be supplemented with more systematic research findings. For example, Stacy Smith's examination of the 101 top-grossing G-rated films from 1990 to 2004 found that less than one in three speaking characters, and less than one in five members of a crowd scene, was female.[29] The total percentage of female characters overall was only about one in four. This imbalance was consistent both across film companies and over the entire fourteen-year span of the films considered.

Rubina Ramji has similarly examined the presentation of Muslims in fifteen Hollywood films from 1987 to 2000. She found that by far the dominant characterizations are of "the dark, violent, male terrorist" complemented by women who are "silent, shapeless bundles under black garb."[30] More allegorically, it is likely that the recent remake of *War of the Worlds* (2005) also has Muslim terrorists in mind, presenting as it does aliens attacking the United States only a few years after the September 11 destruction of the Twin Towers.[31]

Such patterns point to one of the simplest and most important links between movies and religion, namely that both can be highly patriarchal and can marginalize (or even demonize) those who do not belong to the saved or normative group. Both have, from early on, developed canonical texts, forms, and perspectives that naturalize discrimination.[32] Both, in other words, participate in forms of what Raymond MacAfee Brown terms "structural violence." Such violence refers to social structures that promote and perpetuate inequity, such as gender-exclusive language, racist hiring practices, and economic systems that generate poverty and hopelessness.[33]

In the classroom, I have found *The Lion King* (1994) to be a particularly useful example of a film that engages in this kind of violence in a manner connected to religion. As others have pointed out, however, students can often be highly resistant to critiques of Disney films.[34] I have yet to encounter a student who did not watch these movies repeatedly and with great affection while growing up; many of them may consequently find it more difficult to find serious fault with Disney films than with their own religious tradition (should they have one).

For this reason I come at the topic of religion and structural violence in *The Lion King* indirectly, by first asking students to consider the ways in which Mark Pinsky's general points in *The Gospel According to Disney* apply to this film in particular. According to Pinsky, Disney productions embody or promote a wide range of religious beliefs and values, but among these is a "basic canon": rewarding good, punishing evil, having faith in yourself and in something greater than yourself, being optimistic, and working hard to achieve success.[35] Students have little difficulty pointing to illustrations of the basic Disney canon in *The Lion King* in relation to the protagonist, Simba.

A handful may also notice that a few other patterns that Pinsky discusses seem less easily applicable to the film. Pinsky asserts, for example, that Disney movies often encourage the acceptance of difference.[36] Yet in *The Lion King* the characters that are most obviously "different"—Timon, Pumbaa, the hyenas, and Scar—are treated or portrayed in somewhat troubling ways. Timon and Pumbaa live outside the Pride Lands and, while amusing and helpful, they are also clearly subordinated to their ostensible friend Simba, the future king. The hyenas are not only evil outsiders (a notion that seems incongruous with Mufasa's "circle of life" mantra in which all beings have a place), but also live in shadowy "fields of death and deserts of privation, ghettos and barrios populated by unruly hordes. Out there leaders speak in dialect (Whoopi Goldberg and Cheech Marin) or slobber to communicate. In the Pridelands, the good king Mufasa sounds like a Shakespearean-trained actor (James Earl Jones)."[37] As for the villain Scar, I am not always successful in convincing students that he is "animated and voiced in a manner that suggests stereotypes of a gay man's speech patterns, mannerisms, and moods."[38] However, it is not at all difficult to draw attention to the fact that, despite being Mufasa's brother, Scar is suspiciously darker skinned with a black mane.

A second problematic generalization of Pinsky's is that, although early Disney films include "troubling stereotypes" of women, modern productions feature more assertive and accomplished female characters.[39] Without fail students will identify Nala as such a character, who early in *The Lion King* affirms her equality with Simba and even defeats him when they (play) fight. But when the two fall in love as adults and are again playing together, Simba ends up on top this time, a position that confirms both his dominance and his heterosexuality. In a similar but more violent reversal, Simba's mother Sarabi stands up to Scar but is immediately struck down.[40] This scene highlights the most obvious problem with the film's female characters, namely that there is an entire community of (unnamed, silent) adult lionesses who are helpless under Scar's rule, but it takes only a single male lion (Simba) to overthrow him and return order to the land.

The next step is to link the film's structural violence—racism, classism, homophobia, sexism—to its religious aspects. As it happens, the film itself opens the door to this link with Mufasa's explanation of the "circle of life." This belief system asserts that social standing is hardwired into the universe and that it is okay for those higher up on the food chain to prey on those below. As a metaphor for human society, the circle of life's (violent) implications are uncomfortably clear.

The only other explicit religious references in the film are to "African" traditions, namely Timon and Pumbaa's "hakuna matata" outlook and Rafiki's various shamanic activities. Aside from doubting that these constructions are genuinely African— Rafiki's practices seem vaguely "Eastern," for example, including as they do approximations of yogic meditation, Buddhist philosophy, and kung fu—students at first rarely find much wrong with them. But they tend to adopt a different stance when they consider the relationship between these elements and the nonexplicit religious elements of the film, which essentially consist of biblical allegories.

Both Mufasa and Simba are (surprise!) Christ-figures, and both in several instances also evoke the biblical God. Simba takes on even more roles as he reenacts parts of the Eden story (he disobeys an imperial edict in order to acquire knowledge, and is exiled) as well as Moses's narrative arc (he flees his homeland only to experience a theophany abroad, then returns to free his people). Finally, there are the ending's apocalyptic overtones, with Simba/Christ arriving as the warrior savior (Rev. 19:11–13), Scar/the beast cast down into fire (Rev. 19:20), Simba/God as king (Rev. 19:5), and the Pride Lands/city of God (re)established on earth, with rivers, trees, and no more darkness (Rev. 22:1–5).

A critical aspect of these male-centered biblical elements is that they absolutely dominate the film: without the return of the One True King all would be lost. As such the biblical framework also highlights the dangerous ineffectiveness of all other perspectives. Nala's assertions of gender equality are clearly groundless, since only a male lion can stop Scar. Rafiki's shamanism is almost as useless, providing help only insofar as it enables him to locate the savior. And although "hakuna matata" has the catchiest song in the film, this attitude is ultimately exposed as lazy and self-indulgent. If Simba had fully embraced it, he would never have gone home—in a fervor of zealous nationalism—to fight his evil uncle and save the Pride Lands.

The "Disney canon" that provides a kind of blueprint for success has apparently omitted mention of the need to fit into the right categories. In addition to working hard and having faith, that is, we must also be straight, male, and bound in key ways to Christianity. On a larger scale, *The Lion King* teaches that we need to follow the right (biblically based) system of social order, which includes being ruled over by the right (heterosexual male) leaders. Any other formulation will result in unbridled chaos.

Gendered Haunts

My mama, her mama, may they rest in peace, they had the gift.
—Oda Mae Brown, *Ghost* (1990)

In his study of the twenty highest-grossing films each year from 1990 to 1998, Brian Stone found that when these movies posit a connection between religion and violence, the former most often serves "as a force for justifying and legitimating" the latter.[41] In fact, only three of the 180 films he surveyed explicitly show religion "as even remotely leading to the rejection of violence."[42] In making these assessments, however, Stone adopts a fairly restricted understanding of both religion and violence. His commentary on *The Lion King*, for example, concerns only explicit religious elements and physical violence, and makes no mention of the film's biblical symbolism or its various discriminations.[43]

By concentrating on the more obvious examples of the key terms in his study, Stone may have overlooked critical instances of both. I do agree with his overall conclusion that religion in popular film does tend to work in concert with violence, but I also think there may be more than three films in 180 in which religion in some way opposes violence. In fact, I have often attempted to consider this possibility in class by examining one of the movies from Stone's list that he does not discuss, 1990's *Ghost*.

To start, I ask students to tell me—using Tom Ruffles's *Ghost Images* as a guide— what they think the meaning of the ghosts in this film might be. They generally comment that, most obviously, the ghosts point to a desire for or belief in some sort of life beyond the veil, a belief that provides a degree of comfort to the loved ones left behind. This perspective in turn raises the question of a higher power, that is, whether God exists because ghosts do. These issues are further related to concepts of ethics, redemption, and responsibility for others, as the main ghost (Sam) strives in his postmortem state to help his former lover (Molly). Some students may also consider that, precisely because of the presence and importance of the relationship between Sam and Molly, the film is proposing some sort of connection between death and sexuality.

All that said, however, students—even the ones that really like *Ghost*—invariably find that while the movie may raise these issues, it offers little substantive commentary on any of them. In this context, some will quote Ruffles's remark that many ghost films "are routine and their meanings easily exhausted."[44] The cosmology of *Ghost* is embarrassingly simplistic, for example: after death, "good" people are lifted into the air on a beam of light, while "bad" people are dragged down by shadowy demons. Ghostwise, the movie overall appears to be an exercise in wish fulfillment, manifesting the escapist desire to deny reality and cheat death. Students may think the film is dramatic, or funny, or even (unfortunately) romantic, but they also think that it is—in a word—dumb.

This assessment does seem valid in many respects.[45] To suggest that there may be more to *Ghost* than meets the eye, though, I ask students to consider the aspects of being a ghost that cause Sam problems. These problems are related to his goal, which is to protect Molly from his evil ex-friend Carl, the man who had Sam killed. To do this he needs to communicate with Molly, but she cannot hear or see him. Sam is also at first completely unable to affect his physical environment and only learns to have even a small impact with great effort. Ultimately, because he is often unable to really do anything useful at all, he spends a lot of time hanging around (and therefore effectively haunting) his home so he can at least keep an eye on Molly.

With a little luck and some gentle prodding, these details will remind students of Stacy Smith's findings concerning gender in popular film. If so, they have landed upon the thesis promoted by Katherine Fowkes in *Giving Up the Ghost*, namely that the ghostly characteristics of the dead man in this and other films are congruent with the actual situation of live women in movies generally: they are unseen, unheard, powerless, and relegated to domestic spaces. In effect, Fowkes argues, male ghosts in ghost comedies (and she includes *Ghost* in this category) are rendered "female" by their life-after-death status, in terms of a particular construction of what it means to be female.

Another key feature of this construction involves being in touch with, and expressing, one's feelings. While alive, Sam appears to be a "typical man" to the extent that he is emotionally distant. One of his defining traits, in fact, is that he simply replies "ditto" when Molly says, "I love you." He also falls asleep when he goes to the theatre with Molly, refuses to talk to her about marriage (which she wants), and is clearly disconnected from their home life. Until his death Sam, is almost always working, leaving Molly to set up and sort out their newly renovated loft. It is perhaps not coincidental, then, that to accomplish his goal as a ghost—that is, to save Molly from Carl—Sam specifically needs to connect with his emotions.

He does this in two ways. First, he learns that if he really concentrates on his emotions (especially his anger), he can affect his physical environment. This enables Sam to interrupt a moment when Carl seems about to seduce Molly, and, at the end of the film, to fight Carl physically and ultimately avenge his own murder.[46] Second, he learns that he can be heard by a woman named Oda Mae Brown. But this level of interaction is not enough to solve Sam's problems. His attempts to talk to Molly using Oda Mae are unsuccessful until he realizes that he can only convince her of his reality by referencing shared emotional memories.

Ultimately, the gendered nature of Sam's situation is revealed most explicitly through his relation with Oda Mae. We learn that her role as communicator with the dead appears to be an exclusively female one, as she is part of a lineage of women who could see, hear, and speak to departed spirits. Sam needs to bridge this gap in the other direction, which is only possible by connecting to this female tradition. Most important, however, because of Oda Mae Sam not only communicates through a woman, he literally *becomes* one when he possesses the medium's body for a final embrace with Molly.

What we see in *Ghost*, then, is a film that uses a supernatural trope—the ghost—to comment on gender issues. On the one hand, by becoming a ghost Sam is forced to overcome the "male" quality of being stoic, unemotional. This quality threatened his relationship with Molly when he was alive and threatened her life when he was not. On the other hand, by highlighting the ways in which Sam struggles with the inability to be seen, heard, or felt after death, and then connecting him in this state to women, the film implicitly critiques the "ghostly" state of women in cinema generally. In these ways *Ghost* can be seen very much as a film that uses religion to oppose structural violence, employing ideas about life after death to highlight the ways in which gender is often constructed to the detriment of all people.

MYTHIC VIOLENCE
Crime and Parable

First day on the job, you know what I learned? How to spot a murderer.
—Dave Kujan, *The Usual Suspects* (1995)

Perhaps the most overused conception in considerations of myth and film has been Joseph Campbell's theory of the monomyth, or hero's journey. Of course this is not without good reason, and that reason largely has to do with *Star Wars* (1977). In making this film, George Lucas famously adhered to Campbell's model so faithfully that Campbell himself explained how well all the pieces fit during a series of 1980s interviews, which actually took place in Lucas's own home at Skywalker Ranch. These interviews turned into a PBS series and a best-selling book of the same title, *The Power of Myth*.

Star Wars, of course, has been immensely influential, which means that for more than thirty years Campbell's ideas have also had a huge impact on movies.[47] It is no surprise that there are so many works, both academic and amateur, whose point is to identify key elements of the monomyth pattern, including one book that does the job with fifty films.[48] But in the end, simply making such observations is no more meaningful—and only slightly less common—than Christ-spotting.

What I find more engaging about Campbell's work, and its relation to film, is the fact that it absolutely depends on violence. Once the (invariably male) hero accepts his call, he sets out on a series of violent adventures before returning home again. For Campbell these adventures are all about human psychology: they symbolize the process of personal growth, a process that "requires a death and a resurrection."[49] This is "good" violence in other words, the shattering of the old, immature, dependent self and the awakening of the new, adult, creative self. It is an example of what I call mythic violence, which is simply violence that is in some respect bound up with myth ("myth" being subject to varying definitions, of course).

In any given class of first-year undergraduate students, at least a quarter of them are very familiar with Campbell's idea of the hero's journey. Because this idea remains so well known—not to mention so well liked—I instead have students apply a somewhat less common, and less straightforward, model of mythic violence. Doing so not only exposes them to a different way of approaching myth (and film) but also demonstrates more clearly, and concretely, that Campbell's perspective represents only one among many possible ways of understanding myth than if I simply preached that gospel to the class.[50]

The model that I use is John Dominic Crossan's view of myth and parable as outlined in *The Dark Interval*. Crossan puts these types of story on either end of a spectrum. Myth, he states, provides us with a sense of meaning, a way of making sense of the world and reconciling contradictions. Parable, on the other hand, specifically opposes myth: it challenges the actual principle of reconciliation by introducing a piercing doubt, by making us aware that we invented the reconciliation in the first place. Parable is the "dark night of story," then; it subverts the world established by myth. And while myth provides meaning, by unsettling that meaning parable opens up the possibility of transcendence.[51]

In certain key respects, this model represents a very different kind of mythic violence than the one offered by Campbell. Here, myth is "violent" to the extent that it keeps us safe, preventing us from having what are, in Crossan's understanding, the most important religious experiences. Parable offers the chance at such experiences, but only at the expense of those (mythic) beliefs that make our lives worth living. Such an impact represents a kind of positive violence in Crossan's view, as evident in the (biblically based) metaphor he uses to describe it: "Parable brings not peace but the sword, and parable casts fire upon the earth which receives it."[52]

An interpretive model that idealizes the shattering of myth has long struck me as well suited to considerations of noir and neo-noir films. In movies such as *The Big Sleep* (1946), *Out of the Past* (1947), *Blast of Silence* (1961), *Chinatown* (1974), and *Memento* (2000), characters' understandings of themselves and their world are regularly exploded. The impact of such developments is perhaps most pronounced when the film employs an unreliable narrator or point of view with which the viewer identifies. Arguably the most well-known example of a modern film to use this device is *The Usual Suspects*. My prelecture question for students then is relatively simple: Is *The Usual Suspects* a myth or a parable?

The movie itself begins with its own question: What led to a ship's explosion and the deaths of twenty-seven men on a San Pedro pier? There are two survivors of the incident, a fatally wounded Hungarian and a physically disabled con man, who escaped unharmed. Throughout the film the con man, Roger "Verbal" Kint, is questioned by Special Agent David Kujan. He tells a complicated story of his meeting with four other criminals in a police lineup and their eventual involvement in what happened at the pier. He ultimately confesses that all of these events were orchestrated by the master criminal Keyser Söze, an archvillain who is almost supernaturally notorious, whose existence has never even been officially confirmed. Söze's secret plan all along was to kill Arturo Marquez, the one man in the world who could identify him, a man that the Hungarian mob on the ship wanted to buy. Arkosh Kovash, the surviving Hungarian, affirms this; he also states that Keyser Söze killed Marquez and blew up the boat, and then describes Söze to a police sketch artist. Right after Kint's story ends and he is released, Kujan realizes that many key words in his story—Redfoot, Guatemala, quartet, Skokie, Kobayashi— were actually taken from items in Kujan's very office. We then see the sketch of Söze, who bears a striking resemblance to Kint. As the con man walks free, he straightens his gnarled fingers, abandons his limp, gets into a limo, and disappears around the corner.

Inevitably, students will assert that the film is a parable. Their judgment is based on the fact that both the characters and the viewers (or at least a good number of viewers, going by anecdotal evidence) are fooled into thinking that Verbal Kint is helpless and weak, when in fact he is really Keyser Söze himself.

Since parable for Crossan is about doubt, most students will argue that the film facilitates such questioning by undermining our trust in narrators, our tendency to ascribe to them authority and objectivity. We apparently trust narrators so much that we will even believe Kint who, we are told up front, is a professional liar. To the extent that the film attempts to identify the viewers with Kujan—we hear the story just as he does; we are fooled just as he is—it also suggests that our trust in narrators comes in part from overconfidence in our own abilities. Kujan is absolutely convinced of his powers in this respect, that he can separate fact from fiction in a criminal's story, that he knows how to spot a murderer.

Some students will point to another issue at stake, connected to Kujan's a priori conviction that Dean Keaton—one of the criminals in the lineup, and a man Kujan has pursued for years—was the real force behind all the death and destruction at the pier. Eventually the agent pushes Kint to "confess" that Keaton was the true mastermind, but in an earlier conversation Kint also foretells Kujan's failing in this regard: "To a cop the explanation is never that complicated. It's always simple. There's no mystery to the street, no arch criminal behind it all. If you got a dead body and you think his brother did it, you're gonna find out you're right."[53] Kujan's confidence in his abilities and his understanding prevents him from seeing the truth literally right in front of him, the pieces of Kint's story that are posted on his own bulletin board, printed on the bottom of his own coffee cup. To the extent, again, that we are Kujan, *The Usual Suspects* suggests there is a general human tendency to make facts fit theories, rather than coming up with theories that fit the facts; and when we do this we inevitably become at least partially blind. Believing, in this sense, is *not* seeing. If we are legitimately interested in understanding things as they are, we need to doubt not just what others tell us, but our own convictions.

These are all, I think, important points about the film. However, they miss a key aspect of Crossan's definition, namely that a parable is specifically not an "anti-myth"; it "does not, *as parable*, replace one myth with another."[54] And yet showing that the helpless Kint is really a ruthless master criminal does in fact replace one myth, one understanding of the world, with another. A story that provides different answers than expected may have some parabolic effects but it is not, in the strict sense of Crossan's meaning, a parable. In class, then, I suggest a way in which the film *can* fit his definition. Such an interpretation hinges on demonstrating that the story's ending may not really tell us as much as we think it does.

What do we know for sure? We know that Kint lied about his physical disabilities and that he used words found in Kujan's office as part of his story. We also know, from the opening of the film (which is not narrated by Kint, and hence can be understood as "real") that a shadowy figure—whom Dean Keaton addresses as Keyser—sets off the fire at the docks and shoots at Keaton. Finally, we know that Kovash describes Keyser Söze as looking like Verbal Kint. Ultimately, these are the only reliable pieces of information upon which our belief in the new myth is founded.

Even if we accept that Kint was the man who killed Marquez, all we can be sure of is that Kovash *believed* Kint to be Söze. And if, in fact, he was right, that hardly proves that Kint/Söze is any sort of supercriminal. Given that, from Kint's own account, he went to great, convoluted lengths to kill the one man who knew who he was, it seems rather sloppy to have let *another* man not only identify him but live long enough to describe him in detail to the police. The entire reason that Söze "stuck his neck out," according to Kint, was to take care of this one loose thread. However, Kujan now has a sketch he can send anywhere he wants, so soon many, many more people will be able to identify Keyser Söze. Hardly the work of a supercriminal.

Some students may protest. They will cite the complex and brutal web of intrigue and manipulation orchestrated by Kint/Söze as proof of his evil genius. However, that web itself only exists because Kint tells us about it. In fact, we cannot be sure of any part of Kint's story beyond some of the most prosaic details verified by outsiders like Kujan. In other words, in the end we don't really know what happened but we think that we do.[55] So the film works as parable in this way: it lures us into believing a new myth, that Kint is really a supercriminal, but it also gives us enough clues to figure out that this myth too is a construct. It might be true, but we don't know. Whether this realization leads to a transcendental experience is difficult to say, but at the very least it should make us aware of both the temptations and dangers of mythic thinking, and with any luck inspire us to become more cautious, responsible, and scientific scholars.

Colonial Structures

> Our people once were warriors, but not like you, Jake.
> —Beth Heke, *Once Were Warriors* (1994)

Because most considerations of myth in religion and film draw from phenomenologically oriented theories, the violence at issue typically remains rather abstract and individualistic. As with the views of Campbell and Crossan noted above, these theories tend to focus on inward personal journeys, with the cinematic conflicts to which they are applied functioning as symbolic aspects of a religious or psychological path. The discussions generated from such theories thus often remain distanced from actual, historical examples of cruelty, oppression, or abuse.

Despite his interest in transcendence, however, Crossan himself includes a consideration of violence that is grounded in social and political realities: one of his examples of myth is the negative portrayal of Native Americans in Hollywood productions. As he explains, the most critical problem in this regard does not lie with the representation of "Indians" in any individual movie, but with the stereotyping repeated over the course of many years and many films. This pattern creates what Crossan terms "a *structure of contempt*" that perpetuates injustices against Indigenous people.[56]

Crossan's brief comments tie in well with Henry Giroux's consideration of the nature, meaning, and function of cinematic brutality, much of which concerns racism.[57] He argues, for example, that violence committed by young white characters—as in *Single White Female* (1992) or *Natural Born Killers* (1994)—is most often depicted as aberrant, the result of a personal psychological or emotional breakdown. On the other hand, violence committed by young black characters—as in *Menace II Society* (1993) or *Sugar Hill* (1994)—is presented as the normative failure of these characters to take responsibility for their lives. In other words,

> in the racially coded representations of violence in Black films, questions of agency are untroubled by freak individual pathologies but serve instead to indict Blacks as an entire social group while legitimating the popular stereotype that their communities, the urban metropolises, are the central sites of crime, lawlessness, and immorality.[58]

In this respect, popular films depicting youth crime can be seen as constituting a form of mythic violence that in turn legitimates further legal, social, and economic discrimination against black individuals and communities.

With this perspective in mind—along with Crossan's understanding of myth—I ask students to comment on the relationship between myth and violence in *Once Were Warriors* (1994).[59] The film concerns the Hekes, a Maori family living in socially assisted housing in Auckland. The father, Jake, is an alcoholic who loses his job as the opening credits roll and who tends to erupt in bloody fury at anyone in the community who stands against him, including his wife, Beth. The couple have five children, two girls and three boys; the oldest boy (Nig) joins a street gang, and the next oldest (Boogie) is caught by police and placed in a remand home. The eldest daughter (Grace) is a storyteller and the emotional center of the family, taking care of her siblings when her parents are too incapacitated to do so. During one of Jake's many wild parties at home, his friend "Uncle" Bully rapes Grace. She tells no one and suffers in silence, eventually hanging herself. After her funeral, Beth finds Grace's storybook, where she had written about the rape. She gathers the kids and finds Jake at the bar with Bully; Boogie shows Jake the storybook and Jake tears into Bully, smashing his face to a pulp and stabbing him repeatedly with a broken bottle.[60] The film ends with Beth taking the family home to the *marae*, the Maori community she grew up with, while Jake collapses in impotent, drunken frustration outside the bar, whimpering.

In line with Giroux's critique, *Once Were Warriors* presents violence committed by marginalized people as simply part of the status quo. Jake is not aberrant, and he is not the only drunk Maori man beating up people in bars—he just seems to be better at it than most. Similarly, both Nig's gang and Boogie's remand home are filled with other Maori youth who do or did commit criminal acts against property, social institutions, and members of their community. The implication that these people have decided to live this way, the myth that they are wholly responsible for the violence they commit and experience, is embodied mainly by two characters: Boogie and Beth. After being placed in the remand home, the son decides to change his life, committing himself to a very different path from the one that led him to be taken from his family. The mother, similarly, makes a decision in the end she conceivably could have made long ago, before Grace was raped, leaving Jake and the life of violence she shares with him.

What separates this film from the ones that Giroux censures, however, is that it does not present the struggles of the Heke family, or the Maori community more generally, in a vacuum. Colonialism is not addressed explicitly in the film, and yet it forms the background to the violence we see. The opening shot of the movie makes this point with amazing economy: we begin with a scene of pristine natural beauty, but the camera pulls back to reveal that we have been looking at a billboard advertisement, standing alongside a highway bordering a run-down government housing development for Maori families. The billboard speaks to the colonial fantasy that New Zealand was effectively uninhabited when Europeans arrived, similar to the view that Columbus "discovered" the Americas despite the presence of upward of 100 million Indigenous people.[61] Such imagined erasure of entire populations is related in the film to the contemporary relegation of the Maori to the outskirts of "civilization" and to colonial control over their community. This control is nicely symbolized by the fact that the billboard is for a *power* company, and is more directly evident in other aspects of the film, from the visible police presence, to the encouraged dependency on social assistance, to the removal of recalcitrant youths from their families, and even to the name of the local bar: the Royal. The message is that, to the colonizers, the Maori remain nonpersons; instead they are children, criminals, and drunkards, who cannot be trusted to responsibly run their own lives.

As some students will point out, by drawing attention to these issues the film implicitly condemns the colonial myth.[62] The contrast between the bucolic fiction of the billboard and the urban reality in which the Heke family lives speaks to the ways in which both the land and the people were invaded and altered by the newcomers, a kind of environmental and cultural violation that parallels and prefigures Grace's rape. The film thus posits some form of rebuilding links with Indigenous traditions as a way in which Maori people can extricate themselves from circumstances of physical and structural violence. Thus Boogie's ability to choose a different life comes only after he is introduced by a youth worker to rituals such as the *haka*; Beth, similarly, finds the strength to leave Jake only after reconnecting to her *marae* community at Grace's funeral. Until she is assaulted by Bully, in fact, Grace is not just the only fully functioning member of the family, but also the only one actively attempting to bring Maori traditions into their lives. She does this mainly through her storytelling, as in the tale she reads to her younger siblings at the start of the film about the Taniwha, an underwater creature that—like Jake—can be both protector and destroyer.

One of the most important aspects of *Once Were Warriors*, however, is that it does not present this return to tradition—what we could call the Indigenous myth—in simplistic terms. For one thing, the film does not affirm the existence of a pure cultural form to which the characters can reconnect. We see this most clearly in relation to Grace. She is not simply retelling Maori stories, for example; she is incorporating elements from them into her own tales. At Grace's funeral, Boogie sings a mourning song in Maori while his new friends from the remand home perform the *haka*, but they all carry out these rituals wearing European suits. And while Grace is buried at the *marae*, the cemetery is full of Christian crosses. Returning to their own house after the burial, Beth sits down with her children for the first family meal of the movie and says grace—which of course points explicitly to the religious hybridity that runs through the film, since it is the Christian-named Grace who ultimately leads her family back to the Maori traditions that help to address their sufferings.

The film's complexity is also evident in the Maori traditions that are *not* helpfully integrated into the characters' lives. After he is initiated into his gang, for example, Nig receives facial tattoos, or *moko*. However, they remain a superficial marking rather than a signifier of any meaningful connection, a point made by Boogie when he states his disinterest in getting *moko* himself: "I wear mine on the inside." For his part, Jake in some ways represents the Maori warrior tradition indicated by the film's title. Beth, however, asserts that he has got it wrong, that their people were warriors in a different sense than he is. But these somewhat idealized notions of tradition are problematized by Jake himself, who explains that he actually descends from "a long line of slaves"; this is why Beth left the *marae* in the first place, because her family remained prejudiced against Jake's people and would not accept Beth's marriage to a slave.

In the end, one of the most valuable pedagogical aspects of the film is that it offers no simple or clear picture of "mythic violence." On the one hand it speaks to the consequences of colonial myths that violate the personhood of Indigenous people, regarding them as inferior, self-destructive, invisible, doomed. And yet on the other hand the film also shows the potential for institutions resulting from such myths—like the remand home—to function in much more positive ways that help to redress past and present colonial wrongs, even in small ways. Similarly, *Once Were Warriors* affirms the myth that returning to Indigenous traditions to some extent can help individuals remove themselves from situations of economic, social, and domestic violence arising from colonialism. And yet it also hints that such a position can constitute its own form of mythic violence, an essentializing move that ignores aspects of these traditions that may themselves have perpetuated injustice.

Many North Americans remain largely unfamiliar with Indigenous religions or colonialism generally, let alone Maori traditions and New Zealand in particular. My students therefore tend to approach *Once Were Warriors*, unlike the other films examined in this chapter, with few preconceptions.[63] As a result, what they do or do not see tends not to be overly determined by what they believe; taken together, in fact, their responses to this film generally do a good job of exploring its mythic elements in relation to Giroux's points about racism. This in turn means that I rarely try to upend students' readings of *Once Were Warriors* by challenging them with unexpected interpretations of my own. My focus instead is on bringing these readings together into a conversation that highlights the complexity and relevance of the film, while also providing key information about the historical, political, and religious context to the Hekes' story.

CONCLUSION

If you gave me a million years to ponder, I would never have guessed that true romance and Detroit would ever go together.
—Alabama Whitman, *True Romance* (1993)

In my experience, an effective way to introduce a class to the idea that our preconceptions affect what we see is to show the UK video created as part of a public service campaign to increase drivers' awareness of cyclists.[64] The video features two teams of four young people each, one dressed in white and one in black; the members of each group pass a basketball to one another. Viewers are asked to count how many passes the team in white makes. After fourteen seconds the video freezes, and viewers are then asked: "Did you see the moonwalking bear?" The video rewinds and replays and, sure enough, someone in a bear costume moonwalks at normal speed right past all the players. Invariably students will insist that this is a trick, that there was no bear initially, and demand to see the video again from the start. Invariably they will be astounded to realize that they did in fact completely miss the bear the first time around.[65] '

The results of this exercise have clear parallels to students' responses to *Frailty*. Just as they miss seeing the bear, they also do not see that God really is ordering the father of two young boys to kill people identified as demons. For these students, religion and violence in the context of this narrative simply do not belong together. They are as odd a pairing as moonwalking bears and basketball, as incongruous as true romance and Detroit. However, while bears and basketball really do not mix, no such inherent disjunction governs the possible relations between religion and violence.

I see a critical part of my job, therefore, as trying to open students' understanding of these two terms to other perspectives. Jonathan Z. Smith has famously argued that "religion" is a creation of the academy, and so the primary focus for scholars is necessarily "the *imagination* of religion."[66] Similarly, my pedagogical intent is to engage students in discussions on the ways in which films imagine religion and its connections to violence, as seen through the lenses of assorted theorists.

These connections are varied and complex. *The Lion King* draws heavily on biblical symbolism and narrative structures in its depiction of a subjugated community resisting tyranny, yet uses this same symbolism to reinscribe patriarchal social structures and beliefs. A belief in the afterlife helps fuel *Ghost*'s revenge fantasy as well as its indictment against the silencing of women in popular culture. In *Once Were Warriors* the return to Maori traditions allows characters to resist colonialism yet also perpetuate the domestic and communal violence that is in many ways a result of colonialism.

These examples leave students with no definitive understanding of either the films themselves or the relations between religion and violence. In my own view this is a welcome result. Such semantic tension and ambiguity allows me to explore the ways in which meaning is created and the difficulties of interpretation generally. With luck, it will also help me to convince students that when we are open to a variety of perspectives we are more likely to see what is really in front of us. And I, for one, do not want to miss a single moonwalking bear.

NOTES

This essay is dedicated to Lawrence Stern, teacher and friend. Lawrence was the first person who really showed me how and why to look first, and ask questions later. He also showed me so many things worth looking *at*: "Fern Hill," Sankai Juku, *My Dinner with André*, orchids. And on and on. Words will never be enough.

1. Margaret Miles, *Seeing and Believing: Religion and Values in the Movies* (Boston: Beacon, 1996). Although in many ways the idea that seeing leads to believing is central to this text, Miles only explicitly states the point in these terms a few times (x, 29, 55).
2. Mary Bergen with Michael Berger, "Teaching Literature: Rethinking the Socratic Method," in *Teaching Undergraduates: Essays from the Lilly Endowment Workshop on Liberal Arts*, ed. Bruce A. Kimball (Buffalo: Prometheus, 1988), 68.
3. Russell T. McCutcheon, "Redescribing 'Religion and . . .' Film: Teaching the Insider/Outsider Problem," in *Critics Not Caretakers: Redescribing the Public Study of Religion* (Albany: State University of New York Press, 2001), 184.
4. Ironically, in his discussion of these films McCutcheon does exactly what he criticizes phenomenologically oriented teachers of religion and film of doing: he uses them to validate his own views, not to present possible interpretations. McCutcheon similarly asserts that Monty Python's *The Life of Brian* (1979) is "a powerful *example* of how social formations more than likely arise—in a haphazard manner that only later comes to be authorized and mystified" ("Redescribing," 185; my emphasis). Which is to say that, just because these films dramatize the process of creating meaning does not therefore mean that this is the actual process that occurs in any human community, let alone all of them at all times. Such films no more prove the truth of what they depict than, say, *Spider-Man* (2002) proves that great responsibility really does come with great power.
5. For a discussion of visual and verbal learning styles see Richard Felder, "Reaching the Second Tier: Learning and Teaching Styles in College Science Education," *Journal of College Science Teaching* 23 (1993): 286–90.
6. Similarly, many students in Tony's *Frailty* class did not hesitate to challenge his reading of the film. The best of these challenges—in terms of argument quality, use of the film, and connection to other narratives—came from Kate Jenks, who posted the following comments on the course's online discussion board: "As I saw it, the end of the film gestures to the idea that some supernatural force was at play but did not in any way confirm that that force was necessarily 'God,' at least not in the Judeo-Christian sense of the word. With this in mind, it is possible to make a very interesting comparison to *The Lord of the Rings*. In all of the films, but especially in *The Return of the King*, there are seeing stones, which allow Sauron to communicate with whoever is holding them. Through them, he reveals 'truth' but not in its entirety—he shows scenes which are entirely out of context, and, through the power of suggestion, leads characters to jump to very wrong conclusions and act in very bad ways. Now, think about the 'visions' of the crimes committed by the 'demons' that Adam and his father 'destroy' which are revealed at the end of the film—we see the little girl getting into the old man's car, we see the wife sitting beside the dead husband, but we never see any crimes being committed. We do see the FBI agent killing his mother, but we are not given the context in which that happens either. Is it not possible that, like the visions in the seeing stones, the visions that Adam and his father receive are designed to deceive?" To me, Kate's analysis here beautifully throws into question to some extent virtually everyone's reading of the film, both instructors' and students'. More important, it shows, again, a level of confidence with the source material that in my experience is a hallmark of courses that use mainstream films.
7. With luck, such participation will help students move from a "surface" approach to learning toward a "deep" approach; Julia Christensen Hughes and Joy Mighty, eds., *Taking Stock: Research on Teaching and Learning in Higher Education* (Montreal: McGill-Queen's University Press, 2010). The former is normally encouraged by the

traditional information-transmission ways of teaching, whereby students focus mainly on repeating what they are told. The latter emerges as they gradually accept shared ownership of discussion content and develop the skills and interest to investigate material on their own and apply ideas and methods outside the classroom.

8. For other examples, see Gregory J. Watkins, ed., *Teaching Religion and Film* (New York: Oxford University Press, 2008). Although very few of the chapters in this text are explicitly about religion and violence, most of them—like McCutcheon's article—inevitably (perhaps unavoidably?) touch on the topic in some way.

9. In many ways I believe that training students to question their course texts (and teachers) is one of the most important things that we as instructors can do. This importance is well illustrated by William Bigelow's discussion of teaching U.S. history, and the discrepancy between the consistently positive textbook accounts of Columbus's "discovery" of the Americas and the actual history of Columbus's enslavement and massacre of the first Native populations he encountered. A key aspect of Bigelow's course, therefore, is not simply to talk about what happened in the past, but, he writes, "to teach students that text material, indeed all written material, is to be read skeptically. I want students to explore the politics of print, that perspectives on history and social reality underlie the written word and that to read is both to comprehend what is written, but also to question *why* it is written"; William Bigelow, "Discovering Columbus: Rereading the Past," *Language Arts* 66 (1989): 639.

10. A very short list of such films from the past twenty years would include *Single White Female* (1992), *The Cable Guy* (1996), *The Talented Mr. Ripley* (1999), *Kill Bill: Vol. 1* (2003), *Transformers* (2007), perhaps every John Woo film ever made, and the vast majority of superhero movies. For a discussion of Girard's work in relation to the topic at hand, see Ken Derry and Tony S. L. Michael, "On the Pedagogical Benefits of Using John Woo's *The Killer* as a Model of René Girard's Theory on Religion and Violence," *Journal of Religion and Film* 5.1 (2001), http://www.unomaha.edu/jrf/girard.htm.

11. As of this writing, for example, *The Passion of the Christ* remains by far the most referenced production in the *Journal of Religion and Film*. Up to and including the October 2009 issue, thirty-five entries in the journal have included discussion of this film; next in line are *The Last Temptation of Christ* (1988; twenty-seven entries), *Jesus of Montreal* (1989; twenty entries), and *The Gospel According to St. Matthew* (1964; eighteen entries). This embarrassment of riches where Jesus films are concerned is reflected in religion and film work generally, and is why I have not included discussion of any such movies in this chapter, although I do talk about Christ-figures.

12. The title of this subsection is taken from a paper by Laurel Zwissler, "Jesus Christ, Action Hero: Christianity Battles Evil in Canadian Horror Film *Jesus Christ, Vampire Hunter*" (presented at the annual meeting of the American Academy of Religion, Toronto, Canada, November 24, 2002).

13. Thus in 2000, S. Brent Plate called for "a five-year moratorium on interpreting films for their Christic similarities" (S. Brent Plate, Review of *Dancer in the Dark*, *Journal of Religion and Film* 4.2 [2000], http://www.unomaha.edu/jrf/dancer.htm), a plea he reiterated a few years later (S. Brent Plate, "The Re-creation of the World: Filming Faith," *Dialog: A Journal of Theology* 42 [2003]: 158, 160 n. 12). Although that five-year period has long passed, it seems few if any of us heeded the call, and so the point remains an important one: too often identifying a movie's Christ-figure(s) becomes an end in itself, one that can easily overshadow both other key religious aspects and "the much more important ethical, human issues with which [the] film

grapples" (Review of *Dancer*). For a discussion of this topic that specifically relates to teaching, see Christopher Deacy, "The Pedagogical Challenges of Finding Christ Figures," in *Teaching Religion and Film*, ed. Gregory J. Watkins (New York: Oxford University Press, 2008), 129–40.

14. For Baugh's list of Christ-figure characteristics, see Lloyd Baugh, *Imaging the Divine: Jesus and Christ-Figures in Film* (Kansas City, MO: Sheed and Ward, 1997), 205–10.

15. See Michel Desjardins, *Peace, Violence and the New Testament* (Sheffield: Sheffield Academic, 1997) for a detailed discussion of the ways in which both Jesus in particular, and the New Testament more generally, promote these very different perspectives.

16. We can of course also take a more direct route to these same questions by considering films that are actually about specific religious figures, such as *Little Buddha* or *The Passion of the Christ*, and which therefore overtly invite discussion on their historical and theological underpinnings. But in my experience, discussions of such topics resonate more deeply with students when it is the students themselves—rather than the film or the filmmakers—whose questions, objections, and responses push the conversation in that direction.

17. My point here accords with Zwissler's conclusion regarding *Jesus Christ, Vampire Hunter*: "It is the clear linking of Jesus with heroism that validates and legitimizes his Christian message" ("Jesus," 11). See also William Arnal's point regarding both scholarship about, and representations of, Jesus: "Jesus means so much, so differently, to so many people, that it is almost impossible to say anything about him without engaging people's most deeply-cherished feelings—about right and wrong, about who 'we' are, about the meaning of our behaviors and principles"; William E. Arnal, *The Symbolic Jesus: Historical Scholarship, Judaism and the Construction of Contemporary Identity* (London: Equinox, 2005), 7.

18. Not surprisingly, just like Chris Vaughn most superheroes also exhibit, virtually by definition, many Christ-figure characteristics, including having mysterious origins, performing miracles, shedding blood, having followers, opposing authority (acting as a vigilante), and of course saving people. Most superheroes also typically have two natures, both human and superhuman, and with increasing frequency are killed by their enemies only to be reborn later.

19. Superman raises Lex Luthor's kryptonite-infused island and flies it into space, knowing that Luthor and three members of his gang are on the island; two of them don't make it off alive.

20. The authors have made this argument in a number of books, including Robert Jewett and John Shelton Lawrence, *Captain America and the Crusade Against Evil: The Dilemma of Zealous Nationalism* (Grand Rapids, MI: Eerdmans, 2003). For Jewett and Lawrence, the prototype of zealous nationalism is Phinehas (Num. 25), who kills an Israelite man and his Midianite wife in their marriage tent because of his righteous conviction that their intermarriage was impure, a conviction so strong he could not wait for a trial (*Captain*, 169).

21. Ibid., 43.

22. The more recent *Superman Returns* appears in some ways to resist the hero-America identification, most obviously by replacing the comment that Superman stands for "truth, justice, and the American way," with the winking "truth, justice, and all that stuff." And yet despite the film's attempts to paint Superman as a global hero, he remains very much American: he is raised on an American farm and works and lives in an American city, and by defeating Luthor he is specifically saving the continental United States. In his review of the film, Dan Hoy pushes this point fully in

the direction of zealous nationalism by arguing that there is "an implicit proxy within the title of Lois Lane's Pulitzer prize-winning article: 'Why the World Doesn't Need Superman' can be read as 'Why the World Doesn't Need America,' or, more specifically, 'Why the World Doesn't Need America Acting According to Its Idealized Version of Itself.' Yet by the end of the movie it's clear that we're to regard Lois' sentiment as compensatory and false—that is to say, it's the cynics who need to change, not the ideological demiurges who place themselves above a law they swear to protect"; Dan Hoy, review of *Superman Returns*, *Sinlechuga* (2006), http://www. sinlechuga.com/reviews/superman_returns.html.

23. Significantly, Stark gives this speech before his redemption and rebirth as Iron Man, before he realizes that he was wrong to create weapons like the Jericho. Once enlightened, he attempts to correct his former folly, refusing to let his company make further weapons and destroying those that fell into the "wrong" hands. One might think (and students may argue) therefore that he has renounced zealous nationalism; in fact, the opposite seems to have happened. The film suggests that, previously, Stark was not zealous enough; he was too careless, he relied on others, and so allowed evil to flourish. In his new state he creates a weapon (the Iron Man armor) more powerful than any other, a weapon that only he can access, a weapon that allows him to effectively (and illegally) fight and destroy evil.

24. Jane Mayer, "Whatever It Takes: The Politics of the Man Behind '24,'" *New Yorker*, February 19, 2007, http://www.newyorker.com/reporting/2007/02/19/070219fa_fact_mayer.

25. Jewett and Lawrence, *Captain*, 28–35.

26. *The Dark Knight* is rare in this regard, but not entirely unique. The three *X-Men* films also to varying degrees promote prophetic realism, as the mission of the X-Men is itself to use due process to overcome systemic racism. They are opposed in this by the Brotherhood, led by Magneto, who see all humans as evil and so are zealously dedicated to destroying them.

27. Perhaps not coincidentally, Batman's shortcomings as a savior are paralleled by his relative lack of Christ-figure characteristics in other regards. Using Baugh's typology, for example, we can see that while Batman does meet some of the criteria (he sheds blood and is concerned with justice) he clearly does not meet others (he is not an innocent who suffers nor is he really in conflict with authority). Most notably, *The Dark Knight* includes no scene of crucifixion, death, or resurrection. The closest it comes to such a moment is Batman's fall near the end of the film, after saving Gordon's son; however, while lying on the ground he is pointedly not in crucified form and remains there only a moment before getting to his feet, having simply had the wind knocked out of him.

28. In 2009 the worldwide top ten list (according to boxofficemojo.com) comprised, in order: *Avatar*; *Harry Potter and the Half-Blood Prince*; *Ice Age: Dawn of the Dinosaurs*; *Transformers: Revenge of the Fallen*; *2012*; *Up*; *The Twilight Saga: New Moon*; *Sherlock Holmes*; *Angels and Demons*; and *The Hangover*. The only possible exceptions to the straight white male rule in this group are the animated *Ice Age*, in which the main characters are heterosexual *animals* voiced by white males; and *New Moon*, in which the female protagonist, Bella, is arguably so passive she barely registers as a character at all, someone whose fate rests entirely in the undead hands of her straight white male paramour, Edward. Students may enjoy hearing comedian Aziz Ansari's take on the lack of diversity in Hollywood films from his album *Intimate Moments for a Sensual Evening*. He performed a more G-rated version of the routine on the May 8, 2009, episode of *Jimmy Kimmel Live* (http://www.youtube.com/watch?v=hO6oNlierSQ).

Ansari, who was born and raised in South Carolina by parents from India, recounts being asked by an interviewer if he was excited about the success of *Slumdog Million-aire*. Ansari considered the question and thought, "Yeah, I am! And I don't know why. I had nothing to do with that movie. It's just some people that look kinda like me starring in an Oscar-winning film. But I'm excited just to see people like me. And then I thought about it and I was like, man, are white people just psyched all the time?' *'Back to the Future*, that's us! *E.T.*, that's us! *Titanic*, us! Every movie BUT *Slumdog Millionaire* and *Boyz n the Hood*, that's us!'"

29. Joe Kelly and Stacy L. Smith, *Where the Girls Aren't: Gender Disparity Saturates G-Rated Films* (Duluth, MN: Dads and Daughters, 2006), 3.

30. Rubina Ramji, "From *Navy Seals* to *The Siege*: Getting to Know the Muslim Terrorist, Hollywood Style," *Journal of Religion and Film* 9.2 (2005), http://www.unomaha.edu/jrf/Vol9No2/RamjiIslam.htm.

31. In fact, science fiction films about extraterrestrials generally lend themselves well to any discussion of "us" and "them" ideologies. Hostile aliens out to destroy humanity (in films like *Invasion of the Body Snatchers*, *Aliens*, and *Independence Day*) are generally understood to represent any number of "others": those of different cultures, skin colors, worldviews, etc. See, e.g., Peter Biskind, *Seeing Is Believing: How Hollywood Taught Us to Stop Worrying and Love the Fifties* (New York: Pantheon, 1983), 102–59; M. Keith Booker, *Alternate Americas: Science Fiction Film and American Culture* (Westport, CT: Praeger, 2006). On the other hand, friendly aliens who deliberately or incidentally offer assistance (in films like *The Day the Earth Stood Still*, *Close Encounters of the Third Kind*, or *Starman*) are often seen as symbolizing benevolent divine beings rather than *people* who are different from "us." See, e.g., Caron Schwartz Ellis, "With Eyes Uplifted: Space Aliens as Sky Gods," in *Screening the Sacred: Religion, Myth and Ideology in Popular American Film*, ed. Joel W. Martin and Conrad E. Ostwalt Jr. (Boulder, CO: Westview, 1995), 83–93; Hugh Ruppersberg, "The Alien Messiah," in *Alien Zone: Cultural Theory and Contemporary Science Fiction Cinema*, ed. Annette Kuhn (London: Verso, 1990), 32–38.

32. There are of course innumerable examples of the ways in which various religions have authorized the neglect, subjugation, or abuse of "others" based on categories of gender, culture, race, belief system, sexual orientation, etc. For sample commentaries on this topic as it relates to film, see Joel W. Martin, "Redeeming America: *Rocky* as Ritual Racial Drama," in *Screening the Sacred: Religion, Myth and Ideology in Popular American Film*, ed. Joel W. Martin and Conrad E. Ostwalt Jr. (Boulder, CO: Westview, 1995), 125–33; Miles, *Seeing*; Gaye William Ortiz, "Women, Theology, and Film: Approaching the Challenge of Interdisciplinary Teaching," in *Teaching Religion and Film*, ed. Gregory J. Watkins (New York: Oxford University Press, 2008), 165–73; Ramji, "From *Navy Seals*"; Janice Hocker Rushing, "Evolution of the 'New Frontier' in *Alien* and *Aliens*: Patriarchal Co-optation of the Feminine Archetype," in *Screening the Sacred: Religion, Myth and Ideology in Popular American Film*, ed. Joel W. Martin and Conrad E. Ostwalt Jr. (Boulder, CO: Westview, 1995), 94–117. Unfortunately, such studies are actually few and far between; as Brent Plate points out, for example, in religion and film work on popular movies "what often goes unnoticed are the gendered and racial biases of industrial, Hollywood film production" ("Re-creation," 159).

33. Robert McAfee Brown, *Religion and Violence*, 2nd ed. (Philadelphia: Westminster, 1987), 5–12. This understanding is a particular application of his broader definition of violence as a "violation of personhood," in the sense of "infringing upon or disregarding or abusing or denying" another person (7).

34. For examples and discussions of such responses, see Elizabeth Bell, Lynda Haas, and Laura Sells, "Introduction: Walt's in the Movies," in *From Mouse to Mermaid: The Politics of Film, Gender, and Culture*, ed. Elizabeth Bell, Lynda Haas, and Laura Sells (Bloomington: Indiana University Press, 1995), 1–17; Chyng Feng Sun and Erica Scharrer, "Staying True to Disney: College Students' Resistance to Criticism of *The Little Mermaid*," *Communication Review* 7 (2004): 35–55.

35. Mark I. Pinsky, *The Gospel According to Disney: Faith, Trust, and Pixie Dust* (Louisville, KY: Westminster John Knox, 2004), xi–xii. Although I find certain elements of the "Disney canon" highly problematic—such as the easy division of the world into "good" and "evil"—Pinsky does identify numerous other Disney film tendencies that to me are less ambiguously positive. These include promoting joy, play, and friendship; accepting nontraditional family structures; and acknowledging the reality of suffering (*Gospel*, 7–12). I mention this point to suggest that, while Disney films make an easy target for criticism, their value as a teaching example lies also in the fact that often they can be more complex, and even contradictory, than such criticism might suggest. I use these films in class not because I want to tear down students' childhood idols, but in part to illustrate my belief that films can have multiple meanings. It is possible, that is, to have good (nonsentimental) reasons to like a Disney movie and still be able to recognize, and critique, its reactionary qualities.

36. Ibid., x.

37. Joel W. Martin, "Anti-feminism in Recent Apocalyptic Film," *Journal of Religion and Film* 4.1 (2000), http://www.unomaha.edu/jrf/antifem.htm.

38. Ibid. Scar is, in fact, part of a tradition of queer villains in film generally and in Disney movies in particular. For discussions of this issue, see Blog Next Door, "Queering Disney, or How Walt's Villains Play for Our Team," November 19, 2007, http://ablognextdoor. blogspot.com/2007/11/queering-disney-or-how-walts-villains.html; John Weir, "Gay-Bashing, Villainy and the Oscars," *New York Times*, March 29, 1992.

39. Pinsky, *Gospel*, 263–64.

40. As Martin remarks, "in order to undercut feminism, the film must show a female possessing real strength, only to subordinate her to a male" ("Anti-feminism").

41. Brian P. Stone, "Religion and Violence in Popular Film," *Journal of Religion and Film* 3.1 (1999), http://www.unomaha.edu/jrf/Violence.htm.

42. The three films are *Dances with Wolves* (1990), *Pulp Fiction* (1994), and *Pocahontas* (1995).

43. This latter omission is somewhat surprising, given that Stone cites Robert McAfee Brown's broad conception of violence in his own discussion of the term. That is, he understands violence to include all situations when "one individual 'violates the personhood' of another or when social institutions and structures are arranged in such a way as to violate a people's social or personal integrity" (Stone, "Religion"). Throughout his article, however, Stone in fact just twice refers to nonphysical violence, first in regards to various characters' mistreatment of Andrew Beckett in *Philadelphia* (1993) because he has AIDS, and second to the class system depicted in *Titanic* (1997) that results in the disproportionately high number of deaths among the poorer passengers. At no point does Stone discuss racism or gender issues in relation to either religion or film.

44. Tom Ruffles, *Ghost Images: Cinema of the Afterlife* (Jefferson, NC: McFarland, 2004), 8.

45. This assessment is also in agreement with virtually every published review of the film. For reflections on (and samples of) the consistently negative critical reception to *Ghost*, see Katherine A. Fowkes, *Giving Up the Ghost: Spirits, Ghosts, and Angels in Mainstream Comedy Films* (Detroit: Wayne State University Press, 1998), 18.

46. In this way Sam does still fit the stereotypical role of male as protector of the female, whose final solution to the problem at hand is achieved with violence (he keeps hitting Carl, who while trying to escape Sam is killed by a passing car). In fact, in my experience most viewers of *Ghost* tend only to see this aspect of Sam's character, and in this way the film fits with a long tradition of movies whose construction of masculinity is more complex than it first appears. This tradition includes, for example, the B Westerns, which—as Roderick McGillis argues in his thorough and insightful study—present heroes who on close examination surprise us by transgressing binary categories such as insider/outsider, civilized/wild, past/future, sensitive/brutal, and masculine/feminine; Roderick McGillis, *He Was Some Kind of a Man: Masculinities in the B Western* (Waterloo, ON: Wilfrid Laurier University Press, 2009).

47. Campbell's ideas did not penetrate filmmaking only in vague, unformed ways through Lucas's film. Perhaps the most well known way in which this effect occurred in a more direct and calculated manner involved Christopher Vogler, a Hollywood screenwriter, who distributed a memo in 1985 while working as a story consultant for Disney. The memo, "A Practical Guide to the Hero with a Thousand Faces," laid out the basics for writing movies based on Campbell's ideas, specifically using *Star Wars* as the model for these ideas. Vogler has been closely involved with the creation or development of several extremely popular films, including *The Lion King*, and eventually turned his memo into a book that is now in its third printing: *The Writer's Journey: Mythic Structure for Storytellers and Screenwriters* (Studio City, CA: Michael Wiese Productions, 2007). The original version of the memo (according to Vogler) is available online at http://www.thewritersjourney.com.

48. Stuart Voytilla, *Myth and the Movies: Discovering the Myth Structure of 50 Unforgettable Films* (Studio City, CA: Michael Wiese Productions, 1999).

49. Joseph Campbell with Bill Moyers, *The Power of Myth*, ed. Betty Sue Flowers (New York: Doubleday, 1988), 152.

50. This is not to say that I never use Campbell's work when teaching religion and film. However, when I do so I try to turn things around a bit. For example, I will ask students to consider the ways in which *Star Wars* does *not* map onto the hero's journey template, or else I will ask them to compare the template to a movie like 1987's *The Princess Bride* (which pokes fun at the conventions of the hero's journey) or 1990's *Goodfellas* (which uses these conventions to tell the story of a mobster rather than a hero). Such assignments push students both to think about Campbell's ideas in new ways and also to consider how the relationship between these ideas and the films in question affects their understandings of both.

51. John Dominic Crossan, *The Dark Interval: Towards a Theology of Story* (Niles, IL: Argus, 1975), 56. Or to borrow from Leonard Cohen's song "Anthem," parable is the crack that lets the light in.

52. Crossan, *Dark*, 55 (referencing Matt. 10:34 and Luke 12:49).

53. Hanna Roisman provides an excellent, detailed analysis of the ways in which Verbal uses Kujan's preconceptions against him; in the process she makes another link between *The Usual Suspects* and myth by demonstrating parallels between the film and the Phaeacian episode in the *Odyssey*; Hanna M. Roisman, "Verbal Odysseus: Narrative Strategy in the *Odyssey* and in *The Usual Suspects*," in *Classical Myth and Culture in the Cinema*, ed. Martin M. Winkler (Oxford: Oxford University Press, 2001), 51–71. Roisan sums up the rhetorical strategy evident in each work—a strategy congruent with the notion that "believing is seeing"—by quoting Aristotle: "what is convincing is what one can be convinced by" (ibid., 52).

54. Crossan, *Dark*, 60.

55. In the midst of much critical acclaim for *The Usual Suspects*, Roger Ebert offered one of the few negative reviews, and his complaint was largely centered on this point. That is to say, even on the second viewing he found Kint's narrative overly convoluted: "Once again, my comprehension began to slip, and finally I wrote down: 'To the degree that I do understand, I don't care.' It was, however, somewhat reassuring at the end of the movie to discover that I had, after all, understood everything I was intended to understand. It was just that there was less to understand than the movie at first suggests"; Roger Ebert, review of *The Usual Suspects*, August 18, 1995, http://rogerebert.suntimes.com/apps/pbcs.dll/article?AID=/19950818/REVIEWS/508180304/1023.

56. Crossan, *Dark*, 48–49.

57. See Henry A. Giroux, "*Pulp Fiction* and the Culture of Violence," *Harvard Educational Review* 65.2 (1995): 299–314. In addition to its focus on (implicit) racism in modern mainstream films, Giroux's article is useful in its rough breakdown of cinematic violence into three categories: ritualistic ("banal, predictable, and often stereotypically masculine pure spectacle in form and superficial in content," 301); symbolic ("probes the complex contradictions that shape human agency, the limits of rationality, and the existential issues that tie us to other human beings and a broader social world," 303); and hyperreal ("exploits the seamy side of controversial issues [and] isolat[es] terrifying events from wider social context," 304). Giroux also addresses the specifically pedagogical significance of these categories of violence, and the challenges and opportunities presented to educators by violent popular films.

58. Giroux, "*Pulp Fiction*," 306.

59. Although for many years *Once Were Warriors* was the highest-grossing New Zealand film ever made (eventually surpassed by the *Lord of the Rings* trilogy), I find that relatively few North Americans know of this movie, let alone have seen it. As a result students are very often shocked when watching it in class for the first time, as it is violent in a way unlike the movies they are familiar with. Its gritty portrayal of domestic abuse in particular can be quite upsetting, and so I always offer a warning before showing this film.

60. This scene is consistently upsetting to students in a way I did not anticipate when I first taught *Once Were Warriors*. Many who are passionately opposed to violence find themselves cheering Jake's actions, as they too want revenge on Bully for hurting Grace, and are consequently shocked and unnerved by their enjoyment of Bully's intense and graphic suffering. Their reactions provide a great example of how films can offer opportunities to take discussions about violence beyond the theoretical and abstract, to engage and challenge students in more meaningful ways.

61. In this regard, *Once Were Warriors* functions in a way that is arguably very similar to *Unforgiven* (1992), although less directly so. As Giroux comments, Eastwood's film "rewrites the traditional and revisionist Western, and in doing so raises ethical questions concerning how violence has been mythologized and decontextualized so as to reinvent a nostalgic and utterly false version of the American past" ("*Pulp Fiction*," 303).

62. That this condemnation is in fact implicit, not explicit, has inspired a good deal of criticism of *Once Were Warriors* since the film's opening. Detractors argue that, for those viewers who lack an understanding of colonialism, the film may in fact perpetuate negative stereotypes of Maori people in particular and of Indigenous people more generally. Davnia Thornley reviews both sides of this debate in some detail and along the way provides much of the missing context herself; Davinia Thornley,

"White, Brown or 'Coffee'? Revisioning Race in Tamahori's *Once Were Warriors*," *Film Criticism* 25.3 (2001): 22–36. For what it is worth, in my experience teaching the film, students with little or no knowledge of Indigenous religion and history are still able to recognize that *Once Were Warriors* is hinting at the importance of a wider colonial context to the Hekes' story and generally do not see it as reinscribing a picture of the Maori as "inferior" or "depraved" (ibid., 29).

63. This is of course just one of many reasons to include a more diverse range of films and considerations of religion in our classrooms and our writings. Unfortunately, as evidenced in note 11 above concerning the *Journal of Religion and Film*, scholarship in the field remains deeply focused on North American and European movies in relation to Christianity. Rare examples of works that take a broader approach include Part II of Watkins, *Teaching Religion and Film*, and the entirety of S. Brent Plate, ed., *Representing Religion in World Cinema: Filmmaking, Mythmaking, Culture Making* (New York: Palgrave Macmillan, 2003).

64. The video is available on YouTube (search for "moonwalking bear") or from the original site at http://www.youtube.com/watch?v=Ahg6qcgoay4.

65. I always make the point that I also missed the bear the first time I watched this video. I am not sure if students find this information at all interesting or reassuring, but I think it is important to be clear that I do not possess special powers of observation that they lack.

66. Jonathan Z. Smith, *Imagining Religion: From Babylon to Jonestown* (Chicago: University of Chicago Press, 1982), xi (my emphasis).

BIBLIOGRAPHY

Arnal, William E. *The Symbolic Jesus: Historical Scholarship, Judaism and the Construction of Contemporary Identity*. London: Equinox, 2005.

Baugh, Lloyd. *Imaging the Divine: Jesus and Christ-Figures in Film*. Kansas City: Sheed and Ward, 1997.

Bell, Elizabeth, Lynda Haas, and Laura Sells. "Introduction: Walt's in the Movies." In *From Mouse to Mermaid: The Politics of Film, Gender, and Culture*, ed. Elizabeth Bell, Lynda Haas, and Laura Sells, 1–17. Bloomington: Indiana University Press, 1995.

Bergen, Mary, with Michael Berger. "Teaching Literature: Rethinking the Socratic Method." In *Teaching Undergraduates: Essays from the Lilly Endowment Workshop on Liberal Arts*, ed. Bruce A. Kimball, 59–72. Buffalo, NY: Prometheus, 1988.

Bigelow, William. "Discovering Columbus: Rereading the Past." *Language Arts* 66 (1989): 635–43.

Biskind, Peter. *Seeing Is Believing: How Hollywood Taught Us to Stop Worrying and Love the Fifties*. New York: Pantheon, 1983.

Blog Next Door, A. "Queering Disney, or How Walt's Villains Play for Our Team." November 19, 2007, http://ablognextdoor.blogspot.com/2007/11/queering-disney-or-how-walts-villains.html.

Booker, M. Keith. *Alternate Americas: Science Fiction Film and American Culture*. Westport, CT: Praeger, 2006.

Brown, Robert McAfee. *Religion and Violence*, 2nd ed. Philadelphia: Westminster, 1987.

Campbell, Joseph, with Bill Moyers. *The Power of Myth*. Ed. Betty Sue Flowers. New York: Doubleday, 1988.

Crossan, John Dominic. *The Dark Interval: Towards a Theology of Story*. Niles, IL: Argus, 1975.

Deacy, Christopher. "The Pedagogical Challenges of Finding Christ Figures." In *Teaching Religion and Film*, ed. Gregory J. Watkins, 129–40. New York: Oxford University Press, 2008.

Derry, Ken, and Tony S. L. Michael. "On the Pedagogical Benefits of Using John Woo's *The Killer* as a Model of René Girard's Theory on Religion and Violence." *Journal of Religion and Film* 5.1 (2001), http://www.unomaha.edu/jrf/girard.htm.

Desjardins, Michel. *Peace, Violence and the New Testament*. Sheffield: Sheffield Academic, 1997.

Ebert, Roger. Review of *The Usual Suspects*. August 18, 1995, http://rogerebert.suntimes.com/apps/pbcs.dll/article?AID=/19950818/REVIEWS/508180304/1023.

Ellis, Caron Schwartz. "With Eyes Uplifted: Space Aliens as Sky Gods." In *Screening the Sacred: Religion, Myth and Ideology in Popular American Film*, ed. Joel W. Martin and Conrad E. Ostwalt Jr., 83–93. Boulder, CO: Westview, 1995.

Felder, Richard. "Reaching the Second Tier: Learning and Teaching Styles in College Science Education." *Journal of College Science Teaching* 23 (1993): 286–90, http://www4.ncsu.edu/unity/lockers/users/f/felder/public/Papers/Secondtier.html.

Fowkes, Katherine A. *Giving Up the Ghost: Spirits, Ghosts, and Angels in Mainstream Comedy Films*. Detroit: Wayne State University Press, 1998.

Giroux, Henry A. "*Pulp Fiction* and the Culture of Violence." *Harvard Educational Review* 65.2 (1995): 299–314.

Hoy, Dan. Review of *Superman Returns*. *Sinlechuga* (2006), http://www.sinlechuga.com/reviews/superman_returns.html.

Hughes, Julia Christensen, and Joy Mighty, eds. *Taking Stock: Research on Teaching and Learning in Higher Education*. Montreal: McGill-Queen's University Press, 2010.

Jewett, Robert, and John Shelton Lawrence. *Captain America and the Crusade Against Evil: The Dilemma of Zealous Nationalism*. Grand Rapids, MI: Eerdmans, 2003.

Kelly, Joe, and Stacy L. Smith. *Where the Girls Aren't: Gender Disparity Saturates G-Rated Films*. Duluth, MN: Dads and Daughters, 2006. http://www.learcenter.org/images/event_uploads/where.the.girls.arent%5B1%5D.pdf.

Martin, Joel W. "Anti-feminism in Recent Apocalyptic Film." *Journal of Religion and Film* 4.1 (2000), http://www.unomaha.edu/jrf/antifem.htm.

———. "Redeeming America: Rocky as Ritual Racial Drama." In *Screening the Sacred: Religion, Myth and Ideology in Popular American Film*, ed. Joel W. Martin and Conrad E. Ostwalt Jr., 125–33. Boulder, CO: Westview, 1995.

Mayer, Jane. 2007. "Whatever It Takes: The Politics of the Man Behind '24.'" *New Yorker*, February 19, 2007, http://www.newyorker.com/reporting/2007/02/19/070219fa_fact_mayer.

McCutcheon, Russell T. "Redescribing 'Religion and . . . ' Film: Teaching the Insider/Outsider Problem." In *Critics Not Caretakers: Redescribing the Public Study of Religion*, 179–99. Albany: State University of New York Press, 2001.

McGillis, Roderick. *He Was Some Kind of a Man: Masculinities in the B Western*. Waterloo, ON: Wilfrid Laurier University Press, 2009.

Miles, Margaret. *Seeing and Believing: Religion and Values in the Movies*. Boston: Beacon, 1996.

Ortiz, Gaye William. "Women, Theology, and Film: Approaching the Challenge of Interdisciplinary Teaching." In *Teaching Religion and Film*, ed. Gregory J. Watkins, 165–73. New York: Oxford University Press, 2008.

Pinsky, Mark I. *The Gospel According to Disney: Faith, Trust, and Pixie Dust*. Louisville, KY: Westminster John Knox, 2004.

Plate, S. Brent. "The Re-creation of the World: Filming Faith." *Dialog: A Journal of Theology* 42 (2003): 155–60.

——, ed. *Representing Religion in World Cinema: Filmmaking, Mythmaking, Culture Making*. New York: Palgrave Macmillan, 2003.

——. Review of *Dancer in the Dark*. *Journal of Religion and Film* 4.2 (2000), http://www.unomaha.edu/jrf/dancer.htm.

Ramji, Rubina. "From *Navy Seals* to *The Siege*: Getting to Know the Muslim Terrorist, Hollywood Style." *Journal of Religion and Film* 9.2 (2005), http://www.unomaha.edu/jrf/Vol9No2/RamjiIslam.htm.

Roisman, Hanna M. "Verbal Odysseus: Narrative Strategy in the Odyssey and in *The Usual Suspects*." In *Classical Myth and Culture in the Cinema*, ed. Martin M. Winkler, 51–71. Oxford: Oxford University Press, 2001.

Ruffles, Tom. *Ghost Images: Cinema of the Afterlife*. Jefferson, NC: McFarland, 2004.

Ruppersberg, Hugh. "The Alien Messiah." In *Alien Zone: Cultural Theory and Contemporary Science Fiction Cinema*, ed. Annette Kuhn, 32–38. London: Verso, 1990.

Rushing, Janice Hocker. "Evolution of the 'New Frontier' in *Alien* and *Aliens*: Patriarchal Co-optation of the Feminine Archetype." In *Screening the Sacred: Religion, Myth and Ideology in Popular American Film*, ed. Joel W. Martin and Conrad E. Ostwalt Jr., 94–117. Boulder, CO: Westview, 1995.

Smith, Jonathan Z. *Imagining Religion: From Babylon to Jonestown*. Chicago: University of Chicago Press, 1982.

Stone, Brian P. "Religion and Violence in Popular Film." *Journal of Religion and Film* 3.1 (1999), http://www.unomaha.edu/jrf/Violence.htm.

Sun, Chyng Feng, and Erica Scharrer. "Staying True to Disney: College Students' Resistance to Criticism of *The Little Mermaid*." *Communication Review* 7 (2004): 35–55.

Thornley, Davinia. "White, Brown or 'Coffee'? Revisioning Race in Tamahori's *Once Were Warriors*." *Film Criticism* 25.3 (2001): 22–36.

Vogler, Christopher. *The Writers Journey: Mythic Structure for Writers*, 3rd ed. Studio City, CA: Michael Wiese Productions, 2007.

Voytilla, Stuart. *Myth and the Movies: Discovering the Myth Structure of 50 Unforgettable Films*. Studio City, CA: Michael Wiese Productions, 1999.

Watkins, Gregory J., ed. *Teaching Religion and Film*. New York: Oxford University Press, 2008.

Weir, John. "Gay-Bashing, Villainy and the Oscars." *New York Times*, March 29, 1992. http://www.nytimes.com/1992/03/29/movies/film-gay-bashing-villainy-and-the-oscars.html.

Zwissler, Laurel. "Jesus Christ, Action Hero: Christianity Battles Evil in Canadian Horror Film *Jesus Christ, Vampire Hunter*." Paper presented at the annual meeting of the American Academy of Religion, Toronto, Canada, November 24, 2002, http://www.odessafilmworks.com/downloads/JC_Action_Hero.pdf.

CHAPTER 9

༺

Teaching Religion, Violence, and Pop Culture

RANDAL CUMMINGS

INTRODUCTION

Phrases and concepts combining "religion and violence" roll so readily off the lips these days that it takes a concerted act of reflection to recall when the connection was neither so immediate nor so existentially relevant. Since graduate school, "religion in America" had ceased to conjure for me images solely of Sunday go-to-meetings, devotional piety, the pastoral theologies taught in synagogues, churches, cathedrals, or even more esoteric New Age endeavors such as yoga and meditation or the rare occasional media glimpses of American Muslims in public prayer. That's not to say I was trapped in a Norman Rockwell painting as normative of religion. As a teaching assistant in graduate school I spent most of my time explaining ideological differences across a vast variety of worldviews in terms of origins, purposes, meanings, patterns of transcendence, and longed-for futures, all in appropriate ontological, teleological, soteriological, eschatological categories and by means of phenomenologically valid methodologies, *epochē* and empathy abounding. In retrospect, however, in my early teaching days I was temporarily floating in an idyllic post-Vietnam-era solipsistic bubble where the futility of war had seemingly rendered war itself obsolete, except for an occasional peacekeeping police action as enlightened intervention. The Cold War was virtually over; James Bond had to vie with hyperbolized caricatures drawn from cartoon stereotyped terrorists. Fundamentalists were annoying but not lethal. It was a well-insulated, comfort-zone bubble in which I incubated, where religion was isolated as the beneficent force beneath hospitals and hospitality, charity and social justice, empathy and engaged responsibility. I was quick to point out the dharma of Amnesty International, the tao of Greenpeace, the social justice and communal accountability of Alcoholics Anonymous. Oh, the "dharmony" of it all! It was a bubble that contained only half the religious picture, but once I began teaching university courses of my own, it quickly burst. In one of the first courses I taught, Belief and Unbelief, I discovered that the violence of God (or the violence God seemingly ordains in human suffering, or that God is portrayed as commanding, condoning, or ignoring) is one of the on-going objections to the existence of such a being. In Death and Afterlife in the World Religions, I learned from a number of students what directly wrestling with theodicy issues is like, and, in no small part, about the violence of the inner city and the reciprocal violence of the penal system geared to address it. Although I had long since argued for the presence of religious structures in common culture, I was on the cusp of a paradigm shift that would increasingly see violence as engendered, sustained, controlled, fed, fueled, inflamed, and ultimately fluctuatingly repressed and reverberated in and by ostensibly or essentially religious patterns.

Nowhere was this more apparent than in a course I designed titled Myth, Religion, and Culture. Its aim was to apply the full hermeneutical and methodological skills of the historian of religions to aspects of everyday social and cultural phenomena to discover hidden religious and religious-like roots, foundations, structures, dynamics, residues, vestiges, and artifacts richly strewn in the substrata of contemporary culture. I call this endeavor "performing cultural archaeology." When I first began teaching Myth, Religion, and Culture, as a simple exercise in cultural archaeology, I would ask students how they were dressed during their high-school graduation ceremonies. Invariably they were surprised to discover that they were dressed in monastic garb as higher education's inheritance from the monastery-sponsored universities of Europe. It is easy to trace the flow of monastic matriculation from "sacred" locations like the universities of Paris, Oxford, Cambridge, and Tübingen to Harvard, Princeton, Yale, Chicago, Berkeley, and Stanford to its present high ceremonial, ritual status. Although fewer in number than in archaic cultures, there are still a number of similar initiatory rituals that acknowledge shifts-in-being that parallel and are, in fact, borrowed from religious rituals, such as military training and vows like "semper fi." Such initiatory ceremonies may properly be called survivals from more archaic and overtly religious strata. It was a small step to see this same dynamic in gang initiations, with their higher transcendent categories of community, group loyalty, courage, and fearlessness in the face of death, values that group members unflinchingly learn to produce in sacred battles, "jihads" for sacred space bought in blood and ritually sanctified in sacrifice.

An epiphany occurred to me, however, that pop culture was not simply comprised of residues, camouflages, and substitutes for conventional religion, but, if observed objectively through a discerning methodological grid, was indistinguishable from "real" religion and comprised of ideas, activities, and symbols or icons that were religious in their own right. I now argue that popular culture functions like religion and plays a ready-at-hand, pervasive, and even determinative role in identity formation, meaning making, behavior modeling, and the violence modulation, moderation, and mediation traditionally occupied by a variety of conventional religions.

I am hardly alone in this. There has been an accelerating paradigm shift away from the once strong view that Western culture was becoming increasingly secularized and that religion was fading or being replaced by ever-expanding secular modes of thought. Generated by thinkers like Feuerbach and Freud, this idea was proffered by such theologians as Harvey Cox in his classic *Secular City* and further explored and made explicit by such folk as Steve Bruce, among many others.[1] There has also been a steady move away from this position, including a reversal by Harvey Cox in *The Future of Faith*.[2]

An approach adopted by David Chidester in his *Authentic Fakes: Religion and American Popular Culture* goes boldly to the point by defining being religious as "ways of being a human person in a human place."[3] A more cautious and meticulously argued approach to definitions is applied by Jonathan Benthall in his *Returning to Religion: Why a Secular Age Is Haunted by Faith*, where he uses such circumlocutions as "quasi-religion," "para-religion," or "the religioid" to refer to nonmainline, nonconventional, that is, secular, examples of religion.[4] In *Religion and Popular Culture: Rescripting the Sacred*, Richard Santana and Gregory Erickson explore the mutual confluences and cross-insemination of traditional and popular religions with popular culture to spawn a wide variety of new, contradictory, yet thoroughly American religious identities characterized by traceable shifts in what "the sacred" pragmatically entails as touchstones of behavior and identity across numerous cultural endeavors.[5] Another book along these lines that I have used effectively as a course text is Gary Laderman's *Sacred Matters: Celebrity Worship, Sexual Ecstasies, the Living Dead, and Other Signs of Religious Life in the United States*, in which he explores the "living myths" embedded in American consciousness, that, even when devoid of an articulate sense of God, function religiously as the fabric and centrifugal forces of meaning making in everyday life.[6] Perhaps the most ambitious work to appear along these lines is Mark C. Taylor's *After God*, in which he argues that the hidden influence and ongoing tenacity of religion is far more complex and complicated, flowing robustly beneath the surface, than either its apologists and defenders or critics and defamers generally think. Taylor argues that religion has "never been so powerful and so dangerous" as now, having "taken to the streets by filling airways and networks with images and messages that create fatal conflicts which threaten to rage out of control."[7] His definition of religion is meant to encompass secular manifestations in "symbols, myths, and rituals that, on the one hand, figure schemata of feeling, thinking, and acting in ways that lend life meaning and purpose and, on the other, disrupt, dislocate, and disfigure every stabilizing structure."[8]

I argue, therefore, that instead of culture becoming increasingly secularized as a move away from religion, pop culture demonstrates that secularization itself is, in reality, a process of resacralization by which religion constantly reinvents itself and reemerges as dynamic energy, altered, yet manifest in revalorized but recognizable forms. An important corollary to this thesis is the reciprocity between religion and culture and the ever-aspiring role of conventional religions as interpreters and arbiters of pop culture's themes, motifs, and mechanisms. In addition, I argue that violence is the result of deep-structure, paradigmatic myths and metaphysics, and, as Eliade observed, it takes a deeply committed theoretical premise, a theology, or a metaphysic to enable extreme acts of violence such as head hunting and cannibalism.[9] Violence is rarely ever simply a matter of politics or economics, although these may indeed play subsidiary roles. Violence in its fullest form is ultimately a matter of religious significance, interpretation, and motivation. The fact that the "war on terror" is most strongly supported by the religious right and kindred religious-like conservative paradigms serves to support this observation.

PROBLEMATIZING THE ISSUES

In my courses I rarely make distinctions between high and low culture, or among folk, youth, or pop cultures, as those distinctions are increasingly irrelevant for a number of reasons. One is the unprecedented access of the virtual masses to every aspect of the most rarefied essences and finesses of "high" culture, as well as the fact that the loftier achievements of mass culture are increasingly becoming and reflecting sophisticated, high-level art. In addition, the youth culture of one generation often becomes the accepted culture of older generations such as in the triumph of rock or hip-hop music. I will not belabor this point here but just say that the ability of students to visit a virtual Sistine Chapel in an environment like Second Life in order to micro-scrutinize the work of Michelangelo, to visit Internet sites in order to pull up replications of the Dead Sea Scrolls, or to download an increasing plethora of movies, television shows, podcasts, or other events on demand has really leveled the distinction between "high" and "low" culture. Finally, the achievements of cinema and television as masterpieces of visual, auditory, literary, and dramatic achievement are hallmark crossovers of popular media into sophisticated art forms.

Indeed, in contemporary culture there are many overlapping conjunctions, spillovers, intersections, and collisions between multiple stages and varieties of historic strata and media, secular and sacred ideologies, secular spiritualities and scientific mysticisms, and conventional and nonconventional religious patterns. Henry Jenkins calls this "convergence culture," the contemporary context that "refers to a situation in which multiple media systems coexist and where media content flows fluidly across them."[10] I would argue that the terrorist attacks of 9/11 resulted in a consummate convergence culture moment, the result of a brilliant and horrific orchestration of pop culture elements into a graphic, mosaic monstrosity of will, warfare, and identity management incorporating the Internet, cell phones, disaster movie plot structure, private pilot lessons, martial arts training, common household items like cardboard box cutters, how-to checklists, and even Anthony Robbins–style self-help motivational mental momentum mottos and self-encouragements. All of it converged into the will-to-kill payoff moment, and the glorified status of martyrdom identity forever emblazoned in instant-globalization, mass media proclamations before the eyes of the watching world. Along these lines, one should not minimize the power of the martyrdom video (which I sometimes refer to as an anti-Warhol fame claim), an al Qaeda recruiting tool par excellence. Nor should one minimize the powerful glorification of our own casualties in the war on terror as the truly heroic who "have made the ultimate sacrifice."

It is not always easy to say where violence stands apart from, is generated by, spills over, encompasses, or transgresses religious boundaries. Likewise it is difficult to cleanly draw lines between religion and culture or between popular religion and popular culture. From a pedagogical standpoint, these questions would seem to call for precise definitions, lucid overarching theory, and well-wielded methodology. It is readily apparent from a cursory scan of the fields involved, however, that definitions are not precise, no overarching theory currently holds sway, and the pertinent methodologies are at best unwieldy. What I offer here is my category formulation for sorting out the issues with my students.

IS IT LIVE OR MEMOREX? THE RECIPROCITY OF SPIRITUALITY, RELIGION, AND CULTURE

In class discussions, I often start the ball rolling with an exercise I call "Is it live, or is it Memorex?" In other words, is any cultural or religious manifestation spontaneous and pure, or does it reflect new twists on already preexisting reassimilations of traditional categories? The idea behind the question is to try to fathom the distinctions and relationships among the triad of concepts of spirituality, religion, and culture. We start by asking what it means when people refer to themselves as "spiritual but not religious."[11] For my students this line of inquiry invariably takes a variety of spins. For example, one could mean by "spiritual, but not religious" that she does not go to church but she is very disciplined in her pursuit of martial arts and even practices forms of meditation she has modified from various cable shows, martial arts movies, and old episodes of *Kung Fu*. Or perhaps one is a naturalist, a writer of haiku, or very into jazz music with its spontaneous breakthroughs and excursive bursts of inspired improvisation. What is at stake in the popular distinction between spirituality and religion, especially where New Age ideas are concerned, is a distinction between some level of experience on one hand and organized institutions of tradition on the other. Spirituality would then be measured by intensity of experience, the highest degree of which would direct an unmediated experience of the Absolute, some domain of the transcendentally exotic, or an engagement with existential validation. One term for such an experience is mysticism, although we might want to use the language of Maslow and refer to "peak experiences," or the terminology of Rudolf Otto, who speaks of seminal experiences as numinous. The point is that it is, indeed, possible to isolate an experiential moment that could theoretically be distinguished as spiritual as opposed to religious, especially if one has become accustomed to thinking of religion as organized religion in the conventional sense. The distinction might also be made as the difference between private and public religion, but for the moment I generally concede spirituality as a distinct phase or moment apart from systems of tradition that we conventionally recognize as religious. This distinction then provides the makings for a fine theory of religion. The theory proposes that spiritual experience is prior to and the foundation upon which all religious traditions build their edifices. In a way this becomes equivalent to the old chicken-and-egg query. This theory, much in the fashion of William James, would pose the religious genius as the conduit of a primary spiritual experience that must be safeguarded by the subsequent community, who accesses the original spirituality as a sort of second-hand hand-me-down. Thus we have a Moses, a Buddha, a Plato/Plotinus, a Jesus, a Muhammad—all spiritual geniuses who founded or became foundational to the communities, organizations, traditions, and institutions which maintain their memory and bask in the afterglow of their experience. It is a beautiful theory as far as theories go. The one problem is that no spiritual experience takes place in a vacuum. As far as the evidence shows, every spiritual experience takes place in the context of a preexistent religious tradition. As Joachim Wach observed, "every religion is a syncretism."[12] Thus Moses experiences his revelation in the context of the patriarchal tradition of Abraham, Isaac, and Jacob. Jesus experiences and manifests his revelation in the context of Judaism and Hellenistic Greco-Roman culture. Likewise, the transcendent breakthrough of the Buddha takes place squarely in the yogic and metaphysical traditions of ancient India. Is it live or is it Memorex?

To further emphasize this triadic relationship, I then ask my students how culture functions. After they flex and flounder, I offer them my very post-Freudian theory to the effect that the role of culture is to manage our animal drives. I then proceed to delineate what the pioneering ethologist Konrad Lorenz identified as the four basic animal drives, which for mnemonic purposes I call the four Fs: feeding, fighting, fleeing, and frolic—my euphemism for the sex drive. I suggest that if one wants to see the reciprocity of culture and religion, one only need ask what religious influences are exercised on a culture's cuisine, violent conflict generation or resolutions, and sexual patterns and options. Very readily, Jewish kosher, Islamic halal, and various other concepts of taboo foods are suggested. We then move to secular equivalents such as refraining from carbohydrates, refined sugars, caffeine, or non-FDA-approved additives and other controlled substances. Indeed, religious influences will inform a culture concerning what, when, and even whom it can eat. Looking at drives two and three, the fight-flight or "innate aggression" impulses, we discuss such moderating religious patterns as the pacifism and nonviolent philosophies of Mahavira, Buddha, Jesus, the Quakers, Amish, Mennonites, Gandhi, and Martin Luther King Jr., on one hand, and various forms of "just war theory" on the other, which are all predicated in religious contexts that readily spill over into cultural dynamics concerning penal systems, politics, lobbying, and international diplomacy. As for the fourth category, sexuality, one only needs to consider contemporary "cultural wars" over reproductive rights, gender roles, same-sex marriage, and the current crisis over pedophile protection and prevention raging within and against the Roman Catholic Church to see the interplay of religion and culture on sexuality.

Whatever we may discover in this exercise, this triad draws neatly on the board as a triangle in which each component touches upon the other two. Investigating spirituality, religion, and culture together in this way opens the possibility of perceiving "secular spiritualities" that themselves have the form of religion and either draw from or formulate culture, which is why I underscore their mutual reciprocity. Once we consider the vast range of secular spiritualities, from diet disciplines to exercise regimens, twelve-step programs to psychology, from being an artist to being a warrior, we are then in a position to discuss secular religions. This is when I shift the focus to describing what we take as religion.

RELIGION AS THE SYMBOLIZATION OF THE SACRED IN MYTH, RITUAL, AND SYMBOL

All religious traditions have some concept that corresponds to the sacred, some transcendent referent or central point of reference. Typical examples are Nirvana, God, heaven, the Tao, and such. Rather than insisting, however, that the sacred is always represented by the absolutely transcendent (which it often is), I emphasize that the sacred may simply be transcendental, that which is beyond, above, encompassing, overarching, orienting, and exceeding individual personal limitations. One should recall that for Durkheim the most important function of the sacred was as a force for social cohesion, and I would add identity construction. We could multiply the applications of the symbolizations of the sacred across multiple examples, but for now, it is enough to just sample its potential as a methodological grid through which we can sort all kinds of human activities. Across the gamut of their symbolic endeavors, the sacred manifests always as that which is symbolically central and orienting across spiritual, emotional, psychological, economic, behavioral, and political planes.

Let us focus a bit more closely upon three symbolizations of the sacred: myth, ritual, and symbol. Myth is sacred communication, living and paradigmatic reality exemplified by sacred stories and writings such as scriptures, but which might include such descriptors as "worldview," "zeitgeist," "ideological perspective," and "assumptions about reality" as well. I expand on this later. In a nutshell, ritual is sacred behavior in which time, space, and purity codes often play centralizing roles of orientation, exemplified by such acts as prayer, meditation, yoga, sacrifice, baptism, and so forth. Symbols are sacred places, persons, or objects, conventionally exemplified by sites like Mecca, people like Buddha, and objects like crosses. Using these symbolizations as a grid through which to sift phenomena into religious categories, it is possible to expand that which qualifies as religion to include what would appear to be entirely secular endeavors.

Were we to analyze contemporary American culture through this grid, we would first ask, "What is the sacred?" In other words, what is most central and of utmost value in America? Here, thinking of religion as "ultimate concern" or as located in "the nexus of being and meaning" may yield some surprising results. When asked to identify the sacred in American culture, many students will quite idealistically answer God, freedom, or equality, and although these may seem to indeed be true values, many will agree that the God/s of prosperity, money, and power occupy much more of people's energies and thought than the God of liberty, justice, and equality. It is really a matter of the individuals and communities that self-define their own sense of the sacred, although it is possible for the professed sacred to be different from the actual, lived sacred, which is why attention to the implied and tacit myths, rituals, and symbols of the community as crucial determinants of the sacred is important. The perspective shifts subtly depending on whether we examine these phenomena through the lens of the Enlightenment, Judeo-Christian values, patriotism, Greenpeace, Amnesty International, or Raider Nation. We should also not forget the God/s of manifest destiny, just war, or righteous indignation and their avenging angels meting out vengeance and justice in the form of justifiable homicide. Nor should we forget the God/s of empires and emperors like Xerxes or Constantine as candidates for the sacred in America and, although it may seem indelicate, one certainly should not forget the often-invoked God of "Kick Butt" who lives in slogans like "Don't Tread on Me!" or a myriad of bumper stickers to that effect.

Since it is sometimes difficult to be self-lucid, perhaps an example from an all-but-forgotten tradition might be illustrative. Although officially atheistic, in its philosophy of history, Marxism exhibits an intuition of the sacred when it extirpates and co-opts certain aspects of the God of justice, especially economic justice, from the prophets along with the Hegelian synthetic world process as an almost providential historical dynamic. So myth in Marxism centers on dialectical materialism toward the creation of the classless society, a type of utopian kingdom of heaven on earth, as encoded in such seminal texts as *Das Kapital* and the *Communist Manifesto*. Sprinkled, mingled, and punctuated among Marxist mythic concerns are a number of other paradigms and integrated dynamics. A major concept that runs deep in the Marxist myth is the concept of "reification," the attributing of living reality to an abstraction or set of abstractions. In a sense it is a form of idolatry, recognizing as real that which is by nature false. The consequences of reification in human relations is that it creates alienation and "thingification" of individuals, in other words, it falsifies the true human condition by making people into objects and means to ends rather than ends in themselves. This is very close to the prophetic indictment in the biblical book of Amos that "the needy are exchanged for a pair of shoes"; their worth is subjugated to material value. The Marxist ritual par excellence is, therefore, the world revolution that is its soteriology, certain salvation from economic exploitation and the mind-numbing identity denigration of reification. This has been achieved with varying levels of success, sustainability, and scalability in the worldwide labor movements of the nineteenth and twentieth centuries, the achievement of reduced workloads, just compensation, labor dispute boards, work safety standards, retirement plans, and Social Security. Marxism is still the official ideology of China and a looming "threat" or "potential for liberation" in the third world and elsewhere.

We can see that in the symbolizations of the sacred, myth would seem to be the most determinative category since it affects and effects thought-life, interpretations of reality, and definitional determinations of identity, but one should not underestimate the power of rituals and symbols in reinforcing, living out, and succinctly encapsulating the sacred realities myth imagines and idealizes. What myth idealizes, ritual realizes, and symbols succinctly summarize. Such rituals as playing video games, watching television, participating in sports, practicing martial arts, or training for war are replete in pop culture. Symbols function as paradigmatically sacred persons, like James Bond, Jason Bourne, sports heroes, and movie stars. Symbols that function as sacred places or spaces like Washington, Mecca, Vietnam, Iraq, and Afghanistan are heavily imbued with deep significance. Symbols as sacred objects like guns or weapons of mass destruction are the deep objects of desire in the religion of violence that is at the core of the value structure of America's pop culture.

EXPANDING AND EXPOUNDING THE THEORETICAL MODEL OF MYTH

Here is an inclusive, holistic-composite, and heuristically fluid working theoretical model of myth that draws from folks like Mircea Eliade to Kees Bolle and across the spectrum to the likes of Roland Barthes. Myth expresses, encapsulates, or embodies "paradigmatic reality," the codes that a culture takes for granted as well as its meta-language, the largely unspoken assumptions, tacit contracts, and currencies of understanding between the privileged wielders of power, the power brokers of culture, and the masses of individuals in their sway. Thus myth not only unveils reality, it can obfuscate, obscure, and even usurp or hijack it as well. Metalanguage creates an often unchallenged vision of reality that is simply taken for granted if one moves within the confines of its culture and social networks. Myth, however, should not simply be equated with dominating political discourse, propaganda, or even ideology. As a living paradigm, myth is mental engagement in a world of imaginative possibilities. As the code that a culture (or subculture) takes for granted, it also provides freedom and access to the cultural storehouse of treasures, especially confirmation in identity. Thus, although myth is a way of speaking, it more often than not "goes without saying."

Often myth functions so deeply at the core of a culture that there are no compelling alternate myths in conflict with it, but there may be, rather, contests around the application, interpretation, and implementation of the core myth. Take abortion, for example, a popular debate waged with the vehemence of a religious war in many people's minds. Ideologically there are divided camps within a common mythic assumption of human rights. The question is not, "Do humans have rights?" The debate, rather, is over what is human or which humans are candidates for or have the precedent rights. A pro-choice advocate might say, "As a woman, I have a right to determine what takes place in my own body." A pro-life person will say something like, "As a former fetus myself, I wish to champion the rights of all unborn fetuses." To witness this dynamic, one needs to look no further than the debate over Tim Tebow's pro-life/antiabortion 2010 Super Bowl ad.[13] Other examples of pop culture's wrestling with this fundamental myth can be seen in films as various as *Juno*, *Revolutionary Road*, and *Cider House Rules* (the film adaptation of John Irving's novel), as well as many TV shows including *Friday Night Lights*.

The mythic loom of living paradigms juxtaposes multiple constructs and generates vastly variegated yet integrated strands that weave in and out of the grand tapestry of our contemporary culture. What, then, are the myths that run through American history, consciousness, and pop culture? In *Myths America Lives By*, Richard T. Hughes identifies five (actually six) predominant myths that founded and endure in American consciousness.[14] Myths of the "Chosen Nation," "Nature's Nation," "Christian Nation," "Millennial Nation," and "Innocent Nation" with an auxiliary allusion in passing to the myth of "Manifest Destiny" have all given expression to multiple entitlements, exploitations, and elitisms in their powerful identity expansions. The Chosen Nation was an appropriation and application of the idea of Israel as God's People to America as the new Promised Land. Much like the supposedly divinely sanctioned conquest of Canaan and extermination of the presettlement inhabitants, the Chosen Nation myth literally gave birth to the pioneer-savage, cowboys-and-Indians conflicts, domination, and exploitations as though the New World settlers were given divine entitlement to run roughshod over the "savage" populations and landscape. This idea is expanded in the idea of Nature's Nation, which combined Enlightenment values with Rousseau-like naïveté in a return to Eden at the expense of the native populations who were deemed just part of the landscape. (These tendencies and themes provide the deep subtext in the mega-blockbuster film *Avatar*.) The Christian Nation motif continues as a one-to-one correlation with the origins and divinely ordained purpose of the United States as the perfect vessel of God's agenda for the world, further buttressed by its realization of the Kingdom of God and thus the Millennial Nation and consequently Innocent Nation, which means it is always justified in its endeavors and struggles against the forces of darkness that would seek to eclipse it. These themes overlap and dovetail with a host of other similar themes and mythic motifs as developed and expounded in a couple of important treatments.

Although I find a number of texts most illuminating in exploring the foundational myths of American culture, near the top of my recommendations would be *Captain America and the Crusade Against Evil: The Dilemma of Zealous Nationalism* by Robert Jewett and John Shelton Lawrence.[15] The central theme behind this work is that American civil religion and pop culture, like the biblical tradition itself, is characterized by a deeply ambivalent polarity between social justice, exhibited by egalitarian championing of universal human rights on one hand, and repeated attempts to establish the Kingdom of God through apocalyptic-like destruction of its enemies. This dynamic reverberates in comic books, video games, and in practically every stratum of popular culture. The symbolic motif of Captain America is drawn from the comic book hero who was depicted in 1938 as socking Adolf Hitler in the jaw. The symbol of the righteous crusader is an image that flows through the Cold War to the war on terror, sustained by his contemporary avatars. The symbolic Captain America manifests during a dramatic photo-op in the form of the commander in chief, portraying himself as the warrior fighter-jet jockey president, George W. Bush landing on an aircraft carrier to prematurely announce victory in Iraq. The Captain America complex is not limited to a single administration or a few individuals but is an underlying and pervasive syndrome at the core of American identity. Coming to terms with the pervasiveness of this complex helps one to realize how both houses of Congress and close to 90 percent of the American population were such avid supporters of the war on terror right after 9/11. "What is there about American nationalism," ask Jewett and Lawrence, "that encourages such contradictory impulses, leading the nation to repeat the mistakes of the past? The answer lies partly in the biblical origins of American civil religion. Even though separated by centuries in time and by disparities in terminology, these older concepts (i.e., the Kingdom of God and Apocalyptic Triumphalism)—with their inherent contradictions—match, to an amazing degree, their current mythic counterparts."[16] The third chapter, "Popular Culture as a Bearer of the National Complex," is a deep exploration across a multiple variety of genres and a rich resource in examining "the fantastic but credible narratives to which so many

Americans feel a deep emotional attachment."[17] In looking at "the pulp literature, films, television, and video games that receive the steady attention of most American minds," we catch a glimpse via such superhero tales into the mythic matrices that "shape the public sense of what is appropriate in confronting the crises of national and international life."[18] I want to emphasize again what a rich and provocative examination and resource this text provides.

Another extremely helpful text is Bruce Lincoln's *Religion, Empire, and Torture: The Case of Achaemenian Persia, with a Postscript on Abu Ghraib*.[19] Among the many poignant insights contained within this tome is a characterization of the base paradigms that made a colossal and expansive empire like Persia adopt a rationale of intervention, enforced mentoring and patronage, and domination in its plan of global expansionism. Lincoln identifies three characteristics, "dualistic ethics," "a theory of divine election," and "a sense of salvific mission," that combined as strong mythic justifications for a propelling imperative to superimpose the Persian value structure of "the Truth" upon those who even hinted at a "propensity for the Lie." The national and divine imperative to promote "the Truth" necessitated such drastic measures as preemptive military strikes and refined forms of torture and indeed justified the Persian Empire's international imperative to spread "the Truth." Similar sets of imperatives, national characteristics, and mythic dynamics can not only illustrate post-9/11 American reactions, but can provide an interpretive background for much of pop culture as witnessed in a variety of films, TV shows, and video games. This justificatory rationale of a struggle for "Truth" over "the Lie" becomes especially illuminating when one considers the fundamentalist support for the war on terror, films like *The Matrix*, *300*, or television dramas like *24*, the mega-hit series of the *Left Behind* novels, and the video games it has spawned.

An intriguing and alternative attempt to understand the mythic themes running through American pop culture was undertaken in the exhaustively exploratory work of French sociologist Denis Duclos in his *Werewolf Complex: America's Fascination with Violence*.[20] Although written over a decade ago, his examination of pop culture mythic themes bristles with contemporary cogency. Our fascination with vampires, werewolves, violent heroes, and antiheroes is best understood, according to Duclos, in the survival and reemergence of deep-rooted Nordic mythologies that flow from pools of latency at the core of our predominant national character. Like free-floating memes waiting for an opportune milieu in which to flourish, they have most prodigiously erupted in the great melting pot of American pop culture. In answering the question of why he compares a vast array of serial killers, TV-movie heroes, and Odinic warriors, he argues that although seemingly incongruous, "American postmodern society has revived" mythic elements quintessentially "structured as such in the 'free' Nordic European societies, which resisted the Roman Empire and the state controlled societies that came after them."[21] Among the issues he explores is the vastly disproportionate number of serial killers we have produced in comparison to to the rest of the world. In ever-increasing demand, consumption, and exportation of the macabre and grisly in the work of horror producers like Stephen King and our perennial quest for crime fighters and crime drama, we resemble the bloodthirsty penchant of Viking warriors and their propensity for "berserker" possession. Though not without its problems, the work is replete with examples of how "the country that gave the world production line auto-mobiles, nuclear warheads, and multinational business" has succeeded in mass producing "a myth that produces symmetry, doubles, multiples, oscillations, and finally an irremediable conflict between different versions of the self" and thus "should give us pause."[22]

COSMOLOGY, ANTHROPOLOGY, METAPHYSICS

The hermeneutical importance of the three categories of cosmology, anthropology, and metaphysics originally struck me as I read Strasbourg philosopher Georges Gusdorf's *Traité de Métaphysique*,[23] which referred to them as the "Three Traditional Disciplines." Identified more simply by Gusdorf as "The World, the Self, and God," they reside as objects of study in the contemporary subdivisions of the university—namely, in the natural sciences, the social sciences, and the humanities—and in metaphysically inclined subdisciplines within philosophy and theology. The impor-tance of the dynamic relationship that links cosmology, anthropology, and metaphysics is also underscored in Mark Taylor's *After God*,[24] and these three provide a spectrum grid for understanding and, in fact, graphing a variety of nuanced positions intellectually, existentially, and as praxis. Gusdorf challenges us: "Dis-moi quel est ton Dieu, dis-moi quel es ton monde, et je te dirai qui tu es" (Explain your God, explain your world, and I will tell you who you are).[25]

As one strategy to broach the subject, I tell my students that metaphysics function like myths on steroids and have paradigmatic impact and consequence—even though often subtle, hidden, and simply taken for granted—on the way we view the world and our fellow humans. Metaphysical assumptions are often responsible for the "business as usual" destruction that has historically wreaked havoc across different peoples and species. Indeed all senses of justice (including just war and capital punishment) and various senses of entitlement (whether karmic or Calvinistic), propriety, and honor/shame have roots in metaphysical propositions or sentiments.

Although certain hermeneutics of suspicion are justified in their criticisms that metaphysics are indeed anthropological projections, what those hermeneutics often fail to realize is that various anthropologies are reciprocally metaphysical projections. Our models of what comprises "true humanity," the proper roles of women, the proper care and education of children, and questions of life and death (as in who deserves to live and who deserves to die) are metaphysical projections back onto the screen of the human consciousness. Since metaphysics deal with the unseen, the invisible dynamics that provide the innate rationales to existence for people in varieties of ways, one just needs to point out a few examples for students to get the drift. What is important to bear in mind is that metaphysics, whether as sophisticated and complex as Heidegger's "Ontology" or as simple as the patriotic sentiment, "my country, right or wrong," all orbit around concepts of "the real." In some cases the real works itself out paradigmatically to be more real than life itself, and certainly in cases of political conflict, more real than the life of others and often at the expense of others' lives. This fact can give visceral meaning to the old cliché that people can be so "heavenly minded, they are no earthly good," indeed, with a vengeance.

So, for example, feminist hermeneutics have long pointed out that the subjugation of women under the domination of "the patriarchy" is the result of gender-specific privileging of men over women, who are deemed to be "quite properly" subject to men's protection, authority, and control because of their supposed inferior spiritual, intellectual, and rational capabilities. In such a meta-physic women occupy a lower position in the "great chain of being" that flows from God to the lesser beings. One very detrimental consequence of this metaphysic resulted in the medieval "witch craze" that saw the destruction primarily of women in cases by the thousands. A similar metaphysic has seen the domination of women as subject to beatings, imprisonments, and murders as the result of an honor/shame metaphysic and its resultant anthropology of what constitutes "true humanity" or normative human behavior. Given these types of examples, I ask my students to then look for the hidden metaphysics and their anthropological or cosmological implications in movies, television shows, politics, and other popular media. Given the tremendous popularity of crime dramas in American pop culture, some inter-esting discussions ensue around the idea (or metaphysics) of "disposable humanity." There is no way to watch prime-time television and not come away with the impres-sion that some people just deserve to die and are thus disposable.

Or, in the case of sitcoms, that some people are justly the butt of ridicule, deserved objects of scorn or slapstick torture, and thus readily dismissible or demeaned in another form of pop culture disposability that may translate into real-life bullying among adolescents and teens. Other examples can almost function like stand-up comedy.

There are, for instance, extreme fundamentalists whose cosmology denies the age of the universe as anything greater than 6,000 years, who can envision humans on the saddled backs of dinosaurs, and at the same time earnestly and eagerly await the evaporation of history, most of the world's population, and all other metaphys-ical and theological options so they can at last really begin to live. With such a radical cosmology, I would argue, it is impossible for them to have a metaphysic that adequately appreciates human reality or, for that matter, the nature of God. Life itself is as inconsequential as ecospheres and endangered species. Cosmological perspectives have consequences, and it is clear that a particular metaphysical presumption can eclipse even the world. This metaphysical presumption manifests as an arrogant gnosticism that privileges its favorite proof texts and theology at the expense of practically everything else. In the dualistic battleground earth it has virtually subsumed the cosmos and humanity as the combat zone between two op-posing forces, ultimate good and ultimate evil, God and the devil. One is either on the side of God and a vessel of his truth or a demon of Satan. In its most dire, radical form it actively participates in political agendas that would accelerate an apoca-lyptic destruction, containment, and elimination of God's enemies, even at the expense of the earth itself. Indeed, Apocalypticism is one of the predominant themes of modern pop culture; it is dramatic and plays well, especially in video games and in particular science fiction and horror spectacles. According to the apocalyptic scenarios within which this radical dualism originated, or at least found quintessential expression, the world is an afterthought, a temporary trap, a provisional landing strip for the invitational cosmic conflict; Landing Zone Earth, awaiting rescue.

In addition to those discussed above, two other mythic and metaphysical themes that pervade the media, politics, and other forms of pop culture, "six-gun mystique," and "just war theory," bear further scrutiny and fleshing out for their role in creating some commonly unexamined assumptions in American pop culture.

Six-gun mystique is the flowering of the American fascination with guns and their adept users. A gun in the hands of someone who knows how to use it is the equivalent of a Samurai and his sword: armies cannot prevail against such a deft virtuoso when properly armed with his weapon of choice. One might imagine Rambo, or the Terminator. Such an adept often has hero status. In the classic Western drama, the lethal instruments of instant justice nullify greedy cattle barons and their henchmen. As the instant dispatchers of justice, freedom, and the American way, the gun-toting cowboy made the West safe in the taming of the frontier, as does the gun-wielding warrior from the trenches of war to the back-alley shootouts of the inner city; from hard-boiled Humphrey Bogart detectives to SWAT team police action to Armageddon, guns and weaponry are the quintessential tools in the survival of the fittest. Hardware matters. This is evident from the trusty six-shooter of the John Wayne character, Hondo, in *Stagecoach* to Tom Cruise's supersonic jet fighter in *Top Gun*. Iron Man is one extended gun, whereas, in *The Matrix*, guns are metaphors for codes that kill and nullify but ultimately cleanse and sanctify. Generally, in popular culture, six-gun mystique functions in the higher ends of justice though often very thinly distinguishable from vengeance and vendetta. *Gran Torino*, starring Clint Eastwood, evokes gut-level, streetwise, gang-savvy verisimilitude, exploring the vicious cycle of territory-bound, vendetta-laden, macho one-upmanship, smack-down, stare-down bravado in the face of the ever-pending six-gun mystique shootout at the O.K. Corral with a twist. Instead of the usual Dirty Harry, *Death Wish* vindication, the unexpected reversal spins a sacrificial trick play that theoretically pulls the carpet out from under the "bad boys" but ultimately is both less than satisfying and hardly scalable and does not really offer a workable solution, but it does relieve the Clint Eastwood character from getting more blood on his hands, though at the cost of his own life. Nothing seems to get done in pop culture without the death of a victim as a scapegoat.

Six-gun mystique could easily be one of the most characteristic identifying earmarks of American culture. It is everywhere on television, in video games, on the news, in popular vernacular, and in the movies. *Wanted*, for example, with Angelina Jolie and Morgan Freeman, is an acrobatic circus-like exhibition of six-gun mystique on steroids; slinging bullets like curveballs, hypermarksman shots through the crags and valleys of a skyscraper landscape; a video game come to life. The recent TV series *NCIS Los Angeles* opens with beautifully sculpted agents wielding guns in typical lock-and-load commando protocol entrance into potentially volatile and dangerous situations. Shootouts abound. Six-gun mystique functions in the background of the shootout in Waco, Texas, between federal agents and David Koresh, at Columbine High School and Virginia Tech—one can visualize Cho, the shooter, checking his flak-jacket look like the character in Scorsese's *Taxi Driver* as he mutters adoring and iconic references to Eric and Dylan, the shooters from Columbine, as "martyrs." James Bond might well wonder—what is a license to kill if you don't use it?

Just war theory emerged once Christianity moved from its grassroots, counter-cultural, persecuted, underground status to its official position as the religion of the Roman Empire. Where it was once inconceivable for Christians to fight or join the army, in no small part due to the unrelenting pacifism of its founder, an ironic reversal of circumstances made it so that only Christians could serve in the military. Largely due to the rhetoric and argument of Augustine, who worked through the logic of service to others, the Good Samaritan goes from providing aid to a victim of violence to protecting potential victims from the violence that threatens the roads of Jericho. So, though it may be expected that a Christian would lay down his life in following the footsteps of "the Master," it is also then required, in Augustine's logic, that good Christians would risk their lives to prevent others from being killed by evil perpetrators. Just war concepts are everywhere in video games, movies, and on TV. A most popular exhibition of it is in the mega-blockbuster movie *Avatar* as the indigenous population of Pandora must fight to defend their home and lives and the eco-spirituality that binds them together. This theme is found in such popular movies as *Star Wars, The Matrix, Harry Potter, The Lord of the Rings*, and of course the *Left Behind* series of books, movies, and video games. Just war theory often is fed and combines with various forms of Apocalypticism.

RENÉ GIRARD'S THEORY OF SACRED VIOLENCE

Since the 9/11 terrorist attacks, the theories of René Girard have begun to regain momentous cogency in discussions of violence. In *Discovering Girard*, Michael Kirwan states that Girard's theories have had an almost predictive quality, anticipating the "complex interrelation between secular modernity and religiously inspired terrorism," as well as "patterns of provocation and resistance, entrenched and ritualized in long-term conflicts such as Northern Ireland or the struggle for Palestine" along with "the bitter polemics" concerning reproductive rights, "the kinds of stigma which attach to people living with HIV/AIDS," and "the excruciating questions about religion's ambiguous relation to different forms of violence" that have "exploded into our awareness with a new ferocity" in the last half of this decade.[26]

According to Girard's theory, the concept of the sacred itself owes its central position in the mental landscape of humanity to a primal murder, the drives and dynamics that precipitated it, and the mechanics and mechanisms that absorb, channel, and attempt to control its ever-present potential for repetition. Girard's theoretical construct can be very graphically portrayed across practically every stratum of pop culture. One of the powerful pedagogical payoffs of teaching with feature films is to create conceptual and imagistic clotheslines on which to pin these constructs for students. The opening sequence of Stanley Kubrick's cinematic masterpiece, *2001: A Space Odyssey*, provides an excellent portrayal of the Girardian premise, as acknowledged by Girard himself.[27] In the first several scenes of the film, in the chapter called "The Dawn of Man," we witness the protohominid plunge into the mimetic mechanism that spawns the spiral of sacred violence that, according to Girard, lies at the core of every culture and, indeed, at the foundations of not only every civilization but hominization itself, the process by which the path to humanity begins. In the film, the concept of mimetic rivalry is exhibited by a competition of desire for the same water hole by two groups of primates. The protohominids are weaker until they discover the use of tools as weapons and kill the alpha male of the fiercer group. In Girardian theory, mimetic desire leads to mimetic violence, which runs the risk of becoming mimetic contagion, a form of "forward panic."[28] The primal murder provides a mechanism for curbing and controlling the outbreak of this violence, preventing it from becoming a war of all against all, and it thus gives birth to scapegoating rituals and their eventual universal, if temporary, assuaging efficacy. This is the origin of lynch mobs and capital punishment, war, and, alternatively, mechanisms for curbing violence and making peace. On the flip side, according to Girard, one of the unique characteristics of our culture is its concern for the victim. This is an ever-spiraling increase of consciousness toward the plight and from the perspective of the victim. Although it is not without its ironies and paradoxes, the concern for the victim characterizes much of our highest ideals and is evident in all kinds of heightened sensitivities—from wheelchair ramps to accessible technologies to accommodate disabilities in education—and in all kinds of increased awarenesses of victims of rare diseases and victims of child abuse. This ever-increasing spiral of consciousness permeates our society. This is a particular contribution of our Judeo-Christian heritage and can be seen in bundled strands across the biblical tradition in the plight of Israel under imperial oppression, the songs of the suffering servant, the psalmist's pleas for justice and comfort, the lamentations of Jeremiah or Job, all of which reflect a point of view from the eyes of the victim. In the Christian tradition, many of the stories of Jesus ask the reader to adopt the perspective of the other person. The view from the perspective of the victim is extremely focused in such biblical masterpieces as the book of Job and the parable of the Good Samaritan. Ultimately the gospels unveil, illuminate, and unite the variegated strands as Jesus himself becomes the quintessential victim unmasking the mechanism of sacred violence and thus compelling a tradition irrevocably bound to consider the plight of all victims.

The importance of René Girard for understanding violence is manifold. Utilizing Girard's theoretical and anthropological approach to violence has definite hermeneutical and heuristic payoffs when applied to pop culture, for example, in looking at sports as substititionary ritual in its relation to mob violence. An article that does this brilliantly is Darryl V. Caterine's "Curses and Catharsis in Red Sox Nation: Baseball and Ritual Violence in American Culture."[29] An extremely insightful and illustrative book for a Girardian understanding of the relationships among religion, violence, and pop culture is Gil Bailie's *Violence Unveiled: Humanity at the Crossroads*.[30]

Essentially an apologetic for and an application of the theories of René Girard, it encompasses a grand-scale exploration of the origins of violence in human culture as well as a sweeping survey of the contemporary landscape, with numerous illustrative examples from current events, literature, and popular culture in its portrayal of the intimate relationship between the sacred and violence. It is one of the most lucid, comprehensive, and comprehensible expositions of Girardian theory available.

DATA COLLECTING STRATEGIES

One successful strategy for acquiring data to examine is to involve students in a fact-finding expedition by asking them to perform what I call an "environmental scan" exercise. Here is such an assignment description:

> The purpose of this exercise is for you to perform an "environmental scan." Survey aspects of popular culture as they intersect your life. Just keep your eyes open wherever you go and take note of things that might reflect or refract, echo or parallel violent qualities or influences in and on contemporary culture. Simply tell us what you see. Don't hesitate to talk to people as "inside informants" of the traditions of violence to and in which they adhere and cohere. Take stock of the intersections, influences, imprints, vestiges, residues, and evidences of violence in "everyday life." Are there examples from current events, television shows, advertisements, hit movies, pop songs? Do you see the tendencies/effects of violence in and on certain behaviors? Do you hear it in people's speech? Do you see symbols overtly or covertly displayed; hanging as ornaments, adorned in jewelry, part of identity logos, emblazoned as tattoos?

What types of things might students observe? An exemplary posting might describe some macho-posturing Dodge Ram truck replete with gun rack in back of cab, displaying a National Rifle Association logo in the window with a host of bumper stickers plastered on the tailgate and bumper saying things like "Insured by Smith and Wesson"; "Keep honking, I'm reloading"; "An armed society is a polite society"; "My kid can beat up your honor student"; "If I want your opinion, I'll beat it out of you"; "Yes, I do own the whole damn road"; "If you don't like the way I drive, stay off the sidewalk"; "Don't like my driving? Call 1 (800) EAT SHIT!" and a huge pair of plastic testicles hanging from the trailer hitch. Along with all kinds of bumper stickers, T-shirt wit, and cocktail party one-liners, a host of pithy aphorisms bubble to the surface of students' awareness of pop culture like fleeting epiphanies from the ideological substrata of implied metaphysical universes. One poignant jab, obviously aimed at vegans, reads, "I didn't rise to the top of the food chain to be a vegetarian!" Another rather misanthropic T-shirt states, "Some people are like Slinkies, totally worthless but fun to watch tumble down the stairs."

Some students' environmental scans might observe the plethora of karate studios in strip malls, billboards featuring films and TV shows replete with weapons or menacing characters, invading aliens, or advertisements aimed at military recruitment. Perhaps some students might focus on communities of violence; quite possibly some keen observer has been to a sibling's soccer match or Little League baseball game and documented the phenomenon of parents who, in their vicarious projections, have become rabid promoters of their children's imagined professional careers, or perhaps they have seen motorcycle and street gangs flying colors. Some observations will include video games such as any of the many incarnations of Grand Theft Auto that incorporate running over pedestrians, killing police, and beating up prostitutes, combined with all kinds of schemes of vendetta and payback as well as built-in narrative justifications for such actions (the police are corrupt, etc.).

Some students will have observed the Kanye West-Taylor Swift debacle in which West grabbed the microphone from Swift at the 2009 MTV Video Awards and denounced her right to the award she had just won. Swift was flabbergasted, speechless, and quite obviously upset. Subsequently, Mickey Rourke and John Rich appeared on the *Sean Hannity Show* on the Fox Network and suggested that somebody ought to teach the rude Kanye some manners. Mickey Rourke, fresh off his Academy Award–nominated role in *The Wrestler*, stated, "I'd like to see him grab the microphone from my hand." Shortly thereafter at the 2009 Country Music Awards, Carrie Underwood and Brad Paisley repurposed a country song classic as "Mama, Don't Let Your Babies Grow Up to Be Kanye." The culmination of this spiral of symbolic violence appeared on December 12, 2009, when Taylor Swift's boyfriend, Taylor Lautner (one of the stars of the vampire saga *Twilight*), demonstrated his martial arts proficiency by scissor kicking at a life-size effigy of Kanye and eventually knocking the head off of the cardboard body as a demonstration of what he should have done to Kanye at the time he grabbed the microphone, much to the delight of the *Saturday Night Live* studio audience.

Perhaps students will describe comedies about hit men (*Grosse Pointe Blank*), true stories about murder (*Alpha Dog*), or a popular television series about "a beloved serial killer" (*Dexter*) and discover death as the new pornography. Students will no doubt have observed the domestic-abuse ranting and raving of Mel Gibson, the continued debate over the war in Afghanistan, and North Korea's nuclear threats. Perhaps they will discover violence as the ever-present dramatic formula in pop culture and will describe a vast spectrum of violence from peacemaking (antiviolence) on one end and "shock and awe" warfare on the other. As they observe and analyze their surroundings, students will definitely learn to use such descriptive categories as nonviolence, pacifism, aggression, ultraviolence (Alex's term in *A Clockwork Orange*), hooliganism, gang-banging, date rape, gang rape, stalking, domestic terrorism, spousal abuse, child abuse, and urban riots.

THE VIOLENCE OF POVERTY AND RELIGIOUS SIGNIFICANCE IN *NICKEL AND DIMED*

As part of our common readings program on campus, each year we select a book via committee to read across the disciplines as a way to create a common culture on campus—in a sense, our own popular culture. In a recent year we read *Nickel and*

Dimed by Barbara Ehrenreich, a multilayered and intricately woven journalistic exposé of the plight of the working poor in America.[31] Both overt and covert strands of economic violence are evident in its multiple zones, influences, paradigms, assumptions, and inclinations. For our purposes here I will attempt to identify a few of the more prevailing dynamics and structures that jump out of its symphonic sweep. One would have to notice that it is a sustained study of the working poor and their plight of literally being "nickel and dimed" to death, or rather, into substandard and unacceptably impoverished lifestyles. The American Heritage online dictionary lists the meaning of the phrase as "to drain or destroy bit by bit, especially financially." In thus looking at the plight of the poor through their lenses and in their shoes, Ehrenreich adopts an incarnational journalistic approach to her subject matter that functions within a paradigm long recognized as part and parcel of the Judeo-Christian heritage of looking at life from the perspective of the victim. This is a particular genius of the Hebrew Bible as demonstrated in Exodus, celebrated in Passover, and culminating in the social justice denouncements of oppression and class domination. When *Nickel and Dimed* is decried along with the concept of "social justice" as a mere Marxist diatribe, little do its detractors realize that they are simply attributing to it a legacy of social concern long since shared and promulgated by the great Hebrew prophets, Jesus, Muhammad, and many contemporary religious activists such as the authors of *Rich Christians in an Age of Hunger*.[32] In this light *Nickel and Dimed* is a work of deep compassion, a religious and spiritual value also shared by all humans of good will.

In its confrontation with the violence of the American economic system, *Nickel and Dimed* also provides great leaping-off points for discussing patriarchal dominations, historical Jesus research, civil rights movement concerns, labor movement egalitarianism, ecological and environmental sensitivities and sensitizations, flower power, liberation theology, New Age spirituality, ethical theory, psychology, American democracy, the Enlightenment, pop-culture escapism, and Marxist social criticism. Although all of these can be deemed to be "merely" secular dynamics, strong demonstrations can be made of their participation in the tenacity of religion-based dynamics even in their pared-down state as vestiges of or reactions to formerly powerful religious categories and within strongly viable secular spiritualities.

One scene in the book that performs such a demonstration is particularly poignant. After attending an evangelistic tent revival, Ehrenreich's social critique wafts into a meditation contrasting the Jesus co-opted by the fundamentalist preachers to the historical Jesus, "the wine-guzzling vagrant and precocious socialist" whose Sermon on the Mount is an indictment of the status-quo-maintaining, pie-in-the-sky-plying "modern Christianity" that aims "to crucify him again and again so that he can never get a word out of his mouth." She walks to her car from the meeting "half expecting to find Jesus out there in the dark, gagged and tethered to a tent pole."[33] Religion, Ehrenreich reveals, can function as both a mechanism for coping with violence and a device for violent subjugation.

The sheer drudgery and mind-numbing dullness of menial labor takes a toll on the bodies and souls of the workforce she encounters. Ehrenreich wonders, "If you hump away at menial jobs 360 plus days a year, does some kind of repetitive injury of the spirit set in?"[34] The systemic objectification of the worker begins with prescreening personality and aptitude tests that repeatedly reinscribe authority and mind control. Here one should think of many biblical passages and injunctions on behalf of the poor and oppressed and against the exploitation and objectification of the poor by systems of wealth and power.

According to Ehrenreich, this objectification and indeed deep alienation occurs on the level of identity itself. Workers are subsumed, often via an honor/shame dyadic subordination of their identity, into the corporate whole. They are shamed into submission, deprived of acknowledgment and dignity: "As far as I can figure, my coworkers' neediness—because that's what it is—stems from chronic deprivation."[35] And again: "Even in the tightest labor market the person who has precious labor to sell can be made to feel one down, way down, like a supplicant with her hand stretched out."[36] This undermining of self-worth is systemically conducted on a global scale so that the menial worker has no recourse but to assume her own lowliness.

How is their plight portrayed in pop culture?

> The sitcoms and dramas are about fashion designers or schoolteachers or lawyers, so it's easy for a fast-food worker or nurse's aide to conclude that she is an anomaly; the only one, or almost the only one, who hasn't been invited to the party. And in a sense she would be right: the poor have disappeared from the culture at large, from its political rhetoric and intellectual endeavors as well as from its daily entertainment. Even religion seems to have little to say about the plight of the poor, if that tent revival was a fair sample. The moneylenders have finally gotten Jesus out of the temple.[37]

The "money taboo," the unwillingness of workers to compare their wages, "operates most effectively among the lowest-paid people, because in a society that endlessly celebrates" wealth, low earnings "can feel like a mark of innate inferiority."[38]

Ehrenreich paints a landscape of poverty in which alienation and subordination are not limited to individual personalities but spill over into nature itself: "Even the woods and the meadows have been stripped of disorderly life forms and forced into a uniform made of concrete."[39] It is globally ubiquitous in its scale. In looking at labels where clothes are made, for example, in Indonesia, Sri Lanka, or Brazil, she realizes "that none of these places is 'exotic' anymore, that they've all been eaten by the great blind profit making global machine."[40]

How are identity and personhood affected by this condition? Several of Ehrenreich's remarks bring the violence that the working poor must bear into focus. She describes the psychology of debasement: "If you are treated as an untrustworthy person—a potential slacker, drug addict, or thief—you may begin to feel less trustworthy yourself. If you are constantly reminded of your lowly position in the social hierarchy, whether by individual managers or by a plethora of impersonal rules, you begin to accept that unfortunate status."[41] She points to animal studies that demonstrate that "rats and monkeys, for example—that are forced into a subordinate status" fall into humanlike depression and "avoid fighting even in self-defense," and she reminds us that "we depend for our self-image on the humans immediately around us—to the point of altering our perceptions of the world so as to fit in with theirs."[42] In other places, she observes, "If you're made to feel unworthy enough, you may come to think that what you're paid is what you are actually worth," that systemically, "the high cost of repression results in ever more pressure to hold wages down," and that "the larger society seems to be caught up in a similar cycle cutting public services for the poor, which are sometimes referred to collectively as the 'social wage,' while investing more heavily in prisons and cops."[43] Is it any wonder why Jesus saw visiting the imprisoned as a concomitant act of righteousness along with feeding the poor, comforting the afflicted, and clothing the naked? In many ways what Barbara Ehrenreich has accomplished in Nickel and Dimed has some parallel to the attention Charles Dickens (although in fictional form) drew to the plight of the poor in nineteenth-century England. The most famous example is A Christmas Carol, which airs in many versions every year during the holiday season. The power of Ehrenreich's work is its potential for student engagement and as a vehicle to create empathy and sensitize them to economic violence they would not otherwise encounter or observe.

Beyond Ehrenreich there are some other touchstones for evaluating the violence of poverty that I would now like to discuss. Jonathan Kozol's 1988 classic treatment, Rachel and Her Children, was the result of months of on-the-street interviews of families and individuals who had literally hit the skids and were forced to live in their cars, on the streets, and in makeshift dwellings of cardboard and rags.[44] In print since 2006, Rachel and Her Children still functions as case-by-case study and counterpoint to the misguided characterizations of the homeless as lazy, drug-addicted alcoholics, degenerates, and reprobates, or, in systemic flights of fantasy, as volunteer romantic knights of the open road. Still poignant in today's economically insecure environment, it documents the landmines built within the welfare systems of the 1980s that created huge holes so deep that many families who fell into them never recovered.

A much more recent work focuses upon the issue of public space and an accelerating global march toward policies and sweeping systemic overhauls that eliminate the homeless from the open available spaces in the public sector. In Lost in Space: The Criminalization, Globalization, and Urban Ecology of Homelessness, Randall Amster unveils the wave-of-the-future trend to make homelessness a crime by commercially driven vested interests that render "panhandling," "urban camping," or even "sitting or lying on public sidewalks" offenses liable to incarceration.[45] Very akin to this work is the almost title-tells-all book The Rich Get Richer, and the Poor Get Prison, now in its eighth edition, by Jeffery Reiman.[46] A particularly poignant and heart-tugging portrayal of the plight of the working poor can be viewed in the HBO documentary Homeless: The Motel Kids of Orange County, which aired in the summer of 2010.[47] These considerations lead to a deep structural examination of issues concerning America's heritage-laden debates concerning social justice, class conflict, politics, economics, and religion. Bound to this heritage is the prophetic dynamic with its challenge to authority, power, and dominance through a combination of social and religious critique to produce intensive indictments of the systemic violence that threatens the weak and unprotected. The prophet Amos condemned his society's power brokers "because they sell the righteous for silver and the needy for a pair of shoes" and, in the name and voice of God, indicted those "that trample the head of the poor into the dust of the earth, and turn aside the way of the afflicted" (4:6–7). It is the prophet's task to expose the oppressive works of the powerful and to preach relief for the impoverished and downtrodden. Poignant expositions of this dynamic can be found in Isaiah 58, where true service to God is "to loose the chains of injustice and untie the cords of the yoke, to set the oppressed free and break every yoke, to share your food with the hungry and to provide the poor wanderer with shelter."

This resistance to economic violence, of course, finds powerful secular expression in Marxism and its many refractions in the labor movement and social reforms, as well as the writings of Charles Dickens and Upton Sinclair, among others. One can explore this dynamic and the struggle against power, dominance, exploitation, and corruption in many films. Some that come to mind are *Erin Brokovich, Silkwood, Do the Right Thing, Reds, Wall Street, The Boiler Room, Malcolm X, Michael Clayton*, and a myriad of others. For an environmental scan assignment I ask students to find a film or TV episode and make an argument for its inclusion as a further ripple in the prophetic dynamic or an example of the interplay of social justice, class conflict, politics, economics, and religion. Significantly, this is a great departure zone to send students off to research the debate between Glenn Beck, a popular radio show and TV commentator, and Jim Wallis, author and human rights advocate, about the concept of social justice. Google searches and YouTube videos are replete with the polemics. In a nutshell, Beck maintains that social justice is a foreign import from socialist and communist agendas, whereas Wallis demonstrates that the Bible literally falls apart if you cut out passages referring to the concept.

CONCLUSION

David Walker Foster tells the story of a couple of young fish swimming in a stream. An older fish going the opposite direction passes them and asks casually, "How's the water, fellas?" A couple minutes later, one of the younger fish turns to his companion and asks, "What the hell is water?" The point of this story is that sometimes we really are not aware of the environs in which we swim, in which we move, live, breathe, and find our being. One of the objectives of my courses is to awaken students to the currents in which they are entirely immersed but which they take for granted without recognizing them. Religion in pop culture is much like water for fish: it is in many ways invisible until you come to something like a waterfall (a church or an obviously religious or spiritual tradition) but in reality it is everywhere. In this essay I focused upon the violence latent or explicit in pop culture that is sometimes informed by traditional religion but more often functions as religion. If students fail to recognize that culture, even popular culture, functions much like, resembles, usurps, replaces, and functionally becomes "religion," then they will not completely understand who they are, why they hold some of the attitudes they do, and why some things just seem so evidently true to them. Clearly mainstream religion has long since recognized the power of popular culture as the medium and means by which and to which it increasingly pitches its messages amid the plethora of secular spiritualities that abound. Life meaning is vehemently debated as the religion of no-religion with such evangelical fervor as to rival Billy Sunday in his prime. The airwaves and the iPod, the video games and movies, the Internet and social networking are the new lines of connection in the nexus of being and meaning that mediate identity and purpose. We swim in streams that we do not always recognize for what they are. To become aware of our environs and influences is to move toward becoming more lucid, self-critical, and potentially in control of our own destinies.

NOTES

1. Harvey Cox, *The Secular City* (New York: Macmillan, 1965); Steve Bruce, *Religion in the Modern World* (New York: Oxford University Press, 1996).
2. Harvey Cox, *The Future of Faith* (New York: HarperOne, 2010).
3. David Chidester, *Authentic Fakes: Religion and American Popular Culture* (Berkeley: University of California Press, 2005).
4. Jonathan Benthall, *Returning to Religion* (New York: I.B. Tauris, 2008).
5. Richard Santana and Gregory Erickson, *Religion and Popular Culture: Rescripting the Sacred* (Jefferson, NC: MacFarland, 2008).
6. Gary Laderman, *Sacred Matters: Celebrity Worship, Sexual Ecstasies, the Living Dead, and Other Signs of Religious Life in the United States* (New York: New Press, 2009).
7. Mark Taylor, *After God* (Chicago: University of Chicago Press, 2007), xiii.
8. Ibid., 12.
9. Mircea Eliade, *The Sacred and the Profane: The Nature of Religion* (San Diego, CA: Harcourt Brace Jovanovich, 1987), 104.
10. Henry Jenkins, *Convergence Culture: Where Old and New Media Collide* (New York: New York University Press, 2006), 322.
11. Charles Taylor, *A Secular Age* (Cambridge, MA: Belknap, 2007), 504–35.
12. Joachim Wach. *Religionwissenshaft* (Leipzig: J. C. Hinrichs, 1924), 86.
13. Brinda Adhikari, "Tim Tebow Superbowl Ad," ABC News, January 26, 2010, http://abc-news.go.com/WN/tim-tebow-super-bowl-ad-cbs-air-controversial/story?id=9667638.
14. Richard T. Hughes, *Myths America Lives By* (Champaign: University of Illinois Press, 2004).
15. Robert Jewett and John Shelton Lawrence, *Captain America and the Crusade Against Evil: The Dilemma of Zealous Nationalism* (Grand Rapids, MI: Eerdmans, 2009).
16. Ibid., 8.
17. Ibid., 27.
18. Ibid., 2.
19. Bruce Lincoln, *Religion, Empire, and Torture: The Case of Achaemenian Persia, with a Postscript on Abu Ghraib* (Chicago: University of Chicago Press, 2008).
20. Denis Duclos, *The Werewolf Complex: America's Fascination with Violence* (New York: Berg, 1998).
21. Ibid., 207.
22. Ibid., 211.

23. Georges Gusdorf, *Traité de Métaphysique* (Paris: Librarie Armand Colin, 1956).
24. Mark Taylor, *After God*, 19–33.
25. Ibid., 165.
26. Michael Kirwan, *Discovering Girard* (Cambridge, MA: Cowley, 2005), 5.
27. René Girard, Michael Kirwan, Pierpaolo Antonello, and Joao Cezar de Castro Rocha, *Evolution and Conversion: Dialogues on the Origins of Culture* (New York: T & T Clark, 2008).
28. Randall Collins, *Violence: A Micro-sociological Theory* (Princeton, NJ: Princeton University Press, 2008).
29. Darryl Caterine, "Curses and Catharsis," *Journal of Religion and Popular Culture* 8 (Fall 2004): http://www.usask.ca/relst/jrpc/art8-redsox-print.html.
30. Gil Baille, *Violence Unveiled: Humanity at the Crossroads* (New York: Crossroads,1995).
31. Barbara Ehrenreich, *Nickel and Dimed: On (Not) Getting by in America* (New York: Holt, 2008).
32. Ronald Sider, *Rich Christians in an Age of Hunger* (Nashville, TN: Thomas Nelson, 2005).
33. Ehrenreich, *Nickel and Dimed*, 69.
34. Ibid., 106.
35. Ibid., 117.
36. Ibid., 150.
37. Ibid., 117–18.
38. Ibid., 206–7.
39. Ibid., 178.
40. Ibid., 179.
41. Ibid., 210.
42. Ibid., 211.
43. Ibid., 211–13.
44. Jonathan Kozol, *Rachel and Her Children: Homeless Families in America* (New York: Three Rivers Press, 2006).
45. Randall Amster, *Lost in Space: The Criminalization, Globalization, and Urban Ecology of Homelessness* (El Paso, TX: LFB Scholarly Publishing, 2008).
46. Jeffery H. Reiman and Paul Leighton, *The Rich Get Richer, and the Poor Get Prison: Ideology, Class, and Criminal Justice* (Boston: Allyn and Bacon, 2006).
47. Alexandra Pelosi, *Homeless: The Motel Kids of Orange County* (HBO documentary, Summer Series 2010), http://www.hbo.com/documentaries/homeless-the-motel-kids-of-orange-county/index.html.

BIBLIOGRAPHY

Abramsky, Sasha. *American Furies: Crime, Punishment, and Vengeance in the Age of Mass Imprisonment*. Boston: Beacon Press, 2007.
Adhikari, Brinda. "Tim Tebow Superbowl Ad: Anti-abortion Commercial to Air." ABC News, January 26, 2010. http://abcnews.go.com/WN/tim-tebow-super-bowl-ad-cbs-air-controversial/story?id=9667638.
Agamben, Giorgio. *The Signature of All Things: On Method*. Brooklyn, NY: Zone Books, 2009.
Allman, Mark J. *Who Would Jesus Kill? War, Peace, and the Christian Tradition*. Winona, MN: Anselm Academic, 2008.
Amster, Randall. *Lost in Space: The Criminalization, Globalization, and Urban Ecology of Homelessness*. El Paso, TX: LFB Scholarly Publishing, 2008.

Armstrong, Karen. *A Short History of Myth*. New York: Canongate, 2006.

Bailie, Gil. *Violence Unveiled: Humanity at the Crossroads*. New York: Crossroad, 1995.

Bellinger, Charles K. *The Genealogy of Violence: Reflections on Creation, Freedom, and Evil*. New York: Oxford University Press, 2001.

Benthall, Jonathan. *Returning to Religion: Why a Secular Age Is Haunted by Faith*. New York: I.B. Tauris, 2008.

Bolle, Kees W. *The Freedom of Man in Myth*. Nashville, TN: Vanderbilt University Press, 1993.

Bousquet, Antoine J. *The Scientific Way of Warfare: Order and Chaos on the Battlefields of Modernity*. Critical War Studies, Vol. 1. New York: Columbia University Press, 2009.

Bruce, Steve. *Religion in the Modern World*. New York: Oxford University Press, 1996.

Buss, David M. *The Murderer Next Door: Why the Mind Is Designed to Kill*. New York: Penguin, 2005.

Cahn, Edgar S. *No More Throw-Away People: The Co-production Imperative*. Washington, DC: Essential Books, 2004.

Caterine, Darryl. "Curses and Catharsis." *Journal of Religion and Popular Culture* 8 (Fall 2004): http://www.usask.ca/relst/jrpc/art8-redsox-print.html.

Cawelti, John G. *The Six-Gun Mystique*. Bowling Green, OH: Bowling Green State University Popular Press, 1984.

Chidester, David. *Authentic Fakes: Religion and American Popular Culture*. Berkeley: University of California Press, 2005.

Collins, Randall. *Violence: A Micro-sociological Theory*. Princeton, NJ: Princeton University Press, 2008.

Cox, Harvey G. *The Future of Faith*. New York: HarperOne, 2009.

Davis, Richard L. *Domestic Violence: Intervention, Prevention, Policies, and Solutions*. Boca Raton, FL: CRC Press, 2008.

Detweiler, Craig, ed. *Halos and Avatars: Playing Video Games with God*. Louisville, KY: Westminster John Knox Press, 2010.

Duclos, Denis. *The Werewolf Complex: America's Fascination with Violence*. New York: Berg, 1998.

Eakin, Paul John. *Living Autobiographically: How We Create Identity in Narrative*. Ithaca, NY: Cornell University Press, 2008.

Eliade, Mircea. *The Sacred and the Profane: The Nature of Religion*. San Diego, CA: Harcourt Brace Jovanovich, 1987.

Epstein, Jonathan S., ed. *Youth Culture: Identity in a Postmodern World*. Malden, MA: Blackwell, 1998.

Fishwick, Marshall W. *Popular Culture: Cavespace to Cyberspace*. New York: Routledge, 2001.

Garot, Robert. *Who You Claim: Performing Gang Identity in School and on the Streets*. Alternative Criminology Series. New York: New York University Press, 2010.

Gay, Paul du, Jessica Evans, and Peter Redman, eds. *Identity: A Reader*. Thousand Oaks, CA: Sage, 2000.

Gilligan, James. *Violence: Reflections on a National Epidemic*. New York: Vintage, 1997.

Gilmore, Ruth Wilson. *Golden Gulag: Prisons, Surplus, Crisis, and Opposition in Globalizing California*. American Crossroads. Berkeley: University of California Press, 2007.

Girard, René, Michael Kirwan, Pierpaolo Antonello, and Joao Cezar de Castro Rocha. *Evolution and Conversion: Dialogues on the Origins of Culture*. New York: T & T Clark, 2007.

Grossman, Dave. *On Killing: The Psychological Cost of Learning to Kill in War and Society*. New York: Back Bay, 2009.

Gusdorf, Georges. *Traité de Métaphysique*. Paris: Librairie Armand Colin, 1956.

Gwenllian-Jones, Sara, and Roberta E. Pearson, eds. *Cult Television*. Minneapolis: University of Minnesota Press, 2004.

Herrick, James A. *The Making of the New Spirituality: The Eclipse of the Western Religious Tradition*. Downers Grove, IL: InterVarsity Press, 2003.

———. *Scientific Mythologies: How Science and Science Fiction Forge New Religious Beliefs*. Downers Grove, IL: IVP Academic, 2008.

Hoffman, Shirl James. *Good Game: Christianity and the Culture of Sports*. Waco, TX: Baylor University Press, 2010.

Hoover, Stewart M., and Knut Lundby, eds. *Rethinking Media, Religion, and Culture*. Thousand Oaks, CA: Sage, 1997.

Hughes, Richard T. *Myths America Lives By*. Champaign: University of Illinois Press, 2004.

Jenkins, Henry. *Convergence Culture: Where Old and New Media Collide*. New York: New York University Press, 2006.

Jerryson, Michael, and Mark Juergensmeyer, eds. *Buddhist Warfare*. New York: Oxford University Press, 2010.

Jewett, Robert, and John Shelton Lawrence. *Captain America and the Crusade Against Evil*. Grand Rapids, MI: Eerdmans, 2009.

Jones, Gerard. *Killing Monsters: Why Children Need Fantasy, Super Heroes, and Make-Believe Violence*. New York: Basic Books, 2002.

Kirwan, Michael. *Discovering Girard*. Cambridge, MA: Cowley, 2005.

———. *Girard and Theology. Philosophy and Theology*. New York: T & T Clark, 2009.

Kolakowski, Leszek. *The Presence of Myth*. Chicago: University of Chicago Press, 1989.

Kozol, Jonathan. *Rachel and Her Children: Homeless Families in America*. New York: Three Rivers Press, 2006.

Lefebure, Leo D. *Revelation, the Religions, and Violence*. Maryknoll, NY: Orbis, 2000.

Lincoln, Bruce. *Holy Terrors: Thinking about Religion after September 11*. Chicago: University of Chicago Press, 2006.

———. *Religion, Empire, and Torture: The Case of Achaemenian Persia, with a Postscript on Abu Ghraib*. Chicago: University of Chicago Press, 2008.

———. *Theorizing Myth: Narrative, Ideology, and Scholarship*. Chicago: University of Chicago Press, 1999.

Long, Charles H. *Significations: Signs, Symbols, and Images in the Interpretation of Religion*. Series in Philosophical and Cultural Studies in Religion. Aurora, CO: Davies Group, 1999.

Lynch, Gordon. *Understanding Theology and Popular Culture*. Malden, MA: Blackwell, 2005.

Maalouf, Amin. *In the Name of Identity: Violence and the Need to Belong*. New York: Penguin, 2003.

Maier, Charles S. *Among Empires: American Ascendancy and Its Predecessors*. Cambridge, MA: Harvard University Press, 2007.

McCracken, Grant David. *Transformations: Identity Construction in Contemporary Culture*. Bloomington: Indiana University Press, 2008.

Ness, Peter H. van, ed. *Spirituality and the Secular Quest*. World Spirituality, Vol. 22. New York: Crossroad, 1996.

Page, Benjamin B., ed. *Marxism and Spirituality: An International Anthology*. Westport, CT: Bergin and Garvey, 1993.

Pelosi, Alexandra. *Homeless: The Motel Kids of Orange County*. HBO documentary. Summer Series 2010. http://www.hbo.com/documentaries/homeless-the-motel-kids-of-orange-county/index.html.

Perry, Barbara. *Silent Victims: Hate Crimes Against Native Americans.* Tuscon: University of Arizona Press, 2008.

Philpott, Daniel, and Gerard F. Powers, eds. *Strategies of Peace: Transforming Conflict in a Violent World.* Studies in Strategic Peacebuilding. New York: Oxford University Press, 2010.

Poole, W. Scott. *Satan in America: The Devil We Know.* Lanham, MD: Rowman and Littlefield, 2009.

Reiman, Jeffrey, and Paul Leighton. *The Rich Get Richer and the Poor Get Prison: Ideology, Class, and Criminal Justice.* Boston: Allyn and Bacon, 2010.

Rogeau, Vincent D. *Christians in the American Empire: Faith and Citizenship in the New World Order.* New York: Oxford University Press, 2008.

Santana, Richard W., and Gregory Erickson. *Religion and Popular Culture: Rescripting the Sacred.* Jefferson, NC: McFarland, 2008.

Schneider, Steven Jay, and Daniel Shaw, eds. *Dark Thoughts: Philosophic Reflections on Cinematic Horror.* Lanham, MD: Scarecrow Press, 2003.

Segal, Robert Alan. *Myth: A Very Short Introduction.* New York: Oxford University Press, 2004.

Sharpley-Whiting, T. Denean. *Pimps Up, Ho's Down: Hip Hop's Hold on Young Black Women.* New York: New York University Press, 2007.

Sider, Ronald. *Rich Christians in an Age of Hunger: Moving from Affluence to Generosity.* Nashville, TN: Thomas Nelson, 2005.

Storey, John. *Inventing Popular Culture: From Folklore to Globalization.* Blackwell Manifestos. Malden, MA: Blackwell, 2003.

Strinati, Dominic. *An Introduction to Theories of Popular Culture.* New York: Routledge, 2004.

Taylor, Bron. *Dark Green Religion: Nature Spirituality and the Planetary Future.* Berkeley: University of California Press, 2010.

Taylor, Charles. *A Secular Age.* Cambridge, MA: Belknap, 2007.

Taylor, Mark C. *After God.* Chicago: University of Chicago Press, 2009.

Valenti, F. Miguel. *More Than a Movie: Ethics in Entertainment.* Boulder, CO: Westview, 2000.

Vries, Hent de, and Samuel Weber, eds. *Violence, Identity, and Self-Determination.* Stanford, CA: Stanford University Press, 1997.

Watkins, Gregory J., ed. *Teaching Religion and Film.* AAR Teaching Religious Studies Series. New York: Oxford University Press, 2008.

Weber, Eugen. *Apocalypses: Prophecies, Cults and Millennial Beliefs Throughout the Ages.* London: Random House, 1999.

William, James G. *The Bible, Violence, and the Sacred: Liberation from the Myth of Sanctioned Violence.* New York: HarperCollins, 1991.

Winston, Diane, ed. *Small Screen, Big Picture: Television and Lived Religion.* Waco, TX: Baylor University Press, 2009.

Yoder, Howard John. *When War Is Unjust: Being Honest in Just-War Thinking.* Eugene, OR: Wipf and Stock, 2002.

CHAPTER 10

⌒◯⌒

Religion, Violence, and Politics in the United States

JASON C. BIVINS

"Why do you always talk about the bad stuff?" she asked. This question from a student in one of my introductory classes left me a bit taken aback. Stalling, I asked her to clarify her question. She explained that it was her impression that I spent far more time talking about the "negative aspects" of religion, especially Christianity, in America than I did about "the positive." I fumbled my way through an answer, suggesting that I might spend slightly more time emphasizing conflict and violence in American religion only because conventional historical accounts have under-accentuated these features. But I left my classroom uncertain of the accuracy of my answer, and I have since pondered my student's question on many occasions.

Most of us who teach wrestle, if we are honest with ourselves, with the degree to which we want to change our students. Only a very few people actually want to alter their students' opinions, particularly on matters as personal and important as religion. Yet most of us have an enthusiasm for the shared exploration of ideas, texts, and contexts we pursue with our students each semester; the majority of teachers believe that the processes themselves, those things central to the academy, are worthy and ennobling. Aside from those few whose books and articles trickle out beyond the close quarters of academic reading audiences, most of us know, too, that we reach many more people with our work in the classroom than we do with our writings. With this recognition, however, comes a moral edge. What precisely are we doing with our students, beyond the mere transmission of data? Do my classes— a religion in America survey, a class on "cults," a few on political religions, and one on theories of religion—accomplish more than simply informing my students about who protested against what, about when famous religious people died, or how to distinguish Reform from Orthodox Jews?

The answer to this question is obvious, its implications less so.[1] If things were simple, we could simply decide to avoid encumbering ourselves with the hand-wringing and second guessing that come with framing and shaping materials, and instead strive to convey to our students "just the facts." But as everyone reading this knows, things are not this simple and this idea is a fantasy. When we decide which facts to shoehorn into a short semester, how to order them, and which details are or are not inessential, we are already involved in framing ideas and information for our students. So are there any goods—pedagogic or otherwise—that can come from constructing frames, partial looks, emphases, or provocations for our students? The answer, in my judgment, is clearly yes. With my student's question in mind, along with all the associated issues it raises for those who teach religious studies, this essay justifies this answer by focusing on theoretical debates, historical narratives, and pedagogical experiences and possibilities.

I do this in the context of my work in the religions of the United States, which focuses on political matters as these are broadly construed. That is, I focus not only on topics conventionally associated with this subject (religions and the state, constitutional issues, or religious interest groups) but also on a wide range of activities that might be grouped under the heading of cultural politics: protests, discourses, the establishment of resistance communities, civil disobedience, or interreligious exchanges and exclusions. Political life involves contact and conflict, the sort of antagonism that may be regarded as violent; and expressions of violence in the United States, those that hinge upon religions and those that do not, tend often to be framed in political ways. My classes have therefore often included descriptions of these religious expressions, just as all classes tend to privilege whatever research preoccupies their teacher, along with the kinds of issues they raise for thinking about religion and politics in American life and for making connections between the different types of actions or practices these intersections have generated. Such things are the stuff of politics in America, and religious practitioners have always participated in these activities. While questions still remain about balancing "the bad stuff" with other materials, there is clearly something about this conjunction of religions, politics, and violence that captures important dimensions of American culture.

How might we make sense of this conjunction? If we look to theories of religious violence and to conventional American religious histories, we see that they themselves are in conflict. There is one long-standing lineage in the historiography of American religion—one that has clearly shaped pedagogy in the field—which has focused on pluralism. Since the publication in 1973 of Sidney Ahlstrom's seminal *A Religious History of the American People* (which, roughly speaking, chronicled the rise and decline of the Puritan establishments of New England and, later, of Protestant hegemony in American culture), the study of American religions has thrived through an exploration of those religious actors left out of earlier narratives.[2] So in the works of William Hutchison, Charles Lippy, Martin Marty, and Stephen Prothero, among other sources that directly engage the subject of pluralism, we see extensions of these kinds of post-Protestant considerations and an opening not just to Judaism, Catholicism, Islam, Buddhism, and Hinduism, but to new religious movements, separatist groups, atheists, popular religions, and more.[3] Even beyond specifically oriented texts, surveys of American religious life, both popular (Diana Eck's *A New Religious America*) and those oriented to the classroom (Catherine Albanese's *America: Religions and Religion*) seem to privilege pluralism both as manyness and as a specific kind of public experience.[4] The more deft of these synthetic volumes focus on the intimate relation between pluralism and antagonism—not just on the national level but on the communal or even the individual levels—and show that "the one and the many" (to use a well-worn formulation) has been achieved, if at all, through rancor and bloodshed as well as through conciliation and consensus.

Narratives of American religious pluralism, manyness, and multiculturalism are everywhere, normative both in the culinary metaphors they seem to inspire and in university classrooms. And while some of these narratives privilege political order and socioreligious harmony, others do not. The question is not whether scholars have adequately grappled with expressions of violence in American religious history; in my opinion, the field has done so, even if not exhaustively.[5] This essay, though, is about teaching. What good can we impart to our students, whether at a large public university like mine or at a small liberal arts college, by challenging the presumption that religious violence is an irruption into normally stable public life, into the generally coherent fabric of religious or political pluralism? What pedagogical, even civic values are realized by pursuing the notion that American religious and political histories have been constituted by violence and are themselves histories of violences? In proposing, in place of the historical narrative of ordered religious pluralism, one emphasizing religion, politics, and violence in the United States, do we do more than simply flummox our students? Below I suggest that the registers of conflict emerging in such a narrative—rhetorical, theological, and physical, among others—can serve as useful theoretical tools around which to orient conversations addressing religion and violence while also functioning as pedagogical tools in the university classroom.

VIOLENCE IN RELIGIOUS STUDIES

Public interest in religions tends often to follow in the wake of, perhaps even as a product of, spectacle, danger, and controversy. While this characterization might not capture every spike in publishing habits or audience consumption (the frenzy for matters pertaining to the historical Jesus may elude this formulation), there is little doubting that the presence of violence—whether it is communal and self-directed as in Jonestown, directed at internal Others as in the Oklahoma City bombing, or externally terroristic as in the bombings of September 11, 2001—can drive inquiries into the role of religions in creating, motivating, and justifying such actions. These inquiries shape, at least on some level, the students who enroll in our classes, just as surely as they shape teachers, albeit in different ways. A willingness to engage such matters directly in the classroom can assist in a certain kind of demystification of public discourse even as it may contribute to the construction of what I have been calling the historiography of "bad stuff."

The possibilities of such an engagement take on a sense of urgency, or at least they can be pedagogically powerful, in the context of the sharpened methodological attention (or anxiety) recently resurfacing in religious studies. The field has benefited from fruitful conversations across the subdisciplines and a growing sense of reflection about what constitutes the academic study of religion. In a certain sense, of course, we are always talking about ourselves and about the limits of what we do (and always, always about what makes this discipline distinct—in methods, in object of study, in institutional location—from, say, history, anthropology, or sociology). Such metareflections may be useful as we prepare materials for our courses, but they can also prove tedious and confusing to students who are not yet familiar with what the conversations bring into question—in other words, they can lead us to lousy teaching. Yet this remains a moment of real opportunity to take stock of issues or categories like violence.

Religious studies has always been characterized by, and has probably mostly benefited from, its methodological multiplicity. Currently, however, many in the field are especially preoccupied with methodological and occasionally even normative considerations. I consider this largely a positive undertaking, when shorn of solipsism or self-indulgence. Rigorous scrutiny of terms, narratives, and procedures taken for granted is clearly beneficial to scholarship, and they may yield pedagogical benefits too. Although the questions are usually posed in a chastened fashion, which is appropriate given the post-postmodern suspicion of "big questions," scholars of religions today are actively engaged in a kind of cataloguing or assessment of what it is we actually do.[6]

In recent years, scholars from across the discipline of religious studies have entered a period of renewed reflection on the methods and goals of the profession, even as some would reject the notion that anything as coherent as a discipline or a field exists. Some of these reflections have concerned the relationship between confessional modes of scholarship and the "naturalistic tradition" of inquiry, while others have centered on the potential of new critical terms or categories in the study of religion. While I do not necessarily regard *violence* as a critical term as central to the study of religion as, for example, *bodiliness* or *ritual*, I nonetheless believe that using this concept to generate specific inquiries or narratives (as opposed to broad-stroke categories like "religion and violence") is both theoretically and pedagogically fruitful.

There are, however, clear problems in thinking generally about both religion and violence. Questions about the status of religion as a general category are, as indicated above, familiar ones, but engaging them in this context can help usefully to both ground and provoke questions about violence, questions that hover over all conversations in religious studies classrooms.[7] What kinds of actions, beliefs, institutions, and histories can be considered religious? Is it even meaningful to think of religion in the singular, as opposed to a proliferating and unstable ensemble of religions? As Jonathan Z. Smith has memorably written, it is not so much that our understandings of religions are too narrow and that it is impossible to settle on a useful definition thereof, but rather that with some effort it is possible to generate dozens of workable definitions.[8] Is violence any less problematic to define and locate on the map of American religions? Conventional definitions of the term often privilege the physical use of force, one agent's violation of the will of another, improper treatment or the infliction of damage, or simply even a dramatic intensification of the strength, valence, or power of an action (a punch) or a physical state (heat).[9] Yet this leaves open a number of questions of potential significance in orienting ourselves to religions. Is violence only constituted by direct, physical acts of aggression between individuals or communities, as with the 1834 attack on an Ursuline convent outside of Boston? Or are defensive actions also violent? Are there moral or analytical differences between those two modes? Can violence also consist of exclusion, marginalization, or rhetorical or symbolic misrepresentation?

What undergirds all these considerations of violence is the centrality of boundaries, both the physical ones of bodies and territories and the more abstract ones of identities and truths. Through the exertion of strength or the intensity of coercion, such boundaries are problematized in a frequently uneven engagement between hostile agents: communities or individuals are provoked, threatened, or injured against their will; denunciations or symbolic otherings (alterity) are deployed as means of violating the boundaries of identity; or certain modes of behavior are constrained or modified as a result of such coercion. In addition to the various ways in which boundaries are problematized, one must also consider the scale on which violence is being enacted. When thinking through the intersections of religions and violence in American history, we see that the expressions extend from group to individual conflict, all the way to a whole range of questions involving the nation-state and political order, not only the ways in which these entities can sanction violence but the ways in which specific governmental policies (most obviously military ones) raise questions about violence to which religious practitioners have fashioned a range of responses.

I certainly do not aspire here to propose a working definition for either religion or violence, but simply to establish that neither term is historically given or analytically fixed. By situating this understanding of the relation between religions and violence in the broader context of the political cultures of the United States, my aim is not only to call for more comparative thinking about such matters but to suggest that in some sense we cannot avoid thinking about such matters in political terms. It is not much of a stretch to suggest that—due to the ubiquity of the oft-cited factors of cultural and religious pluralism, immigration, and the separation of church and state—one cannot think of American religion independently of politics, nor indeed of politics outside of the religious. But consider further that these relationships and encounters between persons and communities in the public sphere can be characterized by disruptions, violations, breaches, or effacements. If this is the case, as I contend it is below, then religion and violence in America exist in a fluid relationship where perhaps that most central boundary—the one distinguishing American from religious identities—becomes problematized and provoked through (1) conflicting roles and duties, (2) participation in shared institutions, and (3) public encounters with political or religious Others. These issues may promote harmony in certain instances. But they also just as regularly shape religious resentments (over perceived conflict between political and religious obligations) or the intergroup conflicts that have long attended American religious pluralism.[10]

As Elizabeth Castelli notes, conflicts deemed religious are "often viewed as occurring outside of concrete historical conditions."[11] But in fact, religious conflict and violence are obviously products of their material conditions and histories. Any decent pedagogy must note that religions are, like other dimensions of human experience, always intersecting with, for example, race, gender, political order, and so forth. Religions are never discrete realities sealed off from the messiness of lived (political) experience but contribute to that experience either directly or indirectly, in providing rationales for certain courses of action. Whether or not these expressions occur specifically in the context of religious antagonisms against the nation-state, as Bruce Lincoln describes, they can meaningfully be understood as political expressions.[12]

Such concerns hang over every course I teach. How do we, as scholars and teachers, make sense of the possibility that the very manyness of American religions has so often generated violence? How specifically might we help students analyze and interpret the sources or the meanings of these intersections? Put differently, what distinguishes religious from nonreligious violence? Jean Rosenfeld proposes a threefold typology:

> 1) Religious groups that initiate violence or revolution because they believe they are called or chosen to play an active role in the transformation of the social world.
> 2) Religious groups that commit suicide or homicide because, paradoxically, they believe it is the only way to achieve their collective goal or ultimate well-being.
> 3) Religious groups that are stigmatized and directly assaulted because they are believed to threaten society.[13]

This scheme is quite useful and is widely applicable. However, I supplement it by answering the aforementioned questions with an additional distinction: religious violence is distinguished by the specific motivations and justifications for violence invoked, often pitched in absolutist or cosmological terms where those articulating violence are convinced ontological stakes are high; and religious violence is distinct in the ways it identifies and interprets its targets, generally religious competitors or heretical policies or practices whose presence convinces those articulating violence that both political and ontological stakes are high. This distinction, at least as far as the religions of the United States are concerned, reveals something about the relationship between a political order that facilitates a high degree of religious interactions and specific participants therein, who on occasion feel compelled to act violently.

This method of justification and targeting often turns on a specific conception of identity, one in which the self can be perceived as not only an agent upon whom moral legitimacy is conferred (owing to affiliation with or participation in righteousness) but conceivably also as a vehicle for the divine will. If one's religion must be defended against the encroachment of wrong believers or wrong sociopolitical developments, then actions undertaken in the name of such defense may be, however violent, potentially justifiable. As Tazim Kassam suggests, religious autonomy and identity may be experienced as particularly vulnerable in societies characterized by religious diversity, in response to which certain religious practitioners may experience alienation, social grievances, or fears of chaos.[14] Further, as Kassam writes, "Exclusive monotheism premised on visions of scarcity promotes a competitive and violent worldview by reducing divinity to a jealous God whose favors are confined within boundaries guarded by insiders against outsiders."[15] The command morality often associated with religious convictions conveys a sense of ultimacy that may be seen to validate actions regarded as extreme by outsiders, but may be felt necessary by defenders of the faith.

Additionally, this privileging of certainty and clarity can be achieved by naming, scapegoating, and targeting specific causes that have—in the minds of practitioners—led to a compromise of righteousness, to minority status, or to porous identities. Identifying targets—whether in the form of secular humanism, "heathen" sectarians, or moral backsliders—works to establish both an explanation for social distress or indeterminacy and a coherent self-representation. Both the justificatory distinction of religions and the specific Others they single out are central to understanding the ways in which they can manifest in violence. Significantly, each turns on a sense of identity and autonomy at risk.

HISTORIES

These kinds of methodological considerations are open-ended, and the terminological difficulties in particular are likely irresolvable. Considering the subject of my reflections, however—the construction of a narrative of American religious violence, specifically one shaped by political factors—a new set of considerations looms. Immediately the question posed by my student returns: how can teachers justify using a historical narrative that is oriented to or that foregrounds violence? In highlighting these religious expressions, for noble reasons or not, do we skew, undermine, or misrepresent things fundamental to our pedagogical responsibilities as teachers of American religions, political religions, or new religious movements? Furthermore, is it even desirable to conceive of scholarship and pedagogy in terms of narrative, with all of its teleological resonances, its formulaic properties, and its promise of order and structure? Certainly much has been done to problematize the prospect of telling a single story, constructing a single narrative, as if there is an accepted version of events—Puritans to revivals, revivals to pluralism—that can be modified and tweaked until it is theoretically or morally as inoffensive as we can imagine.[16] As everyone reading this surely knows, the audacity of mapping out a syllabus is inevitably accompanied by much methodological hand-wringing: whatever our subject matter, we cannot help but do a kind of violence to the richness and multiplicity of what we teach when we shoehorn it into fifteen weeks, thirty lectures, and so forth.

In other words, as noted at the outset, each attempt to generate a new category to anchor or orient teaching and research, a new interpretation of a recognizable area, or a new narrative calls attention to the pitfalls of limits, exclusions, and reductiveness; even a well-meaning effort to open up conversations brings with it risks not only epistemic (do we exclude even when we seek to become more inclusive?) but also pedagogical (does such endless qualification constitute precisely the kind of pursuit that can overburden and muddy an introductory class?). So as I describe the contours of a history that looks consciously at "the bad stuff," I keep these cautions in mind. And as I argue in the concluding section, however reductive an examination of American religion through the lens of violence may be, it seems important to engage in such examination, perhaps especially now. If we can generate such a narrative or pursue such an exploration while maintaining a sense of limits, and while acknowledging the necessity of remaining open to other narratives, we may be able to avoid or at least temper their dangers.

Conventional Narratives

This approach to the religions of the United States participates in and draws from the multiple interrogations of conventional narratives of American religion, conventions that function more or less in the way a ready-to-hand past awaits travelers and tourists visiting a new city for the first time. Just as newcomers to cities encounter, and have likely already heard much about, a specific range of museums, monuments, or historic sites, so too does the student of American religious history encounter "major" figures and events that function similarly to orient them. It is not the case that these ready-to-hand figures are detached from the lived social history of a place, just as those persons and moments invoked frequently and routinely in conventional narratives truly are important and in many ways defining. I make this analogy to suggest that familiar guideposts such as these shape expectations prior to sustained engagement with a place or narrative, and that in this sense they cater to the images that both tourists and students have prior to their encounter with the messiness of history, as it were. Thus, these archaized, sterilized, and simplified histories are in some important ways constituted by the projections of the visitors (and even residents) themselves. One wanders through neighborhoods whose architecture one recognizes from images seen beforehand, sits in gardens about whose manicured grounds one has read, checks off of one's list a Louvre, a National Archive, a Space Needle, or an Alamo. Such well-lit, abundantly described locations stand in visible relief on our conceptual maps; we have been prepared to encounter them as important, representative spaces that can be singled out to stand in for their larger contexts.

If we approach the United States in this fashion, we find that there are several ready-to-hand narratives whose horizon is established by landmarks that are commonly invoked to chronicle and explain what is described as an imperfectly achieved but usually ordered American religious pluralism. We encounter Anne Hutchinson's and Roger Williams's dissent from the authority of the Puritan magistrates as, in the formulation of Isaac Kramnick and R. Laurence Moore, a kind of early peti-tion for religious freedom, a pre-echo of the Constitution.[17] William Penn's treaties with Native Americans in Pennsylvania might be cited as harbingers not simply of what would in time be described as peaceable relations between the descendants of European settlers and Native Americans, but a kind of legal template outlining the ways in which a civil polity could be maintained as hospitable to disparate cultures and religions.[18] The Revolutionary period itself has been depicted as a time when clear-eyed sages decided through rational debate which procedures and norms best guided what would become a religiously pluralist and tolerant republic.[19] Some tellers of these tales might shrug off the bitter sectional conflicts and religious an-tagonisms of the nineteenth century, seeing them as mere bumps on a road ulti-mately arriving at a public flowering of religious tolerance and cooperation, seen for example in the World's Parliament of Religion in 1893, the ecumenical movement, or in the unceasing array of religious exchanges, combinations, and consumerism that characterize post-1960s American culture.

Yet the very factors I cite above as key indices of the political character of Amer-ican religious life—church-state separation most obviously—can be invoked to do very different narrative and figurative work. A narrative of settled religious plu-ralism may cite this category not only as if its meanings were self-evident but as if it has historically served for the most part to guarantee expressions of harmony such as those just enumerated. Violence is certainly not written out of pluralist narratives like these, but its position therein suggests that it should be seen as an exception to political tranquility or as a hurdle successfully cleared along the path to settled civic order.

I take it as obvious that no scholar worth her salt would write such a one-dimensionally rosy portrait of religious manyness; indeed, writers in the human-ities love no words better than *contest*, *hegemony*, and *conflict*. Yet outside of our own writing, we must confront the fact that not only is it more frequent for something like this narrative of happy religious pluralism to issue into classrooms, it is also the narrative embraced by a considerable majority of our incoming students. Such a con-ventional pluralist narrative caters to a specific set of desires and interests. It sup-ports a particular species of American self-representation, one resistant to less than optimistic strains of memory and nervous about the admission of any collective wrongdoing.[20] Through management of the past, a singular social identity is con-structed through a series of inferences which together suggest that pluralism is a happy reality as long as its difficulties, its injured bodies, its social harms do not have to be confronted; and religious tolerance is an acknowledged first principle pro-vided no special accommodations (either practical or perceptual, behavior in the present or new reckonings with the past) are required of us. Americans tend to think about violence, disorder, and calamity selectively, allowing it to puncture the smooth surface of the orderly everyday only provided that it legitimates a self-understanding that we are people to whom violence only happens when we do not deserve it and in ways for which we bear no responsibility. Willing to acknowledge racism in the past, Americans collectively seek to avoid its continued presence in our culture and rely tacitly on the notion that the problems of racism were solved with the Civil Rights

Act of 1964–65. So too there are tacit assumptions about the achievement of religious pluralism and toleration in the United States: while early eras of Protestant hegemony may have been achieved partly through exclusions and interreligious contests, American religious history evinces a steady flowering of both pluralism and tolerance.

This is the narrative writ large and abundantly available; it is the tourist section of American religious history. Yet it is not entirely accurate, or even persuasive. What would American religious history look like from a different perspective, one that is messier and more "local"? We find that not only has there been considerably greater violence than one might believe (something that arguably characterizes the present as well as the past), but that the terms taken for granted in conventional historiography—church-state separation, pluralism, and so forth—have themselves been subject to often radical contestation. It is not simply the case, for example, that Americans in the twentieth century suddenly discovered the relevance of the First Amendment to considerations of religious freedom; rather, the very notions of religious freedom, of establishment, of community, and of publicity have changed frequently.

By looking specifically into the unsettling links between the centrality of often very public religion to American life, the perennial American obsession with militarism, the popularity of an enduring moral language centered around the tropes of retribution and righteousness, and the awkward and frequently bloody ways in which American political order has reckoned with racial, sexual, ethnic, political, and religious difference, teachers of American religion would not be proposing a replacement narrative so much as a supplementary one. Examinations of these links, and of "the bad stuff," would simply constitute an angle of vision onto extant accounts of pluralism, public life, and conflict. That violence assumes such different forms, and erupts into the world of religions in so many ways, should help to construct a historical map of American religion and violence. What, then, would American religious history look like if configured in this way? What would we gain in the telling? The differing responses to this question might shape divergent histories of religion and violence in the United States.

Rosenfeld's Typology

A first orientation to such a narrative can be generated by reintroducing Rosenfeld's typology. She suggests that religions may act violently out of a desire to transform the social world, in order to achieve a collective goal (or well-being), or may be targets of violence if religions are seen as a threat to social order. Broadly speaking, this typology captures what we might call the justificatory grammar of religious violence, giving us one way of mapping the territories that helps us account for the self-understandings of actors and participants. One persistent current of religious energy in the United States, one mode of public religion's enduring self-expression, is reformism. Most reform actions, like the campaigns undertaken by the Temperance Movement or the houses of hospitality inspired by the

Progressives, do not involve violence or even necessarily protest. Nor is it the case that the transformations to which Rosenfeld refers are necessarily reformist. But underlying these differences, and implicit in Rosenfeld's formulation, is the experience of religious difference. In the United States specifically, with its prohibitions surrounding the public expression of religion and the long saga of religious minorities and assimilation, certain groups of religious practitioners have—under circumstances of marginalization, oppression, or undue constraint—felt that society demands that they act in ways antithetical to their religious commitments. Reaching their limits, when forced to choose between religious and political obedience, some of these practitioners have responded with attempts to resist the source of constraint, challenging its legitimacy or removing it altogether. Thus, violence has sometimes seemed an appropriate response to social or political misery, as in obvious examples such as the slave revolts of the early nineteenth century or less obviously in the religious motivations underlying examples of self-immolation (Norman Morrison's 1965 action was inspired by those undertaken by Buddhist monks in Vietnam). Similar experiential conditions can, when the stakes of an endeavor seem likewise high, lead to the use of violence in seeking to realize collective goals or fulfillment; we see this, for example, in the coercion and intimidation tactics once used by the militant antiabortion group Operation Rescue. It is also visible in the destruction of property (by Catholic pacifists affiliated with the Catholic Worker or Plowshares movements) or even symbolic acts of violence (William Lloyd Garrison's burning of a copy of the Constitution) designed to catalyze public will. Examples of alterity as violence, or targeting religions that are seen as threats, are multiple, ranging from sanctions against the practice of traditional African religions on plantations (which, if discovered, would result in punishments and occasionally death), the jailhouse murder of Mormon founder Joseph Smith, the U.S. military actions against Native American practitioners of the Ghost Dance in the late nineteenth century, or the actions of the ATF and FBI at the Branch Davidian compound in 1993.[21]

Sources That Shape Religious Violence

Beyond the orientation provided by Rosenfeld's typology, another angle of vision onto the range of expressions of American religious violence comes from a consideration of shaping and situating factors. While Rosenfeld provides a way of understanding the motivations of the actors, in other words, turning to broader contextual and historical factors is also necessary to understanding—and narrating—these expressions. These factors include the embattled status of public, political religions in the United States; the history of political violence in American history; the preponderance of retributive moral languages in public discourse; a persistent nervousness about pluralism, at times shading into outright resistance to difference; and finally, a symbolic and literal preoccupation with militarism.

Contests surrounding the public expression of religiosity have taken normative, interpretative, and embodied forms throughout American religious history. While little has been more commonplace than to see religions express themselves politically—via protests, public rituals, or gatherings to witness—these enactments have, however normalized or acceptable according to constitutional standards, frequently been met with antagonism, not just from public authority but from other citizens. Examples come from across the ideological spectrum, and include harassment of Catholic Worker protesters outside of IRS offices, threats and recriminations issued between evangelicals and neo-pagans over the rights to display religious imagery in public spaces, and the rancor that has often surrounded public expressions of religious will (consider, for example, the beating of James Reeb during the Civil Rights Movement).

These sorts of tensions and uncertainties characterizing the nature of public life obviously do not eventuate regularly in violent actions or even flareups of hostility. But I raise the issue in order to suggest that one way to understand American religious violences is as nourished by, and resounding in, the context of a public that is always contested and frequently characterized by antagonisms in which the religious have often participated. Related to these expressions, and often fueling them, is what I refer to above as a resistance to difference. The tensions between what the literature on pluralism calls "the one and the many" is frequently contained by larger debates about American identity and assimilation or about civil religion; yet they also erupt in English-only rallies in the contemporary period, raids by Nativists in the nineteenth century, or attacks on obviously "marked" religious Others such as Muslim women wearing hijab.

The antagonisms of public life, as well as such resistance to difference, are part of the long history of political violence in American life, certainly a shaping factor in American religiopolitical identities. Examples of such political violence run deep, from state-sanctioned coercion of particular political ideologies (in the Alien and Sedition Acts or the "red scare" of the 1950s) to expressions of worker radicalism like the Haymarket riots or the romanticization of revolution by 1960s radicals like the Yippies and the Diggers. Above even this contextual level, any narrative of American religious violence must consider the ways in which two enduring symbolic preoccupations—with the moral languages of retribution and with military might—serve as crucial factors. The languages of vengeance and judgment stem clearly from specific expressions of Christian public concern. These were shaped and nurtured first in the Puritan commonwealths, where Cotton Mather boasted proudly of the number of souls brought to hell in the Pequot War. They survived in subsequent expressions of demonological fervor, most notably in the Salem witch trials but also surfacing in certain periods of revivalism, in the cycles of reform coursing through nineteenth-century American religion, and in the virulent antimodernism of first-wave fundamentalism, for example. Whenever they have been uttered, these languages have been driven by warnings to backsliders of God's impending wrathful judgment or by promises to purge society of those who fall outside of good order, wreaking vengeance on those who do not comply with the will of the cultural or political sovereign.

These languages, and the readiness to exact punishment promised in them, may in part stem from and resonate with the larger cultures of violence so evident in

American history. The religions of the United States have surely been shaped in important ways by this culture's fascination with or even sacralization of violence, vigilantism, and firearms. They have also been influenced by the exclusivist concepts of expansionism (conquering lands settled by others, making normative an "American way of life") and exceptionalism (once described as the "armed" sense that we are God's people, a sense that "recreates the nation as a voice of power and self-righteousness").[22] While these latter categories may not initially seem to constitute forms of violence, they are clearly part of what I above suggest is the centrality of boundaries and the role of coercion against autonomous wills to any violent engagements. What is more, these categories have certainly played a role in shaping America's ongoing zeal for and commitment to military actions and interventions. Certainly these engagements have been as contested as any other, and it is important not to fall into the trap of generating a sophomoric caricature of the American *imperium*, seeking to grind the planet under its authoritarian heel.[23] Yet it is equally obvious that American national and civic identities have frequently, sometimes overwhelmingly, been associated with general support for military service, the expansion of American interests abroad (or even internally, as with the violence accompanying Western expansion and the closing of the frontier), and a cultural fetish for rugged individualism, where lone tough guys like Davy Crockett or "Dirty" Harry Callahan solve problems through heroic violence. These orientations have been reflected not just in militarism but in the way spectacular violence touches a huge number of spaces in American life: the fetish for failure and pain that masks itself as reality TV, paintball and other recreational "war games," Civil War reenactments or various other pursuits of the so-called weekend warriors, and shooting ranges, to cite just a few examples among many.

These thematic expressions of violence interact with American religions in the spheres of politics: not only do many of these modes of religious violence exist in the political sphere and with reference to political matters, broadly speaking, one of the most lasting modes of religious conflict has been that which directly challenges the legitimacy of political authority itself, focusing on the state, juridical conceptions of personhood, economic distribution, and so forth. The late twentieth-century presences of the so-called Christian militias and new religious movements like the Branch Davidians are only some of the most obvious examples of these contests; each represents an instantiation of American traditions of long standing. But elsewhere, some of the most powerful religious creations of this era have been manifestly political and have sought to disrupt public politics through agonistic forms of protest, such as street dramatizations of state-sponsored torture, spilling blood on the steps of the Pentagon, and blockades.

The Practices of Religious Violence

Taking the first two orientations into account, Rosenfeld's typology and the sources of American religious violence, both of which are broadly comparative, it is now possible to think about the mechanics or the specifics of religious violences, examples of which abound in American religious history. Even commonly cited founding events are themselves characterized by violence. The encounter between Spanish Catholic explorers and indigenous peoples exemplifies this, as do the religious exclusions of the early colonies, whether in the recurring anti-Catholicism of the lower colonies or the religious mania for order in the Puritan commonwealths. Even the violent events of the Revolutionary period, first resistance and then war, were undergirded by Protestant foundations.[24] As noted above, the eighteenth and nineteenth centuries were notable for similar kinds of religious conflicts (anti-Catholicism, anti-Semitism, Nativism) as well as social or political violence carried out in the name of or legitimated by religions, with territorial expansion and the displacement of Native Americans, and slavery being the most obvious examples.[25] These modes of religious conflict and exclusion have continued into the twenty-first century, their place in any narrative of American religious history a central one, whether we like it or not.

While examples of physical violence—in wars, revolts, riots, beatings, burnings, and bombings—loom obviously, American religions have also been engaged in rhetorical and representational violences that have proven equally significant in their impact on public life. One way in which this manifests is in cultural and intellectual conflicts that have shaped the religious landscape. Examples here might include the scandals and conflicts surrounding Darwinian theory since the mid-nineteenth century or those concerning homosexuality more recently, in which Topeka's Reverend Fred Phelps proclaims "God Hates Fags!" while San Francisco's Lesbian Avengers release insects into the offices of conservative Christian ministries, hoping that God will begin judgment against the conservatives.[26] It is more broadly visible in the ways American public discourse has become, especially abetted by the power of the mediascape, increasingly focused on combat rather than suasion and has even appropriated the imagery of conflict; important to the latter trend have been American religious critics, like David Barton's Wallbuilders or the War on Christians Conference, who decry the "war on faith" or cast their interlocutors as "enemies."[27] Furthermore, it is worth noting the degree to which the important rhetoric and imagination of the apocalyptic may constitute a kind of symbolic violence, or a spirit of vengeance, that captures themes located elsewhere in the "sacroscape" of American violence.[28]

It is even possible to follow these new modes in a more conventionally chronological manner. Even if one adheres to a relatively conventional narrative in the classroom, it can be supplemented by the suggestion that extant iterations of American religious history show that each period of pluralist growth can be seen as the result of three processes involving violence. First is a dialectic between painful expansions and contractions of public, political inclusivity, where political processes can be both welcoming and exclusive. Second, each period takes shape through difficult arrivals of new citizens, whose presence is often met by force and denunciation (e.g., the frequently violent encounter between European colonists and Native Americans mentioned above). Third, many responses to interreligious encounters have generated violence, including forced segregation, martyrdom, or political criticism of the establishment. Looking further, into the nineteenth century's explosion of religious creativity, it is obvious that there is no way to tell the story of new religious movements, during this or subsequent periods, without the violence that has often accompanied their formation and especially their public expression, in conflagrations like Mountain Meadows as well as Smith's murder and later examples such as the harassment of Jehovah's Witnesses during World War II.[29] It may also be pedagogically interesting to make explicit, consciously adopted nonviolence a part of this history, by introducing, among others, Quakers (even as they were imprisoned and beaten), Jesuit responses to the torture of Native Americans, or the establishment of churches and communities (from the Seneca Indian Mission Church to the Catholic Worker houses) as ways of containing violence.

There are more themes that could be generated, and more examples to be added to these laundry lists. I have spent time on these details to substantiate my claim that while the conventional history of American religious pluralism remains a useful one, in terms of both scholarship and pedagogy, it fails to identify and analyze sufficiently the violent dimensions that accompany and often oppose American religious pluralism. However, the strategies described above—Rosenfeld's tripartite distinction (capturing the motives and justifications for religious violences), the external contexts that shape specifically American iterations thereof, and the particular shapes these expressions have assumed in American history—have been useful in the classroom, as together they help to trace alternate histories that either stand alongside pluralist models or may be used to expand them. For where the post-Ahlstrom literature has usefully been keen to add voices, to explore registers of contact, and to unpack new dimensions of religious subjectivity, there remains much more to say about religious power and violence.

PEDAGOGICAL MEANINGS

This expanded historiography and pedagogy seeks to explore why American religious identities have so often expressed themselves through violence. The benefits of such exploration are multiple. I have written throughout about the expectations students inevitably bring with them to our classes, and specifically about the religiopolitical commitments I often encounter among my students. The majority of students enter religious studies courses with a number of expectations, clearly identifiable beyond any preoccupation with "spectacle"; in my courses on American religion and political religions particularly, I frequently encounter assumptions that American religious history is church history rather than social history, that it is the story of Protestant hegemony rather than religious pluralism, or that it is the story of tolerance alone rather than of conflict. Awareness of these expectations and compulsions can enable teachers to join students in engagements with complexity, ambiguity, and multiplicity, with the results often challenging presuppositions (both about religion's purported essence and about social history) and resisting simplification or generalization.

The positionality of the scholar is routinely acknowledged in humanities research, and one common way of reckoning with the epistemological (indeed, even moral) complexities of this positionality is to engage in frank self-inventory and self-disclosure in our writings themselves. We seek—whether engaged in descriptive or evaluative writing, critical or distanced—to disclose our points of origin and of arrival, to lay bare the principles and methods by which we do our work, to show our awareness of other narratives and methodologies, then attempt to justify our choices and move forward. Yet is this so easy a position to transfer to the classroom? Most of us, particularly those of us who work in public universities, believe there is some pedagogic good in, if not concealing our subject position in the classroom, then at least deflecting it, following a strategy of avoidance whereby we simply convey data and interpretive strategies to our students. And surely our training permits us to bracket our own beliefs in an effective manner; whereas in scholarship we may justify moving out of such bracketing, in the classroom there seems to be a moral imperative to bracket, not simply an epistemic choice.

And yet there she is again, asking me why I always talk about the bad stuff. So these considerations demand that I (we) reflect not only on methodology but on our intentions as scholars of religion. Is there some intellectual, even social violence bound up in talking about the bad things? Is a seemingly good-natured attempt to redress historical inattention likely to become zealotry, coercion, or even a form of intolerance itself? What do we gain, or possibly lose, from foregrounding violence? How are we to measure the value of a historical narrative? These questions (which are also cautions) must be considered, if the classroom is to be preserved as a democratic space. One must not tip the evidence too much to one side. One must not lose sight of the fluidity of ideas and histories in the attempt to foreground the significance of violence. And one must never commit so much to a pedagogical theme or idea that one closes down conversations rather than prompting them. As teachers we must continually reflect on our motives, strategies, and goals, performing the same kind of self-inventory we ask of our students. In supplementing extant narratives, my pedagogical goal is not to portray American religious history as exclusively violent—for that would be as deceptive as emphasizing harmony alone; nor am I suggesting that simply because we can identify and complicate our students' expectations and presuppositions, we should also dismantle them. Rather, pluralizing the narratives of American religion can unsettle and reframe students' understandings, hopefully resulting in the mutual development (between teacher and students) of a vocabulary that is both rigorous and supple enough to engage the problems presented by recognizing the roles of violence in American religions.

The story of violence is one story among many, and it is one that should not be overdone in our classes. Yet I believe that it merits specific attention in classes on American religion because such a focus can undergird important civic or political goods that can be achieved in the classroom. In this sense, I am an idealist as a teacher, a latter-day Deweyan who believes in the transformative power of classroom conversations and contends further that the skills of the academy, specifically those focused on dialogue and criticism, are those that enable good citizenship in a pluralistic culture. So affinities for pluralism, respect, empathy, and active listening are democratic virtues as well as those of religious studies. And they are hard won, just as is the knowledge that violence runs through American history. But why are they worth such efforts? Are we different, even better, for knowing that Puritans occasionally celebrated the deaths of others as opposed to possibly believing they acted benevolently? Why do we need to know such things, to develop a language for violence?

I suggest first that we need a language for violence, not to be used in writing violence out of our narratives or in suggesting that it is everywhere, but precisely because it needs to be addressed in its specificity if one is to avoid the temptation of Othering violence through ignoring its significance. Attempts to avoid the interconnection of religion, violence, and politics constitute intellectual or even political dishonesty: such efforts to displace violence and its sources largely express the abiding fear of the proximity of violence, its regularity, its intimate relation to the familiar. Keeping it safely buried in the past, locating it elsewhere in our expressions or conversations, produces comforts but absolves us of the responsibility—intellectual, moral, political—of reckoning with the causes of religious violence.

Considering the intersections of religions, violence, and politics in the United States sharpens these foci as comparative categories in the discipline. But it also usefully encourages the interpenetration of historiography and theory, helping us to think about the role of violence beyond isolated events and traditions, and to investigate violence in its multiple expressions while still employing it as a discrete category. The work to be done on violence in American religious history cannot hope to generate simple answers to the questions I have raised throughout. And yet, as a professor of mine once told me (and as I tell my students each semester), there is something edifying about existing in a meaningful state of confusion, where things taken for granted are suspended, rendered fluid. Raising more questions than answers, and generating a series of terms by which future conversations may be oriented, can not only situate the study of American religious violence alongside previous contributions but also point in new directions for future scholarship. As we work in the space of the classroom, if we together begin to question ourselves and our role in these histories, then perhaps there is something greater than scholarship to be achieved.

Hannah Arendt once wrote that violence is the antithesis of true politics.[30] Does it follow that writing and teaching and talking against violence is a way of achieving some political good? That is certainly what I have been writing about herein. It has always been my hope that by engaging these issues with rigor in my classes, I am contributing to the reduction of the very violence I describe, calling into question some of its central tropes and images with the aim of reducing their power. I try to do this not because I feel teachers should hold up every idol to reveal its feet of clay, nor because I feel unique or exalted in these endeavors. I make these efforts out of my broader pedagogic and democratic commitments, which I regard as largely coterminous. Salman Rushdie insists that "the responsibility for violence lies with those who perpetrate it."[31] But the responsibility for understanding violence lies with all those who would seek to put an end to it. This is why I talk about the bad stuff.

NOTES

1. Tony Edwards has reckoned provocatively with the quandaries surrounding hopes to transform students, laying out five strategies in "The Teacher's Dilemma: Redescription in the Teaching of Religious Studies," *Teaching Theology and Religion* 2/1 (February 1999): 40–44.

2. Sidney Ahlstrom, *A Religious History of the American People*, 2nd ed. (New Haven, CT: Yale University Press, 2004). John Frederick Wilson's *Religion and the American Nation: History and Historiography* (Athens: University of Georgia Press, 2003) is an excellent survey of these transformations in the literature.

3. See, among others, William Hutchison, *Religious History in America: The Contentious History of a Founding Ideal* (New Haven, CT: Yale University Press, 2003); Charles H. Lippy, *Pluralism Comes of Age: American Religious Culture in the Twentieth Century* (Armonk, NY: M.E. Sharpe, 2000); Martin Marty, *The One and the Many: America's Struggle for the Common Good* (Cambridge, MA: Harvard University Press, 1997); and Stephen Prothero, ed., *A Nation of Religions: The Politics of Pluralism in Multireligious America* (Chapel Hill: University of North Carolina Press, 2006).

4. Catherine Albanese, *America: Religions and Religion*, 4th ed. (Belmont, CA: Wadsworth, 2006); and Diana Eck, *A New Religious America: How a Christian Country Has Become the World's Most Religiously Diverse Nation* (New York: Harper Collins, 2002).

5. Examples include texts as wide ranging as John Hall, *Apocalypse Observed: Religious Movements and Violence in North America, Europe, and Japan* (New York: Routledge, 2000); Rosemary Radford Ruether, *America, Amerikkka: Elect Nation and Imperial Violence* (London: Equinox, 2000); Oren Baruch Stier and J. Shawn Landres, *Religion, Violence, Memory, and Place* (Bloomington: Indiana University Press, 2006); and Ann Taves, *Religion and Domestic Violence in Early New England: The Memoirs of Abigail Abbot Bailey* (Bloomington: Indiana University Press, 1989).

6. The most obvious examples of such considerations are well known: Pascal Boyer, *Religion Explained: The Evolutionary Origins of Religious Thought* (New York: Basic Books, 2002); Russell McCutcheon, *Manufacturing Religion: The Discourse on Sui Generis Religion and the Politics of Nostalgia* (New York: Oxford University Press, 2003); Susan Mizruchi, ed., *Religion and Cultural Studies* (Princeton, NJ: Princeton University Press, 2001); Kimberley C. Patton and Benjamin C. Ray, eds., *A Magic Still Dwells: Comparative Religion in the Postmodern Age* (Berkeley: University of California Press, 2000); Mark C. Taylor, ed., *Critical Terms for Religious Studies* (Chicago: University of Chicago Press, 1998); and Thomas A. Tweed, *Crossing and Dwelling: A Theory of Religion* (Cambridge, MA: Harvard University Press, 2006).

7. See Russell McCutcheon's interesting meditations on the "religion and" problem in "Redescribing 'Religion and . . . ' Film: Teaching the Insider/Outsider Problem," in *Teaching Theology and Religion* 1/2 (June 1998): 99–111.

8. See Jonathan Z. Smith, *Relating Religion: Essays in the Study of Religion* (Chicago: University of Chicago Press, 2004).

9. See David Apter, ed., *The Legitimization of Violence* (New York: New York University Press, 1997); and Sudhir Kakar, *The Colors of Violence: Cultural Identities, Religion, and Conflict* (Chicago: University of Chicago Press, 1996).

10. René Girard's *Violence and the Sacred* (New York: Continuum, 2005) and *The Scapegoat* (Baltimore, MD: Johns Hopkins University Press, 1989) remain indispensable in these considerations. For fine resources on religious conflicts in early America, see John Demos, *Entertaining Satan: Witchcraft and the Culture of Early New England* (New York: Oxford University Press, 1983); Timothy Hall, *Contested Boundaries:*

Itinerancy and the Reshaping of the Colonial Religious World (Durham, NC: Duke University Press, 1994); Christine Leigh Heyrman, *Southern Cross: The Beginnings of the Bible Belt* (Chapel Hill: University of North Carolina Press, 1998); and R. Laurence Moore, *Religious Outsiders and the Making of Americans* (New York: Oxford University Press, 1987).

11. Elizabeth Castelli, "Religion after 9/11: Hijack It, Exonerate It, Get over It?" *AAR Spotlight: Teaching Religion and Violence* (October 2003).

12. Bruce Lincoln, "Conflict," in *Critical Terms for Religious Studies*, ed. Mark C. Taylor (Chicago: University of Chicago Press, 1998), 57–58. I also address similar antagonisms in Jason C. Bivins, *Religion of Fear: The Politics of Horror in Conservative Evangelicalism* (New York: Oxford University Press, 2008) and *The Fracture of Good Order: Christian Antiliberalism and the Challenge to American Politics* (Chapel Hill: University of North Carolina Press, 2003).

13. Jean Rosenfeld, "Violence," in *Religion and American Cultures: An Encyclopedia of Traditions, Diversity, and Popular Expressions*, Vol. II, ed. Gary Laderman and Luis Leon (Santa Barbara, CA: ABC-Clio, 2003), 671–80. Similar themes are explored in Mark Juergensmeyer, *Terror in the Mind of God: The Global Rise of Religious Violence*, 3rd ed. (Berkeley: University of California Press, 2003); Jonathan Kirsch, *God Against the Gods: The History of the War Between Monotheism and Polytheism* (New York: Viking Press, 2004); Barrington Moore Jr., *Moral Purity and Persecution in History* (Princeton, NJ: Princeton University Press, 2000); and Rodney Stark, *One True God: Historical Consequences of Monotheism* (Princeton, NJ: Princeton University Press, 2003).

14. Tazim R. Kassam, "Teaching about Religion and Violence," *AAR Spotlight: Teaching Religion and Violence* (October 2003).

15. Ibid.

16. On the theoretical questions associated with such narratives, see Winnifred Fallers Sullivan, "American Religion Is Naturally Comparative," in *A Magic Still Dwells: Comparative Religion in the Postmodern Age*, ed. Kimberly C. Patton and Benjamin C. Ray (Berkeley: University of California Press, 2000); and Thomas A. Tweed, ed., *Retelling U.S. Religious History* (Berkeley: University of California Press, 1997).

17. Isaac Kramnick and R. Laurence Moore, *The Godless Constitution: A Moral Defense of the Secular State*, updated ed. (New York: Norton, 2005).

18. See William Lee Miller, *The First Liberty: America's Foundation in Religious Freedom* (Washington, DC: Georgetown University Press, 2003).

19. This portrait emerges as more complicated in Frank Lambert, *The Founding Fathers and the Place of Religion in America* (Princeton, NJ: Princeton University Press, 2006).

20. On nostalgia and forgetting, see Stephanie Coontz, *The Way We Never Were: American Families and the Nostalgia Trap* (New York: Basic Books, 2000); Michael Kammen, *Mystic Chords of Memory: The Tradition of Tradition in American Culture* (New York: Vintage, 1993); and Daniel Marcus, *Happy Days and Wonder Years: The Fifties and Sixties in Contemporary Cultural Politics* (New Brunswick, NJ: Rutgers University Press, 2004).

21. On Native American conflicts, see Joel W. Martin, *Sacred Revolt: The Muskogees' Struggle for a New World* (Boston: Beacon Press, 1991); and Ronald Niezen, *Spirit Wars: Native North American Religion in the Age of Nation-Building* (Berkeley: University of California Press, 2000). On Identity Christianity, see James A. Aho, *The Politics of Righteousness: Idaho Christian Patriotism* (Seattle: University of Washington Press, 1995); and Michael Barkun, *Religion and the Racist Right: The Origins of the Christian Identity Movement* (Chapel Hill: University of North Carolina Press, 1996). On the Branch Davidian standoff, see James D. Tabor and Eugene V. Gallagher, *Why Waco?*

Cults and the Battle for Religious Freedom in America (Berkeley: University of California Press, 1997).

22. Greil Marcus, *The Shape of Things to Come: Prophecy and the American Voice* (New York: Picador Books, 2006), 7.

23. On the changing shapes of patriotism in America, see Cecilia Elizabeth O'Leary, *To Die For: The Paradox of American Patriotism* (Princeton, NJ: Princeton University Press, 1999).

24. See Mark Noll, "The American Revolution and Protestant Evangelicalism," *Journal of Interdisciplinary History* 23/3 (Winter 1993): 615–48.

25. On Nativism, see John Higham, *Strangers in the Land: Patterns of American Nativism, 1860–1925* (New Brunswick, NJ: Rutgers University Press, 2002). See also Frederic Jaher, *Scapegoat in the Wilderness: The Origins and Rise of Anti-Semitism in America* (Cambridge, MA: Harvard University Press, 1994).

26. See Michael Cobb, *God Hates Fags: The Rhetorics of Religious Violence* (New York: New York University Press, 2006); and Michael Lienesch, *In the Beginning: Fundamentalism, the Scopes Trial, and the Making of the Antievolution Movement* (Chapel Hill: University of North Carolina Press, 2007).

27. See Tom De Luca and John Buell, *Liars! Cheaters! Evildoers! Demonization and the End of Civil Debate in American Politics* (New York: New York University Press, 2005).

28. I borrow this term from Thomas A. Tweed, *Crossing and Dwelling: A Theory of Religion* (Cambridge, MA: Harvard University Press, 2006).

29. Particularly useful to my reflections here is Eugene V. Gallagher's "Responding to Resistance in Teaching about New Religious Movements" in David Bromley's fine volume *Teaching New Religious Movements* (AAR Teaching Religious Studies Series) (New York: Oxford University Press, 2007), 273–90.

30. See Hannah Arendt, *On Violence* (Orlando, FL: Harvest Books, 1970).

31. Rushdie, *In Good Faith*, quoted in Greil Marcus, *The Shape of Things to Come*, 5.

BIBLIOGRAPHY

Ahlstrom, Sidney. *A Religious History of the American People*, 2nd ed. New Haven, CT: Yale University Press, 2004.

Aho, James A. *The Politics of Righteousness: Idaho Christian Patriotism*. Seattle: University of Washington Press, 1995.

Albanese, Catherine. *America: Religions and Religion*, 4th ed. Belmont, CA: Wadsworth, 2006.

Apter, David, ed. *The Legitimization of Violence*. New York: New York University Press, 1997.

Arendt, Hannah. *On Violence*. Orlando, FL: Harvest Books, 1970.

Barkun, Michael. *Religion and the Racist Right: The Origins of the Christian Identity Movement*. Chapel Hill: University of North Carolina Press, 1996.

Bivins, Jason C. *The Fracture of Good Order: Christian Antiliberalism and the Challenge to American Politics*. Chapel Hill: University of North Carolina Press, 2003.

———. *Religion of Fear: The Politics of Horror in Conservative Evangelicalism*. New York: Oxford University Press, 2008.

Boyer, Pascal. *Religion Explained: The Evolutionary Origins of Religious Thought*. New York: Basic Books, 2002.

Castelli, Elizabeth. "Religion after 9/11: Hijack It, Exonerate It, Get over It?" *AAR Spotlight: Teaching Religion and Violence* (October 2003).

Cobb, Michael. *God Hates Fags: The Rhetorics of Religious Violence*. New York: New York University Press, 2006.

Coontz, Stephanie. *The Way We Never Were: American Families and the Nostalgia Trap*. New York: Basic Books, 2000.

De Luca, Tom, and John Buell. *Liars! Cheaters! Evildoers! Demonization and the End of Civil Debate in American Politics*. New York: New York University Press, 2005.

Demos, John. *Entertaining Satan: Witchcraft and the Culture of Early New England*. New York: Oxford University Press, 1983.

Eck, Diana. *A New Religious America: How a Christian Country Has Become the World's Most Religiously Diverse Nation*. New York: Harper Collins, 2002.

Edwards, Tony. "The Teacher's Dilemma: Redescription in the Teaching of Religious Studies." *Teaching Theology and Religion* 2/1 (February 1999): 40–44.

Gallagher, Eugene V. "Responding to Resistance in Teaching about New Religious Movements." In *Teaching New Religious Movements*, ed. David G. Bromley, 273–90. AAR Teaching Religious Studies Series. New York: Oxford University Press, 2007.

Girard, René. *The Scapegoat*. Baltimore, MD: Johns Hopkins University Press, 1989.

———. *Violence and the Sacred*. New York: Continuum, 2005.

Hall, John. *Apocalypse Observed: Religious Movements and Violence in North America, Europe, and Japan*. New York: Routledge, 2000.

Hall, Timothy. *Contested Boundaries: Itinerancy and the Reshaping of the Colonial Religious World*. Durham, NC: Duke University Press, 1994.

Heyrman, Christine Leigh. *Southern Cross: The Beginnings of the Bible Belt*. Chapel Hill: University of North Carolina Press, 1998.

Higham, John. *Strangers in the Land: Patterns of American Nativism, 1860–1925*. New Brunswick, NJ: Rutgers University Press, 2002.

Hutchison, William. *Religious History in America: The Contentious History of a Founding Ideal*. New Haven, CT: Yale University Press, 2003.

Jaher, Frederic. *Scapegoat in the Wilderness: The Origins and Rise of Anti-Semitism in America*. Cambridge, MA: Harvard University Press, 1994.

Juergensmeyer, Mark. *Terror in the Mind of God: The Global Rise of Religious Violence*, 3rd ed. Berkeley: University of California Press, 2003.

Kakar, Sudhir. *The Colors of Violence: Cultural Identities, Religion, and Conflict*. Chicago: University of Chicago Press, 1996.

Kammen, Michael. *Mystic Chords of Memory: The Tradition of Tradition in American Culture*. New York: Vintage, 1993.

Kassam, Tazim R. "Teaching about Religion and Violence." *AAR Spotlight: Teaching Religion and Violence* (October 2003).

Kirsch, Jonathan. *God Against the Gods: The History of the War Between Monotheism and Polytheism*. New York: Viking Press, 2004.

Kramnick, Isaac, and R. Laurence Moore. *The Godless Constitution: A Moral Defense of the Secular State*, updated ed. New York: Norton, 2005.

Lambert, Frank. *The Founding Fathers and the Place of Religion in America*. Princeton, NJ: Princeton University Press, 2006.

Lienesch, Michael. *In the Beginning: Fundamentalism, the Scopes Trial, and the Making of the Antievolution Movement*. Chapel Hill: University of North Carolina Press, 2007.

Lincoln, Bruce. "Conflict." In *Critical Terms for Religious Studies*, ed. Mark C. Taylor, 55–69. Chicago: University of Chicago Press, 1998.

Lippy, Charles H. *Pluralism Comes of Age: American Religious Culture in the Twentieth Century*. Armonk, NY: M.E. Sharpe, 2000.

Marcus, Daniel. *Happy Days and Wonder Years: The Fifties and Sixties in Contemporary Cultural Politics.* New Brunswick, NJ: Rutgers University Press, 2004.

Marcus, Greil. *The Shape of Things to Come: Prophecy and the American Voice.* New York: Picador, 2006.

Martin, Joel W. *Sacred Revolt: The Muskogees' Struggle for a New World.* Boston: Beacon Press, 1991.

Marty, Martin. *The One and the Many: America's Struggle for the Common Good.* Cambridge, MA: Harvard University Press, 1997.

McCutcheon, Russell. *Manufacturing Religion: The Discourse on Sui Generis Religion and the Politics of Nostalgia.* New York: Oxford University Press, 2003.

———. "Redescribing 'Religion and . . .' Film: Teaching the Insider/Outsider Problem." In *Teaching Theology and Religion* 1/2 (June 1998): 99–111.

Miller, William Lee. *The First Liberty: America's Foundation in Religious Freedom.* Washington, DC: Georgetown University Press, 2003.

Mizruchi, Susan, ed. *Religion and Cultural Studies.* Princeton, NJ: Princeton University Press, 2001.

Moore, Barrington, Jr. *Moral Purity and Persecution in History.* Princeton, NJ: Princeton University Press, 2000.

Moore, R. Laurence. *Religious Outsiders and the Making of Americans.* New York: Oxford University Press, 1987.

Niezen, Ronald. *Spirit Wars: Native North American Religion in the Age of Nation-Building.* Berkeley: University of California Press, 2000.

Noll, Mark. "The American Revolution and Protestant Evangelicalism." *Journal of Interdisciplinary History* 23/3 (Winter 1993): 615–48.

O'Leary, Cecilia Elizabeth. *To Die For: The Paradox of American Patriotism.* Princeton, NJ: Princeton University Press, 1999.

Patton, Kimberley C., and Benjamin C. Ray, eds. *A Magic Still Dwells: Comparative Religion in the Postmodern Age.* Berkeley: University of California Press, 2000.

Prothero, Stephen, ed. *A Nation of Religions: The Politics of Pluralism in Multireligious America.* Chapel Hill: University of North Carolina Press, 2006.

Rosenfeld, Jean. "Violence." In *Religion and American Cultures: An Encyclopedia of Traditions, Diversity, and Popular Expressions*, Vol. II, ed Gary Laderman and Luis Leon, 671–80. Santa Barbara, CA: ABC-Clio, 2003.

Ruether, Rosemary Radford. *America, Amerikkka: Elect Nation and Imperial Violence.* London: Equinox, 2000.

Smith, Jonathan Z. *Relating Religion: Essays in the Study of Religion.* Chicago: University of Chicago Press, 2004.

Stark, Rodney. *One True God: Historical Consequences of Monotheism.* Princeton, NJ: Princeton University Press, 2003.

Stier, Oren Baruch, and J. Shawn Landres. *Religion, Violence, Memory, and Place.* Bloomington: Indiana University Press, 2006.

Sullivan, Winnifred Fallers. "American Religion Is Naturally Comparative." In *A Magic Still Dwells: Comparative Religion in the Postmodern Age*, ed. Kimberly C. Patton and Benjamin C. Ray. Berkeley: University of California Press, 2000.

Tabor, James D., and Eugene V. Gallagher. *Why Waco? Cults and the Battle for Religious Freedom in America.* Berkeley: University of California Press, 1997.

Taves, Ann. *Religion and Domestic Violence in Early New England: The Memoirs of Abigail Abbot Bailey.* Bloomington: Indiana University Press, 1989.

Taylor, Mark C., ed. *Critical Terms for Religious Studies.* Chicago: University of Chicago Press, 1998.

Tweed, Thomas A. *Crossing and Dwelling: A Theory of Religion.* Cambridge, MA: Harvard University Press, 2006.

———, ed. *Retelling U.S. Religious History.* Berkeley: University of California Press, 1997.

Wilson, John Frederick. *Religion and the American Nation: History and Historiography.* Athens: University of Georgia Press, 2003.

CHAPTER 11

M. K. Gandhi: A Postcolonial Voice

PAUL YOUNGER

For the past thirty years a course called Mohandas Gandhi's Life and Thought has been taught in our university in Canada. Although it is taught within the Religious Studies Department, it is considered a thematic course, which means that it has no prerequisites and is expected to appeal to a wide range of student interests. Many thematic courses last only a few years, but enrollment in this course has grown steadily over the years and is now limited by the university to 150 students. The main reason for the growing interest in the course is that students with South Asian backgrounds now make up a significant percentage of the university population, and, especially since 2001, they have shown a determined effort to understand the role violence and religion play in South Asian societies.

In Canada, people of South Asian background are encouraged to create their own cultural enclaves as part of the multicultural society, and for some groups, such as the Sikhs and Sri Lankan Tamils, that sometimes means remaining actively involved in day-to-day political contact with the homeland. On the other hand, Muslims from Pakistan and Bangladesh and both Muslims and Hindus from India tend to avoid the day-to-day politics of the nation-state from which their ancestors came. For all, the deeper question is, "What were the historical circumstances that allowed religion and the threat of violence to get so deeply involved in the political life of the nations of South Asia?"

This particular way of framing the issue should be identified as one that arises within the Canadian branch of the Indian diaspora, which in turn is one segment of the postcolonial world of South Asia. By going back to some of the foundational questions of that world, as Mohandas Gandhi saw them, the students feel they gain a perspective on their cultural heritage that makes their own choices about the role of religion or violence clearer. What this does to the course itself is to turn it into an open dialogical conversation. The instructors tell the students something about Gandhi's views, and they tell the instructors how his views impact theirs. Because we try to present his views as the end product of an extended conversation with both the colonial rulers and other voices within the Indian community, the conversational atmosphere in which the course is held brings the sense of agency into the present time. The students often sum up this atmosphere by saying: "This is the only course I have that is about the real world" or "This course was a life-changing experience."

When I teach this course, I follow the lead of scholars such as Leela Gandhi (*Postcolonial Theory*, 1998), Ashis Nandy (*The Bonfire of Creeds*, 2007), and Susan Abraham (*Identity, Ethics and Nonviolence in Postcolonial Theory*, 2007) and interpret M. K. Gandhi as an early postcolonial thinker, someone who understood the challenges that would be involved in forming a nation-state within the Indian subcontinent. His great manifesto in this regard is the little booklet *Hind Swarāj*, which he wrote in 1909 on a ship returning to South Africa after months of waiting in London for the colonial authorities to guarantee the rights of the Indians of South Africa, and months of bitter conversation with V. D. Savarkar, the "other" prominent postcolonial Indian voice at the time.[1] Even at this early date, the lines of this triangular debate were clearly drawn, and the colonial and postcolonial voices involved had already found the vocabulary in which their long drawn out arguments would be conducted.

A careful reading of Gandhi's 1909 manifesto allows the students to see what he thought the limits of the debate were and who he thought his real enemy to be. The colonial era was a difficult one for Indians of Gandhi's generation because India had been under colonial rule for generations and people understood that they had no vocabulary in which to analyze their situation other than the one that had been bequeathed to them by those who despised their culture. Gandhi's autobiography, even though written in the 1920s, seems to begin with politically innocent vocabulary as he recalls how his mother and father went about their lives and how he went about his as he allowed the landladies of Britain to teach him the routines of adult behavior. Only in his account of life in South Africa do the students begin to realize that an alternative consciousness is trying to find a way to express itself through this story. When Gandhi writes a polite letter to the railway authorities after the brute force of colonial violence threw him off the train in Pietermaritzburg, we begin to listen to this new voice. A few days later, in a gesture that would eventually differentiate him from Savarkar and other postcolonial voices, he called a meeting of all Indians in Pretoria and asked how they "imagined" themselves when they had to deal with the kind of violence he had just suffered at the hands of the railway authorities. By the time he met Savarkar in 1908, Mohandas Gandhi had been in South Africa for fifteen years. During that time, he had taken many daring steps to challenge the colonial authorities and had been instrumental in the development of a vibrant and new community identity among the Indians of South Africa. A few years later, as he set his face to return to India in 1915, he recognized that he would have to flesh out a full postcolonial worldview if his voice was to prevail in the complex fight against colonial thought just beginning in India.

While Mohandas Gandhi himself was not a systematic thinker and preferred to surprise those around him with well-thought-through "actions" or karma, it is clear that, by the time he returned to India, he had recognized how difficult the challenge was and had ways of dealing with matters sociological, religious, and political that were consistent and had far-reaching implications. In matters sociological, Ashis Nandy describes Gandhi's initiatives as "a continuous attempt to change the definitions of centre and periphery in Indian society."[2] Gandhi had learned in South Africa how hard it is for a diverse population group to become what Benedict Andersen would later call an "imagined community." When he returned to India, he carefully arranged all his actions so that he had both time and occasion to discover how the imagination of every distant corner of Indian society was making its contribution. In matters religious, the negative work of the Orientalist critique had had more opportunity to force the issue, and the sensitivities of an elite group like the Chitpavan Brahmins that Savarkar represented were deeply hurt and prepared to answer back with simple physical violence. Gandhi once again went to the periphery and encouraged those there to answer in their own voice. Finally, in matters of politics, Gandhi was from the beginning suspicious of the "nation-state" because of its close links with the colonial monster everyone was trying to get rid of. He knew, however, that nationalism had at least an interim role in raising the enthusiasm of the community, and he was only partially successful in helping people see what the dangers of nationalism were and what a postnational world might look like. As we watch how Gandhi opposed the Chitpavan Brahmin leadership in each of these areas, I try to give the Canadian students of South Asian background an opportunity to figure out why the postcolonial debates were so complicated in the South Asian context, and why some groups still turn to violence long after the postcolonial era has begun. In the next three sections, I outline how our course presents the nature of Gandhi's conversations with the colonial authorities and with his postcolonial contemporaries in the three areas of sociology, religion, and politics. Sometimes the students find these accounts specific to the period in which the discussions took place, and at other times they recognize the issues as ones that continue to impact on their lives.

SOCIETY

Because of India's geographical isolation, the sociology of India is distinctive in certain ways, and observers sometimes conclude that patterns of family, caste, and region changed very little as a result of the social disruption associated with the colonial era. While that kind of long-range perspective has some validity, it must also be remembered that the Orientalist critique of Indian society launched by the colonial rulers focused (one might almost say mischievously) on the role of women, the role of caste, and the effeminate or martial characteristics the colonizers thought they saw in the various regions.[3] Discussion of these social issues was crucial in the overall postcolonial debate because the British thought their criticisms of India on these grounds were fatal, and Gandhi felt that their criticisms were based on misinformation and were for the most part mistaken. Many other Indians felt the sting of the British criticisms and were inclined to react defensively. While the specific social issues of the colonial era have not been reproduced in the debates diaspora Indians have been having with their host societies, the students find Gandhi's way of redefining these issues before answering them an interesting model for approaching the social controversies they do find themselves engaged with in the diaspora.

In seeking to establish its own adventurous and brave masculinity, the colonial ideology made all colonized Others either "female" or "childlike," but in the Indian case it tended to interpret the tolerance of colonial rule as evidence of an effeminate cultural fabric. Rather than allowing its imagination to reflect on this impression and learn something about the role of women in different parts of Indian society, the colonial logic assumed that in such a "primitive" setting women were badly treated. It particularly focused on unfamiliar customs such as the *devadāsīs*, who served as endowed specialists in temple ritual, and the *satīs*, who chose to immolate themselves along with their husbands, and called for legislation to abolish what it considered those extreme forms of gender oppression.

In Bengal, where both the effeminate characterization and the quarrel over *satī* were focused, both cultural and political controversies over gender raged for some time. As long as the question about the role of women was asked in the colonial way, and concentrated on the question of legislation, an Indian leader such as Ram Mohan Roy found himself with little choice but to support the legislation banning *satī*.[4] As an artist, Bankim Chandra Chatterjee had more time to find his voice, and his hymn, "Bande Mātaram" (Hail to the Mother), equated the land of Bengal (later understood as all of India) with a mother goddess, for whom the ascetics of the story were happily prepared to spill their blood.[5] Vivekananda, a generation later, was still mixing philosophical lectures on Vedanta with calls for India to show her "manhood" by asserting her spiritual superiority.[6]

By the beginning of the twentieth century, however, the leadership of the anticolonial struggle had shifted to Maharashtra, and the Chitpavan Brahmin leadership was much less confident in addressing the controversy over gender than the Bengalis had been. Chitpavan Brahmins, such as B. G. Tilak and V. D. Savarkar, were always aware that their great-grandfathers had served in the Peshva Brahmin government of Maharashtra, the one Brahmin government in Indian history, before it had been overthrown by the British in 1818. They, like the British, wanted to believe that they had the proper masculinity and martial tradition to make them natural rulers. While both Tilak and Savarkar borrowed the phrase "Mother India" from Bengal to boost their nationalist rhetoric, they desperately avoided the gender issue, and in their voluminous writings never referred to either their mother or wife as having any role in their political struggles.[7] As we will see when we go on to discuss the politics of caste and region, this social conservatism limited the options the Chitpavan Brahmin voice would have as the debate with the colonial rulers moved into the realms of religion and politics.

Gandhi was fortunate in that he first learned about how gender issues might be posed in colonial-era discourse from the gentle landladies he encountered during his student days in Britain.[8] By the time he arrived back in India permanently in 1915, he was able to ignore the early questions about reform legislation and to playfully topple the Orientalist logic on gender back into the nervous hands of those who had tried to use it as a cultural bludgeon a century earlier. In the culturally calmer context of the twentieth century he could carefully provide the world with extensive accounts of the roles of his mother and wife. He then went on and set aside the common Indian reaction to the British charge that Indians were effeminate by making a counterclaim of masculinity. Instead, using the more open language of the postcolonial world to come, he simply ignored the Orientalist criticism and defined his role as essentially a feminine one and insisted that he had found the women around him to be stronger than men and the heart of his political movement.[9] In his view, women were no longer objects to be governed and protected in this way or that, but subjects leading the effort to define the political forms of the future. In setting forth his views on this social issue, Gandhi had already undermined the colonial obsession with its masculinity and its natural right to use violence, but, more important, he had undermined Savarkar's nervous dream of outdoing the colonizers in this regard by enabling his secret society members to sacrifice their own safety as they made homemade bombs and surprised the world with their penchant for violence.[10]

The students in the course find this aspect of Gandhi's conversations with his British and Indian contemporaries a surprise. They recognize that the colonial-era thinking that linked masculinity and violence so closely was based on a special logic that is no longer widely accepted. At the same time, gender issues continue to haunt their life within the diaspora community and they see the current tensions between feminist theory and postcolonial theory as somehow linked to the discussions of the earlier era.

If the meanest and most self-reflective claim of the colonial Orientalist was that the Indian Other they wanted to create was effeminate, the feature of Indian society that gave them the most difficulty and was the hardest to caricature was the institution of caste.[11] Puzzled at first that these tribelike units of society were not interested in going to war against one another, colonial voices eventually concluded that the whole caste system must have an oppressive pattern. Marx would eventually label that system "the Oriental mode of production" and link it (mistakenly, following studies of China) with despotic state power, and Weber would link it (again mistakenly) with Brahminical priestly control.[12] As it turned out, the colonists did not have to understand this institution of caste very well in order to disrupt it. As soon as textual scholars discovered that there were linguistic similarities between some Indian languages and those of Europe, the door was open for some Indians to claim colonial connections through the back door of race. Brahmins and Kayasthas in Calcutta, Brahmins in Maharashtra, and Brahmins in Madras were suddenly not only Brahmins but also "Aryans" and entitled to an English education and a position of significance in the ruling bureaucracy.

There were now new, "racial" divisions running through Indian society. The new centers of society were within these newly awakened Brahmin enclaves, and the middle castes, lower castes, and especially the South Indians were in the "non-Aryan" darkness. Some non-Aryan leaders, such as Ambedkar for the Dalits or Untouchables and E. V. Ramaswamy Naicker for the Dravidians or South Indians, decided to accept the first part of the colonial logic in the hope that they could then go on and use other Western forms of group formation that encourage minority groups to use the threat of violence to fight for their rights.[13] Chitpavan Brahmins followed B. G. Tilak in trying to shore up this Aryan status by studying the Vedic texts for themselves.[14] They tried to use the racial term Aryan at every opportunity, and, to give themselves a more prominent role in this elite racial community, they pushed the dates of the Vedic texts back to an earlier time and defined the elite community as originating in India.[15]

Gandhi's approach to this caste problem is characteristically complex precisely because he refused to follow the colonial logic in describing it in the first place. He did not understand the land tenure systems in various parts of the country much better than others in his day did, but he knew that they involved some kind of *jaj-mani* or reciprocity between land owner and laborer, and that the tax-hungry colonial rulers had disrupted those relationships by siphoning off the profits from the land as fast as they could.[16] Even more important, he realized that the racially defined divisions the British had introduced served only colonial purposes in identifying an elite of "brown Englishmen" that could enforce colonial authority on their behalf.[17] He knew that the masses of the Indian people would never benefit by that kind of land tax system or that kind of racial division. On these two important social issues, he felt the colonial view of caste was simply wrong, and its actions based on these assumptions were very disruptive to society.

The part of the Indian system that the missionaries had been able to highlight, by cynically concentrating their conversion work in that sector, was the treatment of the very bottom rungs of the social system that they called the "untouchables." Gandhi's effort to address this problem was characteristically postcolonial in that he refused to use the demeaning colonial word for these people and redefined them as Harijans or "God's people," and he undertook a major public effort to change their status. Because most of his effort in this regard came in the 1930s, well after he had been established as the leader of the Indian masses, his work in this area became recognized, both for the social and political awakening it entailed at the time and for the universal political participation it would foreshadow after Independence. Ambedkar's different style of in-group leadership appealed to his own Mahar caste fellows, as well as some others among the castes of low status, which became a challenge to Gandhi's Harijan endeavors at the time.[18] In the later postcolonial analyses, however, both Gandhi and Ambedkar are credited with having set aside the tricky colonial initiatives in this regard. Although the Chitpavan Brahmins continued to fight on in a variety of ways,[19] the colonial plan to elevate the Brahmins by giving them a separate racial identity and then to use them as the English-educated civil service was considered an embarrassment as soon as Gandhi, Ambedkar, and E. V. R. Naicker began to challenge it in the 1920s and 1930s. By the time a democratic government was put in place in the 1940s, full participation from every sector of society was taken for granted, and the colonial experiment with giving Brahmins the leadership role was set aside without any need for social violence.[20]

Colonial tampering with the regional identities of India was thought at the time to have the most potential for producing civil strife. It was assumed in colonial circles that "primordial" loyalties such as language and religion were the natural bases for the formation of nations, and that most societies would follow the example of Europe and fight for nation-states based on those factors. The regional societies of India were a bit of a puzzle in this regard because the colonial authorities could see that they had both deep local loyalties and strong all-Indian loyalties. The colonial strategy was to divide the society wherever possible and see if loyalties based on language or religion would make a military unit fight better or a political unit easier to administer. In dividing Bengal along religious lines in 1905, the British thought they could nip in the bud the growing political restlessness of that region, partly because they still believed the wild Orientalist speculation that the Bengalis had an effeminate culture. By praising the Sikhs as a "martial race," while taking away from them the kingdom they once ruled, the British got some short-term help putting down the 1857 rebellion, but they stirred up a hornets' nest in the northwest without providing any wisdom on whether or not a religious group was entitled to its own nation-state. In the western region, the British effort to divide and rule included issues around history and caste, as well as language and religion, and it was there that the local political imagination was fully stirred and violent forms of anticolonial political activity were seriously discussed.

We have already mentioned M. K. Gandhi's encounter with V. D. Savarkar in London in 1908, just as Savarkar was sending agents of his secret society to various parts of the world with instructions on how to make bombs and blow up a variety of colonial installations. It was a generation earlier that the inspiration for these activities was set in motion when B. G. Tilak (1856–1920) stirred up the first wave of Chitpavan Brahmin resistance to British rule and developed the conviction that Indians could only fight back effectively if they learned to redefine their heritage in terms the colonial power would understand. Tilak's great-grandfather had been a tax collector for the Peshva Brahmin government of the Marathas that was conquered by the British in the second decade of the nineteenth century. Tilak's own parents had died before he got to university, but the bitterness in the family heritage had been passed along, and as a student he was known for quarreling with his British teachers. By 1880, he and some friends thought there should be an alternative to the many missionary schools in the city of Pune, and they opened the "new English school." Less than a year later the teachers of that school became responsible for an English paper, *The Mahratta*, and a Marathi-language paper, *The Kesari*.

Tilak was a restless young man in 1883 when he began to wonder why Hindus made donations for the Muslim procession of Muharram and why there were no equivalent public displays of Hindu faith. Using the opinion pages of the two newspapers, he and his friends launched an annual Ganesha Festival that quickly became popular throughout Maharashtra. The festival included processions from town to town and was characterized by political speeches and stirring music. It gradually became a kind of national festival for that region. By 1894, the festival was the occasion for sparking major riots between Hindus and Muslims. Instead of looking for ways of avoiding trouble in the future, the next year Tilak responded to the controversy around the riots by initiating the more directly political Shivaji Festival to honor the legendary seventeenth-century Hindu king of that region.

During the preparation for this new festival, Tilak wrote in his newspaper that the legendary act in which Shivaji stabbed the Muslim ruler, Afzal Khan, during a private meeting was justified in that it brought about a higher good. By 1897, as famine swept through Maharashtra and the British stubbornly proceeded to celebrate Queen Victoria's jubilee, two brothers heeded the logic of Tilak's newspaper articles about Shivaji's act and shot two British officials as they celebrated the jubilee. Tilak spent two years in prison for what he wrote in this context, and the brothers were hung in 1899.

Hearing of the violent act of the two brothers, the sixteen-year-old V. D. Savarkar in nearby Nasik took a vow to continue their work. He had already led a stoning of the local mosque at ten years of age after he heard about Hindu-Muslim riots in north India, and at sixteen he organized a secret society called the Mitra Mela or Group of Friends that had its own distinctive dress and vowed to defend "Aryans" or "Hindus." By 1904, he was in Fergusson College, Pune, and meeting regularly with B. G. Tilak. By then his secret society was called the Abhinava Bharat or Young India and was trying to spread its revolutionary ideas all over India. By 1906, Tilak had arranged for Savarkar to receive funding from Pandit Shyamji, who operated the India House for Indian students in London, and it was soon from London itself that the bomb-making schemes and various terrorist acts were being arranged.

Gandhi was appalled by what he saw among the Abhinava Bharat group in London. He was finding in South Africa that it takes enormous courage to challenge colonial tyrants that claim to be the pinnacle of all civilization, but he profoundly believed that the Indian people would be no better off if they replaced that form of tyranny with a tyranny of their own. He understood that the Chitpavan Brahmins felt a special need to retaliate against the Peshva's defeat at the hands of the British, but Gandhi saw the violent actions being planned in London as blind forms of retaliation against randomly chosen examples of British power. He could not see how they could be understood as being taken on behalf of the Maharashtrian people, let alone the Indian people. Savarkar had met some other elites from other parts of India during his time in London, so the Chitpavan Brahmin base had expanded somewhat, but these individuals were still not part of local Indian communities and would not be in a position to create a new India by their actions. The "Hindu community" that the rationalist Savarkar was now working for was an empty category defined only by its opposition to a Muslim presence in India, and Gandhi realized that unless the postcolonial discussion about the future could be handed on to a wider community, "India" would never come into being.

Gandhi himself was busy in South Africa for some more years, and he could only hope that the annual meetings of the weakened Indian National Congress would keep discussions going until some new social movements would come into place. When he did get back to India, he carefully traveled the country and studied what was going on in different regions and different levels of society. Fortunately for him, the first people that really needed him were the peasants of Champaran in the north Indian state of Bihar. Working with these impoverished folk, who were obliged to grow indigo when they did not even have food to eat, stirred not only his imagination but that of the entire country. In an important sense, a postcolonial

Indian community was born the moment that event took place. While it would be decades before the redefining of the role of religion would be complete and a nation-state would be achieved without the use of violence, the inclusiveness that would characterize postcolonial India was imagined for the first time as news spread about what was happening in Champaran.

The characteristics of postcolonial Indian society are now largely taken for granted. Debates about gender roles are more or less similar to those in other parts of the world. Castes of all kinds actively engage in an ever-changing economic and political scene. And, while there are unresolved problems about religion and nationalism that I discuss next, the early fear that the regions would constantly be at war with one another has proven wrong. What Gandhi recognized about the initiatives the colonial authorities were taking in these sociological areas was that they did not know what they were doing. They were acting on the basis of their distorted, we would say Orientalist, analysis, and most reasonably thoughtful Indians were, like Gandhi, trying to ignore their analysis and pushing back against their efforts to meddle. The problem was that other Indians wanted to retaliate against the insults and violence the colonial social initiatives entailed, and they were inclined to retaliate blindly and with violence. Tilak and Savarkar were personally offended by all three of the colonial social critiques, and they desperately thought that their "masculinity" would be restored if they could once again show that Chitpavan Brahmins were the ones who could restore the "motherland." The fact that they were deep inside the colonial mind-set seemed to them to be an advantage, and, instead of rebuilding ties with their traditional community, they borrowed styles of violence from the colonial arsenal and hoped that would get them some revenge.

By contrast, Gandhi chose to slow down the pace of response and see if it were possible to sidestep these wild colonial initiatives and let the traditions already in place answer the criticisms in due time. Eventually he would, ironically, be known for what appears in retrospect to be radical social initiatives. After all, it was his wife and other women around him that were transforming the role of women; it was his insistence that he would attend only intercaste marriages that challenged the deepest barrier to a transformation of caste; and it was his heroic fight to keep the different regions within the Indian community that marked his final days. Gandhi was able to address each of these troubling social issues with actions that surprised and confused the colonial critics, and in doing so he won the support of the new polity of persons he truly cared about. That growing support was crucial because the postcolonial debates on these social questions turned out to be much easier than those around the more explosive issues of religion and nationalism.

For the students in the course, these discussions of century-old social conflicts can be confusing. The content of the social conflict does not often affect their life in the diaspora, but they recognize the odd nature of the conversation in that the dominant, or Western, voice analyzes and critiques Indian social practice, and Indians are then forced either to fight back in kind or to find a new, postcolonial voice with which to chart a fresh path. Many are surprised to see how effective the postcolonial voice of India was on these social issues, and how thoughtless the original Orientalist critiques now seem.

RELIGION

The colonial attitude to religion is difficult to characterize. The European Enlightenment accompanied the early years of colonialism, and, at the beginning, the East India Company was in charge and was not sure it was a good idea to link religion with the scientific exploration and trade it was interested in. When the British government took over the colony at the beginning of the nineteenth century, it, too, was happy to make the soft rationalism of Benthamite utilitarianism its major excuse for not interfering in other people's culture.

It was, however, not long before a variety of excuses for religious initiatives were found. The first colonial voices most Indians encountered were those of the evangelical missionaries that flooded into the hinterland. These people were a bit of an anomaly. Back in Britain they were already somewhat marginalized by the impact of the Enlightenment, but they were able to skirt that issue in the colony because their schools and hospitals were central to the utilitarian-driven civilizing mission. It was from these people that the Indians first heard the crude and violent criticisms of "idol" worship and the totalizing discussions of "heathen darkness." A somewhat less demeaning, but more confusing, colonial initiative on religion was set in place when the classical European scholars began to study Indian texts and came up with the idea that a tiny bit of Indian religion might be included in the European religious family if the "Aryan invasion" was understood in a certain way. This suggestion eventually set off a seemingly endless need to classify Indian religion into Vedic and non-Vedic, Big Tradition and Little Tradition, Jnana and Bhakti, Sruti and Smriti, Astic and Nastic, and Aryan and Dravidian, and those classifications have become almost the central interest of the scholarly study of Indian religion. A third, even more confusing, colonial initiative in matters of religion had to do with the link that was gradually established between state authority and religion. In spite of the Enlightenment, by the time the British government took over in India it was thought that maybe the empire itself needed divine justification. Once Hegel had placed Christianity at the head of an evolution of religious forms,[21] and cathedrals and cantonment chapels were erected throughout India to provide for the religious practices of the important persons in the colonial hierarchy, the utilitarian basis for colonial rule had been given a distinctly Christian aura. This was a hollow superstructure with little religious content, but it did provide a kind of justification for the naked use of colonial violence.

This threefold barrage of colonial religion worked as a kind of tag-team critique of Indian religion that was very difficult to respond to wisely. The missionaries' conversion efforts had little effect, but their mocking of the much-loved objects of worship stung personally and made the overall civilizing effort of the colonial authorities seem brutal and unfair. The flattering invitation to break up the traditional religious system and have a few elements praised as fitting within a European understanding proved attractive to a few, but responding to that invitation implied that there really was no traditional system and that much religious practice would not provide a sound basis for a postcolonial discussion. It was, however, the link between state power and religion that provided the last crippling blow.

In the mid-nineteenth century this link may have appeared to be idle ceremony, but as the new century started and the prospect of a postcolonial state dawned, it appeared to the Indian leaders to raise many new issues. It would have to be dealt with wisely, partly because it was a political structure that was foreign to the local population, but also because it would somehow have to disappear if the postcolonial state was to serve a religiously diverse population and function as a territorially defined democratic state.

For Indians this three-part barrage of religious questions would indeed prove troubling. Colonial authorities quickly legislated religious institutions and customs such as *devadāsīs* and *satī* right out of existence, and with the missionaries allowed to mercilessly mock the poor education of the village priests and the great number and unusual forms of the images they encountered, it looked for a while as if other religious activities might also be outlawed one at a time. The first responses to these critiques from within the Hindu fold tended to accept the missionary argument that image worship was not a good thing. Ram Mohan Roy, for instance, agreed with the missionaries on this, but he took full advantage of the Aryan link and, following the lead of the Unitarians, established a post-Enlightenment form of religion that he derived from the Vedas. Dayananda Saraswati also agreed with the critique of images, but he tried to imagine how to use the Vedic references to a fire ritual to establish a ritual form that was more clearly linked to India. He also saw how important it would be to challenge the sociology of missionary religion, and so he set up his own religious communities with their own initiation rituals and forms of community education. It was, however, V. D. Savarkar who first recognized the way in which the empire linked religion and the state, and it was he who tried to adopt that formula and set forth a Hindu claim to be the pinnacle of civilization and the religious basis for holding the reins of power. As we will see, he was personally a rationalist who had little interest in the practice of "popular Hinduism," but he did think that a true anticolonial movement would have to cloak itself in primordial religious claims, much as the British did with their state ritual. Looking ahead to a time when there would be a need for a Hindu justification of a nation-state, he launched the Hindutva movement in 1924.[22]

As we saw earlier, Savarkar went to London in 1906 as a twenty-three-year-old and brazenly led a terrorist movement against the British Raj at the height of its power. From 1910 to 1924 he was locked away in the Andaman Island prison, and from 1924 to 1937 he was under house arrest in Ratnagiri and forbidden from taking an active part in politics. It was in 1924 that he published the book *Hindutva* and launched the strange nonreligious defense of the "Hindu community." Savarkar was not a traditionally religious man. During his time in Ratnagiri this part of his rationalist nature was easier to see because many traditional folk came to him with suggestions and he quickly dismissed anything having to do with the keeping of auspicious days or making appeals to traditional deities as superstitions that would inhibit the cause.

What Savarkar's highly rational and modern discourse about Hindutva had really uncovered was a set of unresolved questions around the social issues of defining leadership roles within society. Unlike Tilak, he was not able to do research on the Vedas, but he thought the racial connection and the Aryan identity was central to defining Hinduism, and that it was the racial identity that should define the religion and, in turn, the nation. Over and over he used the terms *race, religion,* and *nation* in a variety of combinations and as synonyms of one another, and then, like other pure racists, he insisted that the polity these terms referred to be "homogenous," with no room for diversity. Not unlike the logic being used in Germany about the same time, Savarkar's actual day-to-day obsession was with the removal of a minority, in this case the Islamic minority, from the Hindu motherland. In spite of his house arrest, he actively pushed the development of the ritual of *suddhi* or reconversion to bring Muslims back into the Hindu fold, and he fiercely opposed every political concession to the Muslim League.

Gandhi was well aware of the three-pronged barrage of criticism the colonial authorities had unleashed against Indian religion, and he was also well aware of the hurriedly put together "reforms" Indians were setting out in the hope of meeting those criticisms halfway. His reaction to this kind of public debate about religion and the political use of religion was that it was inappropriate. He took religion to be a personal matter that involved the cultivation of the soul, and he rarely even used the political labels Hinduism, Islam, or Christianity or engaged willingly in the discussion of the political rights of those so labeled. Gandhi's own religious ideas developed quietly and were influenced by conversations with many different persons. He had listened carefully to his mother, but also to the many Christian and Muslim friends he worked with as he started his work in South Africa. The use of the title *The Story of My Experiments with Truth* to describe his life was his way of stating his conviction that an open, dialogical approach to truth was the way he had chosen to live. While he passed that off as a personal conviction, we also know how fiercely he protected the rights of every religious group to be part of the society and the coming postcolonial nation.

While such an open approach to religious ideas is an essential element of a critical and postcolonial society, Gandhi's personal religious life probably owed more to the commitment he had already made to imagine Indian society as an inclusive one where the periphery functioned as the true center. Gandhi was no elitist, and in religion more than anywhere else he recognized that the wisdom of tradition quite outweighed the calls for "re-form" that might come from those trained up by outsiders to serve the interests of an alien empire. English-educated reformers might pick and choose from the Vedic or non-Vedic branches of tradition, but in the end they would be creating a religious package that was intended to impress someone and not to provide sustenance for the masses who needed it.

The sustenance Gandhi felt he needed as he faced down the political authorities of South Africa he began to find in his own naive reading of the Bhagavad Gītā. Many Hindu teachers have provided "interpretations" of the Gītā in recent years, but Gandhi's translation into Gujarati in the late 1920s, his later *Talks on the Gītā* given to villagers in 1933, and the many allusions to the Gītā in his autobiography made no pretense to be a new interpretation.[23] He actually had little interest in the myth underlying the text and little interest in the philosophical schools' interpretations of the text. Gandhi's use of the text centered on his effort to discuss religious forms of self-discipline.[24] In this regard he adopted the traditional Indian way of understanding the psyche as a hierarchy in which the senses, feelings, and mental activities provide the basis of experience. It is in these three domains that the initial struggles over self-discipline normally rage. Then the higher parts of the psyche, namely the *samskāras* or character marks derived from one's previous karma, the personal character or *ahamkāra*, and the universal wisdom or *buddhi*, provide the ranges of experience that allow the person to approach to the awakened self or *ātman*.[25]

Gandhi took very seriously the role of the senses and feelings, and he experimented endlessly with vows regarding food and sexual habits that he thought might free him from their control. In his view, it is the undisciplined person who resorts to violence. When one simply retaliates against oppression or injustice, one is still operating at the level of the senses, and one has not begun to utilize the higher levels of the psyche to develop a true personality or a *svadharma* (spiritual path). To respond at a higher level is to respond with discipline and to invite a higher level of response from the opponent. Eventually the disciplined person will be capable of acting with *nis kāma karma*, or action that is not motivated by passion. The religion Gandhi finds in the Gītā is a religion of action, and it is only as one learns how that system of action works that one is able to initiate actions of nonviolence or *satyāgraha*.

The section of the course on Gandhi that the students like best is this one. They comb through the Gītā looking for verses they think Gandhi may have interpreted in a certain way, and then search through Gandhi's writings to see if, in fact, they find a reference to that verse. Students from every religious background seem to enjoy this exercise with equal abandon. Later, when they reflect on the fact that students with varying backgrounds were able to participate in this exercise, they often wonder out loud if Gandhi understood the Gītā as a text that belonged to a particular religious community, because they certainly did not as they went about this exercise. Having reached that conclusion, they then sometimes raise the final question in the sequence and ask if postcolonial religion is necessarily pluralistic. They recognize that their participation in this class and in a diaspora community, where they visit each others' places of worship, is pluralistic, but wonder if this result is directly related to the religious direction Gandhi found himself taking soon after he moved to South Africa.[26] These classroom discussions on the Gītā make clear how postcolonial Gandhi's view of religion seems to these students. In the 1920s and 1930s he was deeply involved in the nationalist cause and trying to prove to himself and others that he understood the local religious practice, but the views he expressed in that context still seem to fit comfortably with those of the Indian diaspora students in Canada—of whatever religious background.

The postcolonial discussions on the role of religion were not that clear in the India of the 1930s and 1940s. Many postcolonial theoreticians would argue that a true postcolonial society is almost certainly pluralist in religious practice and should provide a public arena that is religiously neutral. Jawaharlal Nehru, India's first prime minister, held such a position very firmly, and India's Constitution defines the Indian state as secular and provides guarantees of religious neutrality.

One might describe Gandhi's style of religious practice as postcolonial in a softer sense in that it took for granted a religiously plural polity. He was prepared to share examples of verses from the Gītā that he tried to live by with others, and he assumed they might share verses from other texts they tried to live by with him. Most people in the Indian National Congress probably shared his religious style (although few had his range of friends coming from other religious traditions), and they were happy to have the guarantees of religious neutrality written into the Constitution. Others in South Asian society were less comfortable with this formula, and we need to look next at the concerns they had.

Most of the doubts about the Congress's formula for establishing religious neutrality may be traced in some measure to Savarkar's speculations on Hindutva. His view was that centuries of Muslim and British rule centered on the hollow religious ceremonies that went with imperial grandeur, and it was now the Hindus' turn for imperial grandeur. By defining Hindutva as a combination of race, religion, and nation, and insisting that the society be homogenous, he allowed no space for religious minorities. His views were shared by only a small percentage of people within the developing Indian polity, but that minority disagreed with the growing consensus that a postcolonial nation-state would have to be religiously neutral. Such views were, however, forcefully expressed and accompanied with threats of violence, and they made some of the religious minorities of India concerned about their future. What the religious minorities found during the 1930s was that it was not easy to ask for protection within the not-yet-formulated postcolonial polity. Among the three minorities concerned (the Christian minority at the time naively believed that, somehow, the British would look after them), the Buddhists, Sikhs, and Muslims each developed separate strategies for survival, but all three felt that in some sense they would have to appeal to a primordial religious group loyalty if they were going to negotiate a secure special status for their group.

One important religious minority that we tend to forget about was the elite community of Buddhist monks in what was then called Ceylon. The racial speculations of the nineteenth century had awakened them to the bizarre idea that they might be racially different from the non-Buddhists on the island because the inland language of Singhala was a member of the so-called Aryan family of languages, and the Tamil language, used in the coastal areas by later arrivals, was not. Buddhist leaders close to the British began a reform movement to define a purer religious community and get rid of the many religious practices that they shared with the rest of the population and that were not clearly based on the early Buddhist texts written in India.[27] Although the postcolonial state that appeared officially in 1948 seemed to recognize religious and linguistic plurality, some Buddhist leaders adopted the notion—taught to them by British racism and Savarkarite speculations—that a state needed a primordial religious foundation, and they began to introduce legislation about a Buddhist nation with one national language. Given the nonrational nature of the discussion about this new religious and national identity, it is not a surprise that both the state and the minority community of Tamils soon started to debate the matter with guns.[28] A violent civil war was mounted within Sri Lanka that did not end until 2009.

Many students in our class are refugee immigrants to Canada from that war zone, and they feel directly affected by this blind resort to violence.

In the relatively small religious community of the Sikhs, change began to come about when the ex-army officers, who had been influenced by close contact with British traditions, launched a reform movement called the Singh Sabha in the 1920s. They insisted that their formal organizational wing, the Shiromani Gurudwara Prabandhak Committee, be given government-sanctioned control of all the *gurudwāras*, so that they could abolish traditional practices that they felt did not reflect pure and original teachings, and so that they could create a new leadership responsive to centralized control and alert to the new political environment.[29] They were not in a position to ask for a separate nation at the time of Indian Independence in 1947, but, with the whole community resettled in India a few years later, they did ask for a state reserved for themselves. Even though the separate state within the Indian nation-state was formed (ostensibly on the basis of language use), some Sikhs felt a true religion-based nation-state was still needed, and they began to plan for an armed effort to establish the nation-state of Khalistan.[30] Once again, many students in our class feel directly affected by this unresolved problem and wonder if the potential violence they hear about in the youth meetings they attend could not have been avoided if the discussion of options had gone in a different direction.

The most severe blow to the idea of a religion-neutral postcolonial polity was the long struggle to find a way of accommodating the large Muslim minority in South Asia. The initial prospects seemed good, partly because Muslims were not mocked as brazenly as Hindus were in the Orientalist analyses of the colonized people, and most Muslims were well aware that they would be a minority in the postcolonial South Asian world. M. A. Jinnah, the first clearly postcolonial figure in the Muslim community, was recognized from the beginning as an all-Indian figure within the Indian National Congress and was for a long time not even a member of the Muslim League. He had even served as the lawyer for B. G. Tilak during his trial in 1908 and once again in the confusion about granting Tilak a passport to go to Britain in 1918. As time went on, however, Jinnah became concerned about Savarkar's taunt that all Muslims could leave his Hindutva if they wanted. He was also impatient with Gandhi's innocent, but rather traditional, religiosity. He carefully suggested at first that India might be divided into a number of nation-states much as Europe was, but he was soon cornered into a situation where the British said that they would only grant a separate nation-state for Muslims if it were founded on the primordial principles of their religion. He ended up with little choice but to become the reluctant founder of a "Muslim nation" when Pakistan was brought into being in 1947.

The postcolonial confusion that comes from linking the term *Muslim*, which referred to different kinds of polities in earlier eras, with the modern word *nation* has plagued the history of Pakistan, and indirectly India, ever since. When the "nations" of Bangladesh and Pakistan were separated, the postcolonial understanding of nation as a territorially defined community came into play and resolved a major problem. On the other hand, Syed Abūl-'a'lā Maudoodī's call for a shari'ah-based state in Pakistan raises complicated issues about the role of Islam in the whole postcolonial world that are far from resolved. What is most troubling is that discussions of these issues regularly include threats of violence both within and without national borders, and it is very difficult to bring the issue back within the postcolonial conversation. The Muslim students in the class usually agree that defining a nation-state as having an exclusively Muslim identity was a tragic mistake, and that they, as diaspora Muslims, have many more options than their relatives in Pakistan as they continue with this many-faceted conversation.

Gandhi was appalled by what he saw in 1947, partly because of the violence on every side but, more important, because he did not understand how "religion" could have been so redefined by postcolonial events that it now referred not to traditional practices of self-cultivation and the quest for truth, but to a polity's self-label and excuse to use violence against others. By recognizing the mischievous meddling of the colonial authorities in the areas of gender, caste, and region, he had responded wisely to those challenges, brought new understandings of those issues into Indian polity, and given it a much more inclusive sense of itself. One might have argued that in the area of religion he had also responded with postcolonial insight because of his openness to dialogue and the way his simple reading of the Gītā made it unlikely that he would intrude on anyone else's way of life. In fact, however, the very "modern" figures of Savarkar and Jinnah deeply resented his simple traditionalism because it did not seem to take seriously the new way in which the colonial experience had sanctified a wedding of religion with politics. Gandhi had first met Christians among the landladies of London, and their religious practices seemed innocent enough to him. What he had not figured out at the time was how those same Christians had joined in the civilizational critique that mocked Hindu practice and argued that India could never have a coherent polity until it had a new religious base. Others, unfortunately, had concluded that the colonial critique had some basis, and that a new style of religious life could indeed be the handmaiden of a new polity. For Gandhi, that seemed to be the wrong way to go, and he hoped that a careful examination of the nature of the polity taking shape would lead people to turn away from this mistaken colonial and postcolonial linking of religion and the state.

For students in the diaspora, any linking of religion and the state seems outrageous. They live in a pluralist society and as minorities in that situation they are extra sensitive to majority insensitivity to their religious practice. They expect the state to be the enforcer of religious neutrality, and they are usually able to get either the courts or the government to support the minorities in the case of a dispute. They are almost unanimous in the view that the Buddhists of Sri Lanka were mistaken in trying to create a national religious ethos after Independence, but they are not sure that such outdated action is sufficient grounds for the style of violence utilized by the Tamil Tigers, because its violence, in turn, increased the difficulty of finding a new form of polity. The ongoing Sikh and Muslim efforts to find ways of participating in the diverse avenues of postcolonial discourse while not giving up the threat to use violence do get some support from the diaspora students, because, while they disappoint Gandhi, they do reflect the political reality of South Asia where neither religious community has become comfortably integrated into the postcolonial polity.

POLITICS

When Gandhi arrived back in India in 1915, he made no announcement indicating that he was about to get involved in politics. He was busy in what might be called "social activity" as he attempted to assist the Champaran peasants and to recruit soldiers for the British, who were deeply involved in World War I. Indian leaders had been hoping that more power would be given to elected legislatures at the end of the war, and the Montagu-Chelmsford reforms, when announced, seemed to be a step in that direction, even though a small one. Much to his surprise, Gandhi then read in the newspaper that the Rowlatt Acts proposed to keep the limitations on civil freedoms adopted during the war in place, and something within him turned deeply anti-empire and deeply political. He called for a one-day boycott of all public activities for March 30, 1919 (later postponed to April 6) to demonstrate the all-India opposition to this arbitrary action of the imperial power, and the boycott was upheld in every corner of the country. Gandhi's political engagement was underway.

The British government's decision to take over the rule of India in the early nineteenth century was the most calculated of the many colonial decisions made during that century. The debates in Parliament were extensive and the decisions to use military might to finish the conquest of the country and to use English education to create an elite corps of administrators to reform and manage the country were carefully taken. The Orientalist assumptions about the weaknesses of the Indian polity have been alluded to earlier, but they essentially held that because of caste and an effeminate cultural outlook, India had not been able to develop a rational view of political responsibilities and no effective system of political life had been developed. Given this political opportunity, the British had hastened to push the last of the Mughals off their throne, take down the two remaining regional empires of the Sikhs and the Marathas, and make treaties with the dozens of local kings who continued to have ceremonial control in certain regions.

Once the colonial rulers had established this vast empire, those who served it worked with utilitarian zeal to make it as efficient as any great polity could be, and the police, tax collectors, and census takers all took pride in the divine purpose that brought them to this civilizing mission. Those being civilized had never seen this kind of energy devoted to an abstract entity or nation before. While at first this arrangement seemed only odd and intrusive, as the state apparatus became more and more efficient, it became clear that Indians were having all their agency taken from them and the prison doors were being locked. The military and the threat of violence were at the center of this colonial arrangement, and when elements of the military mutinied in 1857, a crude and embryonic counternationalism was born. By 1905, the odd and intrusive colonial state decided to split the region of Bengal into its urban Hindu west and its rural Muslim east. Those being manipulated in this way awoke and said that Indians, too, could have a national consciousness and would one day rule themselves. From that moment on, every action of the colonial authorities felt oppressive to the Indian, and it was only a matter of time until a postcolonial state would be brought into being.

The Indian conversations about a postcolonial state were long and complicated. As we have said already, the first aspiration for Indian independence came out of the bitter protests against the decision to divide Bengal in 1905. At the Indian National Congress meeting of 1906, however, two very different pictures of how that aspiration might be realized were set forth in what came to be called the camps of the Moderates and the Extremists. The Moderates, led by G. K. Gokhale, recognized that it was the colonial power that had united India in one polity, and they argued that if the British could be convinced to gradually hand over power to elected Indian officials, a healthy Indian polity might come into being without resort to violence. The Extremists, led by B. G. Tilak, held that colonial rule was based on violence, and only violence and Indian-based state structures could form the proper foundation of an Indian state. The nationalist endeavor had not started well, and it got only worse as Tilak was thrown in jail and Gokhale's health started to fail. Gokhale finally died just after Gandhi arrived back in India in 1915.

Gandhi found it hard to know how to proceed. Gokhale had warned him that the anger he had shown in the manifesto *Hind Swarāj* would not be appropriate in the complicated political situation of India. Gokhale had also advised him to travel the country. Gandhi did that, and it gave him a sense of the penchant for action arising from the masses, from whom neither the colonial rulers nor the Congress leaders were expecting to hear. Patterns of communication had been changing rapidly, and everyone seemed to have heard about the mass rallies of 1905 and were expecting more.[31] Gandhi knew he needed some special kind of leverage if he was to put a scare into the colonial power and, more important, if he was to disarm the argument he had first heard in London, that violence was the answer. What he had been able to do over the past decade was to "imagine a community," as Benedict Anderson would put it later, that was eager to become a nation.[32] When he called for a total boycott on March 30, 1919, he was calling for that community to take action, and it did.

What Gandhi found out the morning after the boycott was that, in India, even more than in South Africa, politics is hard work, and the community's aspirations could not be turned on and off at the leader's convenience. Violence had broken out in a few places, and Gandhi realized how limited the conversation about the true goals of nationhood had been. Just days later, the mass shooting in Jallianwalla Bagh occurred, and it became clear that legislative reforms were not going to matter and that "noncooperation" with this colonial monster was the only way to move forward. Progress would be slow that way, but the posture of Opposition was in place and India was in many ways a new polity from 1919 onward when the boycott gave the people a new voice.

Almost as soon as he had made his commitment to the national urges of the people, Gandhi found himself trying to stave off the voices that saw the nation in very different ways. The nationalist movement had two very different styles of leadership. On the one hand were Indian-educated leaders in every region who stepped forward in 1919, again in 1930 during the Salt March agitation, and once again in 1940 during the Quit India campaign. These were able leaders with deep local roots, and, while they were united throughout the Freedom Struggle, they had a decentralized picture of postcolonial India and would help build strong state governments after Independence. Gandhi worked closely with these people.

He had the Muslim scholar Maulana Azad lead the Salt March agitation, and he supported C. Rajagopalachari from the south as the first Indian governor-general, Rajendra Prasad from Bihar as the first president of independent India, and Vallabhai Patel from Gujarat as the first home minister. On the other hand, students educated in the West were regularly arriving back looking for leadership roles. These leaders thought in national terms: they wanted to take over the nation-state that had already been established by the British; they wanted to do so quickly; and, if need be, they were prepared to use violence. Gandhi was a kind of mediator between these two groups. While he had a natural political alliance with the first group in that he, like they, had good contacts with the masses of the people in all regions of the country, he was also well aware of the reasons for the impatience of those arriving back from the West. In order to see his growing doubts about the long-term benefits of nationalism, we need to look at some of the conversations he had with this latter group.

Savarkar, of course, was a member of this latter group that Gandhi had come to know well, and the two of them remained deeply suspicious of one another right to the end. After Savarkar moved from prison to house arrest in 1924, Gandhi paid him a visit, but, if Savarkar's biographer is correct, the visit was mostly a quarrel, with Savarkar taunting Gandhi to help with the *suddhi* effort to reconvert Muslims to Hinduism. Gandhi despised Savarkar's penchant for violence but also thought his idea of redefining Hinduism in the image of an imperial state religion was mistaken and a crippling imitation of colonial policy.

Jawaharlal Nehru had been in Britain at much the same time as Savarkar had, and he became a close associate of Gandhi's when he returned to India in the early 1920s. Like many of the students from abroad, Nehru was fascinated by the polity the British had put together in India, and he simply wanted to speed up the reforms and push the utilitarian secularism the reformist side of British rule entailed. In spite of his reformism, the state Nehru envisioned was a centralized polity, very like the empire itself.[33] Gandhi tried to convince him that there were serious questions about language and religion that would better be decided in a less centralized fashion, but Nehru came to see himself as the agent of history and remained unbending on these cultural issues when he later became prime minister.

While the choices Savarkar and Nehru represented remain symbolic of the choices still before the Indian electorate today, Gandhi's conversations with two other students, returned from Germany and the United States respectively, engaged him more deeply in the theoretical questions surrounding the nationalism of the day. Subhas Chandra Bose was a Bengali raised in the Westernized atmosphere of Calcutta at the beginning of the century, but as a rebellious student, he thought of using religion to mount an anticolonial movement. Instead he went off to Germany and imbibed radical ideas on nationalism. Bose briefly thought that he and Nehru might take over the leadership of the Indian National Congress when he first returned to India in 1929. When he realized that local leadership was reasserting itself and reestablishing its more grassroots style, he returned to Germany for ten years. Arriving back in India in the late 1930s, he immediately moved to take over leadership of the Indian National Congress, and only a determined effort by Gandhi and the local leadership kept that from happening. Bose made his way back to Nazi Germany, organized the Indian National Army with help from both Germany and Japan, and set up a Free India government based in Singapore, where he began planning a military conquest of India. In 1943, the Japanese plane he was in went down, and the fascist-style nationalism he came to believe in died with him.[34]

Jaya Prakash Narayan was a student in the United States when he met leaders of the Communist Party International and became convinced that the way forward for India was not through a takeover of the colonial state but through a true social revolution. He had good contacts among the locally educated youth of India, and after returning he joined with Achyut Patwardhan, R. M. Lohia, J. B. Kriplani, and others to form the Congress Socialist Party as a branch of the Indian National Congress. In Gandhi's mind, this was an ideal arrangement because they were grassroots leaders pushing for grassroots change, but he pointed out to them that the guns they had collected had no role in bringing about social change among the unarmed populace of India, and he argued that mass demonstrations would have a much bigger impact on weakening British rule than a few random assassinations.[35] Narayan especially liked this argument and was soon the underground leader of the Quit India movement sweeping across the country. It was Narayan who would carry forward the critique of the centralized state after Gandhi was shot. In a series of roles, running from Opposition leader, to Bhoodan or land reform leader, to leader of the agitation to bring down the Emergency (the suspension of civil rights implemented by Indira Gandhi in the mid-1970s), Narayan became the symbol for that part of the Indian polity that would remain critical of state power in the postcolonial era.[36]

The final aspect of Gandhi's politics that needs to be given some attention is his internationalism. Gandhi, of course, learned his politics outside of India, and there was never doubt in anyone's mind that while his "experiments with truth" took him deep within the Indian political scene for a long time, he was searching for ways of doing postcolonial politics that should make sense in any part of the world. He kept in close touch with developments in the six societies where Indians had been taken as indentured workers (Mauritius, Guyana, Trinidad, South Africa, Fiji, and East Africa), and he was pleased to find that in each case the Indians remained nonviolent and took an active role in the emergence of a pluralist community that would eventually evolve into a nation-state. Gandhi especially knew about the South African story and the way Mandela was building a multicultural consensus, even though he consciously modified Gandhi's commitment to nonviolence and chose to use violence in certain circumstances.[37]

The drama surrounding Gandhi's death drew international attention to his life in a way that sometimes distorts that story. In India, the death led to a thorough police investigation and the recognition that N. V. Godse, the assassin, was part of a conspiracy that was continuing the long-standing quarrel Gandhi had had with the Savarkar faction of the Chitpavan Brahmin community. In the Indian setting, Gandhi's continuing voice remains true to the postcolonial goals he set for the nation. Some continue to reflect on his voice, while others have come to define those goals differently. In the international community, his story is focused more on the sacrifice symbolized by his death, and he is seen as an uncompromising champion of nonviolence. In this regard Martin Luther King Jr. is often cited as a worthy follower of Gandhi's path, and the fact that he also met a violent death tends to be used as evidence of the similarity. North American students, more often than students with South Asian backgrounds, tend to pick up this part of the story and write papers on how Gandhi serves as a symbol for nonviolent social movements in many parts of the world.

Within the South Asian diaspora community, Gandhi is available both as a thoughtful model of postcolonial thinking and as a symbol of a peaceful pursuit of mutual understanding that they can offer to the society in which they now live. In Canada, where there are more or less equal numbers of Sikhs, Muslims, and Hindus, the discussions in the university are often about how all South Asian religious groups are developing into a common community. The popular explanations for the emergence of this new sense of community have to do with the social life of the high schools and the prominence of fusion music groups and comedians that play up their South Asian backgrounds. The older generation of leaders in the Sikh and Sri Lankan Tamil subcommunities resist the development of this new sense of community because they remain keen to assist those in difficult political situations in the homeland. Although the *dhoti*-clad Gandhi might seem a long distance from the diaspora youth of Canada, Gandhi does often serve as a symbol of this newly emerging community, both in the sense that he had a religious posture that respected pluralism (and, of immediate relevance to some, that he encouraged intermarriage), and he seems like a pioneer in supporting what is now called "human rights" or "minority rights." In Canada it was a *pandit* from a Guyanese temple, Dr. Bupendranath Dubey, who saw the many-sidedness of the Gandhi symbol and led a march across the city to demand that a statue of Gandhi be placed in front of a school. The school board refused, thereby showing the limits of making multiculturalism a public policy, but the statue eventually became the centerpiece of his temple's museum garden and a symbol of the emerging South Asian community of Canada.

CONCLUSION

After September 11, 2001, there was a tendency in the public media to use the term *Muslim* carelessly to describe a whole range of terrorist movements around the world. The scholarly use of phrases like "terror in the mind of God" compounded the murkiness arising from the first usage and left us with a whole set of questions to sort through.[38] Our university's regular course on Gandhi started on September 12 in 2001 and the classroom was packed. Six girls in the front row, wearing *hijab* for the first time, told me that coming to that class was the only thing they could think of doing that would start to sort out their confusion. What these six girls, and the dozens of Muslim males in the back rows, found out is that Gandhi is no antidote to violence, but that his careful discussions with his contemporaries does serve as a model of how one might debate the range of possible actions a person might take.

The idea, sometimes suggested by the public media, that Muslims teach the kind of terrorist violence that is now so prevalent is, of course, nonsense, but it is difficult to explain the sequence of logical mistakes that leads to that kind of nonsense. All the major religious traditions have, of course, been involved at times with ancient empires and with feudal lords who used violence in pursuing their goals. Modern terrorist violence is a different kind of thing in that it arises as a reaction to colonial violence and uses religion only as a shorthand way of giving identity to the group it pretends to speak for. As early as 1908, in his London conversations with Savarkar, Gandhi recognized the nature of this new craze for violence and clearly identified it as a modern phenomenon whose anticolonial intentions might be credible but whose links with traditional religious practice were twisted. He chose at that moment to challenge the pretention of those persons to speak for the emerging Indian polity.

The most important dimension of Gandhi's approach is that he saw religion as part of a social whole. As the above discussion shows, he dealt with social issues, religious issues, and political issues all at the same time. As the community became comfortable about how he was dealing with social issues, they watched more carefully as he addressed religious issues, and then accepted his political leadership as the postcolonial nation-state came into view. Put another way, he did not use his energy to challenge the arguments about the essence of Hinduism, as they were put forward by either the British or the Chitpavan Brahmins. He recognized that the colonial era left massive social destruction in its wake and that rebuilding a society with a healthy range of religious practices and a working polity would require an open form of community building that we would now label postcolonial discourse.

Gandhi's challenge to people like Savarkar or Bose was that when they took a shortcut and seized power in their own hands on behalf of the people, they inevitably had to use violence not only against the colonial power but against those in their own polity who disagreed with them. The colonial power had claimed to have reached a pinnacle of civilization and had adopted ceremonial religious forms that gave credence to that claim, so it seemed natural to those who hoped to simply seize that power that they too would use the name of religion to give credence to their claim. Gandhi undertook a long fight to ensure that Savarkar and his friends would not be able to enforce their will in this way, and while he was killed in that endeavor, the Indian polity appears to have heeded his voice. What might have happened in India without that fight is all too evident in nearby Sri Lanka. There one group did seize power, and it did use religion, in much the same way the colonial rulers had, to define the cultural monopoly it wanted in the nation. Twenty percent of the population were given no place in the polity, and a war of attrition became the inevitable outcome. Had the same thing happened in India, the 20 percent minority would have been Muslim, but the available outcomes would have been much the same.

The final question that continues to bother the students in Canada is "What about Islam?" The Sri Lankan Buddhists had their choices and made the wrong one. The Hindus of India listened to both Savarkar and Gandhi and then chose a secular state. Jinnah found that time was running out and his options were limited, so the nation-state of Pakistan was formed before there was any clear idea of what kind of "imagined community" underlay it. The postcolonial discussion seems to end with one big area unresolved, and considerable violence results from that unfinished discussion. This question of Islam, of course, also brings in a flood of new issues. Osama bin Laden, U.S. policy, global oil strategy, and global warming are issues Gandhi never imagined. What it also brings into view is Gandhi's thoughtful hesitation about nationalism, and his awareness that while nationalism was a good antidote to colonialism, it was certainly not the only basis for a polity. Nationalism seemed to him far too similar to colonialism in the way religion was manipulated and individual rights were curtailed. What the students gradually realize they need is a new set of discussions, not exactly like those on postcolonialism started in 1908, but concerned more with postnationalism and the world the newly powerful nations are likely to leave for the future a hundred years from now.

NOTES

1. The book *Hind Swarāj* is included in *The Collected Works of Mahatma Gandhi* (New Delhi: Publication Division of the Government of India, 1963) as volume 10 and was sometimes republished as *Indian Home Rule*. Gandhi did not name Savarkar in the text, but it is clear with whom he was disagreeing. Dhananjay Keer, Savarkar's biographer, describes the bitter exchanges they had at that time in *Veer Savarkar* (Bombay: Popular Prakashan, 1966), 64.
2. Ashis Nandy, *Bonfire of Creeds* (Delhi: Oxford University Press, 2007), 64.
3. There was a huge volume of literature on Orientalism after Edward Said's seminal book with that name was first published in 1978. Among the books on Indian Orientalism, Ronald Inden's *Imagining India* (Oxford: Blackwell, 1990) is the most comprehensive. I attempt to picture colonial thought as much as possible as Mohandas Gandhi may have heard about it, in the hope that I can represent his responses as accurately as I can. As a scholar who writes from within India but who is well aware of the larger debates, I find Ashis Nandy's writings helpful in getting this in-India perspective on the postcolonial debates.
4. Nandy, *Bonfire of Creeds*, 33–61, provides a detailed account of this debate and Ram Mohan Roy's role in it. Leela Gandhi, *Postcolonial Theory* (New York: Columbia University Press, 1998), 81–101, provides a helpful overview of the links between postcolonial and feminist debates.
5. The novel was published in 1882 and titled *Ānanda Math*, and the hymn became a kind of national anthem during the first anticolonial demonstrations of 1905.
6. The point is made in many different ways throughout *The Complete Works of Swami Vivekananda* (Almora: Advaita Ashram, 1963), but one of the most emotional is vol. 4, p. 413, where he concludes, "Make me a Man!" The current debates around the sexuality of his teacher, Ramakrishna, are no doubt modern echoes of the Bengal sensitivity to the Orientalist's caricature of Indian genders in his day.
7. Their biographies are interesting to read in this regard. In both cases their mothers died in their childhood. Both were also married in the traditional way at fifteen years of age, and their wives lived primarily in their natal homes. Ram Gopal, *Lokamanya Tilak* (Bombay: Asia Publishing House, 1956); and Keer, *Veer Savarkar*. Later in life Savarkar argued that men and women were of different natures and should have different education. He became fascinated with the idea of eugenics and thought women should be bred for beauty and men for strength; Keer, *Veer Savarkar*, 213–14.
8. This part of Gandhi's autobiography (chapters 13–25) is often skipped because it is of little immediate political consequence, but that would be a mistake when we are trying to understand his way of understanding colonial arguments.

9. Gandhi's links with feminine issues are among the most thoroughly analyzed aspects of his life story. See, for instance, Lloyd Rudolph and Susanne Rudolph, *The Modernity of Tradition* (Chicago: University of Chicago, 1967); Ashis Nandy, "Woman Versus Womanliness," in *At the Edge of Psychology: Essays in Psychology and Culture* (Delhi: Oxford University Press, 1980), and "Final Encounter" in *Bonfire of Creeds*.

10. Savarkar's biographer provides details of the excitement of the twenty-year-old Indian males (he describes only one, somewhat older, female Parsi member named Madame Cama) gathered in London between 1906 and 1910 about the sense of daring their terrorist plans gave them: Keer, *Veer Savarkar*, 28–105.

11. Inden provides a thorough review of the many colonial efforts to address this issue: *Imagining India*, 49–84.

12. Karl Marx, *Pre-Capitalist Economic Formations*, trans. Jack Cohen (London: Lawrence and Wishart, 1857, 1964); Max Weber, *The Religion of India*, trans. H. H. Gerth and D. Martindale (Glencoe, IL: Free Press, 1958).

13. Dhananjay Keer, *Dr. Ambedkar: Life and Mission* (Bombay: Popular Prakashan, 1962); Robert Hargrave, *The Dravidian Movement* (Bombay: Popular Prakashan, 1965).

14. *The Orion or Researches in the Antiquity of the Vedas* was published in 1892 and is a very scientific-like effort to date the Vedas on the basis of astrological calculations. His date of 4000 B.C.E.-plus was probably as good a guess as F. Max Muller's of 1200 B.C.E., which was based on a calculation of how long a literary tradition would take to evolve. *The Arctic Home of the Vedas*, published in 1903, involved a different kind of research that included geology.

15. This line of inquiry has continued among a small group of Indians, who apparently think that it will eventually reverse the impact of F. Max Muller's "Aryan invasion theory" and establish India as the original home of, rather than recipient of, Aryan civilization. This line of argument has sparked considerable interest among diaspora Indians in the United States and has become central to the textbook controversies in California and other states. See Prema Kurien, *A Place at the Multicultural Table: The Development of an American Hinduism* (New Brunswick, NJ: Rutgers University Press, 2007). My students in Canada thought these race-based theories were ridiculous even when the argument was carefully laid out for them.

16. Gyanendra Pandey has published a critique of the way Gandhi quieted a budding peasant rebellion in north India between 1919 and 1922 titled "Peasant Revolt and Indian Nationalism," in *Selected Subaltern Studies*, ed. Ranajit Guha and Gayatri Chakravorty Spivak, 233–81 (New York: Oxford University Press, 1988).

17. This phrasing is based on Thomas Macauley's famous Minute on Education during the debate on the India Act in which he said: "We must at present do our best to form a class who may be interpreters between us and the millions whom we govern; a class of persons, Indian in blood and color, but English in taste, in opinions, in morals, and in intellect." Thomas Babington Macauley, *Prose and Poetry* (Cambridge, MA: Harvard University Press, 1952), 729.

18. B. R. Ambedkar went to the Round Table meetings in London in 1931 and demanded separate electorates for the lowest castes, which he eventually came to call Dalits. Nehru made him the chair of the committee that wrote the Constitution, and the reserved parliamentary seats and other forms of reservation were written into the Constitution. In 1956, just before his death, he converted to Buddhism along with millions of his followers, but that move kept them within the emerging national community and avoided a potential occasion for violence.

19. Chitpavan Brahmins were, of course, directly involved in the assassination of Mohandas Gandhi. They are also still prominent in the Hindutva movement, even though serious efforts are now made to make the RSS youth training and the BJP

political party all-Indian institutions. One place where the "Brahminical" style of leadership seems to have reemerged is in the U.S. Indian diaspora, where a minority voice is pushing issues such as Tilak's fight on the "Aryan" links with India.

20. My students in Canada truly seem embarrassed to imagine their grandparents ever having been interested in caste issues. This attitude seems even stronger among those whose names indicate they are of Brahmin background. Very few write papers on this aspect of the course.

21. See W. Halbfass, *India and Europe* (New Delhi: Motilal Banarasi Das, 1981); and Inden, *Imagining India*.

22. There are many polemical accounts of Savarkar's controversial life. I like the 1966 biography of Dhananjay Keer because, while laudatory throughout, it is thoroughly researched.

23. B. G. Tilak had worked on an interpretation while in prison, which he titled the *Gita Rahasya*. It was translated into Gujarati in 1917, and Gandhi tells us he was given a copy and read it, but there is little evidence that he thought of his own work on the Gītā as a challenge to Tilak's. Mahadeva Desai's extensive commentary on Gandhi's translation is sometimes, mistakenly, taken to be a Gandhian interpretation, but Gandhi in the introduction clearly states that it is not.

24. In his introduction to his translation Gandhi says: "This self-realization is the subject of the Gītā, as it is of all scriptures. But its author surely did not write to establish that doctrine. The object of the Gītā appears to me to be that of showing the most excellent way to attain self-realization"; *Translation of the Gītā* (Ahmedabad: Navajivan Press, 1946).

25. I introduce the students to the sevenfold scheme as it is laid out in the Sāmkhya/Yoga system, just so they have one well-formulated system to examine in more detail. I make clear to them that for Gandhi it was a part of Indian philosophy he had probably absorbed early in life and used unselfconsciously. Many of them have chosen to do research papers in this area and are fascinated at how different the assumptions of this hierarchically designed system are from those of the systems they hear about in psychology class. Many students have gone well beyond Gandhi in developing systematic interpretations of the Gītā as a text on ethical discipline.

26. A particularly interesting example of this sequence of thought occurred just last year. A Muslim student raised in East Africa had been reading Gītā verses and wondering about his own ability to use self-discipline and raise his level of response to potential violence to one of the higher levels of the personality. As he waited in a long line to get into the student pub one night, three Muslim students he did not know pushed into the line beside him. Much to his own amazement, he asked them if they were aware they were offending other students nearby who had been waiting a long time. Two were angry and challenged him to go outside, but the third was intrigued and asked him to say more. As this student later explained, he was even more surprised when he later found that he wanted to explain this experience to a classroom made up primarily of non-Muslims. As he said, "I guess I have found a new community."

27. See Richard Gombrich and Gananath Obeyesekere, *Buddhism Transformed* (Princeton, NJ: Princeton University Press, 1988).

28. This civil war is a model of the way religion and violence are linked in the modern postcolonial world of South Asia. As soon as the British left, the majority community began to imitate the colonial model, and soon named Buddhism as the ceremonial religion of the state. They then used its power to demean Tamils by denying some citizenship, others education and civil service positions, and denying all positions in

the armed services. The Tamils were unable to challenge this clique's denial of their rights in a timely way, and the militarily trained Tamil Tigers of Prabakaran stepped forward and began to insist that violence was the only way forward. Other Tamil voices were soon silenced. Although the Tamil Tigers are sometimes referred to as Hindu because they stand against the government effort to define the nation as Buddhist, Prabakaran discourages the use of popular religion and welcomes both Christians and Muslims into his army. Even more than in the cases of the Muslims and Sikhs, his resort to violence follows a very modern style introduced in colonial times. See S. J. Tambiah, *Sri Lanka* (Chicago: University of Chicago Press, 1986); A. J. Wilson, *Sri Lankan Tamil Nationalism* (Vancouver: University of British Columbia Press, 2000); and M. Trawick, *Enemy Lines* (Berkeley: University of California Press, 2007).

29. See H. Oberoi, *The Construction of Religious Boundaries: Culture, Identity, and Diversity in the Sikh Tradition* (Chicago: University of Chicago Press, 1994).

30. See Veena Das, ed., *Mirrors of Violence: Communities, Riots and Survivors in South Asia* (Delhi: Oxford University Press, 1992).

31. From the 1850s the whole country had been tied together with railways and telegraph lines, and newspapers were abundant both in English and in each of the regional languages.

32. In Benedict Anderson's seminal book on nationalism he used the title *Imagined Communities* (London: Verso, 1983) because he wanted to emphasize the role things like print capitalism and international travel played in enabling communities in a given geographical location to imagine themselves as a community, even when they did not necessarily share the older kinds of ties through kin, language, or religion. The older kind of ties were abundant in India, but the new challenge colonialism brought to the scene, by establishing an all-India polity, overrode those ties, and in many ways the process we are discussing does seem to fit Anderson's way of describing the emergence of nationalism. I think Gandhi was a leader who recognized the way in which this polity was in the process of imagining itself and he tried to follow its lead. Martha Kaplan and John Kelly critique Anderson and offer a different approach to the understanding of nationalism in a book they titled *Represented Communities* (Chicago: University of Chicago Press, 2001). They propose that we concentrate directly on the persons who were instrumental in bringing a nation-state into being. Gandhi, Savarkar, Jinnah, and others might be thought of as instrumental in the Indian story, but emphasizing their separate views tends to take us away from the central story, which is how the masses of the people heard the arguments of these representatives and what the polity eventually looked like.

33. Nehru's own self-description and understanding of Gandhi are well presented in his book *Discovery of India* (New York: Day, 1946).

34. Bose's views are clearly laid out in his book *The Indian Struggle 1920–1942* (Bombay: Asia Publishing House, 1942, republished 1964).

35. The author became well acquainted with both J. P. Narayan and Achyut Patwardhan while working with the Bhoodan Movement in 1957–60. Their conversations with Gandhi in the mid-1930s were described in detail by both men in separate conversations.

36. Narayan's mature views are seen best in *Towards Revolution* (New Delhi: Arnold-Heinemann, 1975) and *Prison Diary* (Bombay: Popular Prakashan, 1977).

37. N. Mandela, *Long Walk to Freedom* (New York: Little, Brown, 1994).

38. Mark Juergensmeyer, *Terror in the Mind of God: The Global Rise in Religious Violence* (Berkeley: University of California Press, 2003).

BIBLIOGRAPHY

Abraham, Susan. *Identity, Ethics and Nonviolence: A Rahnerian Theological Assessment*. New York: Palgrave Macmillan, 2007.

Anderson, Benedict. *Imagined Communities: Reflections on the Origin and Spread of Nationalism*. New York: Verso, 1983.

Bose, Subhas Chandra. *The Indian Struggle 1920–1942*. Bombay: Asia Publishing House, 1964.

Das, Veena, ed. *Mirrors of Violence*. Delhi: Oxford University Press, 1992.

Gandhi, Leela. *Postcolonial Theory: A Critical Introduction*. New York: Columbia University Press, 1998.

Gandhi, Mohandas Karamchand. *An Autobiography: The Story of My Experiments with Truth*. Boston: Beacon Press, 1927.

———. *Hind Swarāj: Collected Works of Mahatma Gandhi*. Vol. 10. Delhi: Publication Division of the Government of India, 1963.

———. *Talks on the Gītā*. Ahmedabad: Navajivan Press, 1933.

———. *Translation of the Gītā*. Ahmedabad: Navajivan Press, 1946.

Gombrich, Richard, and Gananath Obeyesekere. *Buddhism Transformed*. Princeton, NJ: Princeton University Press, 1988.

Gopal, Ram. *Lokamanya Tilak*. Bombay: Asia Publishing House, 1956.

Halbfass, Wilhelm. *India and Europe*. Delhi: Motilal Banarasi Das, 1990.

Hargrave, Robert. *The Dravidian Movement*. Bombay: Popular Prakashan, 1965.

Inden, Ronald. *Imagining India*. Oxford: Blackwell, 1990.

Juergensmeyer, Mark. *Terror in the Mind of God: The Global Rise in Religious Violence*. Berkeley: University of California Press, 2003.

Kaplan, Martha, and John Kelly. *Represented Communities: Fiji and World Decolonization*. Chicago: University of Chicago Press, 2001.

Keer, Dhananjay. *Dr. Ambedkar: Life and Mission*. Bombay: Popular Prakashan, 1962.

———. *Veer Savarkar*. Bombay: Popular Prakashan, 1950.

Kurien, Prema A. *A Place at the Multicultural Table: The Development of an American Hinduism*. New Brunswick, NJ: Rutgers University Press, 2007.

Marx, Karl. *Pre-Capitalist Economic Formations*, trans. Jack Cohen, ed. and intro. E. J. Hobsbawm. London: Lawrence and Wishart, 1964.

Nandy, Ashis. *At the Edge of Psychology: Essays in Psychology and Culture*. Delhi: Oxford University Press, 1980.

———. *Bonfire of Creeds*. Delhi: Oxford University Press, 2007.

Narayan, Jaya Prakash. *Prison Diary*. Bombay: Popular Prakashan, 1977.

———. *Towards Revolution*. New Delhi: Arnold-Heinemann, 1975.

Pandey, Gyanendra. "Peasant Revolt and Indian Nationalism." In *Selected Subaltern Studies*, ed. Ranajit Guha and Gayatri Chakravorty Spivak, 233–87. New York: Oxford University Press, 1988.

Rudolph, Lloyd, and Susanne Rudolph. *The Modernity of Tradition*. Chicago: University of Chicago Press, 1967.

Tambiah, Stanley J. *Sri Lanka*. Chicago: University of Chicago Press, 1986.

Trawick, Margaret. *Enemy Lines*. Berkeley: University of California Press, 2007.

Vivekananda, Swami. *The Complete Works of Swami Vivekananda*. Vol. 4. Almora: Advaita Ashram, 1963.

Weber, Max. *The Religion of India*. New York: Free Press, 1958.

Wilson, A. J. *Sri Lankan Tamil Nationalism*. Vancouver: University of British Columbia Press, 2000.

Younger, Paul. *From Asoka to Rajiv: An Analysis of Indian Political Culture*. Bombay: Popular Prakashan, 1987.

CHAPTER 12

Teaching the Just War Tradition

WILLIAM FRENCH

For a number of years I have taught religious ethics courses on religion, war, and peacemaking at Loyola University of Chicago. My main undergraduate course is titled Moral Problems: War and Peace. It deals with the utter carnage, the devastation, and the stark evil that we humans too often inflict on each other and the ways in which we often ironically appeal to religion or ethical concerns to justify our collective aggression. My course examines how religious and nationalist appeals are frequently employed to mobilize emotional energies that fuel aggression and war making. But also more positively, my course attends to how the world's religious traditions sustain powerful moral resources for restraining the scope of violence and for promoting cross-cultural and cross-national empathy, compassion, and peacemaking.

The just war heritage of reasoning was first introduced by Roman thinkers, but it flowered into mature articulation across the centuries as Christian theologians following in the footsteps of Augustine of Hippo and Thomas Aquinas elaborated its value concerns and criteria for guiding the decision to go to war and also for decisions regarding just or morally appropriate conduct within a war. Augustine gave an influential expression to the notion that, under certain circumstances, it is permissible and indeed morally required for Christians to come to the aid of their innocent neighbors if they are being attacked. The Christian communities of the previous three centuries were, by and large, pacifist and committed to the so-called hard sayings of Jesus urging them "love thine enemy" and "resist not evil," but Augustine and other theologians led the Christian churches to accept that the command to "love thy neighbor" might, in certain situations, require that they defend the innocent against attack. This view came to shape the Western Christian belief that, while war is a mournful enterprise and generally a grave evil, some wars are justified. In addition, this tradition came to enumerate different criteria for the decision to go to war, what we now call, from the Latin, the *jus ad bellum* criteria discerning the justice of going to war in the first place and the *jus in bello* criteria governing the decisions about the particulars of conduct within war. *Jus in bello* contains two key principles to guide responsible conduct in war, namely proportionality and discrimination. The first requires that in the conduct of military operations we seek to achieve generally more good than harm and destruction. The second holds that we must discriminate between soldiers and civilians and restrict our targeting solely to our opponent's soldiers and to their military targets. It affirms the moral immunity of civilians from attack.

While Christian reflection played a considerable role in shaping the just war theory's concerns and principles, during the Enlightenment these concerns and principles were disconnected from any explicit Christian theological backing and the just war ethics came to be discussed, developed, and generalized as having universal validity apart from any explicit religious affiliation or commitment. As the great European powers of the nineteenth and early twentieth centuries engaged in sustained diplomatic efforts to establish international treaties regarding the conduct of war, they, not surprisingly, appropriated much of the moral reflection of the just war heritage both justifying the resort to war under certain tightly circumscribed situations and also establishing sharp constraints on what might count as legitimate conduct within war. The series of Hague Conventions and Geneva Accords attempting to delimit the international rules of war have clearly secularized just war reasoning and to an extent have internationally institutionalized it.[1] Rules prohibiting the use of poison gas, rules regarding the treatment of prisoners, rules about aerial warfare and the immorality of attacks on civilians, and treaties condemning genocide have all extended the reach of the ethical commitments of the just war heritage far beyond its centuries-long home within Christian thinking.

Just war reasoning is relevant, for it articulates many of the key values that any discussion about the decision to go to war will bring to the surface. It does not matter that students may not have heard of any of the criteria of the formal just war theory. What does matter is that, as they ponder the values and potential disvalues—the destruction, lost lives, smashed hopes, squandered resources—of going to war, they will argue about points and issues that have been articulated and codified over the centuries in the just war criteria. While the significance of religious and cultural diversity across the globe is a massive fact, still it does appear that there has arisen in the last century an important, if imperfect, global consensus holding that in warfare the intentional killing of innocent civilians is wrong and that military rules of engagement that allow repeated cases of unintended killings of civilians are deeply suspect. While surely this consensus is not affirmed by all, nor is this a very thick and broadly defined moral consensus, still it is real. Global media help to sustain international attention to war zones and heated discussions and debates about the rightness or wrongness of various actions by various armies and more informal insurgent forces, fighters, and terrorist groups around the globe.

While postmodern thinkers have helpfully highlighted humanity's cultural and religious diversity, across the conflict zones of the globe—on battlefields, at checkpoints, and at the receiving end of bombing runs—a range of important structural similarities is visible to a significant degree. And a helpful resource for engaging in critical moral reflection about such cases in war, regardless of the religious affiliations of the armed agents or the innocent civilian victims, is the just war heritage of reasoning. Even though Gandhi's pacifist nonviolence and commitment to justice was grounded in and energized by his reformist Hindu beliefs, this did not stop people of other religious traditions or of no religious affiliation from seeing the truth, relevance, and power of his views and nonviolent practices. Just as Gandhi's powerful approach of nonviolent resistance over the decades has, for many, been detachable from his specific Hindu and Jain influences, and reattachable to specific Christian, Jewish, Muslim, Buddhist, or secular humanitarian beliefs, so too, I believe, the just war heritage is a cross-culturally and cross-religiously transportable tradition of moral reflection and critical thinking.[2]

COURSE GOALS AND STUDENT RESPONSES

I want my students to appreciate the radical character of the escalation of weapons advances in the nineteenth and twentieth centuries that have so greatly expanded the scope of carnage and human suffering unleashed by war. Likewise I want them to appreciate the power of the emotional forces mobilized during war that push peoples to expand their war effort from a limited war to a total war stance, a stance that multiplies the destruction war unleashes upon civilian populations. Together these dual dynamics—the one rooted in historical dynamism and the other in the psychology of fear and aggression—pose the largest challenges for those who, following the just war tradition, wish to sustain strict moral limits regarding decisions to go to war and decisions regarding legitimate practice within war.

My course attempts to promote a number of pedagogical goals. First, I want my students to develop a critical understanding of the function of religion in general and of the history of Christianity in particular. Religious belief, symbols, and transcendental claims offer powerful motivations for action, action that can be guided by broad compassion for the human suffering of all or constricted narrowly with affection, care, and concern restricted only to some—our kind, our people, our citizens. I have my students consider how modern nationalism often functions like a religion when, in time of war, nationalist appeals are generated to promote solidarity against the enemy. Second, I want my students to understand the particular ways that both modern pacifism and the just war tradition sustain distinctive but powerful critiques of the practice of total war, particularly its belief that war is a sphere in which only power and raw force rule, that the only goal is victory, and that the notion of moral evaluation and ethical restraints is naive and inappropriate.

Accordingly I have my students engage the life and thought of Gandhi, the "father of modern pacifism," to illustrate the creativity of his nonviolent resistance campaigns against British colonial rule and the power of his universalist vision of one human community. This case study helps expose my students to a bit of the history of tension in South Asia between Hindus and Muslims and the conflict between Pakistan and India over Kashmir. I rely on Michael Walzer's classic *Just and Unjust Wars* and a 1983 pastoral letter by the American National Conference of Catholic Bishops, *The Challenge of Peace*, to have my students wrestle with ethical principles and values affirmed by the just war tradition and see how these get applied to various concrete cases of modern war and contemporary conflict—World War II bombing campaigns, nuclear weapons, guerrilla war situations like the Vietnam conflict, and the counterinsurgency and counterterrorism efforts currently underway in Afghanistan, Iraq, and Pakistan. In the study of ethics, if the devil is in the details, so too is the intellectual stimulation. If one simply tries to present a generalistic philosophical sketch of the just war criteria for going to war and for conduct within war, students' eyes rather quickly glaze over from the abstractness of the discussion of ethical theory.

Student reaction over the years has generally been quite appreciative of the relevance of the course material. War, for all one can say about it, is certainly dramatic. Its massive destructiveness and the power of the sentiments unleashed in human conflict capture our attention; its vividness and intensity attract both our fascination and revulsion.[3] As newspaper editors well know: "If it bleeds it leads." Sadly, decade after decade the daily news pounds home to my students the real-world relevance of considering the dynamics of human aggression and the ethics of war and peace. Sadly too, year after year new wars and genocides bring new material for my course.

I teach in a theology department and it seems to come as a bit of a shock to students when I note the diverse perspectives on war and peace down through the centuries of Christianity and also how even Christian doctrine can be, and has been, twisted in times of war to stoke the engines of aggression and hatred. Many of my students are surprised to hear that centuries of Christian anti-Semitism helped legitimate Adolf Hitler's racist ideology that gave us the Holocaust or that the United States could have arguably committed mass murder in its sustained bombing campaigns against German and Japanese cities in World War II. My course asks Muslim students to engage with the realities of Islamic extremist violence even as it asks Christian students to engage with some of the tragic history of appeals to the name of Jesus to justify crusader war, colonial conquest, and pogroms against the Jews. It asks students, as we utterly condemn the Nazi violence in the Holocaust, also to train a critical moral eye on the United States' and Great Britain's bombing campaigns smashing German and Japanese cities. My hope is that this exercise in critical analysis of the history of one's own religious community or one's own country can help promote a deeper understanding of the stark differences between good and bad theology or religious commitment and good or bad versions of patriotism.

Courses in ethics, both philosophical and religious, do well to be rooted in the history of the subject under question because that is what sets the context for the discussion of principles and rules and value conflicts. Over the years I believe that my contribution as an educator to my students lies fully as much in simply focusing their attention on ranges of history that they would otherwise be unaware of as in giving them some neatly wrapped set of ethical or religious guidelines. It is humbling to ponder that perhaps my main contribution over the decades has been the

quality of the movies that I have shown—an hour of the movie *Gandhi* and docu-
mentaries on the Holocaust, Rwanda's horrible massacres, the Balkans' wars, the
Vietnam War, and one post-9/11 on the anti-American sentiments across much of
the Arab world. These movies are pedagogically extremely valuable. They provide
compelling visual narratives of important histories that make course readings
come alive and they help generate class discussion.

A consistent student reaction typically becomes apparent by about the third week.
While my students all tend to love Gandhi—his engaging story and personality—they
hit hard analytical ethical reasoning when they start reading Michael Walzer's
book. At that point they get angry at the just war tradition because it draws tight
ethical lines. They often express anger about the sharp differentiation between
soldiers and civilians, between those who, according to the just war tradition, are
legitimate targets in war and those who enjoy an ethical immunity from attack.
Often the anger is vocalized from some who simply think talk of moral rules and
restrictions of war is naive and stupid. They think that no rules really apply anyway.
Others join in with anger from the pacifist side, charging that all this talk of moral
rules and restrictions really functions as a deceptive mask for a dangerous moral
legitimation of war. I find these reactions actually very helpful in stimulating discussion and engagement with the question of the diverse sets of values that both
the pacifist and the just war traditions seek to uphold.

My course serves diverse groups of students. It counts as one of two required
courses that all Loyola students must take in theology or religious studies. It can
be counted as well toward the completion of a theology or religious studies major,
the peace studies minor, and the minor in international studies. Obviously the
course topics deal with many politically charged issues, and I try to remember
that I have a wide range of political affiliations among my students. If my peace
studies and international studies students tend to the progressive or liberal wing,
and my political science students tend to be a bit more moderate or conservative,
these initial differences seem not to matter much as the course progresses. Consistently over the years I have had small numbers of ROTC (Reserve Officers
Training Corp) students in my classes. Though Loyola does not itself offer an
ROTC program, our students may enroll in ROTC at other universities in the met-
ropolitan area. While my peace studies students get very excited about the Gandhi
readings, a number of ROTC students consistently are most attentive, respectful,
and thoughtfully engaged on the concrete discussions of the moral restrictions on
combat and targeting.

MAIN CONCERNS OF THE JUST WAR TRADITION

It has been rightly said that in war the first casualty is the truth. In war the stakes
are very high and national leaders and peoples often employ systematically distort-
ing language to describe and justify their aims and actions. Different sides will
name acts quite differently. I try to show that the just war tradition offers not just
a distanced moral evaluation of acts in war, but more deeply and primarily a

necessary and fundamental language for describing certain basic actions in warfare. In this way I suggest that the just war tradition offers a classification scheme
that is a critical resource for debunking biased and deceptive attempts in warfare
that seek to mask aggression and murder as humanitarian acts. Where some in the
academy today seem to view the field of ethics as dry, theoretical, and worried
solely about evaluation and judgment, I try to show my students that perhaps the
key ethical function of just war reasoning is that it offers a critical resource for
helping us attempt to properly describe the fundamental character of certain actions and practices in warfare. The just war heritage, I suggest, thus functions as a
critical tool and an important hermeneutical resource for right interpretation of
complex and contested human action.

Just war theory is both a critical moral and interpretive resource. It facilitates
critical evaluation of acts in war in major part because it facilitates accurate argument about and description of such acts. War is a time of massive nationalist or
group bias in which lies proliferate. Just war theory asks questions and shines spotlights on these claims. It pushes them to test their accuracy. It sustains an interpretive classification scheme that helps us name and understand certain actions and
policies in time of war. It performs a critical function by emphasizing an absolutely
necessary distinction between permissible killing and murder, between surgical
bombing and carpet or area bombing, and between military heroism, professional
military practice, and war crimes. If the ordinary usage of terms like *murder* and
war crime are forgotten, then all actions in war are too easily accepted under the
generic justifying rubric of "permissible acts of war."

It is tough to make an ethical checklist of criteria interesting when one tries to
go through them philosophically and explain each in turn. Criteria for assessing
the justice of going to war include just cause (namely, to protect the innocent and
fundamental human rights), legitimate authority (war is declared by proper national leaders), comparative justice (do the values and rights involved justify war?),
right intention (is the war fought to pursue justice, reconciliation, and a negotiated
peace?), last resort (have all other less destructive paths been exhausted?), proba-
bility of success (is the cause possible or a hopeless waste of one's soldiers' lives?),
and proportionality (are the likely damage and costs of war balanced sufficiently by
the good to be achieved by war?).[4]

Lecturing on this checklist of criteria quickly becomes tedious and abstract. But
when these criteria are placed in a sustained engagement with real cases of war, the
class discussions become much more stimulating and relevant. Students quickly
see that if we toss away just war reasoning about limits in war, then we have no
bulwark against a slide into endorsing total war logic where anything goes and
where there are no such things as war crimes.

The just war tradition, I argue, with its middle position between pacifist abso-
lutism and the crusader total war approaches provides the most developed
classification scheme for helping to draw important boundaries and distinctions
when considering war's initial justifications and its subsequent conduct. The tendency of pacifists to articulate an absolutist condemnation of the use of violence
and the decision to go to war tends to end discussion abruptly. Its indictment of

all war truncates an effort to develop a set of distinctions and categories about diverse types of actions and practices in war. When all war is judged strictly evil, then there seems little need to distinguish between relatively more just wars and relatively less just wars. Likewise for the crusader extreme. When the appeal to God or to national security calls one to pursue victory in a total war, then no commonly recognized restraints can be placed on combat practices. For the crusader, the war aims are total, and the evilness of the enemy tends to be viewed as total as well. Again, there seems little need for distinctions to be drawn between just and unjust conduct, between civilian and soldier, or between legitimate targeting and war crime.

An important theme of the course is the just war tradition's ability to provide strong sensitization to the tendency for the moral language of justice itself to be hijacked during wartime by attempts to legitimate evil and aggressive acts. If "God talk" is regularly harnessed to justify aggression, so too is talk about justice. But that does not mean that moral discourse or reasoning about justice is rendered useless. Rather, I argue, the just war categories, with their careful moral line drawing, offer us critical resources for indicting the lies, debunking the distortions, shining spotlights on evil practices, and distinguishing carefully between real justice and bogus, biased, and inadequate claims of justice.

DIVERSE TEACHINGS ON WAR AND PEACE: THE CASE OF CHRISTIANITY

Early in my course I sketch the history of Christianity's general shifts in thinking about war and peace. We attend to the early Church's general affirmation of pacifism and to the general embrace of the just war approach articulated following Augustine of Hippo's influential fifth-century book, *The City of God*, in which he accepts that under extreme conditions going to war to stop aggressors may in fact constitute an act of love aimed at the protection of one's innocent neighbors. Finally, I get my students to consider how in the eleventh century Pope Urban II could appeal to the same God and the same love of Christ as Augustine but now call for Christian princes and knights to end their conflicts among themselves in the West and take up the Crusade to free the Holy Land of Israel from the Turks, whom he dubbed "an accursed race, utterly alienated from God." Here, students can observe how violence in language too often leads to violence in action. Christian chroniclers reported that when Jerusalem was taken in the First Crusade, the Christian army entered the city and put all they found—Muslims and Jews—to the sword. The streets, they said, ran knee-deep in blood.[5] Later wars in Europe between Protestant and Catholic armies kept alive the holy war spirit as each side marched under the banner of Christ. As Sam Keen notes, too often "warfare is applied theology."[6]

It is helpful for students to develop a critical understanding of religion and ethics and an appreciation of the complex history of any one religious tradition. It is important that they see that a religious tradition over the centuries and millennia can sustain radically different understandings of war and peace and different normative conclusions. It is also helpful that by examining this one historical tradition, my students are forced to engage the sharp differences between and among the generally "no-war" ethic of pacifists, the "limited war" ethic of the just war tradition, and the "total war" ethic of the holy war.

Because almost all Christians today reject the crusader approach as a normative option, often courses in theological ethics center on the long-standing and lively debate between Christian pacifist voices and Christian just war types. This has the unfortunate consequence of concentrating attention on the differences between the two positions and suggesting to some that while pacifism is "anti-war," the just war approach is somehow "pro-war." Thus I find it quite helpful to keep a focus on the historical and indeed current power of holy war appeals because in their extremity they constitute a real pro-war ethic. The case of holy war helpfully spotlights the relative closeness of agreement between pacifism and the just war view as genuine antiwar approaches. And sadly, after the 9/11 terrorist attacks, we see all too readily the ongoing power of religious appeal to mobilize extremist violence.

MODERN WEAPONS ADVANCES AND THE RESTRAINT OF WAR

Students often come to my class with little understanding of, or appreciation for, the revolutionary character of our modern era with its ongoing industrial revolutions and its burgeoning scientific, technological, and weapons advances. I use a PowerPoint presentation to help students grasp the sweep of the rise of modern and contemporary war. My aim is to fill my students with awe regarding the rapidity of humanity's expanding firepower and weapons capabilities. We note how World War I was dominated by the superior defensive power of the machine gun and how the mass mechanized armies employed the new technologies of large-scale howitzers, gas attacks, and tanks in efforts to overcome the trench lines of the Eastern and Western Fronts. In World War I (1914–19) the airplane played a role, but mostly in observing enemy troop movements and in dogfights with enemy planes. The planes were too light to be used as effective bombers. But by World War II both the tank and the war plane had matured greatly. Blitzkrieg war brought a highly mobile front of attack. In World War I the effective killing range was roughly nine miles—the range of the most advanced howitzers. Generals and leaders may have wanted to cripple the enemies' industrial centers, but by and large they lacked the means. By World War II, however, the killing range was greatly extended by the bomber fleets' new capacities to reach deep behind enemy lines. The destruction that long-range bombers unleashed against cities during World War II was simply unprecedented in the history of warfare.[7]

World War II ended with the dramatic display of the new super weapon, the nuclear bomb, capable of burning entire urban regions in one explosion. And the 1960s saw the development of intercontinental ballistic missile technology and submarine-launched missile advances that threatened mass death at a range of 10,000 miles. After World War II we also saw the effectiveness of a new style of war, guerrilla war, in which soldiers seek to gain the advantage of surprise against a conventionally more powerful opponent—a national government or an industrialized power—by unconventional tactics. Finally, 9/11 introduced us to the emergence of powerful terrorist organizations capable of destabilizing nations and governments across the globe. With each new technological and tactical advance have come new challenges to humanity's ongoing effort to mitigate and restrain war.

THE PSYCHOLOGY OF AGGRESSION AND THE "RELIGION" OF NATIONALISM

Joining the escalation of raw firepower across the decades is the common dynamic within any single conflict of an escalating hostility that heightens feelings of identification with "our" side, "our" country, "our" cause and contrastingly undercuts any identification with one's enemy or their population. At the beginning of my course I show the film *Faces of the Enemy*, which zeroes in on this dynamic of enemy making. In it Sam Keen introduces insights from the field of the psychology of aggression that help us understand some of the emotional engines of escalation in conflict as rooted in the construction and reification of a thoroughly dehumanized picture of the enemy.

We have a strong tendency in times of conflict to take normal civil relations and reify them into sharply polarized "us-versus-them" understandings that function to curtail any sense of identification with, or connection to, the other. War tends to inflame national or tribal group identification and to mobilize a dehumanized picture of our opponents.[8] The high emotions of war—fear, anxiety, anger—reinforce a starkly dualized frame of understanding: our side is the victim and their side is the evil perpetrator. We are civilized. They are barbaric. Propaganda is often employed to construct a picture of the enemy as faceless, to underscore, finally, that they are not really human like us.[9]

Given how religion is able to employ sacred narratives and symbols to mobilize powerful feelings, meanings, and senses of identity, the frequent appeals to religion and theology to justify individual and national behavior during wartime are not surprising. War between two peoples thus gets framed not as yet another struggle between human communities—humans who have bodies, who have children, and who suffer—but as a drama of "cosmic war," a total war whose opponents are cast in absolutist terms as dualized opposites. The struggle is portrayed as one in which God is on our side and our opponents are in frequent league with Satan.[10] This dynamic of the dehumanization and often demonization of the enemy works powerfully to justify a slide into the unrestrained violence of total war.

It is helpful for my students to see that twentieth- and twenty-first-century nationalism often exhibits many religious and quasi-religious elements in its practice and expression. Ninian Smart and others have rightly suggested that nationalism be viewed as a "secular worldview" that valorizes national rituals and symbols to prompt powerful emotions of patriotism and national pride. These are mobilized especially in time of war to shape individual and collective belief and action.[11] And in time of war nations and peoples employ religious-like claims about the sacredness and ultimacy of "our" national cause in ways that often sadly promote an absolutist holy war stance.

As J. Glenn Gray has noted, part of the problem lies in the way we use the definite article to speak of "the enemy," as if the people of the nation we fight are an "undifferentiated group" bound together in rank hostility against us. An uncritical use of the term "the enemy" over time leads people to feel that there is no important distinction between our opponents' soldiers and their civilians.[12] When this distinction collapses, we slide into total war reasoning.

GANDHI ON THE SHARED COMMUNITY OF HUMANITY

I have my students study Gandhi's life and work to give them a sense of the dynamism of modern pacifism and an appreciation for the discipline required to engage in conflict without adopting a dehumanized understanding of one's opponents. While Gandhi's relevance for inspiring contemporary pacifism is obvious, his emphasis on always respecting the full humanity of one's opponents is, I argue, of equal significance to those who wish to follow the just war heritage and fight the slide toward total war. Gandhi's ethic of ahiṃsā (nonviolence) and his satyāgraha ethic of "truth force" offer critically potent resources for resisting the dangerously emotional attraction of enemy making.

I give my students some background history of India, Hinduism, the British colonial domination over India, and the rise of the Indian independence movement. I have my students read sections of Gandhi's *All Men Are Brothers* and see parts of the movie *Gandhi* to accomplish a number of goals. First, most of my students have little familiarity with this history. Further, the tensions stemming from the trauma of Partition that continue to be present between Hindu and Muslim communities in India and between Pakistan and India over the contested state of Kashmir are directly pertinent to ongoing tensions in Afghanistan, Pakistan, and India today. Second, many of my students have the impression that pacifism is basically a negative ethic whose chief characteristic is a rejection of the use of violence under any circumstances. They know what pacifism is against but little about what it is for, about its values, aims, and concrete tactics. Thus my students often equate pacifism with passivity. Gandhi's ethic, however, is anything but passive, and I have my students pay close attention to his use of demonstrations, boycotts, and fasts to help empower Indians in their cause.

I have my students see how Gandhi's ahiṃsā (nonviolence) agenda derives its force from his understanding of the essential unity of all religions and all peoples. He insists that ultimately there is but one God beyond all the manifestations of the world's religious heritages and, as God is one, so also there is but one common human family. Against the emotional default that pushes for a heightened sense of us versus them, Gandhi insists that fundamentally we can name no opponent as some radically other "them". It is just "us" with all of our diversity in a common human community. For Gandhi, we Hindus and Muslims and British engage each other as "us" and "us" again. Surely there is conflict and surely we have significant differences, but conflicts are placed within an encompassing primary affirmation of ours' and our opponents' common humanity and potential friendship.

Gandhi's views thus offer a powerful resource for fighting the tragic emotional dynamic that promotes an aggressive naming of "us vs. them," that undercuts any identification with or empathy toward our opponents and thereby enables the development of easy consciences about total war. It is important too, I believe, that my students see how a Hindu with a Jain mother could become an inspirational figure in discussions within Christian ethics and in the ethical conversations of all other major religions.

THE ETHICS OF BOMBING: THE IMPORTANCE OF THICK DESCRIPTION

I follow Michael Walzer and many others in holding that the principle of discriminating between soldiers who are legitimate targets and civilians who are not remains a deeply relevant moral core of the just war theory. When nations and their leaders picture their opponents in dehumanized or demonized fashion, then it is an easy step for them to escalate a conflict and make war against civilian populations as well. My class grapples with the clear, searing evil of Adolf Hitler's lust for murder that brought us the Holocaust, but we also study the ease of the slide by which Winston Churchill, Franklin Delano Roosevelt, Harry Truman, and the Allied peoples during World War II came to feel justified in the saturation bombing of German cities—Hamburg, Berlin, Dresden—and then in the use of nuclear bombs on Hiroshima and Nagasaki.[13]

Walzer's analysis is most subtle in his diagnosis of the ways in which the fierce emotions of fear, traumatic loss, resentment, and aggression pervert nationalist sentiments and distort a people's moral perspective. He notes how the appeal to the very evilness of our enemy is often employed as justification for the righteousness of our own escalation of violence. Likewise he highlights the power of a utilitarian calculus that can justify an escalation of aggression by arguing that increasing carnage and destruction in the short term will end a war more quickly and thus save more people—on both our side and our enemy's—overall. By this logic decisions that bring vast destruction to civilian populations can be justified in the name of an overall good as "humanitarian acts."

I have my students wrestle with Walzer's analysis of General William Sherman's conduct during the American Civil War. Sherman famously argued that "war is hell," and that his actions aimed at ending this hell—on the battlefield or by burning Atlanta—were morally justified. Likewise we study Walzer's analysis of President Truman's claim that dropping nuclear bombs on Japanese cities actually saved lives overall by ending the war quickly. While Sherman's and Truman's arguments have an initial persuasive power at the popular level, clearly their appeals obliterate the distinction between soldiers and civilians and thus strike at the heart of the just war tradition.[14] If the burning of Atlanta and the bombing of Hiroshima can be described and evaluated as humanitarian deeds and therefore, on balance, as good, then nothing in war can be finally judged morally as out of bounds, excessive, or a war crime.

The utilitarian ethical reasoning of Sherman and Truman argues that the end justifies the means—and more specifically that by saving lots of lives in the long run a quick end to a war justifies expanding the war's carnage against some civilians in the short run. Utilitarianism tends to aggregate lives lost regardless of their status as soldiers or civilians. The just war's deontological ethics, however, rejects this calculus, this aggregation, and this legitimation of "any means necessary." It insists that there are some actions in war that simply are strictly wrong, like the intentional killing of innocent civilians, which it insists must be named rightly as murder.

Just war principles and rules play an important hermeneutical function by providing a rich classification scheme of action and intention for helping us to attend to important distinctions between and among various sorts of complex acts and motivations in warfare. Just war principles and rules allow a moral description and evaluation of particular combat practices and acts that can be used to test the often biased claims and descriptions employed by national leaders in time of war. Just war theory, in short, grounds moral evaluation in a critical set of normative descriptive distinctions about action and intention. Without the just war tradition's careful array of distinctions and criteria, I argue, we would be left with no resource for challenging lies and deceptions in the justifications vocalized for war and certain practices in war.

NATIONALIST DISCOUNTING OF THE LIVES OF FOREIGNERS AND THE PROBLEM OF COLLATERAL DAMAGE

Another important just war concern lies in the way civilians are frequently killed as the unintended consequence of the morally permissible targeting or bombing of legitimate military targets. The tradition has long differentiated these civilian deaths from cases of murder because these deaths are not directly intended. The principle of the double effect, originating in medieval Catholic ethics, has been used historically to differentiate effects or consequences that are directly intended from those that flow from an act but were not directly intended. Such effects have been dubbed "side effects," for they are understood as lying outside the channel of direct intentionality and thus out of the sphere of direct moral responsibility. Accordingly, these unintended civilian deaths have been termed "collateral damage" to convey that the damage and harm are both outside one's directly intended targeting and thus outside one's direct moral responsibility. At bottom, this term signifies an "accident," a label for a regrettable harm for which no one is directly responsible or morally at fault.

On this question, I have my students return to Walzer and engage his critique of this historic moral understanding of collateral damage. One of the grave issues regarding modern and contemporary war's heavy impact on civilians concerns nations' and armies' attempts to reduce their own soldiers' casualties by relying more and more on aerial firepower. The United States and other countries have long employed airpower to keep the causality rates of their ground troops as low as possible. Walzer rightly challenges the traditional affirmation of collateral damage as pure accident for which no one is directly responsible. He argues that the moral standard cannot be set by the mere absence of actual intent to target civilians. Rather, he holds the standard should require that one's military seek to minimize civilian deaths even if this means higher risks are borne by one's own soldiers. He argues that soldiers have a responsibility to increase their level of due care for civilian lives.[15] In this way, Walzer confronts the traditional classification of collateral damage as pure accident that produces a seductively easy conscience regarding the death of civilians during wartime.

The acceptance of collateral damage as accident arises primarily not from a stance of active hatred of foreign civilians but from what I describe to my students as a "nationalist discounting of the lives of foreigners." It arises from the simple identification with one's country and thus justifies a prioritization of concern for the well-being of one's fellow citizens. Nations understandably focus attention on the lives and value of their own soldiers and civilians. Their protection becomes the highest priority. Unless the protection of foreign civilians is intentionally institutionalized in one's national war policy and one's military rules of engagement, it is very easy for one's own military to take steps that reduce their own risks in combat by increasing the risks they ask foreign civilians to bear.

I have my students consider how advanced modern armies tend to rely on airpower and bombing where they can to minimize the loss of their own soldiers' lives in ground fighting. This reliance on airpower is strongly evident in America's wars of the last half century. A standard tactic of the American military during the Korean War was to have American infantry units fall back when attacked from the front. Air Force bombers were called in to pound the area from which the initial firing had come. In this way American infantry lives were saved, but at the cost of escalating numbers of civilians killed in the bombing zones. America's reliance on airpower remained a dominant feature of our conduct of the war in Vietnam, and high numbers of civilian deaths were again a starkly visible consequence of this favored tactic. Likewise I have my students consider how this same resort to America's strength in airpower in the ongoing wars in Iraq and Afghanistan continues to produce (with disturbing frequency) cases of civilian deaths through bombing accidents or cases of flawed military intelligence making mistakes about the intended targets.

What I have dubbed the nationalist discounting of the lives of foreigners is sadly understandable, but still morally unjust and destructive. By so concentrating our moral concern on the lives of our nation's civilians and soldiers, we too often diminish our attentiveness and concern about the lives, vulnerabilities, challenges, and personal stories of other countries' people. If so much of the problem lies with the abstracted terms by which we speak about foreign populations, then a major resource for fighting such discounting lies in articulating more definitively and attending more deliberately to the wide diversity of the sorts of lives foreigners actually live. Attending to and honoring the diversity of peoples, cultures, and histories seems to be a critical resource for prompting a basic respect for global human rights and respecting their basic value and human rights.

MODERN CHALLENGES: NUCLEAR WEAPONS, COUNTERINSURGENCY, HUMANITARIAN INTERVENTION, AND TERRORISM

Whereas just war principles and criteria seem readily applicable to cases of conventional war like World Wars I and II, the emergence of the threat of nuclear war and the challenge of guerrilla war after World War II appeared to many to suggest that just war reasoning was no longer particularly well suited for offering meaningful moral restraint of these new modes of war. Nuclear weapons detonated a blast of such extreme circumference that civilian lives could not be spared even if the intended targets were military sites. And as the United States and the Soviet Union discovered, the best way to deter the other's first launch involved aiming their missiles at the other's cities. Stability and the prevention of war then became oddly tied to the very targeting of civilians that the just war tradition has so long condemned. Guerrilla war, too, seemed to tear at the heart of the just war theory's soldier/civilian distinction that is the moral core of the tradition. Guerrilla tactics rely on getting combatants out of uniform so that they can blend into the civilian population until such time as the guerrilla unit can attack with the advantage of surprise. Indeed, a core guerrilla tactic is to encourage their opponents to fire into civilian groups to generate civilian casualties and a hatred for the counterguerrilla forces blamed for the civilian deaths. How could counterguerrilla forces be expected to follow just war rules when the enemy's core tactic is to make it impossible to distinguish between enemy soldiers and the surrounding civilian population? In this way it seemed to many that just war reasoning simply was not able to handle the distinctive moral challenges posed by the realities of nuclear and guerrilla war.

I suggest to my students, however, that the just war emphasis on the moral principle of the protected status of civilian lives has allowed it to remain a forcefully relevant frame of analysis across a wide range of cases. I have my students engage these two challenges because each is important in itself and each helps display how just war reasoning frames issues relevant to each case. In addition, the twentieth century introduced two other challenges to the moral logic of the just war tradition: genocide and the terrorist attack. In what follows, I discuss how I address each of these four contemporary problems in the classroom in turn.

Nuclear Weapons and Cold War

The end of World War II displayed the awesome power of nuclear weapons and ushered in a nuclear arms race between the United States and the Soviet Union. Whereas the effective killing range of World War I's heavy howitzers was roughly nine miles, by the 1970s Soviet and American intercontinental ballistic missiles could annihilate targets 10,000 miles away a half-hour after launch. In short, the new technology required that these two superpowers be able to mobilize for war in the blink of an eye. I have my students read Michael Walzer's chapter on nuclear deterrence and also a 1983 pastoral letter from the National Conference of Catholic Bishops, *The Challenge of Peace*. These sources provide an extremely stimulating set of reflections about the balance between the horrific immorality of launching nuclear warheads against civilian population centers and the power of the nuclear threat to function as a buttress for stability and a deterrent against any weapons launch. We study how Walzer, the bishops, and many other moralists and strategists follow the basic just war emphasis on the protected status of civilians to condemn counterpopulation nuclear attacks. We wrestle with the issues of the morality of nuclear deterrence as a strategy for stability and peace. The bishops' pastoral letter remains a stimulating discussion starter because while the bishops condemn any actual launching of a nuclear attack, they shocked many by giving a qualified endorsement to the United States for maintaining its nuclear arsenal as a balance against Soviet and Russian arsenals that stabilize the international system.

While happily the Cold War is over, unhappily, knowledge about how to produce nuclear weapons is spreading. The United States and Russia still have vast nuclear arsenals, and these are joined by other nuclear powers and nations like Iran and North Korea who have nuclear weapons development programs and who seek to join the "nuclear club." Nuclear proliferation decade after decade is now of grave global concern, and surely the 9/11 attacks highlighted the viciousness of globally potent terrorist networks like al Qaeda and the immense harm terrorists could do if they got their hands on a nuclear device. The nuclear threat has changed drastically since the Cold War, but it has surely not gone away, and students need to continue to examine the threats of nuclear weaponry.

The Challenge of Guerrilla War and Counterinsurgency Operations

After World War II, wars of national liberation occurred in which former European colonies sought to wrest themselves free. Guerrilla tactics were employed against the French in Vietnam in the First Indochina War (1945–54) and also in the Algerian War of Independence (1954–62). The first sustained American experience of guerrilla tactics, or what is sometimes now called "asymmetrical warfare," began with the commitment of American troops in Vietnam in the early 1960s.

I have my students read Walzer's analysis of guerrilla war and of the United States' engagement in the war in Vietnam to help my students understand the logic of guerrilla tactics and the misjudgments and mistakes made by American forces in Vietnam. I show my students a PowerPoint presentation on the history of Vietnam and its conflicts from the days of its colonization under the French to its unification after the North Vietnamese victory. I show a one-hour segment of *Vietnam: A Television History* titled "America Takes Charge (1965–1967)," for it displays graphically how failures to protect civilian lives undercut trust and caused the American war effort to lose the "hearts and minds" of too many in South Vietnam.

At first glance it would appear that key guerrilla tactics cut away the heart of just war's distinction between soldiers and civilians. Guerrilla units get out of uniform and mix in with the civilian population intentionally to help blur the line between soldier and civilian and thus make it extremely difficult for a counterguerrilla effort to prosecute the war without killing large numbers of civilians. Thus it would appear that guerrilla units who do not respect this distinction would have a military advantage over a conventional military force in uniform who tries to conduct strategies that target only soldiers and not civilians. It would appear at first that attempts to abide by the just war distinction between soldiers and civilians in a guerrilla war context would put one's side at a severe disadvantage—you would be restraining your targeting and violence according to conventional war rules while your opponent is seeking to cut the very guts out of those rules based on those distinctions.

But interestingly, guerrilla war or counterinsurgency war actually reinforces the moral relevance of the just war theory's traditional emphasis on the need to avoid any targeting of civilians. Counterinsurgency operations require intentional and deeply disciplined efforts to minimize civilian casualties. If the war in Vietnam or our current wars in Iraq and Afghanistan show anything, it is that counterinsurgency forces must be conducted with great discipline in respecting the lives, property, and general sensitivities of the civilian population. One can draw a line between the moral and strategic lessons of Vietnam about the need for winning the "hearts and minds" of the civilian population and the same needs in the conflicts today in Iraq, Afghanistan, and Pakistan. American bombs that hit civilians induce understandable rage and help us lose the hearts and minds of the population at large.[16] Sloppy targeting and cases of mistaken identity that sustain high levels of collateral damage increase popular resentment, thus damaging the legitimacy of the host governments allied to the U.S. forces. Such popular resentment against the American or NATO "aggressors" is easily tapped by insurgent forces to increase their ranks and strength. It has been core U.S. Army doctrine since the end of the Vietnam War that if you want to win counterinsurgency operations then you must honor the key *jus in bello* value sustained by the just war heritage, namely the insistence on the protected status of civilians from attack.[17]

Genocide and Humanitarian Intervention Cases

The twentieth century witnessed many cases of horrific genocide but sadly the powerful nations who might have been able to stop or mitigate this mass murder mostly restricted their efforts to verbal condemnation, diplomacy, and hand wringing. Sometimes I have my students focus on the horror of the Holocaust by getting them to read Elie Wiesel's *Night* and showing a film from the *World at War* series titled "Genocide" that gives a compact and gripping account of the rise of Nazism and the unfolding crime of the Holocaust. We also read an account of the history of the development of anti-Semitism within Christianity, which provides a valuable discussion starter for my students, most of whom have no inkling of how a theology of hatred against the Jewish people was sustained across the centuries.[18]

Sometimes I have my class focus on more recent cases of mass murder like the Balkans conflict or the massacres in Rwanda. I often use Samantha Power's magisterial book *"A Problem from Hell": America and the Age of Genocide*.[19] Power, who served as a journalist in the Balkans War, wondered how the Western powers could have failed to come to the aid of the Bosnian people who were being so torn apart by both Serb and Croatian aggression. After the war she embarked on a historical study of America's response to genocides across the twentieth century, beginning with the Armenian massacres by the Turks during World War I. Her conclusion, reached through a series of case studies, is that for all of America's humanitarian rhetoric, we only commit troops in clear-cut cases of compelling national security or in cases where the president and his advisors conclude that "vital national interests" are at stake. Each president calculates that, without overwhelming public demonstrations of support for armed intervention, placing American troops in harm's way runs grave political risks with little positive political benefit. Accordingly, Power notes, we see decade after decade both Democratic and Republican presidents speaking out eloquently against genocide and for humanitarian concern while showing extreme reluctance to commit America's troops in cases of such so-called humanitarian intervention. For example, President George H. W. Bush quickly committed half a million American troops in the Persian Gulf War to shield Saudi Arabia from the threat posed by Saddam Hussein's Iraqi army and to drive Hussein's army out of Kuwait, but Bush found many reasons not to use American military threats against the Serbs to prevent their guns from hitting Sarajevo and other cities and towns of Bosnia. Oil is a strategic national concern of the United States, and Saudi Arabia and Kuwait have much of it while Bosnia does not. In the priority scale of almost all nations, strategic interests trump humanitarian concerns.

If the just war tradition's criterion of "last resort" highlights the heritage's moral concern to obstruct any premature rush to war, Power's investigation of cases of modern genocide raises a sharp moral criticism against those who delay action when stark and massive aggression is taking place in a different nation. If rushing to war is wrong, Power argues eloquently, so is failing to lift a finger to stop raw aggression.

When I have my class concentrate on the collapse of Yugoslavia and the Serbian campaign for a Greater Serbia at the expense of the Bosnian people, I use either Power's chapter on the carnage or Michael Sells's fine book, *The Bridge Betrayed: Religion and Genocide in Bosnia.*[20] Sells, an Islamic studies scholar, examines how Serbian Orthodox religious leaders anointed President Milošević's mobilization of Serb nationalist sentiment against Muslims in Kosovo and Bosnia. Both Sells and Power examine the role of religious appeal in providing justification for massacre and the sustained use of rape as a tactic to traumatize, dehumanize, and advance the "ethnic cleansing" of Bosnians. They each argue that the West was slow to act in major part because of false claims that the warring between and among Serbs, Croats, and Bosnians sprang from "ancient animosities and hatreds." Furthermore, for years the Western press and leaders described the carnage and atrocities as equal on all sides, suggesting that there was really little to do to stop the violence other than to contain it and let it burn itself out. I use clips from the CNN/Discovery Channel film *Yugoslavia: Death of a Nation* to make the sad events narrated by Sells and Power more immediately compelling to my students.

When I focus on the Rwandan genocide that occurred in 1994, I have my students read Power's chapter on this disaster to see the psychology of aggression played out in detail but also to see the logic and moral excuses employed by European, American, and UN leaders to justify nonintervention. After a period of careful preparation a policy of annihilation was sprung on the Tutsi population of Rwanda by Hutu leaders inciting their people across the land to butcher neighboring Tutsis with machetes neatly warehoused and provided by the Hutu leadership itself. In the course of 100 days Hutus killed over 800,000 Tutsis. I have my class watch the Public Broadcasting System's riveting documentary, *The Ghosts of Rwanda*, to see how a policy of hatred can be constructed and how the politics of moral negligence can unfold, as when the United States and Western European powers failed to commit even modest numbers of troops to stop the ongoing murder in Rwanda.

9/11, Terrorism, and the Wars in Afghanistan and Iraq

On the evening of September 10, 2001, I taught a class in which we focused on how religious claims and identities are manipulated to provide potent rationales for religiously based narratives aimed at mobilizing hatred, aggression, and extremist violence against the dreaded "other." Our main text for discussion was Mark Juergensmeyer's *Terror in the Mind of God*, and we saw a movie, *Arab and Jew: Wounded Spirits in the Promised Land*.[21] The next morning, in their astonishing attack, al Qaeda murdered over 3,000 Americans. Osama bin Laden and others in al Qaeda asserted that none of the Americans killed were innocent civilians—as part of the Great Satan, all were combatants and thus legitimate targets. In the cosmic battles of bin Laden's vision of holy jihad, war is total.

The events of that September morning concentrated the world's attention on the scale of the danger posed by modern terrorist organizations, especially al Qaeda, which had become in the previous decade increasingly violent on a number of continents. That attack also concentrated the world's attention on the continuing power of religious appeal to mobilize powerful motives, emotions, and justifications for spurring recruitment to cells committed to large-scale aggression and violence. Suddenly university religious studies and theology departments were flooded with requests for names of professors who could speak on panels about the power of religion in the contemporary world and religion's capacity to mobilize violence. It prompted an intense worldwide interest in the dynamics of Mideast political concerns, in the teachings and practices of Islam, and especially in the sources of the apparently growing anti-American and anti-Western sentiment in sections of the diverse populations of some Muslim countries.

Since 9/11, I conclude my class with sessions focusing on some key sources of conflict and tension in the Mideast and South Asia. These discussions cover the complex relationships between and among modernization, globalization, heightened religious identification, nationalism, and the religious justification of aggression. I have my students read selections from an anthology of articles from *Foreign Affairs* that highlights post-9/11 concerns about terrorism, the Israeli-Palestinian conflict, and the wars in Afghanistan and Iraq.[22] We examine how religious appeals have contributed to polarizing rhetoric of confrontation between India and Pakistan over the contested territory of Kashmir and between Israel and the Palestinians. This section of the course recapitulates its opening themes about the polarizing dynamics of aggression and "enemy making" and the susceptibility of religious identification to an intentional manipulation that generates powerful emotions and a totalization of conflict.

Just war theory provides a helpful lens for bringing certain key aspects of the goals of terrorist violence and the dangers of overreacting to terrorist attacks and threats into focus. In this way, this concluding section of my course recapitulates a number of familiar themes developed earlier and applies them to a critical set of searing contemporary challenges. Just war theory immediately condemns terrorist attacks that target civilians as simply murder. It does not accept any extremist ideological or religious claim that justifies total war or acknowledge any distinction between combatants and civilians. The just war theory helps break out of the post-9/11 nationalist frame of analysis that foregrounded American suffering and the importance of defending American lives. The just war theory, while deeply concerned about the unjust murder of 3,000 Americans, would devote an equal concern to the civilian lives viciously snuffed out by al Qaeda in Nigeria, Sudan, Jordan, Iraq, Afghanistan, and Pakistan, among others.

As noted earlier, a just war analysis would demand that counterinsurgency efforts by American forces in Afghanistan and Iraq be conducted in accordance with its concern for civilian lives and property. As was true in Vietnam, in Afghanistan and Iraq today a key component of the United States' nation-building efforts lies in winning the hearts and minds of the civilian populations. To do that one must conduct one's missions in combat with discipline and restraint so as to respect the core moral affirmation of the just war heritage, the protected status of civilians.

RECENT DEVELOPMENTS IN JUST WAR THEORY: JUST PEACEMAKING AND NATION BUILDING

There has been an interesting convergence of perspectives over the last two decades. Even as greater attention has been focused on the importance of nation-building and society-stabilizing practices, so too many engaged in peacemaking efforts have begun to analyze and catalog a number of concrete practices that function to mitigate conflict, preempt war, promote sustainable development, and increase social stability. Many activists and development specialists recognize that the peace agenda must include tangible and concrete practices rather than simply a litany of generalistic condemnations of war.

Glen Stassen and many other scholars of religion and ethics have rightly noted that while the just war theory has been developed historically over many centuries, pacifist views have not enjoyed the power of being formulated into an analytic set of criteria that function as concrete decision-making guidelines.[23] Pacifism and the general emphasis on peacemaking efforts have often been visionary and inspirational, but without some organized focus on the range of concrete peacemaking practices, these efforts have often been regarded as more idealistic than realistic. Stassen and his colleagues have been providing an important service by identifying a number of the best available practices developed over the last two decades for promoting international and domestic stability, economic development, and conflict resolution.

Inspired by the success of Gandhi's liberation movement and American civil rights campaigns against racist policies and more recently by successful nonviolent overthrows of unjust regimes in the velvet revolutions of Eastern Europe, South Africa, and the Philippines, many are studying the power of supporting nonviolent direct action campaigns that offer tangible historic gains without the carnage of violence and war. Likewise, the just peacemaking movement highlights the effectiveness of practices that promote "cooperative conflict resolution," "foster just and sustainable development," "reduce offensive weapons and the weapons trade," seek reconciliation via truth commissions and public admissions of repentance, and "strengthen the United Nations and international efforts for cooperation and human rights."[24]

Likewise, another important development in just war theory in the last two decades is its attention to postwar concerns. A number of scholars have suggested a whole new category be added to the historic criteria articulated by the just war tradition—namely, *jus post bellum*, or justice after war.[25] This addition rightly expands the range of the just war heritage's moral scrutiny to new and important concerns. It remembers how the harsh terms imposed on Germany after World War I by the Treaty of Versailles may have helped promote the rise of Hitler and the aggressive steps that led to World War II. *Jus post bellum* would function helpfully to raise awareness of how unjust resolutions to wars simply defer violence for a decade or two via the promotion of resentments and instability that lead to new tensions and new carnage and bloodshed.

Application of *jus post bellum* criteria would encourage a wide range of peacemaking and aggression-reducing practices and also consider the use of modern classes of weapons that have destructive effects long after their battlefield use has ended. The radioactive half-life of nuclear weapons means that the effects of any detonation flow deeply into the next millennium and raise key concerns about any battlefield use. Similarly, *jus post bellum* criteria would condemn the use of land mines, which have often been employed as protective barriers to prevent any potential attacks. Tragically, the laying of mines buries explosives in the ground that continue to maim and kill, but in the years after the conflict, the injured and dead are children and farmers, not soldiers.[26] Likewise, *jus post bellum* focuses attention on the use of depleted uranium shells employed by the United States and NATO forces in recent conflicts, beginning in the 1991 Persian Gulf War. While these shells are extremely effective at piercing the armor of an opponent's tanks, the fragments spread radiation across whole regions for decades and centuries to come.

COSMOPOLITAN EDUCATION FOR GLOBAL CITIZENSHIP

My course employs discussions of war and peace in which students are pushed gently to identify with people of different religions, cultures, and nations. Martha Nussbaum has eloquently called for liberal arts education to center on what she calls "cosmopolitan education," in which students are taught to broaden their appreciation and respect for the dignity, rights, and equal moral value of people beyond our national borders. She follows in the Stoic tradition of envisioning a universal human community of which we are all members.[27] It is the same vision of a universal community affirmed by Gandhi as well. A key element in the escalation of conflict is what I call the problem of the "nationalist discounting" of foreign lives. While nationalist ideologies and sentiment often promote strong identification with and care for one's national grouping, religious identification in times of conflict can also tightly constrict our sense of relatedness, responsibility, empathy, and concern. Against the narrowing of allegiance and compassion sometimes encouraged by nationalism and religious identification, the just war heritage asks individuals and communities to step back and differentiate between combatants and innocent victims regardless of national, ethnic, or religious identity.

For this reason, in my course we try to remember always to look at events not only through the eyes of the decision makers and military actors, but also through the eyes of those being bombed and attacked. Nations may be, as Benedict Anderson puts it, "imagined communities," but the just war theory asks us to break away from the constricting nationalist bias to more broadly imagine a universal community of vulnerable humans, all of whom have equal rights and value.[28] It asks us to imagine plain old human suffering: bodies injured, loved ones dead, homes crushed, cities destroyed. And then to empathize and act.

The world's religious traditions offer many powerful teachings that critique the slide toward total war and toward employing religion as a weapon. Mainstream Islam has long emphasized peace, restraint in war, and the inner jihad.[29] Today, given the powerful examples of Gandhi, Martin Luther King Jr., and Nelson Mandela, appreciation for the power of peacemaking beliefs and practices has spread and at least some adherents of every religious tradition espouse the commitment to nonviolence of various streams of pacifist thought. Likewise, all religious traditions have teachings that seek to restrict violence and war making. Most articulate a limited array of conditions that must be met for war to be accepted as morally proper, even as they set out to check total war escalation by designating certain classes of people as not legitimate targets. Indeed, all religious traditions contain potent resources for supporting their members in condemning the killing of innocent civilians and, in this way, all religious traditions can contribute to the important effort of providing a cosmopolitan education about rights and responsibilities in an oft-troubled world.

APPENDIX

Helpful Instructor Resources

Print

Allman, Mark J. *Who Would Jesus Kill? War, Peace, and the Christian Tradition*. Winona, MN: St. Mary's Press, 2008.

Bellah, Robert N. *The Broken Covenant: American Civil Religion in Time of Trial*. New York: Seabury Press, 1975.

Cahill, Lisa Sowle. *Love Your Enemies: Discipleship, Pacifism, and Just War Theory.* Minneapolis: Fortress Press, 1994.

Childress, James F. "Just-War Criteria." *Theological Studies* 39 (September 1978): 427–45. Reprinted in *War in the Twentieth Century: Sources in Theological Ethics*, ed. Richard B. Miller, 351–72. Louisville: Westminster/John Knox Press, 1992.

Davis, G. Scott. *Religion and Justice in the War over Bosnia.* New York: Routledge, 1996.

Gandhi, Mahatma. *All Men Are Brothers: Autobiographical Reflections.* Ed. Krishna Kripalani. New York: Continuum, 2000.

Johnson, James Turner. *Just War Tradition and the Restraint of War: A Moral and Historical Inquiry.* Princeton, NJ: Princeton University Press, 1981.

Johnson, James Turner, and John Kelsay, eds. *Cross, Crescent and Sword: The Justification and Limitation of War in Western and Islamic Tradition.* New York: Greenwood, 1990.

Kelsay, John. *Islam and War: A Study in Comparative Ethics.* Louisville, KY: Westminster/John Knox Press, 1993.

Kimball, Charles. *When Religion Becomes Evil.* New York: HarperCollins, 2002.

Mojzes, Paul. *Yugoslavian Inferno: Ethnoreligious Warfare in the Balkans.* New York: Continuum, 1994.

Nardin, Terry, ed. *The Ethics of War and Peace: Religious and Secular Perspectives.* Princeton, NJ: Princeton University Press, 1996.

Smith-Christopher, Daniel L. *Subverting Hatred: The Challenge of Nonviolence in Religious Traditions.* Maryknoll, NY: Orbis, 1998.

Stern, Jessica. *Terror in the Name of God: Why Religious Militants Kill.* New York: Harper Collins, 2003.

FILM

Faces of the Enemy: Reflections of the Hostile Imagination. Produced and narrated by Sam Keen. Quest Production, 1987. DVD and VHS, 58 minutes. California Newsreel has rereleased this excellent film, which explores the dynamics of enemy making and the psychology of aggression in individual conflict, ethnocentrism, and nation-state propaganda.

Gandhi. Starring Ben Kingsley, John Gielgud, Candice Bergen, and Edward Fox. DVD, wide-screen two-disc collector's ed., 2007. 191 minutes. Gives students an overall feel for Gandhi's agenda and pacifist nonviolent resistance tactics.

"Genocide," *The World at War*, episode 20. Thames Television, 1973. DVD and VHS. It features first-person testimonies concerning the Holocaust and original film footage and photographs of the events described. Written by Charles Bloomberg and researched by Drora Kass and Susan McConachy. Provides students with an excellent overview of the rise of Hitler and the descent into the Holocaust.

Ghosts of Rwanda, PBS Home Video, DVD. A Frontline coproduction with BBC and Silverbridge Production Limited, 2004. 120 minutes. Deeply moving account of the tragedy of the Rwandan genocide.

Yugoslavia: Death of a Nation. Brian Lapping Associates for Discovery Channel, BBC, and ORF, 1995. Five-part video series, VHS in three tapes. 300 minutes. Powerful account of the tragedy of the Balkans conflict and the reasons why the United States and Europe were so negligent in allowing the conflict to drag on so long.

Why We Fight. Directed by Eugene Jarecki. Sony Pictures Classics, Charlotte Street Film, 2005. DVD, 99 minutes. Uses President Eisenhower's Farewell to the Nation address, in which he warns against the "military industrial complex," to give a post-9/11 analysis of what drives America's war budgets and war machine.

NOTES

1. See Dorothy V. Jones, *Code of Peace: Ethics and Security in the World of the Warlord States* (Chicago: University of Chicago Press, 1991); and W. Michael Reisman and Chris T. Antoniou, eds., *The Laws of War: A Comprehensive Collection of Primary Documents on International Laws Governing Armed Conflict* (New York: Vintage, 1994).

2. See Michael Walzer, *Just and Unjust Wars: A Moral Argument with Historical Illustrations*, 3rd ed. (New York: Basic Books, 2000), 16–20.

3. See Chris Hedges, *War Is a Force That Gives Us Meaning* (New York: Anchor, 2003).

4. National Conference of Catholic Bishops, *The Challenge of Peace* (Washington, DC: U.S. Catholic Conference, 1983), paragraphs 80–109; and Walzer, *Just and Unjust Wars*, 21, 41.

5. Roland H. Bainton, *Christian Attitudes Toward War and Peace* (Nashville, TN: Abingdon Press, 1960), 111–12; and Geoffrey Hindley, *The Crusades: A History of Armed Pilgrimage and Holy War* (New York: Carroll and Graf, 2003), 48.

6. Sam Keen, *Faces of the Enemy: Reflections of the Hostile Imagination* (Cambridge: Harper and Row, 1986), 27.

7. See Sven Lindqvist, *A History of Bombing* (New York: New Press, 2000); and Gwynne Dyer, *War* (New York: Crown, 1985).

8. See Sudhir Kakar, *The Colors of Violence: Cultural Identities, Religion and Conflict* (Chicago: University of Chicago Press, 1996); and Amin Maalouf, *In the Name of Identity: Violence and the Need to Belong*, trans. Barbara Bray (New York: Arcade, 2001).

9. Keen, *Faces of the Enemy*.

10. Mark Juergensmeyer, *Terror in the Mind of God: The Global Rise of Religious Violence* (Berkeley: University of California Press, 2002); and Scott R. Appleby, *The Ambivalence of the Sacred: Religion, Violence and Reconciliation* (Lanham, MD: Rowman and Littlefield, 2000), 57–120.

11. Ninian Smart, *The World's Religions* (Cambridge: Cambridge University Press, 1998), 22–25. See also Ninian Smart, *Worldviews: Crosscultural Explorations of Human Beliefs* (New York: Charles Scribner's Sons, 1983), 48–50.

12. J. Glenn Gray, *The Warriors: Reflections on Men in Battle* (New York: Harper and Row, 1970), 134.

13. See Lindqvist, *A History of Bombing*; and A. C. Grayling, *Among the Dead Cities: The History and Moral Legacy of the World War II Bombing of Civilians in Germany and Japan* (New York: Walker, 2006).

14. Walzer, *Just and Unjust Wars*, 32–33, 264–65.

15. Ibid., 151–57.

16. Richard A. Oppel Jr., "Convoy and Checkpoint Shootings of Afghan Civilians Jump," *New York Times*, Sunday, May 9, 2010.

17. In 1986 the U.S. Army published *Field Manual No. 90–8: Counterguerrilla Operations*, which strongly parallels Walzer's analysis. http://www.globalsecurity.org/military/library/policy/army/fm/90-8/.

18. Elie Wiesel, *Night* (Toronto: Bantam, 1960); and Harry James Cargas, *Shadows of Auschwitz: A Christian Response to the Holocaust* (New York: Crossroad, 1990). See *The World At War* film series episode "Genocide" from HBO Video (Thames Television, 1982). It is narrated by Laurence Olivier and runs 52 minutes.

19. Samantha Power, *"A Problem from Hell": America and the Age of Genocide* (New York: Basic Books, 2002).

20. Michael A. Sells, *The Bridge Betrayed: Religion and Genocide in Bosnia* (Berkeley: University of California Press, 1996).

21. The movie *Arab and Jew: Wounded Spirits in the Promised Land* is based on a book by David K. Shipler, *Arab and Jew: Wounded Spirits in a Promised Land* (New York: Penguin, 1986). See Juergensmeyer, *Terror in the Mind of God.*
22. James F. Hoge Jr. and Gideon Rose, eds., *Understanding the War on Terror* (New York: Foreign Affairs/Council on Foreign Relations, 2005).
23. Glen H. Stassen, ed., *Just Peacemaking: Ten Practices for Abolishing War* (New York: Pilgrim, 2004).
24. Ibid.
25. My colleague Michael J. Schuck was one of the first scholars to suggest the need for a *jus post bellum* category. See his essay "When the Shooting Stops: Missing Elements in Just War Theory," *Christian Century* 111/30 (October 26, 1994): 982–84. See also Mark J. Allman and Tobias L. Winright, *After the Smoke Clears: The Just War Tradition and Post War Justice* (Maryknoll, NY: Orbis, 2010).
26. See Philip C. Winslow, *Sowing the Dragon's Teeth: Landmines and the Global Legacy of War* (Boston: Beacon Press, 1997).
27. Martha C. Nussbaum, "Patriotism and Cosmopolitanism," in *For Love of Country: Debating the Limits of Patriotism*, ed. Joshua Cohen (Boston: Beacon Press, 1996), 3–17.
28. See Benedict Anderson, *Imagined Communities: Reflections on the Origin and Spread of Nationalism*, rev. ed. (London: Verso, 2006).
29. See John Kelsay, *Arguing the Just War in Islam* (Cambridge, MA: Harvard University Press, 2009); and John Esposito, *Unholy War: Terror in the Name of Islam* (Oxford: Oxford University Press, 2002).

BIBLIOGRAPHY

Allman, Mark J., and Tobias L. Winright. *After the Smoke Clears: The Just War Tradition and Post War Justice*. Maryknoll, NY: Orbis, 2010.

Anderson, Benedict. *Imagined Communities: Reflections on the Origin and Spread of Nationalism*, rev. ed. London: Verso, 2006.

Appleby, Scott R. *The Ambivalence of the Sacred: Religion, Violence and Reconciliation*. Lanham, MD: Rowman and Littlefield, 2000.

Bainton, Roland H. *Christian Attitudes Toward War and Peace: A Historical Survey and Critical Re-evaluation*. Nashville, TN: Abingdon Press, 1960.

Cargas, Harry James. *Shadows of Auschwitz: A Christian Response to the Holocaust*. New York: Crossroad, 1990.

Dyer, Gwynne. *War*. New York: Crown, 1985.

Esposito, John. *Unholy War: Terror in the Name of Islam*. Oxford: Oxford University Press, 2002.

Gray, J. Glenn. *The Warriors: Reflections on Men in Battle*. New York: Harper and Row, 1970.

Grayling, A. C. *Among the Dead Cities: The History and Moral Legacy of the WWII Bombing of Civilians in Germany and Japan*. New York: Walker, 2006.

Hedges, Chris. *War Is a Force That Gives Us Meaning*. New York: Anchor, 2003.

Hindley, Geoffrey. *The Crusades: A History of Armed Pilgrimage and Holy War*. New York: Carroll and Graf, 2003.

Hoge, James F., and Gideon Rose, eds. *Understanding the War on Terror*. New York: Foreign Affairs/Council on Foreign Relations, 2005.

Jones, Dorothy V. *Code of Peace: Ethics and Security in the World of the Warlord States*. Chicago: University of Chicago Press, 1991.

Juergensmeyer, Mark. *Terror in the Mind of God: The Global Rise of Religious Violence*. Berkeley: University of California Press, 2000.

Kakar, Sudhir. *The Colors of Violence: Cultural Identities, Religion and Conflict*. Chicago: University of Chicago Press, 1996.

Keen, Sam. *Faces of the Enemy: Reflections of the Hostile Imagination*. San Francisco: Harper and Row, 1986.

Kelsay, John. *Arguing the Just War in Islam*. Cambridge, MA: Harvard University Press, 2009.

Lindqvist, Sven. *A History of Bombing*. New York: New Press, 2000.

Maalouf, Amin. *In the Name of Identity: Violence and the Need to Belong*. Trans. Barbara Bray. New York: Arcade, 2001.

National Conference of Catholic Bishops. *The Challenge of Peace*. Washington, DC: U.S. Catholic Conference, 1983.

Nussbaum, Martha C. "Patriotism and Cosmopolitanism." In *For Love of Country: Debating the Limits of Patriotism*, ed. Joshua Cohen, 3–17. Boston: Beacon Press, 1996.

Oppel, Richard A., Jr. "Convoy and Checkpoint Shootings of Afghan Civilians Jump." *New York Times*, May 9, 2010.

Power, Samantha. *"A Problem from Hell": America and the Age of Genocide*. New York: Basic Books, 2002.

Reisman, W. Michael, and Chris T. Antoniou, eds. *The Laws of War: A Comprehensive Collection of Primary Documents on International Laws Governing Armed Conflict*. New York: Vintage, 1994.

Schuck, Michael J. "When the Shooting Stops: Missing Elements in Just War Theory." *Christian Century* 111/30 (October 26, 1994): 982–84.

Sells, Michael A. *The Bridge Betrayed: Religion and Genocide in Bosnia*. Berkeley: University of California Press, 1996.

Shipler, David K. *Arab and Jew: Wounded Spirits in a Promised Land*. New York: Penguin, 1986.

Smart, Ninian. *The World's Religions*. Cambridge: Cambridge University Press, 1998.

———. *Worldviews: Crosscultural Explorations of Human Beliefs*. New York: Charles Scribner's Sons, 1983.

Stassen, Glen H., ed. *Just Peacemaking: Ten Practices for Abolishing War*. New York: Pilgrim Press, 2004.

U.S. Army. *Field Manual No. 90–8:Counter-Guerrilla Operations*. http://www.globalsecurity.org/military/library/policy/army/fm/90-8/.

Walzer, Michael. *Just and Unjust Wars: A Moral Argument with Historical Illustrations*, 3rd ed. New York: Basic Books, 2000.

Wiesel, Elie. *Night*. Toronto: Bantam, 1960.

Winslow, Philip C. *Sowing the Dragon's Teeth: Landmines and the Global Legacy of War*. Boston: Beacon Press, 1997.

CHAPTER 13

⌀⌀⌀

Understanding the Nature
of Our Offense

A Dialogue on the Twenty-First-Century Study
of Religion for Use in the Classroom

LAURIE L. PATTON AND JEFFREY J. KRIPAL

The deeper the truth, the greater the controversy it creates in the world.
—Rabbi Nahman of Bratslav

This fellow is wise enough to play the fool, and to do that well craves a kind of wit.
—William Shakespeare, *Twelfth Night*, 3.1.66

PERSONAL INTRODUCTIONS AND STRUCTURE
OF THE CONVERSATION

We have on our desks the fall 2006 edition of *Religious Studies News*, one of the major publications of the AAR or American Academy of Religion, an international body of scholars who study religion professionally. This particular issue contains no less than fifteen essays on the present crisis in the field involving challenges to the content, even legitimacy, of scholarship on religion by religious communities and their spokesmen (it is almost always men). Jeff's work on sexuality and religion is named and treated in three of these essays as paradigmatic of the types of scholarship that have been under attack for the last decade. Laurie has been a major player in defending one of her own Emory colleagues from very similar organized campaigns. So we write, alas, with some authority and (too) much personal experience here.

We begin with these anecdotes and this particular periodical not to overdramatize, but to mark the very real moral, emotional, and social contexts in which scholars of religion who work on very difficult subjects teach, think, and write today. This is the way things are. Not that this is a new situation. It is not. Jeff sees this as an ancient dilemma wrapped up in the very psychodynamics of religious belief. In his view, the prohibition against open reflection on what we today call religion within the Western monotheistic traditions begins not with a banned scholarly monograph or a taunted academic, much less with an Internet hate campaign, but with an ancient myth about a transgressive desire for mature moral knowledge and a subsequent sexual emotion, namely, Adam and Eve's shameful sense of being naked after accepting the serpent's gift of the knowledge of good and evil. Laurie sees this dilemma as an ancient question raised again in a new technology: can a culture criticize itself, safely, in public? Can it activate the work of the "fool" as a moral corrective to the potential political and epistemological excesses of its most transcendental claims? Can members of a twenty-first-century religion become their own critics within a public multicultural space?

Jeff has explored some of the ways that both Western religious thought and modern critical theory have adopted the Adam and Eve myth in order to take up the couple's erotic gnosis and explore the problems and promises of sexual desire, gender difference, sexual orientation, divinity, love, mortality, and—today—the inescapably transgressive nature of radical thinking about religion within the contemporary academy.[1] More specifically, he has sought to address some of the epistemological and theological dilemmas that the modern study of religion poses for any traditional religious system. These dilemmas all boil down to a basic human desire to know and not to know the truth about religion. Hence the hissing serpent (who knows), the lovely couple (who want to know), and the jealous and rather petty father god (who wants to stop them from knowing). One can easily recognize each of these characters in our present circumstances. It is a depressingly stubborn story.

Laurie is presently writing about the contemporary study of religion as a form of creative scandal. Her book is about the cultural work of the study of religion through a series of case studies of the extreme cases—the controversies of the late 1980s and 1990s—where the work of the scholar clashed with the views of the public. In these encounters, the classically liberal cultural work of the secular study of religion was passionately refuted and refused. Laurie chose the 1990s not because the decade provides neatly convenient boundaries of time, but rather because it (1987–1996, in fact) circumscribes a set of moments in which such controversies began to emerge fast and furious. Her larger argument is that on the twenty-first-century global stage the scholar of religion fulfills a cultural role similar to that of the fool in classical dramas: speaking insights that no one wants to hear, reviled and embraced by a variety of patrons, never sure of the ground upon which he or she might stand.

So that is who we are and where we stand. With a snake and a fool, it turns out.

Still, we are not alone. The truth of the matter is that it is not at all unusual for scholars of religion to be blacklisted by political and religious communities, to have their names slandered in the press (or, much more likely, on the Internet), or to have their books banned in countries, either officially or unofficially. Some colleagues have even received death threats for their work. We wish that we were exaggerating here. We are not. Hence the fifteen essays of the AAR publication have titles like "Difficult Knowledges: Sexuality, Gender, and Religion," "Convoluted Strategies Attack Academic Freedom," and "The New Blacklists." The general feel one gets from the entire issue is that the study of religion, as a critical rational enterprise essential to any open liberal society, is under a broad cultural attack on a variety of fronts, all of them religiously motivated. Indeed, the essay on Islamic studies and the blacklisting of scholars that routinely occurs in that particular subfield had to be written under a pseudonym in order to protect the author from both angered colleagues and offended believers.

The Internet has provided a radically expanded readership of works of scholarship on religion. It has also expanded those who do not read these works but wish to condemn what they believe is contained in the scholarship. Because of these changes in audience, the nature of public discourse about religion has also changed. Not all of the voices weighing in have the resources to train in the academic study of religion, and those who do may not have the inclination. Through a medium like the Internet, there is a clear democratization of textual interpretation, but also at the same time an intensification of identity politics.

And yet, let us be very clear, not all of those offended by scholarship on religion and who speak out are extremists. Nor would all those who understand themselves as insiders sanction such attacks. And the majority of readers, of course, say nothing at all. It is very difficult, if not impossible, to know, really, where a particular community or subculture stands on a particular issue. Certainly the loudest voices are by no means always the most representative. It is no longer, then, simply a question of insider/outsider, believer/unbeliever, or scholar/layperson. The debates about the interpretation of religion cross all these populations, and not everyone lines up neatly in the communities one would expect. It is also no doubt the case that the vast majority of conversation goes on "below the surface," invisible to almost everyone. This is crucial to keep in mind.

We offer the following thoughts not as unqualified certainties, much less as easy solutions, but as acts of hope that might help us to begin thinking beyond the methodological solipsisms and cultural essentialisms in which these controversies always seem to be locked, as if Western scholars were the first to think and write critically about religion, as if cultures and religions were perfectly sealed systems without histories, complexities, and openings of their own, as if both literal and symbolic migration were not the norm of human history, as if there were no talking snakes or fooling tricksters in other forms of folklore and myth, teasing their listeners and readers out of their own cultural certainties.

We also write in the spirit of what we believe some of the most aggressive critics of the field have lacked: the ability to hold diverse points of view together in a single conversation with a larger aim, the aim of creating the conditions for civil, public, critical discourse about religion. This is a very difficult thing to do. One of us (Jeff) has responded to this challenge with a series of articles and books about the nature of the historian of religion and his or her right to free speech in the academic study of religion before and despite all religious restrictions. Another of us (Laurie) has responded with a heightened public lecture schedule about comparative religion in the city of Atlanta and a set of articles and a book manuscript in process about the need to create a different kind of public space, a space in which common ground about religion is built among citizens who differ.[2]

Our scholarly voices themselves are different, and we have at times disagreed about when and how to emphasize what. But both voices are crucial in addressing the current situation, and both need to be heard as we train generations of students that come after us. In what follows, we present both of our voices as a kind of dialogue for students to consider. At the end of each section, we formulate questions for students to keep in mind in each religion class they take.

More specifically, we wish to treat three themes here: (1) the history and nature of becoming an author in the humanities and the liberal arts; (2) the historical role of Christianity and Judaism in the origin and development of critical theorizing about religion; and (3) the "scandalous" nature of comparison and the study of religion in general.

A Short History of Being an Author(ity)

Jeff

It is my own difficult conclusion that the contemporary problem of threatening responses to scholarship on religion is an understandable, but ultimately dysfunctional and dangerous, response to the transgressive nature of thought itself. Free thought, of course, is just that—free. It is always overflowing, ignoring, or otherwise offending the imaginary boundaries of the particular social or religious system in which it is allowed to develop and be expressed. Such thought applied to the subject of religion (itself a deeply subversive comparative category created by the freedom of this same thought) recognizes all sorts of crucial cultural, linguistic, and historical differences, but it also affirms a shared humanity, a common biology, a single global history of ancient migration and constant change. This "being on the move" or "not fitting into received categories," this willingness to take risks and court the abyss— is this not precisely what it means to be creative or original, to write at the cutting edge of some discipline? Is this not what the liberal arts are all about?[3] Is this not what every intellectual is called to do for the health and vitality of his or her free society? And is this not what it means, literally, to be an author, that is, to become one's own author-ity?

To be one's own authority, of course, is often more or less equivalent to challenging or denying the authority of others, particularly those in power. It is at once a political and an ethical act of real-world consequence. Little wonder, then, that acts of censorship and persecution have been replayed a million times in the modern world in almost every field of study, where intellectuals are routinely harassed, threatened, occasionally even chased out of their professions or countries by those who cannot stand what Virginia Woolf once called "the habit of freedom and the courage to write exactly what we think."

We even have a separate organization today, Scholars at Risk, dedicated exclusively to placing such threatened scholars from around the world and from every discipline in American host universities, where their personal lives can be restored and their intellectual freedoms protected and nurtured. One of the founding insights of Scholars at Risk is that, precisely because intellectuals are public figures who inevitably work on controversial subjects in a necessarily open or published fashion, they are particularly vulnerable to political forces that seek to control or even shut down the free exchange of ideas. Here is how they put it: "Around the world today, scholars are attacked because of their words, their ideas and their place in society. Those seeking power and control work to limit access to information and new ideas by targeting scholars, restricting academic freedom and repressing research, publication, teaching, and learning. The Scholars at Risk Network (SAR) is an international network of universities and colleges responding to these attacks. SAR promotes academic freedom and defends the human rights of scholars and their communities worldwide."[4] In this model, intellectuals are seen to be like the proverbial canaries in the coal mine—they are the first to be identified and marked out as dangerous to the established order of things, as threats to "what is right."

Why do we always need to be reminded of this most obvious of historical truths? Do we imagine that Ludwig Feuerbach, or Friedrich Nietzsche, or Sigmund Freud, or any other radical thinker was happily embraced by the public? Is not the surest marker or sign of any truly original vision precisely its inability to fit into the established system? Have we already forgotten that the Nazis burned Freud's books, then killed his beloved sister, that he died in exile in a welcoming, and still free, London? Have we also already forgotten that much of the American intellectual culture of the 1940s and 1950s was dominated by people much like Freud, that is, European exiles who had fled fascist regimes in Europe to protect their intellectual freedoms and, more practically and pressing, to preserve their very lives? On this side, have we also forgotten the gross censorship campaigns initiated here in the States, for example, the McCarthy paranoia of the 1950s and its attempted purges of the American academy and entertainment industry as somehow "communist" and "anti-American"?[5] Replace "communist" and "anti-American" with "liberal" and "secular humanist" and, alas, you are not too far from the rhetoric of much of the religious right.

Again, not that this is anything new. Alas, it is very old news. Similar patterns go back to the very beginning of the modern study of religion, which has always had to struggle against the religions themselves to defend its right to study them in full freedom. To take just one early iconic example, David Friedrich Strauss, inspired by German mystical thought, attempted to understand Jesus as a pantheistic mystic in his pioneering *The Life of Jesus Critically Examined* (1835). In the process, he also denied the traditional literal understandings of the resurrection and miracle stories (like thousands of scholars since). The result? He found it impossible to get a perma-nent professorship. "His name was anathema in the German universities," Peter Hodgson tells us. Three times his name came up for positions. The third time it was accepted, but only until a public outcry forced a referendum vote "in which the citi-zens of Zürich supported a petition revoking the call by a vote of 39,225 to 1,048."[6]

There are many modern Strausses, and many of them are women. Female scholars have almost certainly suffered far more than the men, as they, having suffered through their own microhistories of culturally sanctioned misogyny and religiously authorized oppression, have generally been much more ready to see and critically analyze the gendered and sexual dimensions of Christianity, or any other ancient religion for that matter, none of which, if the truth be told, can really measure up before the simple moral yardstick of complete gender equity. Here is a difficult truth. Whereas some of our best universities, though hardly perfect, explicitly prohibit discrimination based on gender, sexual orientation, or race (check out your own and see), many religious traditions define themselves on the basis of these very discrim-inations, which they consider to be the epitome of morality. What the academic institution sees, with some reason and more than a little history, as gross bigotry and ignorant prejudice, the religion sees as a brave moral stand against a godless secular world. We should not be surprised, then, when intellectuals clash with tra-ditional religious communities. We should be proud. And careful. And definitive.

Ask Jane Schaberg. Schaberg certainly suffered more grievously than most for her astonishingly insightful and powerful book, *The Illegitimacy of Jesus*. The book's thesis that the mythology of the virgin birth was a later spin on an original illegit-imacy story attracted considerable scorn from both religious and scholarly circles. Her own vice president for academic affairs, whom one would think would defend academic freedom and not judge truth by polls, stated, "I would say 99% of the people at this university disagree with her."[7] We are back to Strauss's referendum vote, I suppose. Vicious hate mail and phone calls flooded Schaberg's office and cam-pus, calling her "whore, feminazi, queen of crapola, pseudointellectual, delusional, bitch, blasphemer, heretic, a spiritual cancer, Satanic, lesbian, and sicko."[8] These same people asked for her resignation, insisted that she had no place on the faculty of a Catholic institution, and, in a couple of cases, called for her death. One night a local terrorist put a flaming rag in the gas tank of her car and blew it up as it sat in her own driveway.

And why? Because she had the audacity to point out the obvious (that Joseph was not Jesus's father) and ground an obvious biological skepticism about a virginal birth in some very solid New Testament scholarship. In the end, it is very much worth pointing out that Jane Schaberg kept her job and her university, where she is now a respected and senior colleague. The tenure system did exactly what it is sup-posed to do: protect intellectuals. But the tenure system is itself imperfect too, and it can only do so much. Hence the feminist theologians Chung Hyun-Kung in Korea, Rosemary Radford Ruether, and Elisabeth Schüssler-Fiorenza, to name just a few, have all entertained similar ideas and have suffered similarly from right-wing, anti-feminist Christian groups. Feminist scholars thus now routinely and rightly speak of a backlash—in essence, another kind of whipping.

This list of offended religious communities and harassed, threatened, or expelled scholars could be extended for a very long time, across virtually every religious tradition in both the West and Asia, from the study of Hinduism, Sikhism, and the Baha'is, to the study of Native Americans and Islam. In truth, although this historical phenomenon of prohibition always takes on the local colors and nuances of its historical contexts, and although the likely dangers involved differ greatly from subfield to subfield (with historical-critical readings of Islam no doubt being the most risky today), this same religious prohibition against critical study also appears to transcend these specific contexts as an extremely common, if not universal, feature of the history of religion itself. In short, we are not dealing with a strictly local or modern problem that can be reduced to this or that political history or ethnic identity. We are dealing with a problem (which is also a promise) inherent in the nature of critical thought itself. We are back to the snake in the garden and the young, beautiful couple.

Laurie

And yet at the same time, attention to those historical contexts is in one sense a crucial way to address the nature of these responses to critical thought. One needs to take into account both the historical context of the university and those who, in all of their various identities, object.

Let us begin with the historical context of the university—its present status in the global economy. Those in Western universities write and speak from a position of profound, and in some views unsustainable, economic privilege. As A. Suresh Canagarajah notes in his recent work, *Geopolitics of Academic Writing*, "third-world" scholars are often relegated to the peripheries of academic discourse because of the conventions governing academic writing. First, their methods of reasoning, their forms of rhetoric, are conducted in a "lesser" form of English, whether it is African or Indian or the English of some other formerly colonized state. Second, their frames of reference are frequently scholars who write in their own countries, and not Western scholars, thus making it impossible to write scholarship "relevant" to a prestigious Western journal. Third, social customs undergirding the academic community might well be different indeed, at best unintelligible and at worst aggressive in Western academic mores. Third, the publishing protocols are different in third-world countries, and the time and resources it takes simply to play the Western publishing game on Western turf are too great for a third-world scholar to afford. In other words, even in the so-called free market of the exchange of ideas, radical economic disparities make it virtually impossible to speak a mutually comprehensible language. Thus, in order to create a civic public global space, we must do two things. Even as we assert the right to freedom of speech, or the "freedom to blaspheme," as Purushottama Agarwal puts it,[9] we would also do well to acknowledge our privilege and take steps to share our research and publishing resources.

Another part of attention to historical context might mean that all parties in a controversy understand the nature of an academic department of religion. Many of those who have criticized university scholars believe that an academic department of religion's job is to present the religion as sympathetically as possible. Every department has an obligation to explain to its publics, both inside and outside the university, that such sympathetic presentation is not its job. At the same time, however, university scholars might acknowledge the need for indigenous institutions where indigenous forms of interpretation can thrive. As Christian and Jewish seminaries have grown alongside university departments, with very different intellectual mandates, so too those of other minority traditions can and should build their own versions of seminaries, where indigenous modes of interpretation are given serious intellectual weight. The two kinds of institutions can and will challenge each other. But university scholars, too, might allow a religious community the right to interpret itself without giving up its own right to interpret in social scientific and literary method.

Finally, attention to historical context means distinguishing between different kinds of attacks on scholars. An attack on a scholar inspired by the ecclesiastical condemnation of an established Christian church looks very different indeed than an attack on a scholar by Sikhs who have themselves just experienced the destruction of their Golden Temple by their own government. This will look different again from an attack on a scholar inspired by Hindu nationalists claiming minority status in their new home and enjoying majority status in their country of origin. And this will look different again from an attack on a scholar by members of a Native American community that has been violently oppressed and disenfranchised by its own government for three centuries. Violence or threat of violence in any of these cases should never be tolerated. However, it is important to note that the root causes of each of these attacks is radically different, and not some inchoate "religious fundamentalism" writ large. Rather, each of these attacks is "writ small" in the specifics of each group—their relative empowerment or lack thereof, their historical relationship to the state, and so on.

Here are some questions for students, then:

- What lies behind the common contemporary refusal and rejection of the critical study of religion?
- Is this different in every case, completely dependent on cultural context and ethnic history? Or are we dealing with a larger global phenomenon here?
- How should a university negotiate "the dilemma of liberalism," that is, how should it promote a core set of social values that encourage tolerance while at the same time not tolerating explicitly intolerant values?
- How can a university retain its crucial right to free speech while at the same time sharing other privileges that right the global imbalance of power?

On the Christian or Jewish Nature of the Enterprise

Jeff

As Laurie's comments illustrate, not everyone agrees, of course, that we are dealing with a problem inherent in the nature of critical thought itself. There are some very intellectual ways to challenge or deny the life of the intellect. More specifically, there are two common criticisms raised at this point, no doubt to get around the liberal structure of thought itself—which is the basic epistemology of all modern universities worthy of the name—and return the debate to a politically understandable, but finally fruitless, exercise in identity politics. The first involves the historical fact that the modern study of religion arose within a Christian environment and is, to this day, supported largely by the same cultural complex. The second involves the universalizing nature of the comparative method, which remains the basis, acknowledged or no and however qualified, of almost all critical theorizing. A few words on each criticism are thus in order.

Those who seek to censor or limit critical theorizing often claim, as if this somehow settles the matter, that the critical study of religion is a Western project, and that it was inspired largely, if not entirely, by Christian categories and institutional histories. Both claims are in fact true, and they need to be recognized as such. Christianity contains within itself a very radical critique, even rejection, of religion itself, at least if we define *religion* as that set of beliefs and social, dietary, and ritual customs inherited from one's cultural tradition or ethnic group, which, of course, well describes something like the Hindu caste system and its purity codes, or the ethnic nature and purity codes of Orthodox Judaism, or conservative Islam, or contemporary American Evangelical Christianity.

It is perhaps not too surprising, then, that the critical study of religion arose within the seminaries and universities of Protestant Europe. It appears that something about the structure of Protestant Christian thinking allowed it to deconstruct and move beyond itself (although, just as clearly, a basic fundamentalism or literalism was built into the structure of the Protestant Reformation that has always posed a serious challenge to this very Protestant liberalism[10]). By the way, this internal reflexivity, this Protestant ability to protest itself, was precisely the point of the early nineteenth-century German Lutheran theologian-turned-radical humanist, Ludwig Feuerbach, who argued that the literally false Christian doctrine of the incarnation—by which Christians assert that the divine became human in the person of Jesus—led finally to the true philosophical realization that God is made in the image of man, that God is a projection of an infinite human potential. Feuerbach's projection theory lies at the base of modern critical theory still.

It not just a matter of Christian thought, though. It could well be argued that Judaism has been far more formative on a theoretical or intellectual plane. The discipline, after all, has been profoundly, and perhaps even more deeply, formed by Jewish intellectuals, who have long sat uncomfortably on the outside of normative Christian culture, particularly in nineteenth-century, anti-Semitic Europe, where the field first formed. And why shouldn't they think much more deeply, much more radically? Outsiders, after all, often see things much more clearly than insiders, who are always imagining that the majority view is the natural view, that their worldview is "the way things really are." It is not, of course, and it usually takes an outsider of some sort to point this out.

Because of these two very different religious factors, the overwhelming majority of critical scholarship is to this day directed at either Christian or Jewish sources and is performed by intellectuals whose methods often trace back to a few select (secular)

Jewish and Christian intellectuals, with Kant, Marx, Feuerbach, Nietzsche, Freud, Weber, and Durkheim perhaps being the most paradigmatic. The Bible, moreover, is easily the single most studied, analyzed, and criticized religious text in the field.

So the critics are correct to note that the study of religion derived from Western religious sources. They are also correct to point out that the same study was historically connected to colonial histories in its early development. It is wrong, however, to suppose that this means that the study of religion goes easy on Christianity or Judaism, that it is aimed primarily at non-Western traditions, or that the methods are necessarily and forever colonial ones. The history and structure of the discipline has, we both believe, been rather grossly misread on these issues, or, perhaps better, has been read only very partially.

In addition, we might note here the frequent reference to Islam as the new most extreme model from which other offended communities might (should?) measure themselves. In the rhetoric of those who wish to deny the very legitimacy of the study of religion, we frequently hear something like this: "If a scholar had done this to Islam, it would not have been tolerated." There is a curious admission here, followed by a double, and doubly dubious, attitude. The curious admission is the implication that whatever of substance is being spoken in the scholarship is more or less true. The base truth of the scholarship is not generally at issue in such remarks. What is at issue is whether such a truth can be spoken without severe punishment, whether the truth can be sufficiently repressed from public view. The doubly dubious attitude then follows: first, there is a reification of Islam as the most violent of all religions; and second, there is a kind of implicit envy before an Islam that is strong and does not tolerate supposedly anti-Muslim discourse. Islam, of course, has its own rich history of counterdiscourses and internal criticism, and there are numerous fine historical-critical studies of Islamic traditions and texts that many conservative Muslims might well find troubling or even offensive, but these are all more or less conveniently forgotten in such moments.

Laurie

The ways in which Judaism and Christianity have been "equal opportunity" objects of critique in the study of religion also provide us with a great opening. With this point in mind, students of religion, and the publics they engage, can think differently about religion in general. Each tradition has endured both life-giving and death-dealing schisms within itself, and thus each tradition must be understood as internally plural. And their internal arguments, indeed, their influence on the study of religions, derives from this inherent pluralism. Tomoko Masuzawa's recent work on the idea of "world religions" as deriving from Christianity actually indirectly makes this point quite powerfully. Without arguments between Christians, there would be no discourse of world religions at all.[11]

And internal pluralism is precisely one of the normative and descriptive challenges that each tradition must face today. When representing itself to itself, a tradition frequently engages in one way. When representing itself to another, a tradition tends to focus on unity, on the uniform commitment that all its members can make. And thus the basic question remains: Can a community whose political and cultural clout depends upon an essentialized identity risk a public conversation with others about its own multiple voices?

But such internal pluralism is inimical to the logic of identity politics. Such logic precludes any participant in a debate from publicly acknowledging the multiplicity of voices within their community; it stifles dissent in the name of dissent. Such a rhetorical situation prevents authentic conversation and allows only for a simplified version of point-counterpoint, simplistic cries for balance on both sides, and an obsession with public image that stifles the practice of rigorous disagreement.

Identity politics, to be sure, is a crucial part of any multicultural democracy. In the 1990s, Charles Taylor, Amy Gutman, and Anthony Appiah, among many others, were putting the issue of cultural identity on the philosophical map. They argued that cultural identity, and the ability to maintain it, should be understood as a natural right to be protected by any democratic state. This was philosophically basic and necessary work. Without it, the situation of many minority groups in the United States would not have progressed and would not be able to refer to both concepts and laws by which they can continue to progress.

Yet there was also a risk, the risk that identity can become so completely fused with rights that one's inherited obligation is primarily geared toward one's ethnic or religious community and only secondarily, if at all, to the larger society from whom one receives those rights. Here I am inspired by the writing of Jedediah Purdy on the idea of a common good. Following in the tradition of social critics such as Wendell Berry,[12] Purdy writes that "American culture begins with the refusal of inherited duty."[13] The idea that one inescapably carries responsibility for the well-being of a place and for the acts of a political community is thus a thing of the past. Even if they are émigrés on the outside, Americans of all kinds are also "inner émigrés, whose first loyalty is to conscience or to some particular, freely chosen, and often dissenting moral community."[14] The best of this tradition is Thoreau; the worst of it is badly interpreted Thoreau, where the assertion of independence, or of a particular identity above all others, precludes the idea of responsibility.

Purdy sees the "shadow side" of American identity politics in just this way. "Identity politics based on sex, sexuality, and mostly, race and ethnicity, suggest that politics should work not so much to give people things such as education and jobs as to give them recognition. . . . In this vein, the greatest of political failures are failures of recognitions, organized insults to particular groups."[15] Religions, for both better and worse, have become counted as examples of those groups.

And so here are some questions for students of religion to ask:

- Is an idea always bound to its social origins?
- Does it make sense to speak of a "Jewish chemistry" or a "Hindu physics"?
- Does it make more sense to speak of a "Christian study of religion" or of a "Muslim anthropology" or a "Buddhist historian"? It well might.
- If so, how do we negotiate these differences between the perspective of the researcher in the natural sciences and the humanities?

- What is gained and what is lost by understanding the Jewish and Christian origins of the Western study of religion?
- How might a knowledge of such origins actually help us rethink the question of internal pluralism in our own time as we study other traditions?

On the Scandalous Act of Comparison

Jeff

But perhaps the real problem, which is also the real promise, of our field lies in that old-fashioned but still highly relevant word—*comparison*. After all, within a truly comparative perspective—be it rendered as cultural anthropology, sociology, political science, comparative linguistics, evolutionary psychology, or the history of religions—words like *blasphemy*, *scandal*, and *offense* are seen for what they are, that is, always contextual and specific terms that make sense only in highly local fields of discourse. They are simply meaningless as universal or general categories. The true scandal of religious studies, then, lies neither in this or that work of scholarship that this or that particular religious community finds offensive (for few, if any, outside a particular community find radical scholarship on that community particularly offensive). It lies rather in the discipline's implied insistence that, for whatever else they happen to express, all religious phenomena can be fruitfully approached as human products and studied with the same literary and social-scientific methods. Put simply, the scandal of religious studies is its keen awareness that for the comparativist there is no such thing as religious scandal, nor can there ever be.

Put differently again, a certain radical egalitarianism and deep humanism is implied in the study of religion that, together, must both affirm and deny the authority of any local truth for the sake of understanding a much greater, if never fully reachable, human nature. That human nature, it turns out, is as infinitely plural as it is universal, containing within itself immeasurably more potentialities than any single culture can nurture and realize, that is, "make real."

Such an approach to the human condition is certainly not accidental, and all of it is historically conditioned, like the religions themselves. Hence we are hardly arguing for some absolute or ahistorical truth of the discipline. Far from it. In the end, we share, we are the same nature as the human beings we study. It is all the same mixing and matching gene pool. There is no final inside or outside. We are all products of our histories and cultures. We are all participant-observers.

To take our own local example, the study of religion in the United States relies intimately on the secular spaces carved out by the legal separation of church and state and the Constitution's democratic principles and practices. Without those spaces or principles, without real legal protection, the field would simply cease to be. At best, it would simply be ignored and would dry up for lack of financial and institutional resources. At worst, it would be persecuted into oblivion by the religions themselves.

Certainly we can find premodern analogues in other cultures and times. The impressive interreligious debates and funded translation projects of Akbar's Hall of Worship and syncretistic "Divine Faith" (*Din-i-Ilahi*) in Mogul India, or the Italian Renaissance's hermetic interest in a *philosophia perennis*, Rabindranath Tagore's mystical-humanist "Religion of Man," or Bahai's theological notions of a "progressive revelation" and a world community all come to mind. But there are many, many more. Practically the entire New Age movement, for example, can be read in a similar light. But such a truly anomalous thing as the professional study of religion has never existed in the history of human civilization in such a developed and permanent form before the nineteenth century. Go back just ten generations, and it is no more. That it exists now, moreover, hardly establishes its (or our) secure future. The truth of the matter is that the discipline and all that it represents constitute some historically new and quite tenuous existential positions, and that most of the planet's seven billion inhabitants (including tens of millions of believing Americans) live within religious worldviews that would deny, sometimes quite violently, its most basic working principles and moral values, not to mention its practitioners and professors. We would do well to recognize this difficult fact. We really are snakes and fools.

Laurie

And millions more live in between the two worldviews, the two poles that would either vigorously defend or passionately deny the scholar of religion's basic working principles and moral values. Many live in a state that Charles Taylor has, in his magnificent work *The Secular Age* called the "state of being pulled in both directions." And scholars of religion have as many of these folks, if not more, in their publics as they do the kind who might deny them their professions.

Scandal, then, not only fits the question of comparison. It fits the uneasy perspective of the scholar of religion today and her many publics, all of whom are pulled in both directions. We embody a particular kind of stumbling block, in the sense that we are historical examples of engagement with tradition while at the same time we do not, in our modes as historians of religion, represent religious authority. This should be an obvious intellectual statement, but it is not an obvious cultural one. We all know the query always silently posed by our students after the lecture or discussion: "Should she be the role model? Should he have had more [or less] empathy?" We all know that the longing of our students to know our religious identities is in part a longing to know from which religious authority we speak, so that the rest of what we say can fall easily into place as coming from that perspective. Surprisingly, then, we find that we are also frequently looked up to as exemplars of a religious tradition, or at least faithful advocates, in a variety of contexts, sometimes even within the academies that we inhabit. And thus, when communities we represent disagree with our assessments, we have fulfilled the earliest definition of scandal, someone "whose religious authority is questioned." Indeed, what is clear to us from the beginning is that we never assumed such religious authority, and yet it is in the nature of many religious traditions to impute such authority to one who is knowledgeable about their texts. Even as secular scholars, we assume a mantle of religious authority, even if it is one step removed from the actual hierarchical authority that is given to those ordained to a priesthood, a rabbinate, or the rank of a sensei. Many of us have questioned our religious authority from the beginning of our training and wish to rebel against any such mantle being bestowed upon us. And yet in many of our teaching contexts we must still wrestle with the question as such. This is the major issue of positionality that we face today, about which Tom Tweed has written so eloquently.[16] If we are doing our jobs, we should also fulfill that second definition of scandal and spark "that perplexity of conscience occasioned by a person who is looked up to as an example." If we know something about a tradition from any source, we are examples of engagement with a tradition. Many of us would rather be engaged with a tradition in a particular kind of way, from a distance, or from a perspective of intimacy. But however we look at such a tradition, by virtue of our degree we have also been given the power to question that tradition, albeit through the authority of secular reason and secular reason alone. Thus, the perplexity of conscience arises because we do, like it or not, embody familiarity with a tradition at the same time as we assume we must question it.

We also embody the form of scandal that asks questions in both directions, of all communities. We are not only Janus-like, but Brahma-like, with four heads, or even Ravana-like, with ten heads. Someone with ten heads might have ten things to say, and what would we do then with the relentless bias toward singular positionality in the academy? It is a singularity so dear to us that we have in recent decades made a singular position out of our multiple positions and have pretended that it will suffice to take care of the scandal that is the study of religions.

It should be clear by now that, for our purposes, scandal is not a bad word. Rather, I am using scandal in the sense that Wendy Steiner uses it in her *Scandal of Pleasure* (1995), in which, in a series of compelling essays, she characterizes scandal as a form of behavior that clarifies, challenges, and invigorates the assumptions of the intellectual and cultural life surrounding it.

In this light, the idea of scandal (and its related trope of public spectacle) is extremely useful for our generation of scholars trained in the study of religion. It is useful because it is so all pervasive: the offense of the study of religion is now a double offense—both to the religious communities who are our old and new readers, and to the academy who reluctantly admitted it into its halls in the mid-twentieth century. Contrary to the opinions of their accusers in the religious world, the works of many historians of religion take religious traditions so seriously that they have come up with deep, passionately held conclusions that get them in trouble on both sides of the fence. The offense in the academy is the usual offense in the study of religion—that any deeply fictive enterprise such as a religious tradition could be taken seriously at all. The offense in the conservative religious community is that religion has been treated only as a fictive enterprise in which eros, history, and ingenuity all play a part in religion's construction.

So, in responding to this double community of critics, the study of religion is forced to partake in the perennial paradox of liberalism. It must insist on tolerance and inclusion of others' religious voices even as it argues with those religious voices that are not tolerant. As Steiner describes this paradox:

> In a state controlled by fundamentalist ideas, the liberal cannot speak, but in a state controlled by liberal ideas a fundamentalist cannot act. The ideas of a fundamentalist are exclusionary and performative, i.e. valid only when turned into actions; an article of faith is not a mere topic of discussion to the believer. Thus, the liberal, in insisting on tolerance, is insisting on not only his idea but his practice. In the considerable commentary about the Rushdie affair in America, the absolute value of tolerance or free speech emerges as a point of dogmatic blindness for some and a logical embarrassment for others. Leon Wieseltier states without irony, "Let us be dogmatic about tolerance," but for Norman Mailer the issue is not so easy: "We believe in freedom of expression as an absolute. How dangerous to use the word absolute."[17]

The scholar of religion insists, and has traditionally insisted, that everyone must practice tolerance even as his or her analytic categories imply judgment.

This liberal paradox is also related to another, more recent feature of our craft: our zeal to "locate" ourselves in the multiple, shifting universe. In the early twenty-first century, we are coming face to face with the failure of the great, unacknowledged Romantic ideal of the postmodern perspective—that if we only located ourselves, somehow it would be all better. Naming our locatedness has not necessarily made it all better. It has not necessarily produced better scholarship. And it has frequently made those who would prefer not to be located more angry. This is the challenge of our generation of historians of religion.

The final questions, then, for students to consider are the following:

- How can we remain committed to a human identity and prepare for the scandal that we create when we do so?
- How can we balance sameness and difference?
- How can we juggle our multiple intellectual commitments and speak to those who would think such multiplicity itself is scandalous?
- What thoughts regarding religion do you have that are "scandalous"?

CONCLUDING THOUGHTS: THE HISSING FOOL

Differences aside, we are not so different. Jeff might see the field as a hissing snake tempting the younger generations out of their dangerous gardens of religious inno-cence. Laurie might see the field as a wise fool performing for a future generation that will desperately need just these sorts of provocations and reflections. But both of us share the conviction that the study of religion will be, must be an integral part of any sustainable human future on this planet. That future will depend partly, maybe largely, on whether this and the coming generations can negotiate sameness and difference, that is, how well they can step back and out of their own ethnic, religious, and cultural identities and learn to live in a world that is irreducibly plural, and irreducibly the same.

We have not yet mastered this difficult art. But we think it is very much worth trying.

NOTES

1. Jeffrey J. Kripal, *The Serpent's Gift: Gnostic Reflections on the Study of Religion* (Chicago: University of Chicago Press, 2006).
2. Laurie L. Patton, *The Scholar and the Fool: Scandal, the Secular Study of Religion, and Its Twenty-First-Century Publics* (Chicago: University of Chicago Press, forthcoming).
3. For an eloquent historical meditation on the real risks and real glory of intellectual freedom, see John Durham Peters, *Courting the Abyss: Free Speech and the Liberal Tradition* (Chicago: University of Chicago Press, 2005).
4. See Scholars at Risk Network, "Mission," http://scholarsatrisk.nyu.edu/About-Us/Mission.php (accessed July 12, 2010).
5. For a discussion, see Floyd Abrams, *Speaking Freely: Trials of the First Amendment* (New York: Penguin, 2005), chapter 6, "McCarthyism and Libel."
6. Peter C. Hodgson, "Editor's Introduction," in David Friedrich Strauss, *The Life of Jesus Critically Examined* (Ramsey, NJ: Sigler Press, 1994), xxxvi.
7. For Schaberg's reflections on the aftermath of her work, see Jane Schaberg, "Feminism Lashes Back: Responses to the Backlash," *Biblicon* 3 (1998).
8. Ibid., 47.
9. Personal conversation, November 2003.
10. See James Simpson, *Burning to Read: English Fundamentalism and Its Reformation Opponents* (Cambridge, MA: Harvard University Press, 2007).
11. See Tomoko Masuzawa, *The Invention of World Religions: Or, How European Universalism Was Preserved in the Language of Pluralism* (Chicago: University of Chicago Press, 2005).
12. See in particular Berry's *Recollected Essays: 1965–80* (San Francisco: North Point Press, 1981).
13. Jedediah Purdy, *For Common Things: Irony, Trust, and Commitment in America Today* (New York: Vintage, 1999), 106.
14. Ibid.
15. Ibid., 64.
16. Thomas Tweed, "Moving Across: Translocative Religion and the Interpreter's Position," *Journal of the American Academy of Religion* 70/2 (2002): 253–77. Also see his *Crossing and Dwelling: A Theory of Religion* (Cambridge, MA: Harvard University Press, 2006).
17. Wendy Steiner, *The Scandal of Pleasure* (Chicago: University of Chicago Press, 1995), 123.

BIBLIOGRAPHY

Abrams, Floyd. *Speaking Freely: Trials of the First Amendment.* New York: Penguin, 2005.
Berry, Wendell. *Recollected Essays: 1965–80.* San Francisco: North Point Press, 1981.
Hodgson, Peter C. "Editor's Introduction." In David Friedrich Strauss, *The Life of Jesus Critically Examined.* Ramsey, NJ: Sigler Press, 1994.

Kripal, Jeffrey J. *The Serpent's Gift: Gnostic Reflections on the Study of Religion*. Chicago: University of Chicago Press, 2006.

Masuzawa, Tomoko. *The Invention of World Religions: Or, How European Universalism Was Preserved in the Language of Pluralism*. Chicago: University of Chicago Press, 2005.

Patton, Laurie L. *The Scholar and the Fool: Scandal, the Secular Study of Religion, and Its Twenty-First-Century Publics*. Chicago: University of Chicago Press, forthcoming.

Peters, John Durham. *Courting the Abyss: Free Speech and the Liberal Tradition*. Chicago: University of Chicago Press, 2005.

Purdy, Jedediah. *For Common Things: Irony, Trust, and Commitment in America Today*. New York: Vintage, 1999.

Schaberg, Jane. "Feminism Lashes Back: Responses to the Backlash." *Biblicon* 3 (1998): 45.

Scholars at Risk Network. "Mission." http://scholarsatrisk.nyu.edu/About-Us/Mission.php. Accessed July 12, 2010.

Simpson, James. *Burning to Read: English Fundamentalism and Its Reformation Opponents*. Cambridge, MA: Harvard University Press, 2007.

Steiner, Wendy. *The Scandal of Pleasure*. Chicago: University of Chicago Press, 1995.

Taylor, Charles. *The Secular Age*. Cambridge, MA: Harvard University Press, 2007.

Tweed, Thomas. *Crossing and Dwelling: A Theory of Religion*. Cambridge, MA: Harvard University Press, 2006.

———. "Moving Across: Translocative Religion and the Interpreter's Position." *Journal of the American Academy of Religion* 70/2 (2002): 253–77.

INDEX